A QUICK OVERVIEW OF THE MAJOR GAME CHANGES UNDER THE 1997-2000 RACING RULES

The new racing rules will result in many changes in the way the game is played. Some of these changes have been made with the intention of improving the game; others are the by-product of the effort to simplify and shorten the rules. For a comprehensive summary of the many rule changes, see **The Significant Changes in the 1997-2000** *Racing Rules of Sailing in Appendix A of this book.*

NOTE: These brief summaries are not intended to be actual representations of the rules.

• A boat that completes a tack less than two lengths from the windward mark must do it in a place that allows other boats to pass the mark with no interference, and without ever having to sail above close-hauled to avoid hitting the boat that tacked. (Rule 18.3)

• There is no more "Mast Abeam." Before the starting signal, L can always sail up to head to wind, even when overlapped with W by only a couple of feet. After the starting signal, L can also sail up to head to wind regardless of W's position, unless L established the leeward overlap from clear astern; in that case L can't sail above her proper course during the overlap (as in the previous rules). (Rule 17.1)

• L can no longer luff as fast as she pleases. Now when L luffs, she must give W "room" (space and time) to keep clear of her. W still needs to act promptly so L will still be able to luff fairly quickly. This requirement is exactly the same both before and after the starting signal. (Rule 16)

• Whenever a right-of-way boat changes course near another boat, she must simply give her "room to keep clear." Therefore, when P is passing near S (upwind or down), S can change her course toward P as long as P can take evasive action that is safe and not too extreme. (Rule 16)

• Now, when a boat is involved in contact that causes any damage at all, and she could have reasonably avoided it, she can be penalized. Also boats (including right-of-way boats) can do a "720" to absolve themselves when they break this rule. Give-way boats (P and W) can now seek redress if they are physically damaged by a r-o-w boat in a way that significantly worsens their finishing place. (Rule 14 and 62.1(b))

• At marks, whenever any inside right-of-way boat's proper course is to gybe around the mark, she has to do so, even when she's not otherwise limited to sailing her proper course. Also, at windward marks, a boat astern can now sail above close-hauled to make it more difficult for a boat ahead to tack around the mark. (Rule 18.2 and 18.4)

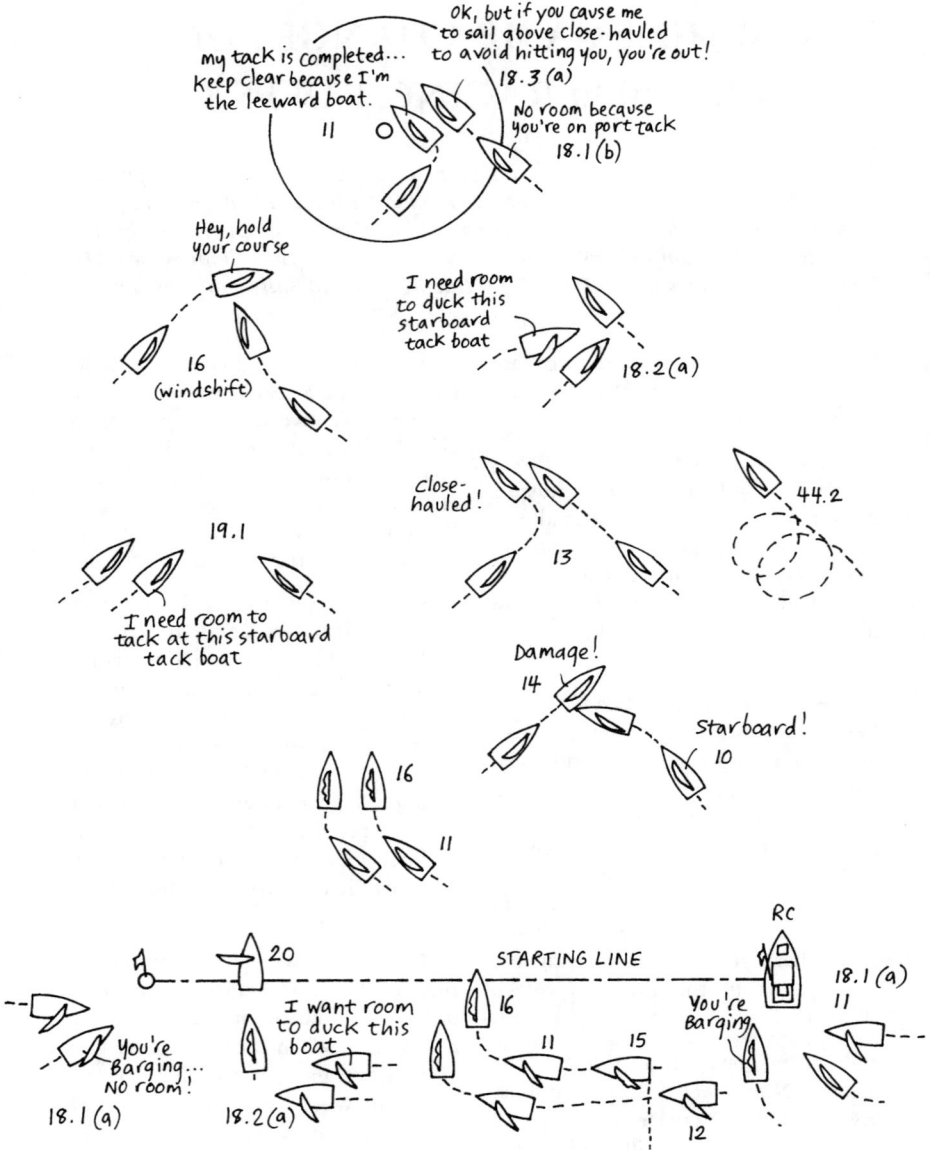

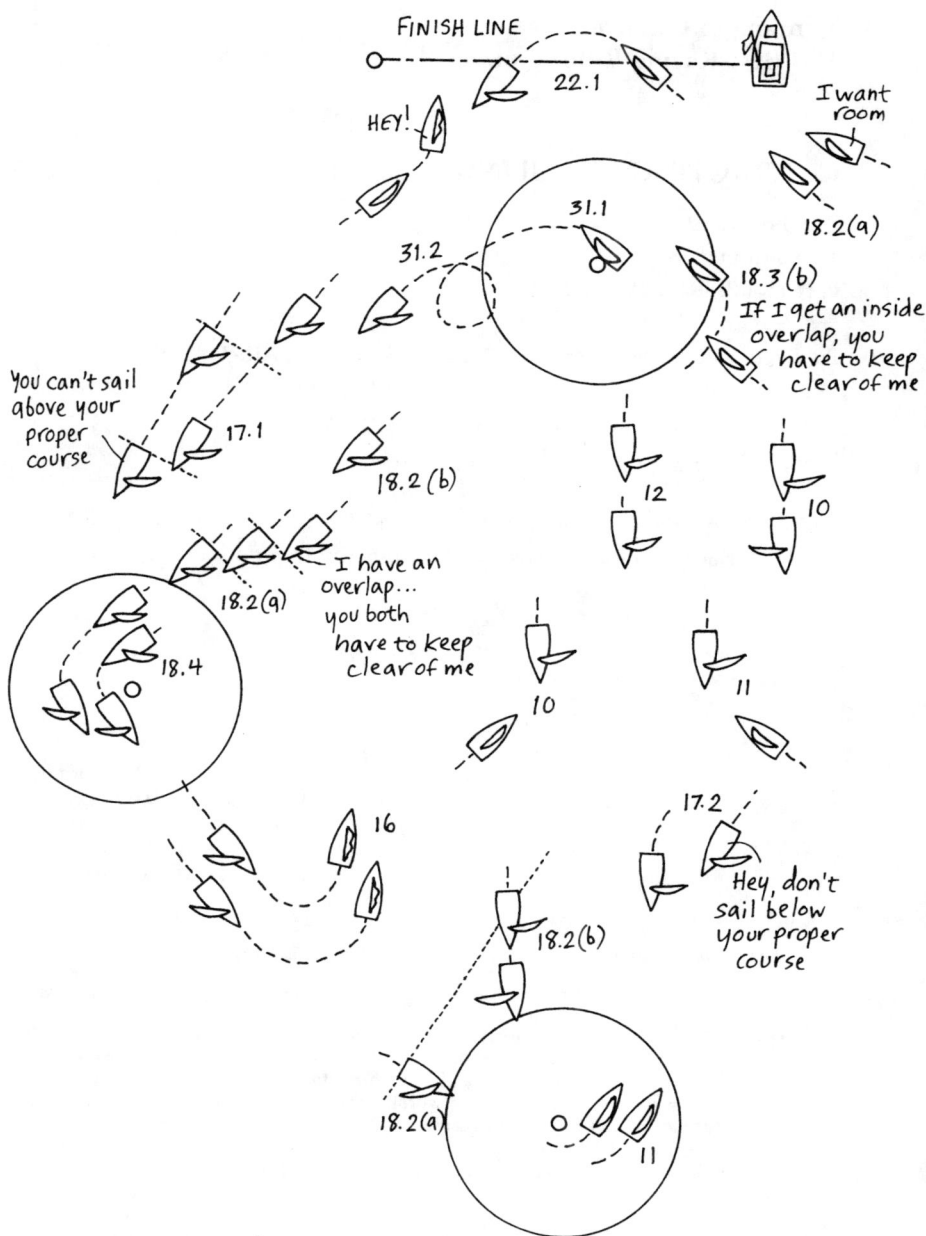

OTHER BOOKS BY DAVE PERRY

Winning in One-Designs
100 Best Racing Rules Quizzes

CONTACTING US SAILING

P.O. Box 1260
15 Maritime Dr.
Portsmouth, RI 02871-6015

Publications & accessories orders*...........1-800-US SAIL-1
Office phone......................................401-683-0800
Fax...401-683-0840
CompuServe.......................................75530,502

* Call US SAILING to order rule books, the US SAILING Book of Appeals and ISAF Racing Rules Appeals Cases, or other publications and accessories.

Published by
UNITED STATES SAILING ASSOCIATION

ISBN 1-882502-44-2

Printed in the United States of America

Previous editions published in 1985, 1989 and 1993

UNDERSTANDING THE

RACING RULES OF SAILING

THROUGH 2000

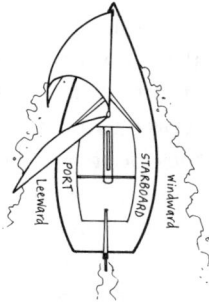

BY
DAVE PERRY

Illustrations by
Brad Dellenbaugh

FOREWORD

We are at a very exciting time for our sport. The worldwide governing body for the sport has changed its name from the International Yacht Racing Union (IYRU) to the International Sailing Federation (ISAF) to reflect the diversity of craft that race and to distance itself from any negative connotations of the words "yacht" and "union" that might act to deter new participants and sponsors from becoming involved in our sport.

In addition, the ISAF has presented the sport with a new code of rules called *The Racing Rules of Sailing*. This new code represents the most major rewrite of the racing rules since the previous code was introduced in 1961. The goal of the ISAF is to provide a shorter and less complex set of rules, using more common language, that conform to ideas of fairness accepted by most sailors and that strive to minimize contact to the greatest extent possible. The rationale for the new code is threefold: 1) that the sport will be more attractive to newcomers if the rules are easier to understand, resulting in more boats on the starting line; 2) that less complex rules will contribute to fewer protests and more consistency in protest committee decisions; and 3) that, given the increase in the average speed of racing boats, simplifying the rules and toughening their requirements regarding contact will lead to fewer expensive collisions and unpleasant confrontations.

For veteran racers, the new code incorporates many interpretations previously found only in the appeals books and covers many situations left uncovered or vague under the previous rules. Furthermore, the rules create some significant improvements to the game, particularly at crowded windward marks.

My hope is that sailors who read this book will feel confident that they do fully know and understand the rules. I realize that a rules book doesn't often make for the best bedtime reading, but I've made a conscious effort to write in an easy to follow, conversational style. In addition, I've taken the time to go into each rule in enough depth so that you can feel confident that you actually do understand what the rule means and how it applies to your racing. Finally, Brad Dellenbaugh has provided his usual clear and humorous diagrams that make understanding the rules even easier. In learning these new rules and their tactical implications I strongly recommend an attitude that is positive about accepting that challenge, realistic about letting go of some of what was previously known about the rules, and willing to make the effort to fully study and understand them.

If you're new to sailboat racing, Chapter 2 covers the basic terms you'll hear throughout the book and around the race course; and it lists the basic rules which you will need to know so you can get out there and start having fun without feeling that you're lost and in everyone's way. But, after reading Chapter 2, I encourage you to take the extra time to read through the rest of the book. Obviously you won't be able to visualize all the situations discussed, but at least you will have been exposed to the big picture right off the bat; and I can promise that your understanding of the rules will happen much faster because you will know how to answer most of your own rule questions as they arise, which they will!

If you are already an experienced racer, I'm confident that you will find this book an informative and useful reference. Wherever possible, I have quoted from the US SAILING Appeals and International Sailing Federation (ISAF) Appeals Cases so that you will know their authoritative interpretation and explanation of the rules. I have also gone into depth in areas which commonly cause the most problems or raise the most questions. As a result, this reference will also be extremely useful to sailors serving as judges on a protest committee. The most useful appeals are quoted or referenced with the discussion of each rule; and each discussion goes into sufficient depth to provide the answers or at least the guidelines to resolve most protests or questions as they come up. Both competitors and judges will find the extensive use and reference to the appeals very useful and timesaving when they are either lodging a protest or trying to resolve one in the hearing.

NOTE: At the time this book was published, US SAILING and ISAF had not yet completed their revisions of their Appeals and Cases; therefore the quotes from the appeals may not be 100% accurate. I expect that the substance of the interpretations are accurate, but encourage you to double-check the actual appeals and cases.

Finally, this book offers explanations and interpretations of a new code of rules. I have given my best studied opinion on the interpretation of these rules and have sought the insight of leading rules authorities around the world, including the authors of the rules themselves. However, as the rules become tested, scrutinized and debated, I recognize that appeals decisions and even ISAF rulings or rule changes may occur during the four years these rules are in effect. Clearly, these take precedence over any conflicting opinion in this book; and I encourage you to note these changes in your copy.

It is nearly impossible to race sailboats without getting involved in some rules-related situations, whether it's in a crowded mark rounding, a protest hearing, a measurement problem or an appeal. It is my hope that this book, which blends the rules and the appeals together, will answer most of your rules questions and expand your knowledge and awareness of what is in the US SAILING and ISAF appeals so that you can continue to satisfy your own rules curiosity into the future, and feel confident that you in fact do understand the rules yourself.

This book will be published every four years with the revisions of *The Racing Rules of Sailing*. As it is my goal to provide a useful and accurate reference for all sailors, I welcome your comments and suggestions concerning improvements and inaccuracies. Please send them to my attention by May 1, 2000, or sooner at: 239 Barberry Road, Southport, CT 06490.

And now, enjoy your understanding of the rules!

Good Sailing,
Dave Perry

DEDICATION
TO F. GREGG BEMIS 1900-1995

Through his lifelong devotion to our sport, and in particular the development of our racing rules, Gregg has touched each one us who has ever raced a sailboat or has otherwise been involved with the racing rules.

Gregg graduated from Harvard in 1922, and spent his working life in philanthropy. He was an active sailor as a member of the Cohasset Yacht Club in Massachusetts, and twice won the 210 national championship. Gregg became a member of the NAYRU Racing Rules Committee in 1950 at the time when the IYRU and NAYRU were working on making their respective versions of the rules the same. Harold "Mike" Vanderbilt and Gregg, representing the U.S., and Gerald Stambrooke-Sturgess, representing Great Britain, worked together for ten years to reach an agreement on a code of rules that ultimately would be adopted by every national authority worldwide. In 1961, their code of rules went into effect, and have been the foundation of the racing rules eve since. Gregg served on the U.S. Racing Rules Committee from 1950-1989 and the U.S. Appeals Committee from 1961-1984. Since 1975, junior double-handed sailors have competed for the Bemis Trophy, symbolic of the double-handed national championship in North America.

I first met Gregg while an active intercollegiate racer in the mid-70's. He was often judging at our regattas and my rules-curiosity was in full gear. When my division was not on the water and he was not hearing a protest, Gregg would sit on the dock with me and anyone else who cared to join in and answer our endless questions on the rules. I will always remember being touched by his patience, his interest in our questions, his deep understanding of the rules and his humility.

Over the years, Gregg and I became regular correspondents on rules-related issues. Then, in 1985 my family and I began a wonderful tradition of visiting Gregg and his wife Marty each summer at their beautiful home in Concord, Massachusetts overlooking the Atlantic Ocean.

While Marty took my wife and our young son for invigorating walks down to the their beach, Gregg and I would sit on their porch overlooking the ocean and discuss current trends and developments in the sport, particularly as they related to the racing rules. He was always extremely current with the sport, even into his 90's; and always genuinely interested in whether the rules were enabling sailors to compete at the highest and fairest level possible.

On one such visit, I had my most memorable and enjoyable occasion with Gregg. On one of those perfect sailing days—sunny and windy—Gregg invited me and our son Alex, who was around three at the time, to go for a sail on his 210. As he adeptly steered off her mooring and out the narrow channel of the Cohasset Yacht Club, I became overwhelmed by the realization that behind Gregg's clear love and sophisticated knowledge of the rules was an even greater love of sailing itself. The three of us sailed for almost two hours that day, talking, laughing and enjoying the sport and each other's company. I will never forget that sail.

In 1986, Gregg was bestowed the highest award of the International Sailing Federation (then the International Yacht Racing Union), the Beppe Croce Award for Distinguished Service to the Sport. At a luncheon reception in Gregg's honor at the Newport, Rhode Island station of the New York Yacht Club, a large group of us were enjoying some refreshment before the luncheon began. Out on the water, a fleet of 20 or so Lasers were just starting a short race. For a few minutes the Lasers were well spread across the harbor. Then as they grew closer to the windward mark, the boats began to converge with each other in what would have looked to be a collision-filled situation to a non-sailor. But, with the smoothness of a well-rehearsed dance, those 20 Lasers intertwined within inches of each other with no contact, and exited the mark in an orderly line headed for the next mark. In a remark that, for me, summed up the acknowledgment of the contribution that Gregg has made to each one of us who races sailboats, a fellow turned to Gregg as the Lasers sailed away from the mark and said, "Thank you Gregg!"

Therefore, it is out of great admiration, affection and gratitude that I dedicate this book to Gregg. He sails with us each time we go out on the water to race.

ACKNOWLEDGMENTS

I'd like to thank the following people, and for the reasons given:

My father, Hop Perry, who began my rules interest and taught me the first rules I knew; my mother, Jan Perry, who, along with her father Northrop Dawson, stimulated and encouraged my desire to write; and my wife, Betsy, who has enhanced this book (and my life) with her contributions and her support.

Bill Bentsen and Dick Rose, two of the principle architects of the concept and substance of the 1997-2000 *Racing Rules of Sailing*, who have generously given me tremendous amounts of their time and insight as I have prepared this book; and who have inspired me to become a strict analyst of the exact word in each rule so as to learn and interpret only what the rule writers wrote.

Harry Anderson, who patiently tolerated my endless rule questions during his every visit to Yale from '73 to '77, and who answered each with the same high care and interest to explain exactly why he gave the answer he did. Gregg Bemis, whose countless hours of conversation on the rules I've cherished. David and Brad Dellenbaugh, who have significantly helped my understanding of the rules by their high-minded approach to analyzing and interpreting the rules. Tom Ehman, who shares my insatiable curiosity to understand the rules. Andy Kostanecki, with whom (along with Dick Rose) I shared my first experience at writing a rule and who was wonderful to work with. Goran Petersson, whose sincere dedication to listening to sailors and welcoming their input on the racing rules I admire and appreciate so much. And my fellow members on the US SAILING Appeals Committee for their high level of rules interpretation and interest in the rules.

I would also like to thank the many friends with whom I've enjoyed much open-minded and friendly, thoughtful debate on the rules, completely devoid of any self-righteousness or the ill effects of taking debate personally; and all the sailors I've met while sitting on protest committees, who have given clear and honest testimonies so that the facts of what happened were clear, enabling everyone involved to learn from and enjoy the more intellectual challenge of applying the rules to the seemingly endless variety of situations we find ourselves in while racing.

I can't say enough about the talent and energy of my friend Brad Dellenbaugh, whose illustrations are an equal half of making this book fun and effective. I also thank Terry Harper, Loren Appel, Chris Museler and Chip Balch of US SAILING for all their efforts towards the publication of this book. Finally, I want to acknowledge all those sailors who took the time to write to me with their critical comments and suggestions for the improvement of this book.

As individual words form together to create a rule, so have all these people formed together to become my teacher in a subject that never ceases to give me pleasure each time I feel I know and understand a rule a little more clearly. To all of you: Thank You!

TABLE OF CONTENTS

THE RACING RULES OF SAILING
TABLE OF CONTENTS

This table indicates where discussion of each rule is located. The text of *The Racing Rules of Sailing* (RRS) and Appendices are printed in the back of this book. "RRS" by a rule indicates that there is no specific discussion of that rule in this book; you will find the text of the rule in the RRS.

PREFACE

by David Dellenbaugh

It was almost 30 years ago when I first sailed with Dave Perry. We were racing a 13-foot Blue Jay in a junior championship, and I was the skipper that time. Though Dave was already known for having a quick paw himself, what I remember most about him was his bubbly enthusiasm. He was a "keener," as they say, and an eager learner.

It didn't take Dave very many years to reach the top of the sport. At Yale, he was a two-time All-American and later did two very successful Soling Olympic campaigns. In 1983, Dave was invited to sail in the prestigious Congressional Cup regatta in Long Beach, California, and asked me to be part of his crew. That was a turning point for both of us.

We ended up winning the regatta; but more importantly, it changed the direction of our sailing lives. Since we had done very little match racing before then, we were exposed to a whole new world of tactical sailing and, especially, to the racing rules. During the regatta we spent many hours, at the home where we stayed, moving empty soda bottles around on the pool table and discussing "what if" situations.

We won the Congressional Cup again the next year, and the following summer Dave decided to write a book about the rules. That first edition of *Understanding the Yacht Racing Rules* required an incredible amount of work, and Dave tackled it with typical passion. He did such a good job he was soon asked to join the US SAILING Appeals Committee. Ever since then Dave has dedicated himself to the task of rules interpretation, and he has amassed an incredible wealth of rules knowledge.

During that time Dave also published two more updated and improved editions of this book. Now he has done it again. This time, however, it took much more than a simple rewrite to explain the most substantial rule changes in at least 40 years. Even though Dave had to work many weekends and late nights in addition to his regular job, he approached this challenge with his usual fervor and perfectionist tendencies.

The result, in my opinion, is the best book on the racing rules ever published. It is a book written for sailors, by a sailor. And that sailor just happens to be a champion racer who is also one of the world's foremost rules experts. Inside you will find a thorough, user-friendly explanation of the new rules. You will hear Dave's authoritative voice and sense the respect he has for his readers. And you will feel the enthusiasm that makes this potentially tedious subject come to life. Enjoy!

*David Dellenbaugh grew up sailing with Dave Perry at the Pequot Yacht Club in Southport, Connecticut. As a racing sailor, David is best known for his role as the tactician on America3 when they won the 1992 America's Cup and for sailing with the women's team on Mighty Mary in 1995. David is also a rules expert, teacher and writer, and he currently publishes a monthly instructional newsletter for racing sailors called **Speed and Smarts**. For more information about **Speed and Smarts** or to get a free sample issue, write to Speed and Smarts, P.O. Box 435, Easton, CT 06612.*

INTRODUCTION
HOW TO LEARN THE MOST
FROM THIS BOOK

*Give me a fish and I'll eat for a day; teach me to fish
and I'll eat for the rest of my life.*

It is one goal of this book to help you learn and understand
the rules and the appeals better. It is an equal goal to help
you see how you can continue to answer your own rules
questions as they arise, whether in the position of a competitor, a race committee member or a judge. Here are
some suggestions that will make it much easier for you to
accomplish both.

DON'T TRY TO MEMORIZE THE RULES

It is the wrong approach to try to memorize the eight situations
where a *port-tack* boat has right of way over a *starboard-tack*
boat, just as it's confusing to try to simply memorize the entire
text of rule 18 (Passing Marks and Obstructions). Each rule has
a clear purpose, which I have tried to explain thoroughly. You'll
learn and remember the rules faster and more clearly if you take
a step back and try to see exactly what actions each rule is trying to produce or eliminate. For example, when you are over the

starting line at the gun you have taken an unfair head start on your competitors. You can remedy your mistake simply by returning behind the line and starting properly; and it makes complete sense that while you are returning you have no rights over boats that have started correctly. This is the purpose of rule 20 (Starting Errors; Penalty Turns; Moving Astern) and rule 29.1 (On the Course Side at the Start), which you can easily understand and apply in your racing without knowing the exact wording of each rule.

LET GO OF PREVIOUS INTERPRETATIONS OF THE RULES THAT DIFFER FROM THE NEW ONES

As frustrating as it may be at first, it is important that sailors let go of previous interpretations of the rules that no longer apply as quickly as possible. This process will be helped by a positive commitment to learning the new rules as opposed to a negative resistance to accepting them. One clear benefit to learning a new code of rules is that previous misconceptions of the rules will be eliminated.

My advice is: read this book with an open mind. Be careful not to hurry through sections that you feel you already know. Read each word and discussion carefully. It's very common and easy to superimpose what you "think" a rule says or should say; and in many cases this causes you to miss a subtle difference in what the rule is actually saying. Sailors seriously interested in understanding the rules will find real pleasure and benefit in learning a rule correctly.

WHEN ALL ELSE FAILS, READ THE DIRECTIONS

It is usually not difficult to answer your own rules questions if you follow this route. When you have a question, first look in the Index of Subjects in the ISAF *Racing Rules of Sailing* (RRS) to see which rule(s) may apply. Also look through the contents of the RRS at the titles of the Parts, then the Sections and finally the rules themselves to find the one(s) that might pertain to your situation. For example, if it involves two or more boats, the appropriate rule(s) are probably in Part 2. To find the rule(s), first determine what the relationships of the boats are just before, during and just after the incident. For instance, have they been converging for some time or does one of the boats suddenly alter course and cause the convergence; are they on the same or opposite *tacks*; are they *overlapped* or not, and so forth. Also determine where they are on the course; i.e. are they behind the starting line, near a *mark* or halfway down a reaching leg? Then look through the titles of the rules in Part 2 for the description most similar to the situation.

When you have found the rule you feel applies, read it out loud. As Bill Bentsen, member of the ISAF Racing Rules Committee for many years, says, "Before answering a rules question I always reread the rule first." Then read the discussion of the rule in this book, along with each appeal referenced in the discussion. It is also good advice to reread the definition of each italicized word in the rule. If you have access to the US SAILING Appeals and ISAF Racing Rules Appeals Cases (available from US SAILING), check the helpful index and read any appeals that may pertain to your situation. If you are still not confident in the answer, write down your question in the back of your rule book and discuss it with the local rules expert or one of the US SAILING Certified Judges in your area.

USEFUL FEATURES OF THIS BOOK

Brad and I have included the following features in the book with the hope that they will be useful to you.

1) A "blimp's eye" chart in the front of the book which shows an entire race course with the rule numbers for the situations that commonly arise in each location. This feature should be very useful when you're involved in a protest but you're not sure what rule number applies.

2) A "question and answer" format, indicated by the icons in the margin, in which I ask and answer the most commonly asked rules questions. Perhaps you'll recognize some as questions you may have.

3) When a term defined in the Definitions is used in its defined sense, I have printed it in *italic* type. To emphasize words or phrases throughout my explanations and discussions of the rules, I have used **bold** type.

4) A Glossary of Terms explaining the meaning of terms commonly used in discussing the rules but not defined in *The Racing Rules of Sailing*. (Located after this Introduction.)

5) A table for calculating boat speed, distance and time that will be useful when preparing for a protest or hearing one. (Located after this Introduction.)

6) The complete text of *The Racing Rules of Sailing*, including its appendices. (In the back of this book.)

7) A detailed index of rule subjects and the rule(s) in which they are located, prepared by the ISAF and included in *The Racing Rules of Sailing*. (In the back of this book.)

8) A complete cross-reference of rule numbers, listing the 1993-96 rule number and title/subject and what number that rule has become in the 1997-2000 rules. This tremendously thorough and useful index was prepared by Tom Farquhar, a US SAILING Senior Certified Judge and member of the US SAILING Appeals Committee. (Appendix B of this book.)

9) An index listing each 1997-2000 rule number and where the primary discussion of that rule is located in this book. (Located after the Table of Contents in this book.)

10) A summary of the significant changes in the rules and how they change the game. (Appendix A of this book.)

GLOSSARY OF TERMS

As part of the simplification and shortening process, the rule writers used common terms when possible ("boat" instead of "yacht," "breaks" instead of "infringes," etc.) and removed five terms from the list of defined terms in the RRS that are used in their ordinarily understood sense (bearing away, close-hauled, gybing, luffing and tacking). They also attempted to remove as many subjective words as possible for better consistency in applying the rules (e.g. "ample," "seriously," "slowly," etc.).

When a term is not defined in the RRS, it is intended to be interpreted in its common, everyday, dictionary meaning.

The following is a glossary of some of the terms you will find in the *rules* and their discussion that are not defined in the RRS themselves.

Bearing Away	turning away from the direction of the wind
Luffing	turning toward the direction of the wind
Heading Up	another term for "luffing"
Can or May	means permissive; have option of doing it
Shall	means mandatory; must do it
Beating to Windward	a boat is "beating to windward" whenever her fastest course to the next mark is close-hauled or above
Close-hauled	the course a boat will sail when racing upwind and sailing as close to the wind as she can.
Gybing (To Gybe)	the maneuver involving changing *tacks* with the boat's bow away from the wind (when sailing downwind, a boat changes *tacks* the moment her mainsail crosses her centerline)
Tacking (To Tack)	the maneuver involving changing *tacks* with the bow toward the wind (when sailing upwind, a boat changes *tacks* the moment her bow passes head to wind)

SPEED, DISTANCE & TIME TABLE

(1 knot = 6076 feet per hour)

Boat speed	Feet per second	Meters per second
1 knot	1.69	0.51
2 knots	3.38	1.01
3 knots	5.06	1.52
4 knots	6.75	2.03
5 knots	8.44	2.53
6 knots	10.13	3.04
7 knots	11.81	3.54
8 knots	13.50	4.05
9 knots	15.19	4.56
10 knots	16.88	5.06

In other words, if your boat is going 4 knots, you will travel 6.75 feet per second. One way to determine your boat's speed is to sail by a buoy or other fixed object and count how many seconds it takes for the buoy to go from your bow to your stern. If in a 24 foot boat it takes 3 seconds to go by the buoy, you are going 8 feet per second, or just under 5 knots.

It's very useful to know your boat's approximate speed on all points of sail in all wind and wave conditions, particularly in a protest hearing. For instance, in the above example you know that the *two-length zone* is about 6 seconds' worth of sailing before the *mark*. You also know that if you tack in front of another boat and she claims to have hit you only 3 seconds after you became close-hauled, you can point out that, by her own testimony, she held her course **for a full boat-length** after you were close-hauled.

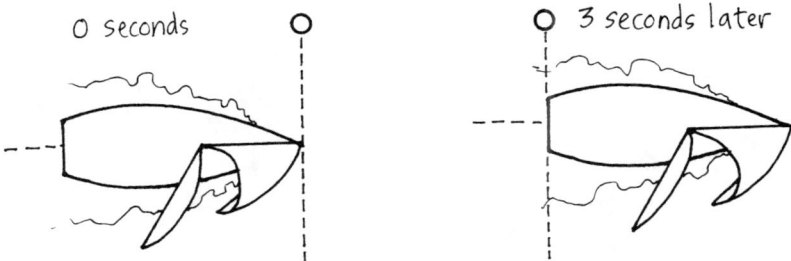

O seconds   3 seconds later

CODE

Throughout this book, in order to consolidate space and to conform to the appeals, I have used the following code:

S   *starboard-tack* boat

P   *port-tack* boat

L   *leeward* boat

W   *windward* boat

A   boat *clear ahead*

B   boat *clear astern* (behind)

M   middle or intervening boat

I   inside boat (at a *mark* or *obstruction*)

O   outside boat (at a *mark* or *obstruction*)

When combined, the codes work like this:

SL   the boat is on *starboard tack* and *overlapped* to *leeward* of the other boat.

PI   the boat is on *port tack* and *overlapped* on the inside of the other boat.

Hey! You can't cause me to sail above close-hauled!

1

AN OVERVIEW OF THE RULES SYSTEM

BRIEF HISTORY

Up through the early 1920s, different parts of the world had their own versions of racing rules. Then, as more sailors started traveling to other countries for international regattas, the European and United States yacht racing associations agreed on a common set of right-of-way rules in 1929. However, as racing grew in popularity and the boats were getting smaller, the existing rules were not clear and precise enough to make them easily enforceable.

In the mid-1930s Mike Vanderbilt, defender of the America's Cup in the J-boats Enterprise (1930), Rainbow (1934) and Ranger (1937) began work on a new draft of the rules based on the three basic relative positions boats can be in: on the same tack, on different tacks and in the act of changing tacks. In 1948 the North American Yacht Racing Union (NAYRU), predecessor to the United States Sailing Association (US SAILING) and the Canadian Yachting Association (CYA), adopted Vanderbilt's draft as their official rules.

In 1949 the International Yacht Racing Union (IYRU) created a Racing Rules Committee to study the various racing rules that were being used throughout the world. From 1950 to 1959,

Mike Vanderbilt and Gregg Bemis of the United States, Gerald Sambrooke-Sturgess of Great Britain and others worked hard to draft one set of rules under which the entire world would race. In 1960 the IYRU adopted a draft, largely based on the "Vanderbilt draft," and these rules came into effect in 1961. Since then, racing throughout the world has been done under the same code of rules.

Beginning in 1961, the IYRU's policy became that the rules would be locked in place for four-year periods lasting through the Olympic Games. During these four-year periods, sailors would communicate their ideas for improvements to their Racing Rules Committees, which would also study the rules for areas of improvement. After each Olympics, the IYRU would adopt a revised set of rules for the next four-year period.

Over the years since 1961, in the process of being revised to clarify their meaning and to meet changes in the sport, the rules became longer and more complex. As newcomers joined the sport, they (and those who taught them) found learning the rules to be a formidable task. It was also acknowledged that the interpretation and application of the rules was not consistent worldwide. In 1991 the IYRU took formal action to simplify and improve the rules. A draft of "experimental rules" was offered to sailors each year from 1993-1996 for their review, trial and input. This worldwide research project resulted in a highly refined and simpler set of rules that went into effect in 1997.

For a more detailed history of the racing rules, read Rob MacArthur's *Room at the Mark*, available from US SAILING.

THE RULES AND HOW THEY ARE UPDATED

The rules are *The Racing Rules of Sailing*. They are published by the International Sailing Federation (ISAF). Each national authority (US SAILING in the United States) adopts these rules for racing in its own country. Some rules permit each national authority to make some additions or modifications, called "prescriptions." So when racing in a different country, a sailor need only learn what prescriptions, if any, that national authority has made. But notice that there are no modifications permitted to the Definitions and "right of way" rules in Part 2, thus ensuring that these remain identical throughout the world.

Notice that the ISAF and the national authorities are very interested in having sailors study the rules for improvements and give their input. In the US, suggestions or comments should be sent to the Racing Rules Committee, c/o US SAILING. Notice also that rule 86 (Rule Changes) restricts which rules the sailing instructions can alter; but rule 86.2 says, "*If a national authority so prescribes, these restrictions do not apply if rules are changed to develop or test proposed rules in local races.*" US SAILING prescribes "*that proposed rules may be tested in local races and that its approval is not required for such tests.*" US SAILING Appeal 278 says, "Local races are those in which normally the same group of people from a limited geographic area regularly race together."

WHERE THE RULES ARE LOCATED

The rules are located in the following places.
(See the Definition Rule.)

1. **The ISAF rule book** (*The Racing Rules of Sailing*) **and any prescriptions of the national authority.** US SAILING sells one "rule book" that includes the ISAF rules, appendices and US SAILING prescriptions. See its Table of Contents for an overview of where each ISAF rule is located and what each Appendix covers. Notice that rule titles are not part of the rules.

2. **Class rules.** Each class publishes rules specific for that class, which are available from the class secretary. (Contact US SAILING for class office addresses.)

3. **Club or "local" rules.**

4. **The Notice of Race.** Rule M1(Notice of Race Contents) lists the information contained in the Notice of Race.

5. **The Sailing Instructions.** Most races you enter will have written sailing instructions. The sailing instructions are required to tell you when class and "local" rules apply, as well as any special rules for the race. They may even change some of *The Racing Rules of Sailing* (see rule 86, Rule Changes). Rule M2 (Sailing Instruction Contents) lists all the information the sailing instructions must contain. Notice

that rule 88.2(c) (Race Committee; Sailing Instructions; Scoring, Sailing Instructions) prohibits any oral instructions unless there is a procedure specifically set out in the sailing instructions; and even then, they can be given only on the water. This is obviously to avoid confusion and potential prejudice to sailors not hearing about a change.

6. **Any other conditions or documents that might apply to a particular race or series.**

    In particular, **every sailor should take a few minutes to read the sailing instructions for a race or event.** Normally, a race committee will not answer oral questions concerning any rule or sailing instruction to avoid possible confusion or prejudice. You should give them your question(s) in writing in ample time for them to consider their answer, seek the judges' opinions (when necessary) and post each question with its answer in writing on the official notice board.

PROTEST SYSTEM

A *"protest"* is merely the means of bringing an incident in which a boat may have broken a rule to a hearing after the race where the sailors involved and the members of the protest committee can review the incident and decide how the *rules* apply.

The rules for how to lodge a *protest* are clearly stated in rule 60 (Right to Protest and Request Redress). Rules concerning how the protest hearing must be run, including a listing of all the sailor's rights, are in Part 5, Section B (Protests, Hearings, Misconduct and Appeals; Hearings and Decisions).

Appendix P contains detailed recommendations for how protest committees should conduct the hearing. The preamble to the Appendix clearly states the fundamental principle in our sport that you are "innocent until proven guilty." It reads:

In a protest hearing, the protest committee should weigh all testimony with equal care; should recognize that honest testimony can vary, and even be in conflict, as a result of different observations and recollections; should resolve such differences as best it can; should recognize that no boat or competitor is guilty until a breach of a *rule* has been established to the satisfaction of the protest committee; and should keep an open mind until all the

evidence has been heard as to whether a boat or competitor has broken a *rule*.

APPEALS SYSTEM

If you are penalized in a protest hearing and you feel that the protest committee applied the *rules* incorrectly to the facts they found or failed to follow the correct procedures in hearing the *protest*, you can "appeal" their decision to a "higher court." All the rules and procedures for submitting an appeal are located in rule 70 (Right of Appeal and Requests for Interpretation) and Appendix F (Appeals Procedures), except that regional sailing associations may have additional procedures as well.

Note that you cannot appeal the **facts** that were found by the protest committee; only their interpretation and application of the *rules* to those facts (rule 63.6, Taking Evidence and Finding Facts; rule 70.1, Right of Appeal and Requests for Interpretation; and rule 71.3, Appeal Decision). If after a hearing you, as a *party* to the hearing, feel the protest committee found the wrong facts, you can ask them to reopen the hearing under rule 66 (Reopening a Hearing) or request redress under rule 62 (Redress).

In the United States the "highest court" is the US SAILING Appeals Committee. When they decide a case that to them sets a precedent or is a clear and useful interpretation of a *rule*, they publish it. They can also submit the appeal and their decision to the ISAF Racing Rules Committee, which in turn can publish the appeal in their book. Notice that the ISAF does not, in most cases, decide appeals; they simply publish ones submitted by member national authorities that they feel are important and useful interpretations.

US SAILING's Decisions of the Appeals Committee and the ISAF's Racing Rules Appeals Cases are available from US SAILING. US SAILING members receive new decisions of the US SAILING Appeals Committee in their magazine, *American Sailor*, as well as in annual supplements.

"What is the status of the appeals published in US SAILING's Decisions of the Appeals Committee and the ISAF's Racing Rules Appeals Cases?"

The appeals decisions of the national authorities (US SAILING in the United States) and the ISAF Appeals Cases are not *rules*. They are "authoritative interpretations and explanations of the rules." However, sailors and protest committees can and should refer to the appeals for guidance. The ISAF's Cases carry supreme weight worldwide. When a situation is identical to a published ISAF interpretation, the ISAF Case serves as a precedent. (See US SAILING Appeal 262.)

Similarly, US SAILING Appeals Committee's decisions carry supreme weight within the United States; and in fact their appeals are highly regarded throughout the world. They do not, however, have the same weight as the ISAF cases, and outside the United States they may sometimes be disregarded in favor of the host country's national Appeals Committee's decisions.

"What's the best way to use the appeals books?"

Both the US SAILING Appeals Committee's Decisions and the ISAF's Racing Rules Appeals Cases are easily designed for quick reference. One index lists each Definition and rule and then each appeal referring to that particular Definition or rule; another gives a short description of each appeal. Instead of reading the appeals book from front to back, you should read each appeal pertaining to a particular rule. The appeals themselves are each very short. You are given the facts, a diagram when relevant, and then the decision. I like to read the facts, close the book, think out what my decision would be, then compare it with the actual decision.

"Can the decision on an appeal change the results of a race or series?"

You bet. Rule 71.4 (Appeal Decisions) states, *"The decision of the national authority shall be final...all parties to the hearing and the protest committee...shall be bound by the decision."* In ISAF Case 131 it was asked, "May an authority organizing a race state in the notice of race or sailing instructions that, while appeal is not denied, final regatta standings and awards will not be affected by any appeal decision? ANSWER: No...An appeal involves not only the adjudication of a dispute on the meaning of a rule but also, in the event of a reversal of the decision of the protest committee, an adjustment of the results of the race and the final standings of the regatta on which the awards are based."

"Can anyone appeal the decision of a protest committee?"

No. Only a *party* to the hearing can appeal the decision in that hearing (rule 70.1, Right of Appeal and Requests for Interpretations). (For more explanation on who qualifies as a *party*, see the discussion of the Definition *Party*.) If you were **not** a *party* to a hearing, but the decision in that hearing affected you and you believe that the protest committee acted improperly, your recourse is to request redress under rule 62.1(a) (Redress). (See US SAILING Appeal 293 and ISAF Case 119.)

"If I'm in a situation where I feel the protest committee is prejudicing, or has prejudiced, the outcome of the hearing by denying me any of my procedural rights under Part 5, Section B (Hearings and Decisions) , do I have to 'object' at the time if I want to retain my right to appeal?"

You are not required to, but I strongly encourage you to do so. Remember that an appeals committee can only base its decision on the facts as presented to them by the protest committee. When a competitor appeals on the grounds that the protest committee made a prejudicial procedural error, generally there is little or no record of it in the protest committee's "facts found." Therefore, it becomes very difficult for the appeals committee to ever learn enough facts to uphold the appeal.

That is why I recommend that if you are in a situation where the protest committee is denying you your procedural rights, you should state your "objection" right then. Hopefully that will result in the problem being corrected and the hearing continuing properly. However, if after the hearing you feel the protest committee has prejudiced the outcome of the hearing by denying you any of your procedural rights, you should request redress under rule 62.1(a) (Redress). The reason for this is that a protest committee must then give you a hearing and, more importantly, must find facts and give you a decision (rule 63.1, Hearings; rule 64.2, Decisions on Redress). Otherwise, you may never get any facts regarding the alleged improprieties on which to base an appeal. Note that in the US, the time limit for requesting redress for a protest committee action is 6:00pm the day **following** the protest committee action, or even later if there is a good reason to extend this time limit (see the US SAILING prescription to rule 62.2, Redress).

Note that, when seeking redress, you must be prepared to point out the "improper" action or omission of the protest committee. ISAF Case146 states, "A boat is not entitled to redress for proper action of a race or protest committee." It is not enough to claim that the protest committee should have taken alternative action which would have given you better standing.

"Are there ever times when I am not allowed to appeal?"

Yes. Rule 70.4 (Right of Appeal and Requests for Interpretations) is very clear on this:

There shall be no appeal from the decisions of an international jury constituted in compliance with Appendix Q. Furthermore, if the notice of race and the sailing instructions so state, the right of appeal may be denied provided that

(a) **it is essential to determine promptly the result of a race that will qualify a boat to compete in a later stage of an event or a subsequent event (a national authority may prescribe that its approval is required for such a procedure),**

(b) **a national authority so approves for a particular event open only to entrants under its own jurisdiction, or**

(c) **a national authority after consultation with the ISAF so approves for a particular event, provided the jury is constituted as required by Appendix Q, except that only two members of the jury need be International Judges.**

2

A SIMPLIFIED VERSION
OF THE RACING RULES
OF SAILING

There's no disagreeing that there are a lot of rules to know when racing sailboats. But just as in every other sport, you don't need to know and completely understand them all before you go racing. I love to play soccer, and I've got the basic rules down: Keep my hands off the ball, try to kick the ball into the goal to score, try not to kick the other guys in the shins and stop when the referee blows the whistle. I'm still a bit hazy on what 'offsides' means, what the difference between an "indirect" and a "direct" kick is, and just how many elbows in the ribs I'm supposed to politely accept as part of the game. But I still have a great time playing, and I learn a bit more about the rules each time I go out.

Here then are a few basic rules you should know so that you can get into racing without feeling like you're just in everyone's way. At first, take the racing easy just to get the feel of how it works, and never be worried about asking too many questions; that's exactly how we all learned what was up. Of course, the one danger in learning just the basic rules is that there will be places on the course where there are exceptions or where the actual rule has more detail. So I encourage you to take the time to read through this book. It's written in language that is easy to understand. The more you race, the more situations you'll run into that are exactly as covered and described here, and the sooner you'll be comfortable enough to get in there and mix it up out on the course.

Now, if you are just getting into sailing and racing, you've probably noticed that there are a few different words and phrases used around the track. Clearly the rules wouldn't be using them if they didn't make things easier; so we've included some illustrations to help you understand what some of these terms mean.

BASIC RULES

These are simplified summaries of the basic rules that apply when you and another boat are about to hit. When one boat has the "right of way," that means that the other boat is required to "keep clear;" in other words to stay out of the way of the right-of-way boat.

1) If you are on **opposite** tacks (booms on different sides), the boat on starboard tack has the right of way over the boat on port tack (just as at a four-way stop, the car on the right gets to go first). (Rule 10.)

2) If you are on the **same** tack (booms on the same sides), the leeward boat has the right of way over the windward boat; and a boat coming up from behind can't hit the boat ahead (just as on the road). (Rules 11 and 12.)

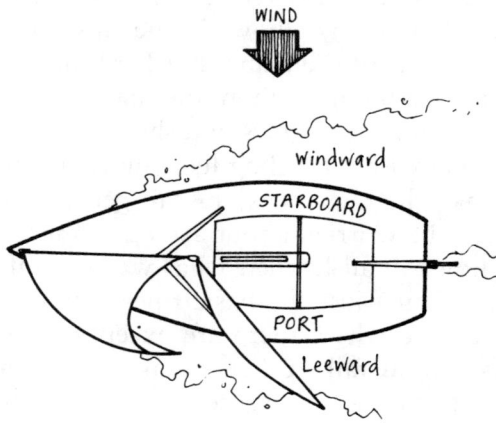

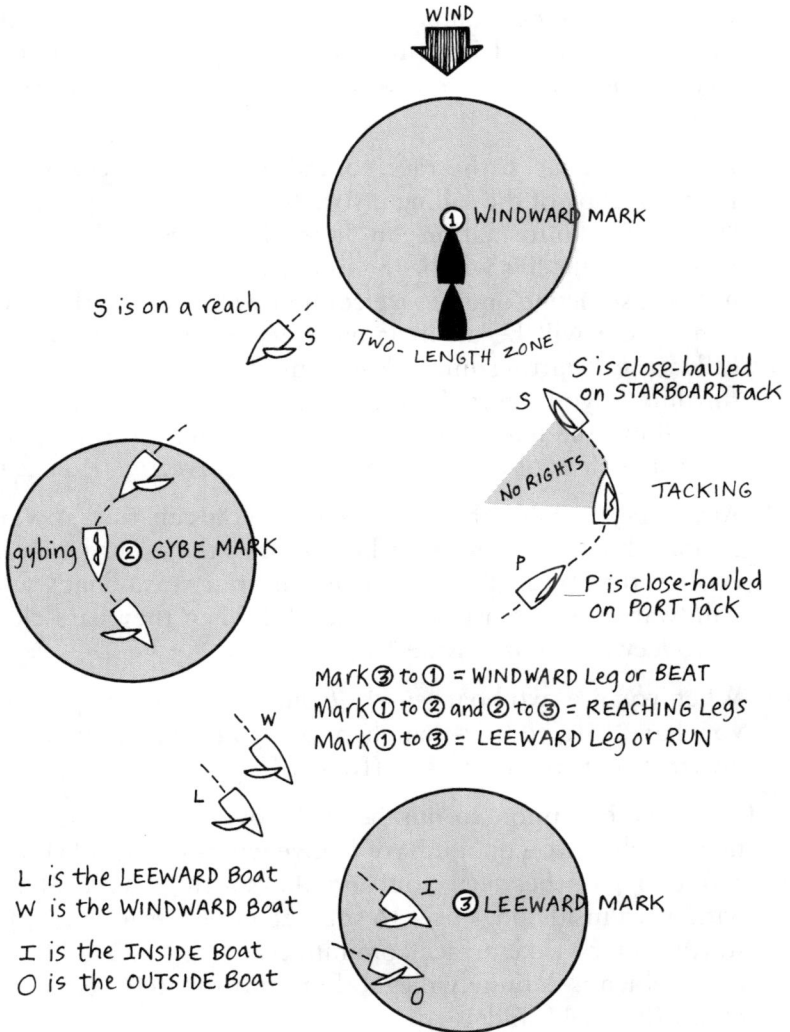

WIND

① WINDWARD MARK

S is on a reach

TWO- LENGTH ZONE

S is close-hauled on STARBOARD Tack

No RIGHTS

TACKING

P is close-hauled on PORT Tack

gybing ② GYBE MARK

Mark ③ to ① = WINDWARD Leg or BEAT
Mark ① to ② and ② to ③ = REACHING Legs
Mark ① to ③ = LEEWARD Leg or RUN

W

L

③ LEEWARD MARK

I

O

L is the LEEWARD Boat
W is the WINDWARD Boat

I is the INSIDE Boat
O is the OUTSIDE Boat

3) If you are **tacking,** you have to stay out of the way of a boat sailing in a straight line (just as you cannot pull out onto a road immediately in front of a car driving down the road). (Rule 13.)

4) Before most races, the race committee will give each competitor a copy of the **sailing instructions** (SI's), which contain the specific information on how the races will be run. Included in the SI's will be the timing system for the starts. If not, ask someone on the race committee to explain their system. There will be an imaginary line between two marks called the "starting line." You must be completely behind this line at your start. If you are not, simply turn back and get behind the line. However, while you are returning, you must stay clear of all boats that started correctly. (Rule 20.)

5) Anytime you have the right of way, you can turn toward another boat; but you must be sure that the other boat has enough **time** and **space** to get out of your way. That's why windward boats must be very careful when they pass close by to leeward boats. (Rule 16.)

6) When you are two boat-lengths from a mark or obstruction, you have to give any boat between you and the mark or obstruction room to pass it. (Rule 18.)

7) One large exception to number 6 (above) is at the starting marks, where you do **not** have to give windward/inside boats room to pass between you and the starting mark. If the windward/inside boat tries to squeeze in between you and a starting mark (like a race committee boat), they are "barging," which is definitely illegal (but unfortunately very common). (Rules 11 and 18.)

8) You must **avoid all collisions** if possible. (Rule 14.)

9) If you make a right-of-way boat **change their course** to avoid hitting you, you must take a penalty. Normally the penalty is to simply get away from the other boats immediately and make two circles (called a "720"). When you're done, get back in the race. (Rule 44.)

10) If you **touch any mark**, the penalty is just one circle. (Rule 31.)

If you have the right-of-way and another boat makes you change course to miss hitting her, she has broken a rule. You can tell her this by "protesting" her. To do this, immediately hail the word "Protest" and put up a red flag. Then at the finish tell the race committee which boat you are protesting, and onshore fill out the protest form the race committee will give you. Soon afterward, the protest committee (usually three knowledgeable sailors) will hold a hearing at which both boats have the opportunity to tell their story; the committee will then make its decision. (Rules 60 to 68.)

Hike hard, sail fast and enjoy!

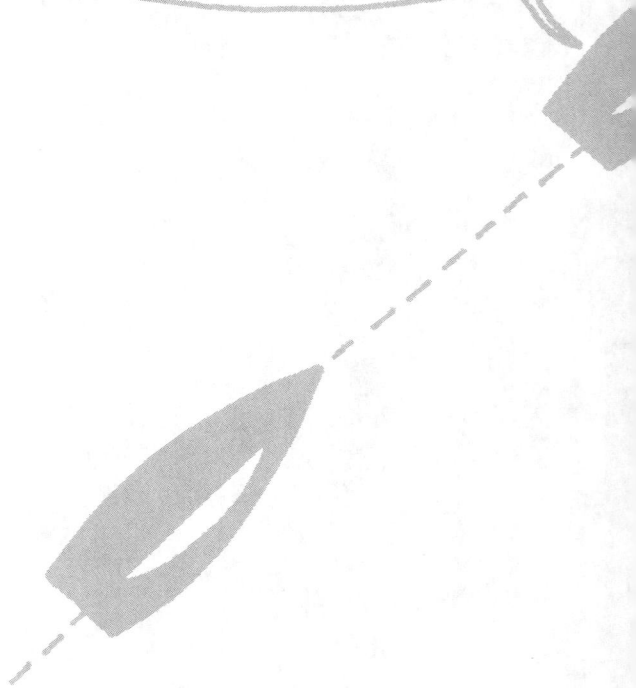

3

SPORTSMANSHIP AND
THE RULES

*"You haven't won the race if in winning the race you
have lost the respect of your competitors."*

FOUR-TIME OLYMPIC GOLD MEDALIST, PAUL ELVSTRÖM

SPORTSMANSHIP AND THE RULES

**Competitors in the sport of sailing are governed by a body of
rules that they are expected to follow and enforce. A fundamental principle of sportsmanship is that when competitors
break a rule they will promptly take a penalty or retire.**

This statement of principle is located in the rule book just before
Part 1 (Fundamental Rules). It is no coincidence that the subject
of "sportsmanship" is given a status above all the rules in our
sport. The history of sailboat racing is filled with the tradition of
exciting competition played out with honor and respect among
the competitors and officials. In keeping with that tradition,
when we race we agree to be fair and honest, to be good sports
and to attempt to win using our own superior boat speed and
racing skills.

At the heart of what makes our sport so fulfilling is the principle that we have a competitor-enforced, "no-referee" rules system. In other words, we have the responsibility to follow the

rules on our own, to self-penalize ourselves when we break a rule and to protest when we believe another boat has broken a rule. In this regard, our sport is unique compared with most other sports. I was watching a pro tennis singles match (two players) and became amused as I counted at least ten referees: one calling each of the four lines on each side, one calling the net, and an umpire to settle disputes. Even at the highest levels of racing we "call our own lines."

The rules are intended to provide for safe, fair and equitable racing world-wide; and to make competitor enforcement as easy as possible by clearly defining which boat has the right of way and which boat the requirement to *keep clear* when boats meet. When competitors know they have broken a rule, they are expected to promptly take a penalty or retire. Competitors who "never drop out," even when they know they are in the wrong, because they think they have a chance to "win" the *protest* in the hearing just waste the time of all the people involved in the *protest* and diminish the quality of the racing.

Rule 44 (Penalties for Breaking a Rule of Part 2) provides that the 720-degree Turns Penalty or other voluntary penalty will always be available to a boat; and rule 31 (Touching a Mark) provides the 360-degree penalty turn for touching a *mark*.

When a competitor believes that another boat may have broken a rule, she can protest. A *protest* is merely the means of bringing an incident in which a boat may have broken a *rule* to a hearing after the race where the sailors involved and the members of the protest committee can review the incident and decide how the *rules* apply. *Protests* that are the result of honest differences of opinions on the *rules* or observations of the incident should never have a negative taint to them. Quite the contrary, protests are an essential part of our competitor-enforced rule system and are expected, particularly in situations where a boat has gained an advantage in the race or series by breaking a rule.

When a boat is forced to break a *rule* through no fault of her own she is known as the "innocent victim," and can be excused from blame under rule 64.1(b) (Penalties and Exoneration). If a boat feels she her finishing place has been made significantly worse by the race committee, protest committee or another competitor, she can request redress under rule 62 (Redress); in this case, rule 64.2 (Decisions on Redress) reminds the protest committee to make as fair an arrangement as possible for all boats affected.

The rule writers have taken some excellent measures to amplify the message that sailing should be synonymous with good sportsmanship and integrity with regard to fair play. However, in the end of the day it is up to us, the sailors, to use the rules as they are written and intended. One problem is that some feel that the rewards from winning justify cheating, such as the "good feeling" of winning, the attention and hype, the benefit to business and sponsors and so on. Obviously, this is a personal decision that all sailors must make for themselves. The hope is that the temptations to cheat can't possibly overpower the realization that once people start bending or ignoring the rules, or develop their own "common law," the whole exercise of playing the game becomes meaningless for everyone involved.

Rule 2 (Fair Sailing) and rule 69 (Allegations of Gross Misconduct) provide the external "weight" to encourage strict and voluntary rule observance. However, people who race should want to know that everyone whom they've spent the time, money and energy to race against is sailing within the rules also; and when they know or suspect that someone isn't, then rather than joining in, they should take action under the rules to encourage the others to stop.

*ure it is. I'm using
ood one-on-one
tactics*

4

FUNDAMENTAL
RULES

PART 1

The first rules in the rule book are appropriately called the "Fundamental Rules;" and they address five very important issues in our sport: safety and helping others when in a position to do so, fairness while racing, acceptance of the rules under which we race, responsibility for one's own safety, and drug use (primarily an issue of caution for Olympic-bound racers).

RULE 1 - SAFETY

Rule 1.1 - Helping Those in Danger

A boat or competitor shall give all possible help to any person or vessel in danger.

This rule is the first fundamental rule, reaffirming that this principle must be the one to which all sailors hold above all others. Remember that the word "shall" means "mandatory." If it were proved that a sailor was in a position to help another, but did not do so, he or she would be liable for disqualification. Note that the rule requires the giving of all "possible" help; this is to leave no question about the extent to which sailors should help each other when in danger.

The rule book is very supportive of this principle.

- Rule 21 (Capsized, Anchored or Aground; Rescuing) reads in part, *"...a boat shall avoid a boat that is...trying to help a person or vessel in danger."*

- Rule 41 (Outside Help) reads, *"A boat may receive outside help as provided for in rule 1. Otherwise, she shall not receive help except for an ill or injured crew member or, after a collision, from the crew of the other boat."*

- Rule 42.3(c) (Propulsion, Exceptions) reads, *"Any means of propulsion may be used to help a person or another vessel in danger."*

- Rule 47 (Limitations on Equipment and Crew) reads in part, *"No person on board shall leave, unless...to help a person or vessel in danger."*

"If I do stop and help a boat or person in danger, can I get some compensation for the places and/or time I may have lost?"

You bet! When you have lost places and/or time as a result of a rescue, you are permitted to request redress under rule 62.1(c) (Redress), and the protest committee, acting under rule 64.2 (Decisions on Redress), can give you appropriate compensation for the places and/or time lost. In the event you go to a rescue, try, if possible, to accurately note the time and your position when you began sailing to the rescue and when you got back in the race. On boats in offshore races it is common to keep a log of times and positions to help the protest committee provide the fairest compensation.

A now famous instance of these rules at work is the rescue made by Canadian Finn sailor Larry Lemieux in the 1988 Summer Olympic Games held in the rough seas off Pusan, South Korea. While in second place midway through a race, Larry noticed a 470 sailor in the water separated from his boat and having great difficulty. Larry went to the sailor's rescue, succeeded in getting him safely back to his boat, and after the race requested redress. The Olympic Jury awarded Larry points equal to finishing second in that race!

Several appeals speak clearly on the subject:

ISAF Case 66 reads, "SUMMARY OF FACTS: Shortly after gybing around a reaching mark, the crew of a boat fell overboard. During the time it took her helmsman to lower the spinnaker and turn back to recover his crew, a spectator boat picked him up and returned him to the boat. She continued in the race and finished, but her helmsman, in consideration of rule 41 (Outside Help), chose to retire. Later, however, he asked to be reinstated, holding that safety was involved in the outside assistance given, and the penalty for retiring was too severe in the circumstances. The protest committee, while sympathetic, believed that, because his boat had received outside assistance, her retirement was appropriate under the terms of rule 41. He appealed.

"DECISION: Rule 41 makes a specific exemption for receiving assistance when it is given under rule 1.1. The latter requires that every boat shall render all possible assistance to a person or vessel in danger. It is in the best interests of safety to consider any person in the water, without clear evidence to the contrary, to be is some degree of danger. The appellant therefore did not break rule 41."

ISAF Case 38 reads: "SUMMARY OF THE CASE: Dinghy A capsized during a race and seeing this, dinghy B sailed over to her and offered help. A accepted help and B came alongside taking the crew of two aboard. Then all hands worked for several minutes to right A whose mast was stuck in mud. Upon reaching shore, B requested redress under rule 62.1(c). The protest committee considered several factors in its decision. First, A's helmsman was a highly experienced sailor. Secondly, the wind was light, and the tide was rising and would shortly have lifted the mast free. Thirdly, she did not ask for help; it was offered. Therefore, since neither boat nor crew was in danger, redress was refused. B appealed, stating that rule 1.1 does not place any onus on a boat rendering assistance to decide, or to defend, a decision that danger was involved.

"DECISION: Appeal upheld. A boat in a position to help another that may be in danger is bound to do so. That she offers assistance not requested is irrelevant. That a protest committee, later assessing the many factors that may cause a vessel or person to be in danger, concludes that help was offered but not requested or that no danger existed is irrelevant."

Rule 1.2 - Life-Saving Equipment and Personal Buoyancy

A boat shall carry adequate life-saving equipment for all persons on board, including one item ready for immediate use, unless her class rules make some other provision. Each competitor is individually responsible for wearing personal buoyancy adequate for the conditions.

Rule 1.2 gives the highest prominence to these safety issues. Note that it is **each sailor's** responsibility to decide when to wear his or her life-jacket. Often class rules and/or sailing instructions will require you to wear your life-jacket any time you go afloat. Be sure to check those rules.

Also, the race committee can require you to wear your life-jacket by displaying flag Y (rule 40, Personal Buoyancy). Note, however, that though the race committee has the option to use this signal, it does not shift away from you any of your responsibility for your own safety. Rule 40 also clarifies that wet suits and dry suits are not adequate personal buoyancy.

Finally, the US SAILING prescription to rule 40 reads, "*US SAILING prescribes that every boat shall carry life-saving equipment conforming to government regulations.*"

RULE 2 - FAIR SAILING

A boat and her owner shall compete in compliance with recognized principles of sportsmanship and fair play. A boat may be penalized under this rule only if it is clearly established that these principles have been violated.

As was discussed in Chapter 3, Sportsmanship and the Rules, when we race we should all agree to hold ourselves to the highest principles of fairness and sportsmanship. Rule 2 is a clear statement of that premise. When a boat or competitor clearly violates these principles before, during or after a race, he or she breaks this rule and is liable to penalty.

Note that a penalty for breaking this rule is more severe than for most other rules. Rule A1.3 (Scores not Discardable) states that if you are in a series which allows you to discard your worst race, a disqualification for breaking rule 2 cannot be discarded. Notice also that a boat can be penalized under rule 2 **even when another rule applies to the situation**. (Under the previous rules this was not the case.) Therefore, in any incident or situation where the principles in rule 2 have been clearly violated, regardless of what other rules may also have been broken, a boat is liable to disqualification under rule 2. This becomes very significant given that a boat has to count that disqualification in her final score.

"Could you give some examples of when you would consider the principles in rule 2 have been violated?"

Sure. But first let me remind that each protest committee is given the discretion to judge what they deem to be "recognized principles of sportsmanship and fair play." In deciding whether a competitor has competed in compliance with the principles in rule 2, I feel it is important to consider the motive for their actions; i.e. was it an intentional violation of one of the principles?

In ISAF Case 107, "An experienced helmsman of a port-tack boat hails 'Starboard!' to a beginner who, although on starboard tack, not being sure of himself and probably being scared of having his boat holed, tacks to port to avoid a collision. No protest was lodged. One school of thought argues that it is fair game, because if a helmsman does not know the rules, that is his own hard luck. The other school rejects this argument, on the grounds that it is quite contrary to the spirit of the rules to deceive a competitor in that way. It is known that such a trick is often played, particularly where novices were involved, and therefore guidance is sought on whether a protest committee should or should not take action under rule 2.

"ANSWER: A boat that deliberately hails 'Starboard' when she is on port tack has not acted fairly and is liable to disqualification under rule 2. When it is clearly established that such a misleading hail was deliberate, the protest committee should also consider taking action under rule 69 (Allegations of Gross Misconduct)."

Other examples:

- A *port-tack* boat is reaching by to *leeward* of a *starboard-tack* boat before the start. Just as the boats are passing, her boom suddenly flies out and hits the *port-tacker*'s shroud. Clearly there is no way for P to *keep clear* at that moment. If it is determined that S's skipper let the boom out **intentionally to hit P,** I would penalize S under rule 2. If it is determined that S was simply sailing her boat, perhaps responding to a gust of wind, etc., I would penalize P for not *keeping clear*.

- Two boats come off the starting line side by side in very light air. Suddenly, the *leeward* boat rocks hard to *windward*, the tip of her mast hitting the tip of the *windward* boat's mast. Again, if it is determined that the action was done solely to try to touch the *windward* boat, I would penalize her under rule 2. I would apply the same reasoning to a *leeward* boat whose crew goes out on the trapeze in light air or otherwise reaches out and touches the *windward* boat for the sole purpose of "fouling the other boat out."

- A boat is on a heavy-air overnight race. Each time the boat tacks, the crew down-below move the sails back and forth to the *windward* side to increase the boat's stability. Not only would I penalize this boat for breaking rule 51 (Moving Ballast), I would penalize her under rule 2 as well (and consider taking action under rule 69, Allegations of Gross Misconduct).

One common practice that is **not** a violation of rule 2 is the tactic whereby one boat tries to make it harder for another boat to do well in a race or series, including by trying to put boats between herself and the other boat at the finish, provided the boat tries to sail within the *rules* and provided her motive is to benefit her own series score.

ISAF Case 155 reads, "On a windward leg near the finish of the final race of a series, boat A is some distance ahead of boat B. Suddenly, A changes course, so that she sails back down the

course towards B and positions herself in a tactically controlling position over B. A then impedes B's progress, resulting in three boats passing them. A had calculated her own and B's score, and had determined that if B were to be passed by three boats A would defeat B in the series (after throw-outs).

"QUESTION: Is the tactic employed by A, turning back to impede another boat's progress, a sportsmanlike action, and is it an acceptable tactic in any race or in any part of a race?

"ANSWER: This tactic breaks no rule, including rule 2 which refers to sportsmanship. It is acceptable for A to make it difficult for B to do well in a race, so long as she does not thereby break a rule...The tactic is acceptable in any race of the series, and at any time or place during the race, only provided it can be justified as benefiting boat A through her series score."

Though some may shiver at the notion that it is okay for one boat to actively try to hinder another boat's race, the racing rules themselves are in no way constructed to discourage, inhibit or prevent this. In fact, it is quite common for one boat to try to start close to *leeward* of another for the purpose of hindering the other's start, to intentionally tack on someone's wind on a beat, or to luff a boat downwind. In addition, it is quite common for sailors to be aware of "who their competition is" from the outset of a race or series and to actively seek opportunities to hinder them early on. As long as it's done within the racing rules, there is no problem.

"What happens if a boat hinders my race and causes me to finish worse than I would have otherwise finished, and is found to have broken rule 2 in the process?"

In that case, you are entitled to redress under rule 62.1(d) (Redress)! You can request this yourself, or the race or protest committee can do it on your behalf (rule 60, Right to Protest and Request Redress).

When a protest committee feels that an individual competitor has acted in a way that is contrary to our sport, they can conduct a hearing under rule 69 (Allegations of Gross Misconduct).

Rule 69 - Allegations of Gross Misconduct

Rule 69.1 - Action by a Protest Committee

(a) When a protest committee, from its own observation or a report received, believes that a competitor may have committed a gross breach of a *rule* or of good manners or sportsmanship, or may have brought the sport into disrepute, it may call a hearing. The protest committee shall promptly inform the competitor in writing of the alleged misconduct and of the time and place of the hearing.

(b) A protest committee of at least three members shall conduct the hearing, following rules 63.2, 63.3, 63.4 and 63.6. If it decides that the competitor committed the alleged misconduct it shall either

   (1) warn the competitor or

   (2) impose a penalty by excluding the competitor, and a boat when appropriate, from a race, or the remaining races of a series or the entire series, or by taking other action within its jurisdiction.

(c) The protest committee shall promptly report a penalty, but not a warning, to the national authorities of the venue, of the competitor and of the boat owner.

Rule 69.1(a) permits a protest committee to call a hearing when it believes that a competitor may have committed a gross breach of a *rule* or of good manners or sportsmanship, or may have brought the sport into disrepute. The protest committee may have first-hand knowledge of the situation, or it may have received a report from someone else. Notice that a boat does not protest under rule 69; however, she can suggest in a protest that a hearing under rule 69 be considered.

If the protest committee decides that the competitor has acted improperly, they can warn him, exclude him (and his boat if appropriate) from one or more races in a series or the entire series, or take other action available to them. Notice that, with the exception of a warning, they must also report their action to the national authorities involved.

Note that when a boat is removed from a series, rule A1.7 (Scores Removed From All or Part of a Series) reads, "*When a boat is penalized by having her scores removed from the results of some or all races of a series, no changes shall be made in the race scores of other boats.*"

Rule 69 is to be used when the competitor's conduct is "gross." "Gross" can be generally interpreted as follows: conspicuously obvious, flagrant, deliberate, referring to offenses or errors so bad they cannot escape notice or be condoned or actions exceeding reasonable or excusable limits.

In my opinion, any **deliberate infringement** of the rules is a gross infringement. For example: S deliberately rams P causing damage (perhaps because the skipper of P had "disqualified" the skipper of S in a protest hearing the night before). Another example is when a competitor deliberately cuts a *mark* or starts ahead of the starting line for the purpose of hindering another competitor's race. (See ISAF Case 78.)

Further examples of a gross breach of good manners or sportsmanship include: **proved lying** in a protest hearing (as opposed to honest differences in recollection of the incident); **intentional cheating** (for instance, racing with an unmeasured sail or removing mandatory ballast, as opposed to class or racing rule violations caused by ignorance or oversight); **intentional damage to another boat** afloat or on shore (for instance, cutting someone's shrouds in the night); **fighting**, particularly where there is injury or damage; **stealing** from another boat or from private property at a club or elsewhere; and **foul or threatening language**, particularly if it is continued after receiving a clear warning.

Obviously rule 69 is an important rule, but its effectiveness relies on the integrity of the protest committee that chooses to invoke it. Each case must be carefully examined to determine, as accurately as possible, exactly what happened, what events led up to the incident, and what the probable motives of the individuals involved were. The hearing and deliberations should be conducted as objectively as possible with an effort to keep emotions out. A competitor's previous actions should not be weighed in the case unless germane and accurately represented. Appeals that are cited as precedent must be closely examined to be sure that they are truly nearly identical in all ways. And before imposing a penalty under rule 69.1(b)(2), the protest committee must thoroughly consider if the weight of the punishment is justified by the competitor's action.

Disqualification from a series for a gross infringement of the *rules* or a gross breach of good manners or sportsmanship is a strong penalty by itself, due to the effect it generally has on the individual(s) and from the adverse publicity it can create. But in addition, this penalty must be reported to US SAILING or the appropriate national authority. In turn they can conduct an investigation and exclude the competitor(s) or boat(s) from the sport for a period of time. This is an extremely strong consequence as it will have an impact on the sailor's life beyond just their sailing, in ways that may extend beyond just the time period of their penalty.

Note that a sailor penalized under rule 69 is a *party* to a hearing (see the Definition *Party*), and as such she has the right to appeal the decision of the protest committee under rule 70.1(a) (Right of Appeal and Requests for Interpretations). A U.S. sailor also may file a grievance under Article XIV of the US SAILING Bylaws when they feel actions have been taken against them that are not in accordance with the *rules*.

RULE 3 - ACCEPTANCE OF THE RULES

By participating in a race conducted under these racing rules, each competitor and boat owner agrees

(a) to be governed by the *rules*;

(b) to accept the penalties imposed and other action taken under the *rules*, subject to the appeal and review procedures provided in them, as the final determination of any matter arising under the *rules*; and

(c) with respect to such determination, not to resort to any court or other tribunal not provided by the *rules*.

Rule 3 states that when you decide to race under the ISAF *Racing Rules of Sailing*, you agree to be governed by those *rules*, and to keep actions made in accordance with the rules within the rules system of the sport; i.e. not to take them to any outside court. Note that Rule M1.2(4) (Notice of Race Contents) requires that the Notice of Race shall include, when appropriate, an entry form to be signed by the boat's owner or owner's representative, containing words such as: "I agree to be bound by *The Racing Rules of Sailing* and by all other *rules* that govern this event."

This agreement becomes especially important when an incident results in a high cost of repair or replacement. Rule 68 (Damages) states, "*The question of damages arising from a breach of any **rule** shall be subject to the prescriptions, if any, of the national authority.*"

In the United States, US SAILING prescribes that "*responsibility for damages arising from any breach of the **rules** shall be based on fault as determined by application of the **rules**, and that she shall not be subject to the legal doctrine of 'assumption of risk' for monetary damages resulting from contact with other boats.*" Furthermore, the prescription states, "*A protest committee shall find facts and make decisions only in compliance with the **rules**. No protest committee or US SAILING appeal authority shall adjudicate any claim for damages. Such a claim is subject to the jurisdiction of the courts.*"

In other words, a protest committee can find only the facts; and a protest committee, or appeals committee acting on an appeal, can decide only which boat was at fault under the *rules*. They cannot decide issues of claims for damages.

When you disagree with a protest committee's application or interpretation of the *rules*, you may appeal under rule 70.1

(Right of Appeal or Requests for Interpretations), unless the right of appeal has been denied under rule 70.4. If you feel that any of your rights as a competitor have been denied by the race or protest committee and it hurt your finishing place in a race or series, you can request redress under rule 62 (Redress) and you can appeal that decision as well.

If you feel you've been aggrieved by an action not under the jurisdiction of the *rules*, you can take your grievance to the organizing authority for the race or series, or to US SAILING through Article XIV of the US SAILING Bylaws.

RULE 4 - DECISION TO RACE

A boat is solely responsible for deciding whether or not to *start* or to continue *racing*.

There have been attempted lawsuits brought unsuccessfully against race committees by sailors who have had accidents during races in strong winds. Their contentions have been, in part, that the race committee has jeopardized their safety by holding races in severe conditions. US SAILING Appeal 209 is crystal clear: "The decision to start, postpone or abandon a race is a matter solely within the jurisdiction of the race committee (see rule 85, Governing Rules). Rule 62 (Redress) should not be interpreted to restrict or interfere with its authority and responsibilities in matters of race management. Under rule 4, each boat has the sole responsibility to decide whether or not to race. If a boat decides not to race, she cannot claim her finishing place was made worse."

Notice that it is the **boat's** responsibility to decide. Every sailor on a boat has the responsibility to voice their opinion as to whether or not to *start* or to continue to *race*. Nothing in this rule protects an owner, skipper or helmsman from a liability suit brought by their crew.

RULE 5 - DRUGS

A competitor shall neither take a substance nor use a method banned by Appendix L. An alleged breach of this rule shall not be grounds for a *protest,* and rule 63.1 does not apply.

Appendix L - Banned Substances and Banned Methods

Introduction

Doping is the taking or using by a competitor of a substance or a method banned by the ISAF. Doping is governed by rule 5, this appendix, and the ISAF *Medical Lists* (containing the official lists of doping classes and methods, medicines that may be taken, and laboratories accredited for doping control) and *Doping Control Procedures* (the medical procedures leaflet). These publications, doping control forms and the ISAF schedule of penalties are available from ISAF to national authorities and competitors on request.

Clearly, this is primarily of concern for Olympic-bound competitors. However, all competitors are wise to recognize that there is a strict rule forbidding the use of banned drugs in our sport.

WI
LI
3) Now I'm the leeward boat so keep it up!
1) Up... You bet to get o my wa

5

THE DEFINITIONS

The Definitions are the "dictionary" of the rule book. Words and terms like "racing," "obstruction" and "proper course" are specifically defined so that there is no question or debate as to their meaning. When a defined word or term is used in a rule, it is printed in *italic* type. Before studying the rules, be sure to study the Definitions and then actively check back to them as you go through each rule; you'll find that in a short time you will be confident of each rule's full meaning.

N

N OVER H

N OVER A

ABANDON

A race that a race committee or protest committee *abandons* is void but may be resailed.

A race committee can *abandon* a race before it starts (rule 27.3, Other Race Committee Actions Before the Starting Signal), while it is under way (rule 32, Shortening or Abandoning After the Start) or even after one or more boats have finished (rule 32). To signal an *abandonment*, the race committee will make three consecutive sound signals and display flag N (meaning return to the starting area for a new start), flag N over H (meaning return to the harbor and await further instructions) or flag N over A (meaning no more races that day). (See Race Signals.) A protest committee, acting on a request for redress, can *abandon* a race (rule 64.2, Decisions on Redress). A race that has been properly *abandoned* may be resailed.

Notice that once the race has started, the race committee is governed by rule 32 when deciding whether to *abandon* a race. Rule 32 lists the five scenarios in which the race committee may *abandon* a race:

a) **because of an error in the starting procedure,**

b) **because of foul weather,**

c) **because of insufficient wind making it unlikely that any boat will *finish* within the time limit,**

d) **because a mark is missing or has moved out of position, or**

e) **for any other reason directly affecting the safety or fairness of the competition.**

"Does rule 32(e) mean that the race committee can abandon a race in progress when a large wind shift occurs?"

Yes, when in its judgment the wind shift has made the race an unsatisfactory test of skill and therefore "unfair." However, in my opinion it is desirable to reduce the number of subjective decisions a race committee can make once the race has started and it can see who is or isn't doing well. Therefore, once a race has been started, race committees should make every attempt to anticipate and react to wind shifts and to reposition *marks* in order to keep the race "fair" before deciding to *abandon*, particularly after the first boat has rounded the first *mark*.

After at least one boat has finished a race, the race committee and protest committee are required, before *abandoning* the race, to consider the probable consequences for all boats affected and to take appropriate evidence when doubt exists (rules 32 and 64.2).

CLEAR ASTERN AND CLEAR AHEAD; OVERLAP

One boat is *clear astern* of another when her hull and equipment in normal position are behind a line abeam from the aftermost point of the other boat's hull and equipment in normal position. The other boat is *clear ahead*. They *overlap* when neither is *clear astern* or when a boat between them *overlaps* both. These terms do not apply to boats on opposite *tacks* unless rule 18 applies.

Putting aside for a moment what *tack* the boats are on, let's look at two boats sailing near each other. To figure out if they are *overlapped*, take one of the boats and draw a line down her centerline. Then find the aftermost point of her hull or equipment in **normal position.** Draw another line perpendicular to the centerline and through the aftermost point. If the other boat's hull and equipment in **normal position** are completely behind that line, she is *clear astern* and the other boat is *clear ahead*. If she is on or across that line at all, then neither boat is *clear astern* of the other; therefore they are *overlapped*.

Now let's say one of the boats was *clear ahead* of the other boat by five feet. Put a third boat in between the two. If the boat that was *clear astern* now *overlaps* this middle boat and the middle boat *overlaps* the boat that was *clear ahead*, the definition says that now each boat is *overlapped* with each other.

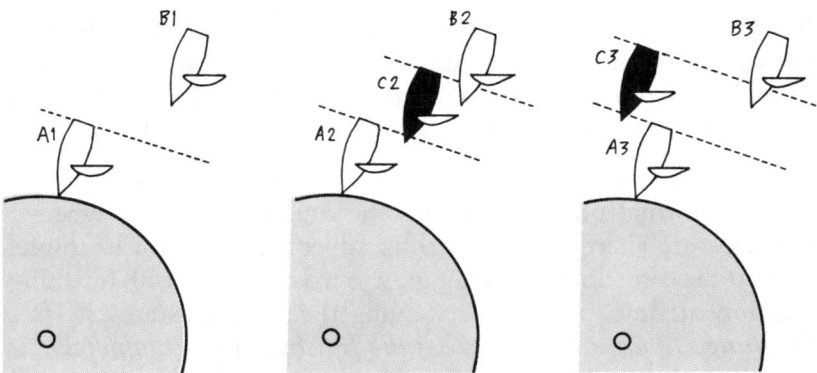

In position 1, A and B are not overlapped; A is clear ahead and B is clear astern. In position 2, C is in between A and B and overlapped with both of them; therefore B has an inside overlap on A. In position 3, C is not in between A and B; therefore B has an inside overlap on C, C has an outside overlap on A, and A and B are not overlapped.

One point worth discussing is determining the aftermost point of the hull and equipment in normal position. It literally means the point on the boat that is the farthest aft, i.e. the point that would hit a wall first if the boat were backed into one.

Notice also the term "normal position" (see the Definition *Finish* for more discussion). If your auxiliary engine is tilted up, then in all likelihood the propeller is the aftermost point; and if you've been sailing the race with it up, you can't come into a *mark* and quickly swing the engine down just to break an *overlap* by making your boat shorter.

Finally, notice that the terms "clear astern," "clear ahead" and "overlap" do not apply to boats on opposite *tacks,* unless they are about to pass a *mark* or *obstruction* (rule 18, Passing Marks and Obstructions). So two boats side by side on opposite *tacks* halfway down the run are not *overlapped,* but when they get down near the "*two-length zone*" at the *mark,* they are considered to be *overlapped.*

It's worth pointing out a deletion from the previous definition. Under the previous rules, when the *leeward* boat *started,* the *overlap* was considered to be a new one at that time. This has been deleted in the new definition. For a full discussion of the implications of this deletion, see the discussion of rule 17.1 (On the Same Tack; Proper Course).

FINISH

A boat finishes when any part of her hull, or crew or equipment in normal position, crosses the finishing line in the direction of the course from the last *mark* either for the first time or, if she takes a penalty, after complying with rule 31.2 or rule 44.2.

You *finish* when any part of your hull, or of your crew or equipment in **normal position,** crosses the finishing line, i.e. when it first crosses. Therefore, in a strong adverse current for example, all you need to do is get your bow across to get your finishing position or time. Rule 28.1 (Sailing the Course) states, "*After finishing, a boat need not cross the finishing line completely.*"

Notice that your crew and equipment must be in "normal position." "Normal position" is generally defined as the position where your crew or equipment is normally located in the

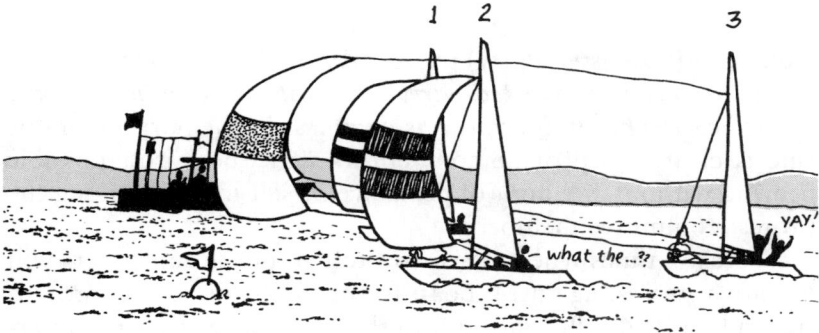

Boat 3's spinnaker is not in normal position.

existing wind and sea conditions. Therefore boats can't come into a close downwind finish and suddenly let their spinnaker halyards and sheets out two feet, or come into a close upwind finish in light air and suddenly have their crews jump out on the trapeze to put their heads across the line.

If you do not *finish* correctly, the race committee is allowed to score you DNF (Did Not Finish) without protesting you (rules A1.1 and A3, Scoring). If you feel they have incorrectly scored you DNF, you can request redress under rule 62.1(a) (Redress). However, if you *finish* but the race committee thinks it saw you touch a finishing *mark* and you do not take a penalty, they must score you as having *finished* and then protest you under rule 31 (Touching a Mark) in accordance with rule 61 (Protest Requirements).

Sometimes, when coming up to a finishing line, it is not always clear which way to go across it. The definition says that a boat *finishes* when she crosses the finishing line in the direction of the course from the last *mark*. The last *mark* means the last *mark* of the course prior to the finishing line. Therefore, simply cross the line in the natural direction from the last *mark* you passed, regardless of any required sides either of the finishing *marks* may have had at other times during the race (see ISAF Case 102).

INTERESTED PARTY

A person who may gain or lose as a result of a protest committee's decision, or who has a close personal interest in the decision.

Rule 63.4 (Interested Party) reads, "*A member of a protest committee who is an **interested party** shall not take any further part in the hearing but may appear as a witness.*" The purpose of this rule is clearly to provide competitors with the fairest possible hearing without any taint of prejudice or self-interest among the protest committee members.

There are times when race or protest committee members will initiate a *protest* against a boat; for example, under the propulsion rule (rule 42, Propulsion). In this context they are not *interested parties*, and they are allowed to be **both** a member of the protest committee as well as the protestor. However, they must give all their evidence and testimony as a witness in front of the *parties* to the hearing (see rules 63.3(a) and 63.6, Hearings, and US SAILING Appeal 209.)

Persons who, in my opinion, **could** be considered *interested parties* are parents (or offspring), instructors or coaches, employers or employees, sponsors or financial contributors, members of the same yacht club or association, or even a fellow sailor with the same nationality. In the right set of circumstances, any of these persons could be judged to be an *interested party*.

"What can I do if I honestly feel a member of the protest committee might be an 'interested party?'"

If you feel any member of a protest committee is an *interested party*, you may object. Rule 63.4 reads, "*A **party** to the hearing who believes a member of the protest committee is an **interested party** shall object as soon as possible.*" The protest committee should then consider your objection before proceeding (Appendix P2, Recommendations for Protest Committees, Before the Hearing). In evaluating members of a protest committee as potentially *interested parties*, the important criterion is: will their hearing of the facts, their finding of the facts and their application and interpretation of the *rules* be hindered by any prejudice or favoritism toward or against any of the *parties* to the hearing? If members of the protest committee honestly feel that any predisposition on their part will affect their decision in the hearing, they should respectfully decline to serve; and when you honestly feel or suspect that a *protest committee* member's decision-making ability might be affected for some reason, you have a right to say so and to state your reasons (rule 63.4).

KEEP CLEAR

One boat *keeps clear* of another if the other can sail her course with no need to take avoiding action and, when the boats are *overlapped* on the same *tack*, if the *leeward* boat could change course without immediately making contact with the *windward* boat.

The rules are structured so that when two boats converge on the race course, one has the right-of-way and the other must stay out of her way, i.e. *keep clear*. The preamble to Part 2, Section A reads, *"A boat has right of way when another boat is required to keep clear of her."* I call the boat that is required to *keep clear* the "**give-way**" boat.

The principle in the definition is clear: right-of-way boats should be able to sail their race without give-way boats getting in their way. That means that not only must a give-way boat not hit a right-of-way boat, she must also not get so close that the right-of-way boat can no longer sail her course because she has to take action to avoid contact with the give-way boat. Though this "action" will normally be a change of course, it could also be a change of speed or some other action.

Note that a give-way boat doesn't need to begin taking avoiding action until she is converging with a right-of-way boat. Before that time she is *keeping clear*.

On the issue of "need," I believe that when the right-of-way boat has a reasonable apprehension that if she continues sailing straight ahead, contact will occur without action on her part, she is justified in saying she "needed" to take action, even if subsequent analysis of the situation shows that the give-way boat would have actually cleared by inches (ISAF Case 169).

Note that this definition now legitimizes a common tactic that previously had been of questionable legality. The scenario is when a *starboard-tack* boat (S) instructs a nearby *port-tack* boat (P) to cross ahead of her and then bears away to avoid P. The tactic is intended to encourage P not to tack on S's lee-bow. In this scenario, S's **chosen** course is to bear away and pass astern of P; therefore P has *kept clear*.

The last phrase in the definition closes a possible loophole caused by rule 16 (Changing Course). Rule 16 requires that when right-of-way boats change course, they give other boats *room* to *keep clear*. The loophole is that a *windward* boat (W) could position herself right next to a *leeward* boat (L) such that the moment L changed course either up or down she would hit W. W could then claim that L had broken rule 16 by not giving her *room* to *keep clear*. The definition closes that loophole by addressing **overlapped** boats on the same *tack* and telling W that she is not *keeping clear* if she allows herself to get so close to L that L couldn't change course in either direction at that moment without **immediately** making contact with her. If L couldn't luff without immediate contact but could bear away without immediate contact, the last phrase in this definition doesn't apply because L "could" change course without making immediate contact.

Note that the second "if" in the definition suggests that L does not need to actually hit W to prove she couldn't change course without contact. If the protest committee decides that L couldn't have changed course without immediately hitting W, then W has broken rule 11 (On the Same Tack, Overlapped) simply by her extreme close proximity to L. Note, however, that this just essentially reinforces the opening phrase of the definition because anytime L cannot sail her course without a need to take action to avoid W, W has not *kept clear* and breaks rule 11.

"Do I have to keep clear of the right-of-way boat's crew, sails, equipment, spars, etc. even when they are clearly out of their 'normal position'?"

Yes. The definition makes no distinction regarding whether or not a boat is carrying her crew, sails, equipment, spars, etc. in "normal position." (See US SAILING Appeal 271.) The only exception is in the rare instance where a boat is *keeping clear* and suddenly something from the right-of-way boat flies out unexpectedly and immediately makes contact with the give-way boat. ISAF Case 153 describes such a case where just after rounding a leeward *mark,* the head of the spinnaker of the boat *clear ahead* (A) came loose and flew back and touched the head-stay of the boat *clear astern* (B). The decision concludes, "Concerning the Definition, Keep Clear, in its terms nothing that B did or failed to do required A 'to take avoiding action.' This is shown by the fact that the contact between them results exclusively from A's equipment moving out of its normal position."

LEEWARD AND WINDWARD

A boat's *leeward* side is the side that is or, when she is head to wind, was away from the wind. However, when sailing by the lee or directly downwind, her *leeward* side is the side on which her mainsail lies. The other side is her *windward* side. When two boats on the same *tack* overlap, the one on the *leeward* side of the other is the *leeward* boat. The other is the *windward* boat.

The definition called *Tack, Starboard* or *Port* tells us that whether we are on *port* or *starboard tack* is determined by our *windward* side, i.e. if our *windward* side is our port side, we are on *port tack.*

This definition tells us that our *windward* side is the side closest to the wind, and that our *leeward* side is the opposite side. If the boat is heading directly into the wind, then whichever side **was** the *windward* side before the boat was head to wind is still considered the *windward* side.

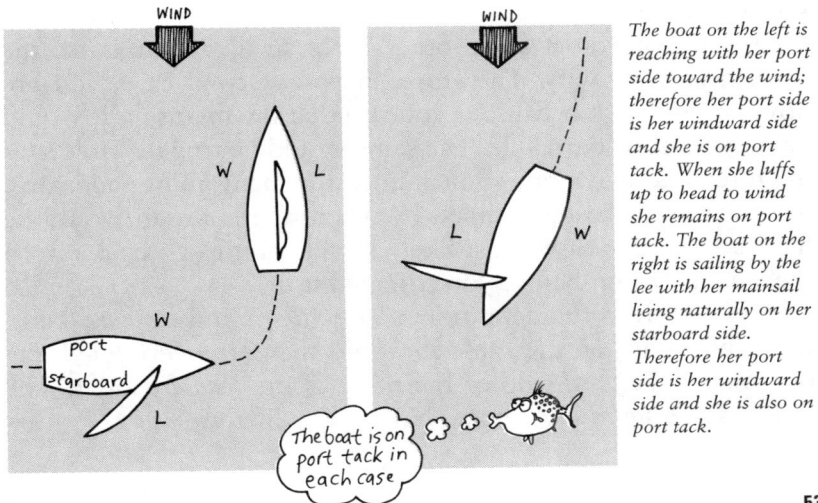

The boat on the left is reaching with her port side toward the wind; therefore her port side is her windward side and she is on port tack. When she luffs up to head to wind she remains on port tack. The boat on the right is sailing by the lee with her mainsail lieing naturally on her starboard side. Therefore her port side is her windward side and she is also on port tack.

The boat is on port tack in each case

The only exception is when the boat is heading directly down-wind or "by the lee" (which means the boat has continued to turn past directly downwind without the boom changing sides). In that case, the *windward* side is the side opposite the side the boom is on.

"If I'm sailing close-hauled on port-tack in light air and heel the boat sharply to windward such that the boom falls to the port side of the boat, am I now on starboard tack; or if I'm sailing by the lee and forcibly holding the mainsail over the port side with my arm, am I still on starboard tack?"

No. Remember that when you are not sailing directly downwind or by the lee, your *tack* is determined by the side of the boat the wind is blowing over. In your first case, when you are sailing close-hauled, the wind is blowing over your port side regardless of where your boom is located; therefore you are on *port tack*. The same would be true if you are sailing along on *port tack*, and then go head to wind and push your boom out on the port side to back down. You are still on *port tack* as long as your bow doesn't **pass** head to wind. The moment it **passes** head to wind, you are now on *starboard tack*.

When you are sailing directly downwind or by the lee, your *lee-ward* side is the side on which your mainsail "lies." "Lies" is used intentionally to indicate that it is the side where your main-sail would **naturally** lie, i.e. be pushed by the wind, as opposed to by the control of some other force such as your arm, the mainsheet or gravity. Therefore, in your second case, you are now on *port tack* because if you released the mainsail, it would lie on your starboard side. The same would be true if, while sail-ing directly downwind, you trimmed the mainsail in amidships. Your *tack* will be determined by where the mainsail would lie naturally; in this case, most likely it will want to go back out to the side it was on before you trimmed it in.

Finally, there is the definition of *windward* and *leeward* boat. If the boats are **on the same** *tack* and they are **overlapped**, the one on the *leeward* side of the other is the *leeward* boat. The other is the *windward* boat. Notice that if they are not *over-*

lapped, they are not *windward* and *leeward* boats; they are *clear ahead* and *clear astern.*

MARK

An object the sailing instructions require a boat to pass on a specified side, excluding its anchor line and objects attached temporarily or accidentally.

A *mark* can be an inflatable ball, a bell buoy, a large power boat, an island or any object the sailing instructions so indicate. Notice that often the sailing instructions require that government *marks* be passed on their required side as you sail from one turning *mark* to the next. These government *marks* are *marks* of the course as well. On a starting line between a race committee boat and a buoy, the **entire** race committee boat is a *mark* even though the actual end of the line is marked by a flag or some other specific point on the boat. Anything that is normally attached to the object is also part of the *mark,* for instance, a flag, a long antenna or a mizzen boom; but something temporarily attached, such as a Whaler tied up to the race committee boat, is not part of the *mark* **unless** the sailing instructions indicate otherwise. Note that a race committee will often hang a "stand-off buoy" off the transom of their race committee boat to keep boats farther away, and that they will commonly indicate in the sailing instructions that these "stand-off" buoys are to be considered part of the *mark.*

Also note that the entire object is the *mark,* not just the above-water part. The 1949 NAYRU rules read, "Every ordinary above-water part of such object...is part of the Mark, but no part below water." This was changed in the 1961 international rules and has remained so since.

OBSTRUCTION

An object that a boat could not pass without changing course substantially, if she were sailing directly towards it and one of her hull lengths from it. An object that can be safely passed on only one side and an area so designated by the sailing instructions are also *obstructions.* However, a boat *racing* is not an

obstruction to other boats unless they are required to *keep clear* of her or give her *room.*

An *obstruction* is **anything** on the race course, including another boat in your race or other vessel in the racing area, large enough to require you to make a substantial alteration of course to avoid it if you are about to hit it. In determining whether the object can be considered an *obstruction,* the definition offers three criteria:

1) the object must be large enough to require you to change course substantially **if** you were aiming right at it, regardless of whether you actually are or not. In other words, it's a hypothetical test. An object does not become an *obstruction* or cease to be an *obstruction* based on where on it you are actually aiming at the time.

2) the amount of course change required is determined from a point one of your boat's overall lengths away from the object. This strongly suggests that you keep a lookout for anything ahead of you, as opposed to suddenly finding yourself about to hit something right in front of you and needing to slam your tiller over to miss it.

3) the size of the course change must be "substantial," i.e. a large course change. In a twenty-foot boat, a course change of 10 degrees moves the bow about three and a half feet. Done when one boat-length away, a 10-degree alteration will clear a seven-foot object on either side. **As my general rule** I would say that a course change less than 10 degrees is not "substantial;" i.e. a stationary object clearly less than one-third your boat's length would not be an *obstruction,* though a moving object will require a larger alteration to get around it. Obviously, a lobster pot or an average-size channel marker is not going to require you to alter your course substantially, but a race committee boat, a breakwater or another sailboat in a race will.

A powerboat can be an *obstruction* if it's large enough. When a race committee decides to use a powerboat as one end of the starting line, the powerboat becomes a *mark* also. Notice that it doesn't cease to be an *obstruction*. It is always an *obstruction,* but now it also happens to be a *mark.*

Notice also that in a three or more boat situation, another boat in a race is an *obstruction* when the other boats in the incident are required to *keep clear* of her or to give her *room*. Therefore, a right-of-way boat can be an *obstruction* to giveway boats, and an inside boat entitled to *room* while passing a *mark* or *obstruction* can be an *obstruction* to outside boats. Other boats in the race are not considered *obstructions*.

PARTY

A *party* to a hearing: a protestor; a protestee; a boat requesting redress; any other boat or competitor liable to be penalized, including under rule 69.1; a race committee in a hearing under rule 62.1(a).

It is important to understand exactly who is, and is not, a *party* to a protest hearing. The primary reason is that the rules in Part 5, Protests, Hearings, Misconduct and Appeals, provide many specific rights and obligations for *parties* to a hearing and many requirements of a protest committee regarding *parties* to a hearing. Furthermore, only a *party* to a hearing may appeal a decision of a protest committee under rule 70.1 (Right of Appeal and Requests for Interpretations).

When boats or the race or protest committee protest, they automatically become a *party* to the hearing (protestor), as do the boats they are protesting (protestee). The same is true when boats request redress under rule 62 (Redress); and when the claim is that an improper action or omission of the race committee made their finishing place significantly worse, the race committee also becomes a *party* to the hearing.

Often, in the course of a hearing, a third yacht will become a "suspect." Rule 61.1(c) (Protest Requirements) says, "*During the hearing of a valid **protest**, if the protest committee decides to protest a boat that was involved in the incident but is not a **party** to that hearing, it shall inform the boat as soon as reasonably possible of its intention and of the time and place of the hearing.*" Once the protest committee protests the third boat, that boat becomes a *party* to the hearing.

"If, after acting on another boat's request for redress, the protest committee abandons the race in which I was first, can I consider myself a 'party to the hearing' because I was 'penalized,' and as such appeal the decision?"

Absolutely not. Rule 64 (Protest Decisions) discusses "penalties," using disqualification as the usual penalty. You were not given a specific penalty when the race was *abandoned*. Obviously *abandoning* the race changes series results, moving some competitors up and some down. You may have been disappointed by the *abandonment*, but you were not "penalized" by it. A "penalty" results from a rule breach either accepted voluntarily or imposed by a protest committee decision. Because you were not liable to be penalized in the incident, you are not a *party* to the hearing and are not entitled to appeal.

On the other hand, you certainly can request redress under rule 62.1(a) (Redress). You must be prepared to demonstrate what **"improper** action or omission" the protest committee made in reaching its decision to *abandon* the race, and how the action/omission made your finishing place significantly worse through no fault of your own. Then, once the protest committee has made a decision on your redress request, you may appeal **that** decision. Note, however, that a boat is not entitled to redress for proper action by a race or protest committee simply because alternative action would give her a better standing. (See also ISAF Case 119.)

M is surfing waves in order to increase her speed in an attempt to arrive at the next mark and ultimately the finishing line as quickly as possible. Therefore, her luffing and bearing away are justifiable changes in her proper course. M has not broken any rule.

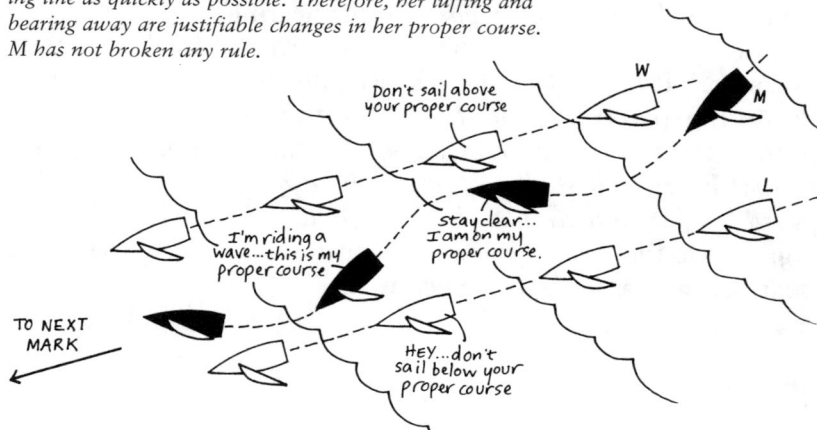

Finally, a boat or competitor who is liable to be penalized under rule 69.1 (Allegations of Gross Misconduct, Action by a Protest Committee) is a *party* to a hearing, thereby giving her standing to appeal the protest committee's decision should they want to do so.

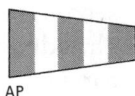

AP

POSTPONE

A postponed race is delayed before its scheduled start but may be started or *abandoned* later.

AP OVER H

A race can be *postponed* only if it has not been started. Once a race has been started, it can only be stopped by *abandoning* it. To signal a *postponement*, the race committee will make two consecutive sound signals and display flag AP, flag AP over H (meaning return to the harbor and await further instructions) or flag AP over A (meaning no more races that day). (See Race Signals.)

AP OVER A

PROPER COURSE

A course a boat would sail to *finish* as soon as possible in the absence of the other boats referred to in the rule using the term. A boat has no *proper course* before her starting signal.

This is the most subjective definition in the book. It is also very important, particularly in applying rule 17 (On the Same Tack; Proper Course). The concept is very straightforward: your *proper course* is the course you think will get you from the starting line to the finishing line as quickly as possible, taking into account all the factors that will affect your speed. Typically, different sailors will have different ideas on what their fastest course is; thus different boats will have justifiably different *proper courses*.

One way to visualize this concept is to imagine a Time Trial. You and nine other sailors show up to race around a fixed-length triangle course, one at a time; the one with the fastest time wins. Around the windward-reach-reach course there are wind shifts, grandstands and a small man-made island on the second reach for the press and photographers. You start. You've already calculated the fastest path up the first beat, accounting for wind shifts, waves, current, time lost while tacking and so on. Down the first reach, as you approach the grandstand area you notice it's creating a huge wind shadow so you bear away to avoid the light air and break through to leeward as quickly as possible. On the second reach, you've calculated that passing to leeward of the press island is the shortest, fastest route to the leeward mark. You finish.

The next boat starts. But this boat goes a different way up the beat. And it doesn't think the grandstand's wind shadow is that bad, so it doesn't bear off as much. And finally it passes the press island to windward and finishes. Both boats were trying to race and finish as quickly as possible and so they were both sailing *proper courses*. In fact, all the boats may have had different opinions as to the fastest course that day. The course each boat sailed was a *proper course*.

Clearly it is possible that there may be several proper courses at any given moment, depending upon the particular circumstances involved. However, because it is often difficult to prove when someone is actually on a *proper course* as opposed to sailing extra high or low for tactical purposes, ISAF Case 25 suggests, "Which of two different courses is the faster one to the next mark cannot be determined in advance and is not necessarily proven by one boat or the other reaching the next mark ahead." For protest committees, two reasonable criteria for judging a *proper course* are whether the boat sailing it has a logical reason for its being a *proper course* and whether she applies it with some consistency.

The phrase *"in the absence of the other boats referred to in the rule using the term"* clarifies which boats to "remove" when determining whether a course is a *proper course* or not. Note that it certainly does not mean "in the absence of all the boats in the race." Let's say you and another boat are sailing down a reach. You catch up and establish an *overlap* to *leeward* of the other boat (W). Rule 17.1 (On the Same Tack; Proper Course) tells you that you cannot sail above your *proper course* while *overlapped* with W. Because W is the other boat referred to in rule 17.1, your *proper course* is your fastest course in the absence of W.

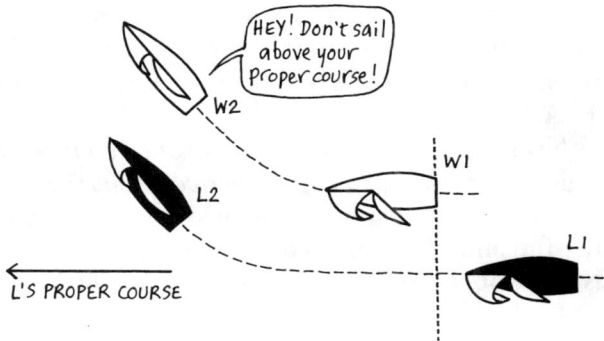

L has established the overlap from clear astern and then luffed above her proper course solely to make it more difficult for W to stay ahead of her. In W's absence L would not have luffed at all. Therefore, L has broken rule 17.1 by sailing above her proper course.

As you and W continue down the reach, you begin catching up to a group of boats in front of you going slowly. Now you have to decide whether to head up and try to pass the group to *windward*, or bear away and try to pass them to *leeward*. You decide that you will arrive at the gybe *mark* faster by heading up and passing the group to *windward*, but by heading up, you will collide with the *windward* boat. In this case, heading up can be considered your *proper course* because you would do so even in the absence of W.

The point is: your *proper course* should be based on what will get **you** to the next *mark* and ultimately to the finishing line as

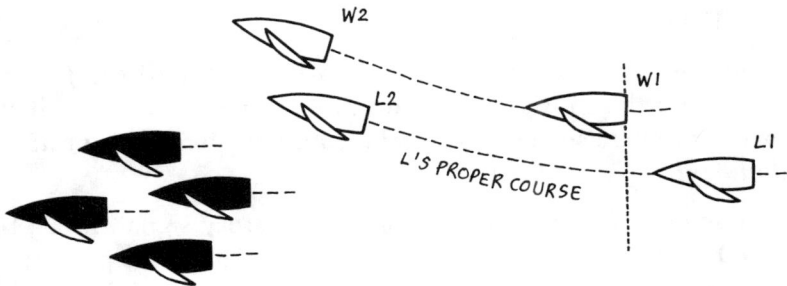

L is "limited" to sailing no higher than her proper course because she has established the overlap from clear astern. However, L decides that she will arrive at the gybe mark faster by luffing and sailing to windward of the pack in front of her. Because she would do this even in the absence of W, it is a legitimate proper course for L and W must keep clear under rule 11.

quickly as possible, not on a tactical consideration such as heading up to cut off a nearby *windward* boat. Note that the rules referring to *proper courses* are rules 17.1, 17.2, 18.1(b) and 18.4.

Notice also that there is no *proper course* **before** the starting signal. That is because a *proper course* is the course sailed to *finish* as soon as possible. Obviously, you can't start racing toward the finishing line until you are allowed to *start*; therefore, there is no *proper course* until after the starting signal is made.

PROTEST

An allegation by a boat, a race committee or a protest committee that a boat has broken a *rule*.

For the most part, allegations and decisions on whether boats have broken any rules are handled after the race in a hearing called by a protest committee. The procedure to ask for such a hearing is called a *protest*. Rules 60 (Right to Protest and Request Redress) and 61 (Protest Requirements) clearly outline the rights and requirements for boats, race committees and protest committees who wish to protest.

Note that a "request for redress" under rule 62 is not a *protest*. For you to "request redress," you must make your request in writing and comply with the time limit of rule 61.3 or within two hours of the relevant incident, whichever is later. You don't need to fly a protest flag (rule 62, Redress).

RACING

A boat is *racing* from her preparatory signal until she *finishes* and clears the finishing line and *marks* or retires, or until the race committee signals a general recall, *postponement*, or *abandonment*.

You actually begin *racing* at your preparatory signal. In a "10-5-GO" sequence, the five-minute signal is usually the preparatory (rule 26, Starting Systems 1 and 2). In a "3-2-1-GO" sequence, it's usually the two-minute signal. Check the sailing instructions for the race to find out when your actual preparatory signal is.

You are no longer *racing* when you have *finished* and cleared the finishing line and *marks*. US SAILING Appeal 99 reads, "When no part of a boat's hull, equipment or crew is still on the finishing line, she has cleared it."

"When am I considered to be clear of the finishing marks?"

You have "cleared the finishing *marks*" when you have left them astern without hitting them during an incident that occurred while you were *finishing*. US SAILING Appeal 136 says, "The official diagram showed the boat in this case to have finished six boat-lengths from the mark that she subsequently touched. When she cleared the line, she was well clear of the mark. Thus, her contact with the mark occurred after she had finished and cleared the finishing line and finishing marks. Since she was no longer racing, rule 31.1 no longer applied."

ROOM

The space a boat needs in the existing conditions while manoeuvring promptly in a seamanlike way.

This definition is central to applying rule 15 (Acquiring Right of Way); rule 16 (Changing Course); rule 18 (Passing Marks and Obstructions) and rule 19 (Room to Tack at an Obstruction).

Note the word "promptly" which means "performed readily, quickly, immediately." This builds in a time element to the definition. Therefore when a *leeward* boat (L) luffs or bears away near a *windward* boat (W), rule 16 requires L to give W *room* to *keep clear*, but W must respond "promptly" or risk losing the protection of *room*. Note also the word "while." This also builds in a time element in that it defines the duration of time a boat must give another "room."

To expand on "seamanlike," I would say "seamanlike" means "responsible, prudent, safety conscious." In other words, it is "seamanlike" never to put your or another boat's crew, boat or equipment at risk of injury or damage.

US SAILING Appeal 119 talks about tactical *mark* roundings and says in essence that *room* does not include all the room an inside boat might like to take to make a tactically desirable rounding.

ISAF Case 40 gives further interpretation of room:

"QUESTION: What is the maximum amount of room an inside boat without right of way is entitled to take in passing a mark or obstruction? What is the minimum amount that an outside boat is required to give? The possible answers vary widely. To suggest the extremes, they might be:

1. as a minimum, enough room with sails and spars sheeted inboard, for the hull to clear by centimeters both the mark and the outside boat;

2. as a maximum, all the room the inside boat takes, setting her course as far abeam of the mark as she wishes.
"Between these extremes are two more moderate possibilities: next to the minimum enough extra clearance to allow for some error of judgment or execution; or, next to the maximum, enough room to make a tactically desirable rounding. Perhaps the most reasonable answer would fall roughly between these two.

"ANSWER: In accordance with the definition, the word 'room' in rule 18.2(a) (Passing Marks and Obstructions) means the space needed by an inside boat, which, in the existing conditions, is handled in a seamanlike way, to pass promptly and safely between the outside boat and a mark or obstruction.

"The term 'existing conditions' deserves some consideration. For example, the inside one of two dinghies approaching a mark on a placid lake in light air will need and can be satisfied with relatively little space beyond her own beam. Contrariwise, when two keel boats, on open water with steep seas, are approaching a mark that is being tossed about widely and unpredictably, the inside boat may need a full hull-length of room or even more to ensure safety.

"The phrase 'in a seamanlike way' applies in two directions. First, it addresses the outside boat, saying that she must provide enough room so that the inside boat need not make extraordinary or abnormal maneuvers to keep clear of her and the mark. It also addresses the inside boat. She is not entitled to complain of insufficient room when she fails to execute with reasonably expected efficiency the handling of her helm, sheets and sails during a rounding."

RULE

(a) The rules in this book, including definitions, race signals, the Introduction, preambles and the rules of an appendix when it applies, but not titles;

(b) the prescriptions of a national authority, when they apply;

(c) the sailing instructions;

(d) the class rules except any that conflict with the rules in this book;

(e) any other documents governing the event.

This is the complete list of the *rules* that govern a race. Note that sailing instructions are *rules* so it is important to read them carefully before entering a race. Sailing instructions can change certain racing rules, but they must refer specifically to the rule being changed and state the change (see rule 86.1(b), Rule Changes).

   Also note that if a class rule conflicts with any of the ISAF *Racing Rules of Sailing*, **the class rule does not apply.** Furthermore, in accordance with rule 86.1(c), class rules are only permitted to change certain rules of *The Racing Rules of Sailing*, specifically: rule 42 (Propulsion); rule 49 (Crew Position); rule 50 (Setting and Sheeting Sails); rule 51, (Moving Ballast); rule 52 (Manual Power); rule 53 (Skin Friction) and rule (Forestays and Headsail Tacks).

"Is it true that weight jackets have been banned from the sport, and that class rules cannot change that rule?"

Yes! Rule 43.1(a) (Competitor Clothing and Equipment) now forbids competitors from wearing or carrying any clothing or equipment for the purpose of increasing their weight. And as this rule is not listed in rule 86.1(c), class rules are not permitted to change it.

START

A boat *starts* when after her starting signal any part of her hull, crew or equipment first crosses the starting line and she has complied with rule 29.1 and rule 30.1 if it applies.

You cannot *start* until after the starting signal for your class. If any part of your hull, crew or equipment is on the course side of the starting line at the starting signal, you must return completely behind the line to *start* correctly (rule 29.1, Starting; Recalls). If you don't, the race committee can score you OCS (On the Course Side) or DNS (Did Not Start) without needing to protest you (rules A1.1 and A3, Scoring). If you feel they have incorrectly scored you OCS or DNS, you can request redress under rule 62.1(a) (Redress). (Note that the phrase "premature starter," used in the previous rules, has been eliminated as it was in fact a misnomer.)

Notice that you *start* when, **after** the starting signal is made, **any** part of your hull, crew or equipment first crosses the starting line. There is no mention of **normal position** here. If your bow person is calling the line from the pulpit and inadvertently sticks his or her hand over the line just before the gun, or if your crew, by going out on the trapeze, mistakenly puts his or her head over the line one second before the gun, you are "on the course side." The same is true if anchored and your anchor and anchor line are over the starting line.

The definition refers to rule 30.1 (Rounding an End of the Starting Line) or more commonly known as the "One Minute Rule." Notice that the race committee can signal the "One Minute Rule" on any start it wants simply by displaying flag I **before or with** the preparatory signal. When it is lowered one minute before the starting signal, accompanied by one long sound signal, it means that the one-minute period of rule 30.1 has begun.

The purpose of the rule is to keep people from charging over the line early and making it difficult for the race committee to have a fair start. The way it works is, if you are on the course side of the starting line or its extensions during the minute before your starting signal, you must return behind the line by going **around one end or the other at some point before** *starting* correctly. Notice you can get back around an end immediately.

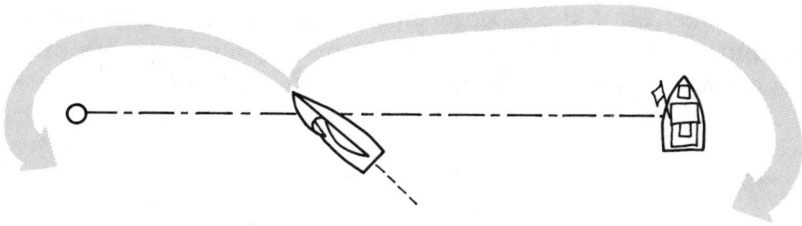

When rule 30.1 (the "One Minute Rule") is in effect, a boat that goes across the starting line at any time during the final minute before the starting signal must go around one of the ends before starting. She may do this immediately if she chooses; i.e. she does not need to wait for the starting signal before going around an end. While doing this, she must keep clear of all other boats until she is completely on the pre-start side of the starting line, under rule 20.

You don't have to wait for the starting signal to be made.

Notice also that while doing this, you must *keep clear* of all other boats (other than boats similarly sailing around an end) until you are completely on the pre-start side of the starting line (rule 20, Starting Errors; Penalty Turns; Moving Astern).

The rules now also include more stringent starting penalties available to race committees in rules 30.2 (Z Flag Rule) and 30.3 (Black Flag Rule).

TACK, STARBOARD OR PORT

A boat is on the *tack*, *starboard* or *port*, corresponding to her *windward* side.

When *racing*, you are **always** on either *starboard* or *port tack*, even when you are in the act of tacking or gybing. Your *tack* (*starboard* or *port*) is determined by your *windward* side, i.e. if your port side is your *windward* side, you are on *port tack*. For discussion on how to determine your *windward* side, see the Definition *Leeward* and W*indward*.

Though this is a slight change from previous rules, there is no game change here. When a *port-tack* boat begins to tack, the moment she passes head to wind her starboard side becomes her *windward* side; therefore she is instantly on *starboard tack*. However, rule 13 (While Tacking) requires her to *keep clear* of other boats until she is on a close-hauled course; and rule 15 (Acquiring Right of Way) requires her to initially give other boats *room* to *keep clear* once she gets the right of way.

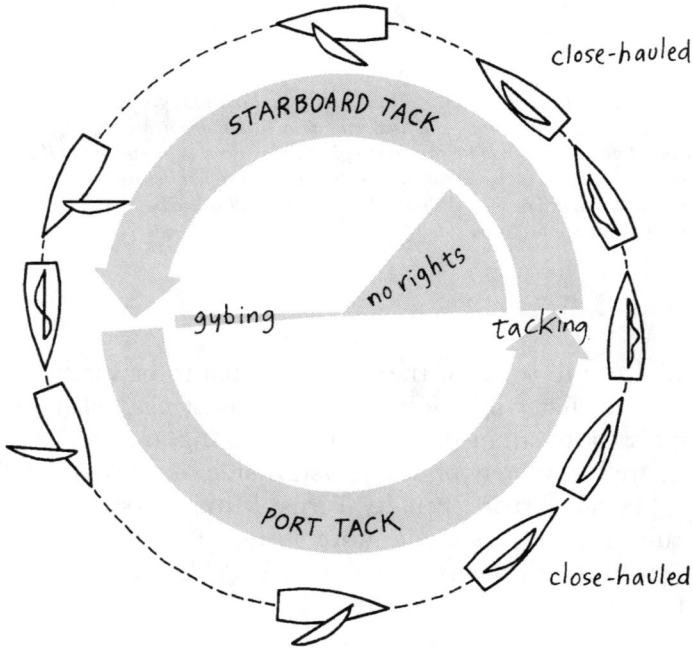

TWO-LENGTH ZONE

The area around a *mark* or *obstruction* within a distance of two hull lengths of the boat nearer to it.

As boats are about to pass a *mark* or *obstruction*, rule 18 (Passing Marks and Obstructions) provides specific instructions regarding which boats are entitled to *room*, which must give *room* to others, etc. Most of these instructions are based on the relationship of the boats when they are two lengths away from the *mark*. To make the rules themselves cleaner to read, the rule writers have created a defined area around a *mark/obstruction* called the "*two-length zone*." Previously, sailors called this the "two boat-length circle."

The *two-length zone* is a circle with the *mark/obstruction* at its center whose radius is two hull lengths of the boat that is nearest to it. Therefore, if a 24' boat and a 30' boat are approaching a *mark* and the 24' boat is nearer the *mark*, the *two-length zone* is 2 x 24' (48') from the *mark*.

The use of the term "hull length" is intended to clarify that the *two-length zone* is based solely on the length of the hull, and not the additional length of bowsprits, overhanging mizzen booms, etc. Webster's dictionary defines the "hull" of a boat as its "frame or body, exclusive of masts, yards, sails and rigging." Note, however, that two boats *overlap* when any part of their hull or equipment in normal position are alongside each other. Therefore, a boat with a 3' bowsprit can have a 2' *overlap* on a boat nearby, although her bow is still a foot from the other boat's stern.

The Two-Length Zone is an imaginary area with the mark or obstruction at its center, and extending out a distance equal to two hull lengths of the boat nearest the mark or obstruction.

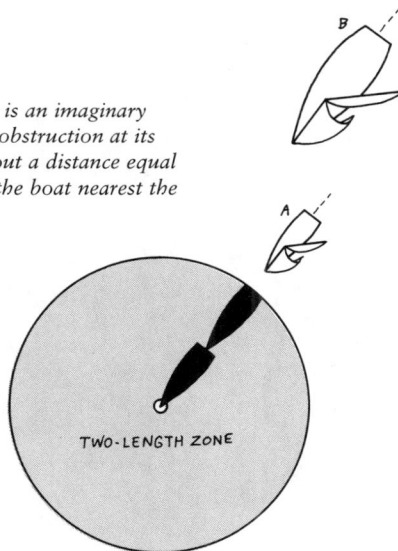

TWO-LENGTH ZONE

WINDWARD

See *Leeward* and *Windward*.

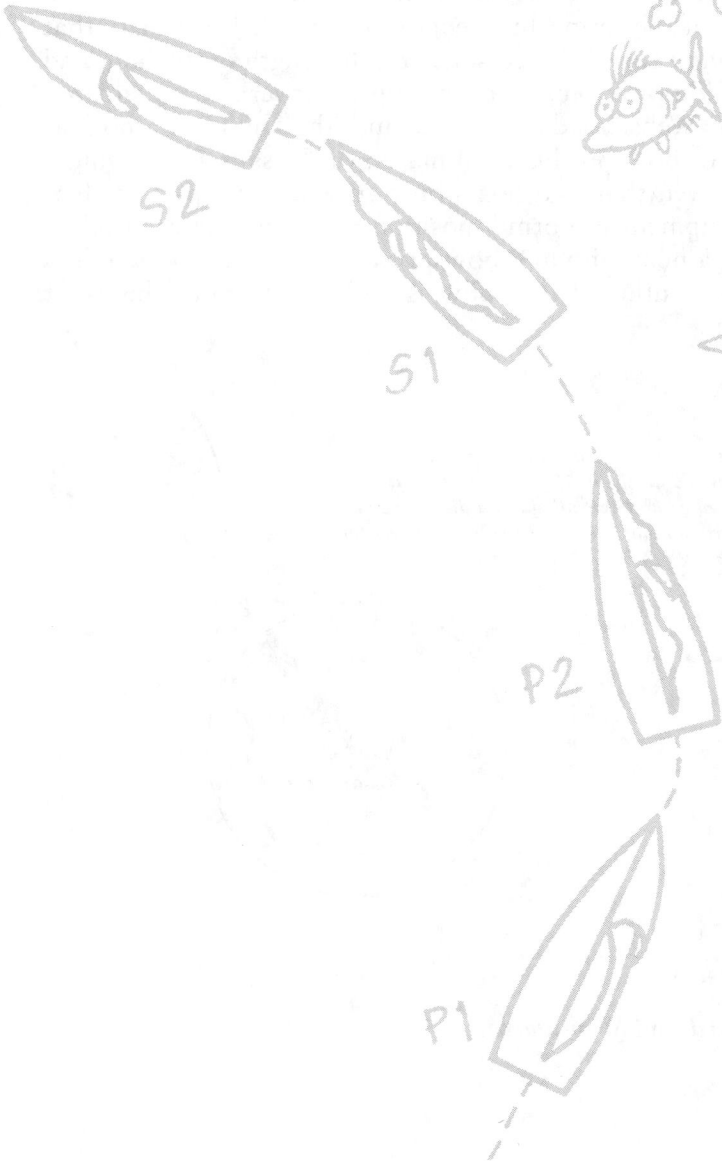

6

WHEN BOATS MEET
RIGHT OF WAY

PART 2 - SECTION A

When boats that are **both** *racing* meet, the rules that govern are in Part 2 of the rule book.

Preamble to Part 2

The rules of Part 2 apply between boats that are sailing in or near the racing area and intend to *race*, are *racing*, or have been *racing*. However, a boat not *racing* shall not be penalized for breaking one of these rules, except rule 22.1. The International Regulations for Preventing Collisions at Sea or government right-of-way rules apply between a boat sailing under these rules and a vessel that is not, and they replace these rules if the sailing instructions so state.

The preamble clarifies **which** rules apply **when** and **to whom**. Note that the "preambles" rank as *rules* (see the Definition *Rule*). When the Inland Navigational Rules (in U.S. waters) or the International Regulations for Preventing Collisions at Sea (outside of a country's waters) are to replace *The Racing Rules of Sailing* (e.g. when the race will continue after sunset) the sailing instructions must specifically contain the numbers of the applicable INR or IRPCAS and state the time(s) or places(s) they will apply, as well as any night signals to be used by the race committee (rule M2.2(3), Notice of Race and Sailing Instructions). Sailors wishing a complete copy of the INR or IRPCAS should contact the US SAILING office for information on how to get one.

Notice that the racing rules apply to boats even when they are racing in different races. Rule 63.7, Protests Between Boats in Different Races, reads, "*A **protest** between boats sailing in different races conducted by different organizing authorities shall be heard by a protest committee acceptable to those authorities.*"

Also, notice that when you intend to *race,* the rules of Part 2 only apply from when you begin to sail in or near the racing area until you have left the racing area; and they only apply between boats intending to race. This distinction may be important in resolving a financial claim after a serious collision when the boats were not actually *racing.*

"I realize I am technically 'racing' after my preparatory signal, but what happens if I accidentally foul a boat before or after I am racing?"

The preamble to Part 2 says, "*a boat not **racing** shall not be penalized for breaking one of these rules, except rule 22.1.*" (Rule 22.1, Interfering With Another Boat, says that even if you aren't *racing*, you can't interfere with a boat that is; see discussion of rule 22.1.) Rule 44.1 (Taking a Penalty) says, "*A boat that may have broken a rule of Part 2 **while racing** (emphasis added) may take a penalty at the time of the incident (720 Turns Penalty, percentage penalty, etc.).*" Therefore, if you break a rule before your preparatory signal, simply apologize and continue on.

Remember, under the definition of *racing*, you are *racing* from your preparatory signal until you have *finished* and cleared the finishing line and finishing *marks* or retired. So if your preparatory signal is five minutes before your starting signal and you foul someone with four and a half minutes to go, you can be disqualified if you don't take a penalty. Remember also that you are no longer *racing* the moment your transom clears the finishing line and finishing *marks* (US SAILING Appeals 99 and 136 and rule 28.1).

Note, however, that if you are not *racing* and break any other *rules* other than those in Parts 2 and 4 and rule 31 (Touching a Mark) you will receive a penalty under rule 64.1(a) (Penalties and Exoneration). For instance, you will be penalized before or after you are *racing* for breaking the sailing instructions, or for violating the principles in rule 2 (Fair Sailing), or for committing a "gross breach of a *rule* or of good manners or sportsmanship" under rule 69 (Allegations of Gross Misconduct) or for not complying with the *rules* of Part 6 which include rules 75, 78 and 79 which concern eligibility, measurement compliance and advertising. Also note that rule 64.1(c) (Protest Decisions) reads, "*If a boat has broken a rule when not **racing**, her penalty shall apply to the race sailed nearest in time to that of the incident.*"

"If five minutes before my preparatory signal I'm near the starting line on starboard tack and despite my best effort to avoid the collision my boat gets holed by a port tacker who is also intending to race, and as a result I can't sail in the race, do I have any recourse under the rules?"

You sure do. You should protest them under rule 10 (On Opposite Tacks) and request redress under rule 62.1(b) (Redress). Both of you were intending to *race* and were sailing in the racing area; therefore you were both governed by *The Racing Rules of Sailing*. The *port-tack* boat (P) was required to *keep clear* of you while you were on *starboard tack* under rule 10. Though P cannot be penalized for breaking this rule as she was not *racing* at the time, the protest committee is required to hold a hearing, find facts and determine which boat, if either, was at fault (rules 63.1, Hearings; 64.1, Penalties and Exoneration and 65.1, Informing the Parties and Others). Once P is found to have broken rule 10, the protest committee must turn to your request for redress (rule 63.1); and you should be granted redress as your finishing place was made significantly worse (you were unable to race!) through no fault of your own due to the physical damage caused by P, a boat that was breaking a rule of Part 2 at the time. Furthermore, the question of financial responsibility for damages may hinge on a finding of

UNDERSTANDING THE RACING RULES OF SAILING THROUGH 2000

facts and fault by the protest committee (see rule 68, Damages).

"If I'm racing and a boat definitely fouls me, and later in the race I am converging with them and I don't have the right of way, do I have to keep clear of them even though they were wrong in the first incident?"

You bet! In simplifying and shortening the rules, the rule writers removed the previous rule that specifically addressed this (old rule 34, Retention of Rights). However, the principle remains. When competitors know they have broken a rule, they are expected to promptly take a penalty or retire (see Sportsmanship and the Rules in the Introduction). But while a boat continues to *race*, she maintains all her rights just as any other boat. US SAILING Appeal 4 reads, "Pilgrim (X) and Y were involved in an incident early in a race, and each protested the other. Later in the same race, Maori (Z), which had observed the incident and believed X to have been in the wrong, refused to yield right of way to her. X protested Z. The protest committee disqualified X in the first hearing and Z in the second, despite Z's contention that because X had been disqualified for a breach of a rule in the first incident she was no longer entitled to her rights under the rules. Z appealed.

"DECISION: Rule 63.1 (Hearings) provides that a boat shall not be penalized without a hearing. Boats that have observed an incident in which a breach of a rule may have occurred cannot know with certainty that there was such a breach or which boat was at fault until the protest committee hears a protest and finds facts. Therefore, X retained her rights under the racing rules and Z was required to honor those rights. One such right, provided by rule 60.1(a) (Right to Protest and Request Redress), allowed X to protest Z, whether or not X broke a rule in the earlier incident."

ISAF Case 2 reads, "Boats A, B, and C are racing with others. After an incident, boat A hails and displays her protest flag, but boat B neither retires nor takes a penalty. Later, B protests a third boat, C, after a second incident. The protest committee hears A's protest against B and disqualifies B; does this disqualification invalidate B's protest against C?

"ANSWER: No. When a boat continues to race after an alleged rule breach, other boats shall continue to accord her such rights as she has under the rules of Part 2. Consequently, even though A's protest against B is upheld, B's protest against C is still valid and, when the protest committee is satisfied from the evidence that C broke a rule, she must be disqualified."

"So do I understand it correctly that the rules of Part 2 apply even between boats that are racing in different races?"

Yes. The rules of Part 2 apply between boats in different races as long as they both fit the description in the preamble of Part 2. Rule 63.7 (Protests Between Boats in Different Races) reinforces this point by saying, "*A protest between boats sailing in different races conducted by differing organizing authorities shall be heard by a protest committee acceptable to those authorities.*"

Preamble to Section A

A boat has right of way when another boat is required to *keep clear* of her. However, some rules in Sections B and C limit the actions of a right-of-way boat.

The rules of Part 2 are written to clearly say which boat must *keep clear* of the other. (See the Definition *Keep Clear* for a full discussion of the meaning of this phrase.) For example, rule 10 says, "*When boats are on opposite **tacks**, a **port-tack** boat shall keep clear of a **starboard-tack** boat.*" Therefore, in learning the rules, it is helpful to learn which boats do **not** have the right of way in meeting situations, as these are the boats with the requirement to stay out of the other's way.

There are just four basic right-of-way rules (rules 10-13), and they are found in Section A. They cover the three basic relationships boats can be in (on the same *tack*, on the opposite *tack* or changing *tacks*), and they are:

* on opposite *tacks*..rule 10
  port tack keeps clear of starboard tack

* on same *tacks*, overlapped.................................... rule 11
  windward keeps clear of leeward

- on same *tacks,* not overlapped.....................................rule 12
  clear astern keeps clear of *clear ahead*

- changing *tacks* by tacking..rule 13
  boat tacking *keeps clear* of other boats

RULE 10, ON OPPOSITE TACKS

When boats are on opposite *tacks, a port-tack* boat shall *keep clear* of a *starboard-tack* boat.

This basic rule applies to boats that are on **opposite** *tacks.* When boats are on the **same** *tack,* rules 11 (*windward/leeward*) and 12 (*clear astern/clear ahead*) apply. Thus, if on a run a *starboard-tack* boat comes up from *clear astern* and runs into a *port-tack* boat (assuming no damage), who is disqualified? The *port-tack* boat, because the two boats are on **opposite** *tacks.*

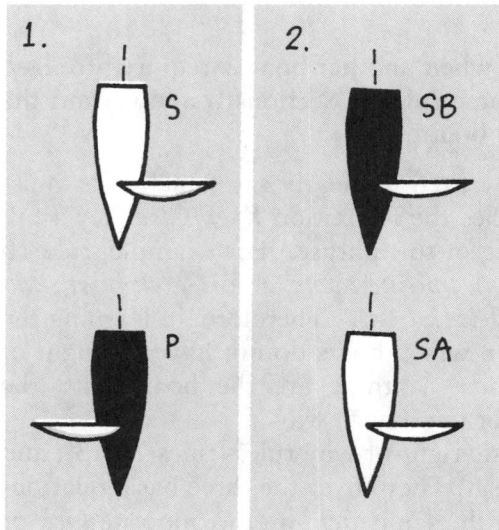

In position 1, the boats are on opposite tacks; therefore S has right of way over P under rule 10. In position 2, both boats are on the same tack; therefore, as the boat clear astern, SB must keep clear of SA under rule 12.

"If I'm on a beat converging with a port-tack boat and she hails 'Hold your course,' is that hail binding on me?"

US SAILING Appeal 137 reads, "In response to the questions regarding a boat that has been hailed to hold course, it is permissible to hail but the rules do not recognize such a hail as binding on the other boat. S can tack or bear away at any time she is satisfied that a change of course will be necessary to avoid a collision."

My opinion is that in order for the *port-tack* boat to be liable for failure to *keep clear*, it is important that as they approach each other, the *starboard-tack* boat hold her course as long as she can do so with safety. I recommend that when *port-tack* boats are about to cross close in front of *starboard-tack* boats, P should always hail "Hold your course" to S to alert her that P is there, that P realizes it will be close, and that P wants S to hold her course for as long as possible.

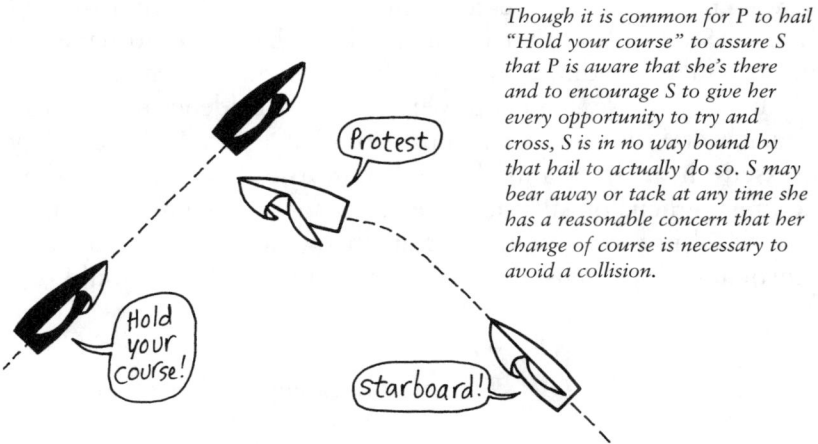

Though it is common for P to hail "Hold your course" to assure S that P is aware that she's there and to encourage S to give her every opportunity to try and cross, S is in no way bound by that hail to actually do so. S may bear away or tack at any time she has a reasonable concern that her change of course is necessary to avoid a collision.

"OK, but do I have to hit the port-tacker to prove there was a foul; and if there is no contact, whom is the 'onus of proof' on?"

S does NOT have to hit P to prove that P failed to *keep clear*. S should avoid the collision and protest. Though the rule itself contains no specific "onus" (i.e. an assignment of responsibility to one boat or the other to prove the other boat's guilt), ISAF

Case 113 discusses the whole issue, including the question of "onus of proof:" "Rule 10 protests involving no contact are very common, and protest committees tend to handle them in very different ways. Some place an onus on the port-tack boat to prove conclusively that she would have cleared the starboard-tack boat, even when the latter's evidence is barely worthy of credence. No such onus appears in rule 10. Other protest committees have been reluctant to allow any rule 10 protest in the absence of contact, unless the starboard-tack boat proves conclusively that contact would have occurred had she not altered course. Both approaches are incorrect.

"A starboard-tack boat in such circumstances must not hold her course so as to prove, by hitting the port-tack boat, that a collision was inevitable. Moreover, if she does so she very likely will break rule 14 (Avoiding Contact). At a protest hearing, S must establish that either contact would have occurred, if she had held her course, or that there was enough doubt that P could safely cross ahead to create a reasonable apprehension of contact on S's part and that it was unlikely that S would have 'no need to take avoiding action' (Definitions, *Keep Clear*).

"In her defense, P must present adequate evidence to establish either that S did not alter course or that P would have safely crossed ahead of S and that S had no need to take avoiding action. When, on all the evidence, a protest committee finds that S did not alter course or that there was not a genuine and reasonable apprehension of collision on her part, it should dis-

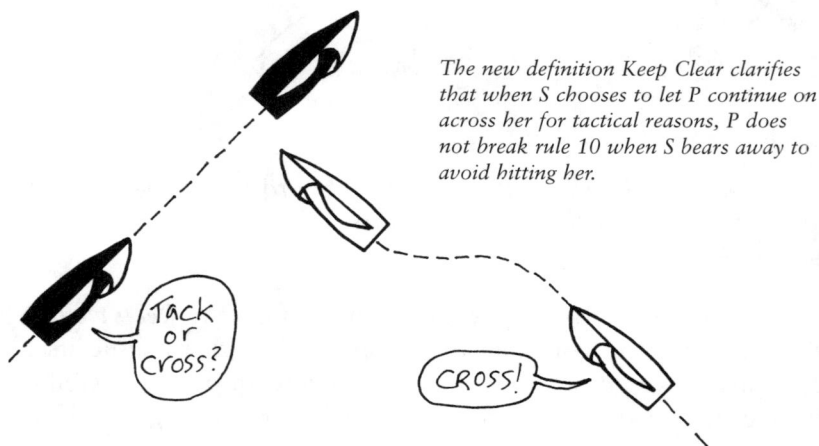

The new definition Keep Clear clarifies that when S chooses to let P continue on across her for tactical reasons, P does not break rule 10 when S bears away to avoid hitting her.

allow her protest. When, however, it is satisfied that S did alter course, that there was reasonable doubt that P could have crossed ahead, and that S was justified in taking avoiding action by bearing away, then P should be disqualified." (See also ISAF Case 169.)

In tight racing, the situation often arises where a *port-tack* boat cannot cross a *starboard-tack* boat, but can tack close to S's lee-bow, causing S to drop back or tack away. Often in this situation, the *port-tack* boat will hail "Tack or cross?" meaning "If you don't let me cross you, I will tack on your lee-bow; what will it be?" When S wants to continue on her chosen course, a common tactic for S is to say "Cross!" (along with a vigorous wave of the arm), telling P to hold her course while S ducks her. In this situation, P has *kept clear* of S under the Definition *Keep Clear*, as S is able to sail her **chosen** course without interference.

RULES 11 and 12 - ON THE SAME TACK

Rules 11 and 12 are the basic rules for boats on the **same** *tack*. When boats are on the same *tack* they can either be *overlapped* or not *overlapped*. If they are *overlapped*, they are either a *windward* boat or a *leeward* boat. If they are not *overlapped*, they are either *clear ahead* or *clear astern*.

RULE 11 - ON THE SAME TACK, OVERLAPPED

When boats are on the same *tack* and *overlapped*, a *windward* boat shall *keep clear* of a *leeward* boat.

When boats on the same *tack* are *overlapped*, rule 11 applies. When boats are on much different angles of sail, it is often difficult to know which is the *leeward* boat. The boat that will hit

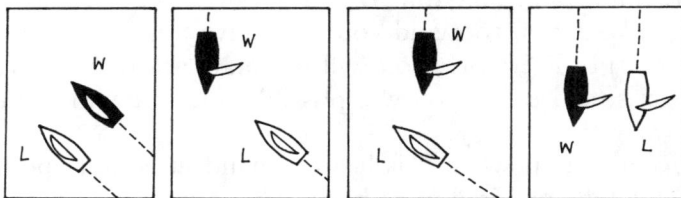

In each situation, both boats are on the same tack. The white boat is the leeward boat and the black boat must keep clear under rule 11.

the other's *leeward* side or be hit on her own *windward* side is the *leeward* boat. As a good rule of thumb, the boat that is on the point of sail closer to the wind is the *leeward* boat; i.e. between a boat sailing downwind and a boat sailing close-hauled, the close-hauled boat is the *leeward* boat.

"I realize that when I'm the windward boat I have to keep clear of the leeward boat, but how far away do I need to stay?"

Far enough away so that while the *leeward* boat (L) is sailing on a straight line, you do not hit L or force L to take any avoiding action to miss you, e.g. have to alter her course, ease her spinnaker pole forward or require any of her crew to duck or move to avoid being hit.

Furthermore, you need to be far enough away so that the *leeward* boat can change course in at least one direction without **immediately** making contact with you. If you allow yourself to get so close to L that she couldn't change course in either direction at that moment without **immediately** hitting you, you are not *keeping clear* under the new Definition *Keep Clear* and are breaking rule 11. (Note: if L couldn't luff without immediate contact but could bear away without immediate contact, the last phrase in this definition doesn't apply because L "could" change course without making immediate contact.) Note also that the second "if" in the definition suggests that L does not need to actually hit you to prove she couldn't change course without hitting you. If the protest committee decides that L couldn't have changed course without immediate contact, then you have broken rule 11 (On the Same Tack, Overlapped) simply by your extreme close proximity to L.

More importantly, **anytime** L cannot sail her course without a need to take action to avoid you, you have not *kept clear* and break rule 11. Therefore, you will be smart not to allow yourself to get so close that you will possibly interfere with L in the least.

Notice also that when L is head to wind, it is quite possible that you will be required to go **beyond** head to wind (i.e. change tacks) in order to *keep clear*. If this is the case, you must do so.

Also, if you are converging with L and both of you are sailing on what you each believe to be your *proper courses*, rule 11 requires you to *keep clear* of L.

RULE 12 - ON THE SAME TACK, NOT OVERLAPPED

When boats are on the same *tack* and not *overlapped*, a boat *clear astern* shall *keep clear* of a boat *clear ahead*.

In 1949 the rule read, "A yacht Overtaking another shall keep clear while she is Clear Astern." Now the rules only talk about boats that are *clear ahead* or *clear astern*; however, the concept is still the same. A boat, just like a car on the highway, coming up from behind another boat, must not hit her.

Rule 12 clearly identifies a boat or boats *clear ahead* as right-of-way boats, therefore making them *obstructions* to boats coming up from behind. See the Definition *Obstruction*. ISAF Case 91 reads, "With respect to A [clear ahead], both boats astern must keep clear of her under rule 12. However, A is also an *obstruction* to both, as the last sentence in the Definition *Obstruction* makes clear. When they are 'about to pass' A, still overlapped, rule 18 will come into effect."

RULE 13 -WHILE TACKING

After a boat passes head to wind, she shall *keep clear* of other boats until she is on a close-hauled course. During that time rules 10, 11 and 12 do not apply. If two boats are subject to this rule at the same time, the one on the other's port side shall *keep clear*.

Remember that under the new definition *Tack, Starboard or Port*, you are always on one *tack* or the other. So if you are on *port tack* and turn your boat towards the wind, the moment your boat passes head to wind you are **instantly** on *starboard tack*. Though this is a new concept from the previous rules, there is no game change here, i.e. no change in the way the rules govern a boat that tacks near other boats.

As part of the process to simplify and shorten the rules, the previous definitions of "tacking" and "gybing" have been deleted because it was felt that the concepts were commonly well

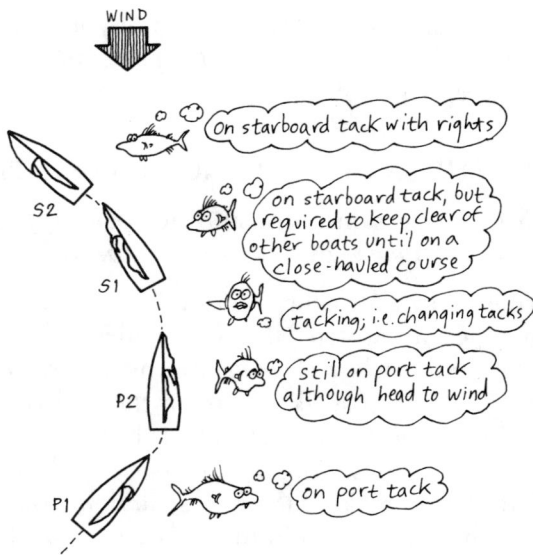

understood. "Tacking" is the maneuver by which a boat changes *tacks* with the bow passing head to wind. Generally that involves an approximately 90 degree turn from close-hauled to close-hauled.

Rule 13 simply says that while you are tacking, you must *keep clear* of other boats from the moment you pass head to wind until you are on a close-hauled course (on **either** *tack*). A "close-hauled course" is the course a boat will sail when racing upwind and sailing as close to the wind as she can. Notice that to be on a close-hauled course, the sails don't need to be full nor does the boat need any headway (see ISAF Case 32). If, after you pass head to wind and before you're on a close-hauled course, another boat hits you or has to alter her course to avoid you, you have not *kept clear* and have broken rule 13.

In the rare instance where two boats are tacking near each other and both are past head to wind but neither is close-hauled yet, the one on the other's port side must *keep clear*; or put another way, the boat on the right has the right of way.

"Gybing" is the maneuver by which a boat changes *tacks* with the bow turning away from the wind. When sailing downwind, the moment the foot of your mainsail crosses the centerline, you are on *starboard tack*. (see the Definition *Leeward* and *Windward* for a discussion on determining a boat's *tack* when sailing downwind or by the lee). Because the act of "gybing" is generally so momentary, it was decided that no special rule for "gybing" was needed.

"Under the previous rules, when I tacked or gybed into a right-of-way position I had to give other boats room to keep clear of me; has that changed under the new rules?"

No, not at all. For a full explanation of the obligations of boats that acquire right-of-way, see the discussion of rule 15 (Acquiring Right of Way).

"Will you be discussing how the new rules affect Slam Dunks?"

You bet. That explanation occurs at the end of the discussion of rule 17 (On the Same Tack; Proper Course).

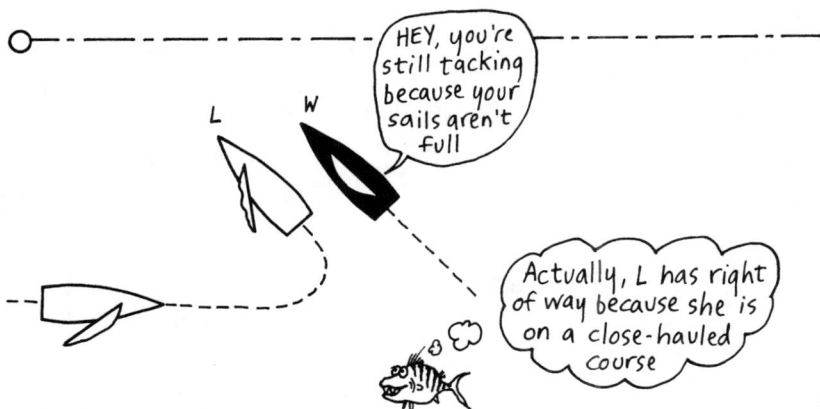

HEY, you're still tacking because your sails aren't full

Actually, L has right of way because she is on a close-hauled course

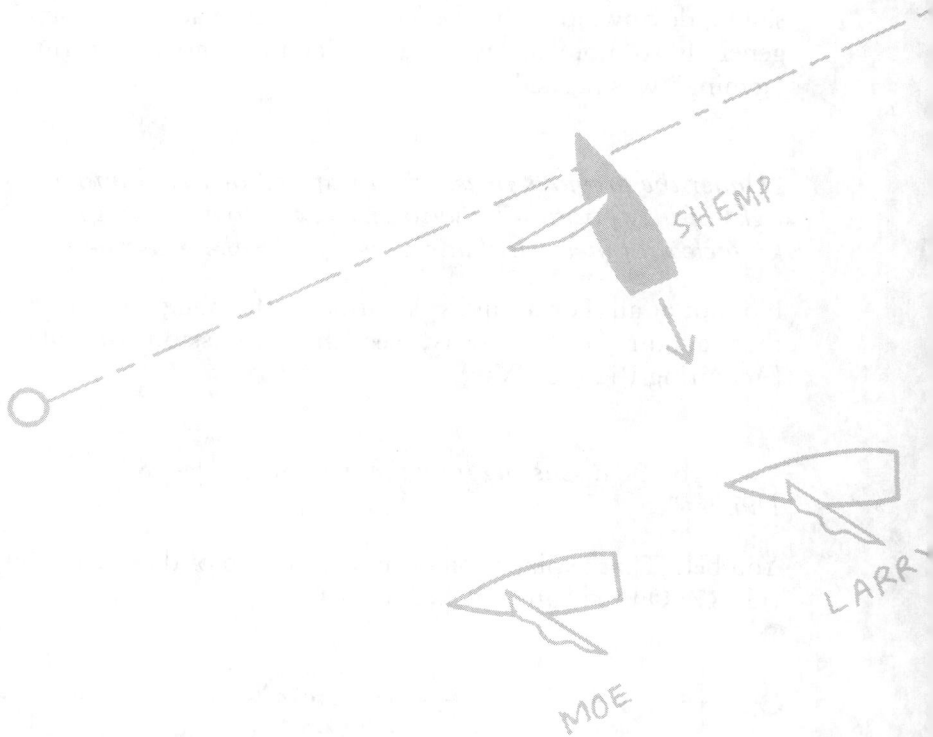

7

WHEN BOATS MEET GENERAL LIMITATIONS

PART 2 - SECTION B

In addition to the right-of-way rules, Part 2 also contains rules that **limit** the actions of right-of-way boats (rules 14-17). In other words, a right-of-way boat cannot just go anywhere she wants. These limitations are found in Section B. One example is that a right-of-way boat can be penalized when she's involved in contact that causes any damage (rule 14). Another is that whenever a right-of-way boat changes her course, she is required to give the other boat *room* to *keep clear* (rule 16). Therefore, it is equally important to know what limitations the rules place on right-of-way boats in various situations.

RULE 14 - AVOIDING CONTACT

A boat shall avoid contact with another boat if reasonably possible. However, a right-of-way boat or one entitled to *room*

(a) need not act to avoid contact until it is clear that the other boat is not *keeping clear* or giving *room*, and

(b) shall not be penalized unless there is contact that causes damage.

This is a much stronger rule regarding contact than the previous rules. It talks to all boats in a race, including right-of-way boats, and tells them to avoid any contact whatsoever if reasonably possible. The intent of the rule is to minimize the number of collisions that occur during a race, **and particularly the intentional ones.** Collisions can be dangerous, expensive, frustrating to all sailors and especially intimidating to newcomers and novice sailors. The message from the rule writers is: sailing is not a "contact" sport!

When two or more boats converge, the possibility of contact exists. The rules clearly assign the right-of-way and the requirement to *keep clear* or to give *room* in each situation where boats could hit. A basic principle of navigation is that when one boat is required to keep clear, the other shouldn't do anything to make the situation more dangerous. Rule 14(a) makes it clear that the right-of-way boat or the inside boat entitled to *room* can hold her course until it becomes "clear" that the other boat is not going to avoid contact. At that moment, the right-of-way or inside boat must take action herself to avoid the contact if reasonably possible. For instance, take a *port-tack* boat crossing a *starboard-tack* boat. If S holds her course and damages P, with no attempt to avoid or minimize the contact, P has broken rule 10 (On Opposite Tacks) and S has broken rule 14.

Finally, rule 14(b) states that a right-of-way boat or one entitled to *room* can be penalized under this rule if the contact causes any "damage" whatsoever. On the other hand, these boats cannot be penalized under this rule if no damage occurs. Notice that it is immaterial whether the damage has any effect on the speed or handling of the boat. Under the previous rules, a boat could only be penalized if the contact resulted in "serious damage," so clearly rule 14 is much stricter and will apply to many more situations where "damage" occurs.

Note that if the give-way boat fails to avoid contact, she technically can be penalized under this rule; however, this is a moot point because she will be penalized under the Section A rule she broke, and a boat can only be penalized once per incident, regardless of the number of rules she may have broken in that incident (rule 44.4(b), Penalties for Breaking Rules of Part 2, Limits on Penalties).

"If I'm involved in contact that causes damage, can I do a 720 or put up a yellow flag to avoid disqualification?"

Yes! This is a big change from the previous rules. Rule 44 (Penalties for Breaking Rules of Part 2) permits a boat that may have broken any rule in Part 2 while *racing* to take a penalty at the time of the incident. The penalty is the 720-degree Turns Penalty unless the sailing instructions specify the use of some other penalty (rule 44). So if you are a right-of-way boat or an inside boat entitled to *room* and you cause damage to the give-way boat, you can quickly do a "720" and continue in the race. If you are the give-way boat, you can also do a "720" which absolves you of all Part 2 rule breaches you may have committed in the incident. There is one exception, however. Rule 44 goes on to say, *"if* [a boat] *caused serious damage...she shall retire."* In other words, you can't absolve yourself with a "720" if the damage was "serious."

See the explanation of rule 44 for a discussion on how to properly do a "720," and what constitutes "serious damage."

"I understand that if I'm the right-of-way boat, I can now be penalized for causing any damage at all; what constitutes damage?"

ISAF Case 36 offers an interpretation of the term "damage." "It is not possible to define 'damage' comprehensively, but one current English dictionary says 'harm or injury impairing the value or usefulness of something, or the health or normal function of a person.' This definition suggests questions to consider. Examples are:

1. Was the current market value of any part of the boat, or of the boat as a whole, diminished?

2. Was any item of the boat or its equipment made less functional?

3. Was a member of the crew injured, and was first aid required?"

In my opinion, a related question to number 1 above is, "Did the contact result in something needing to be repaired or replaced?"

Clearly, boats will have contact that will cause no damage to either boat or crew. Examples will include two boats having light side to side contact while rounding a *mark*, or incidents where the crews fend off and the hulls never touch. On the other hand, there will be contact that clearly causes "damage:" a hole or dent in the boat, a torn sail, a bent stanchion, a nick out of the rudder, a broken finger, etc. The hard calls will be the situations where the gel coat gets scratched, the sailors hear the fiberglass "crunch" though there is no visible sign of "damage" or a crew member gets a temporary soreness from fending off, etc. Protest committees will need to exercise their best judgment in these situations. Notice that the judgment that "damage" occurred is not a "fact found;" it is a conclusion based on the "facts found" and therefore subject to appeal.

"As I understand the rule, even if I'm involved in contact that causes damage, but it was not reasonably possible for me to avoid the contact, I won't be penalized under this rule; correct?"

Correct. The rule acknowledges that there may be times when it is simply not reasonably possible for a boat to avoid contact. However, this should not be viewed as a rationale for not making every effort to avoid collisions. Ultimately, whether or not it was reasonably possible to have avoided the contact will be decided by the protest committee.

The dictionary defines "reasonable" as "agreeable to reason; possessing sound judgment; not extreme or excessive." In judging whether it was "reasonably possible" for a boat to have avoided contact, it is implicit, to me, that as two boats near each other, the right-of-way boat settle on a straight-line or compass course or risk breaking rule 16 (Changing Course); and the giveway boat begin to take avoiding action. However, when, in her judgment, the right-of-way boat has a reasonable apprehension that contact will occur if she continues to hold her course, she may alter her course to avoid the collision (ISAF Case 113). Rule

14(a) reinforces this by telling right-of-way boats they need not act to avoid contact until it is "clear" that the other boat is not *keeping clear*.

Therefore, as boats approach each other, they must continually assess the situation in terms of "What are the probable chances that I may hit this other boat or vice versa?" This judgment should factor in:

- what the response(s) have been from the other boat,

- whether the other boat is keeping a good lookout,

- what the sailing conditions are like and how well a boat of the class involved maneuvers in such conditions,

- who the sailors in the other boat are, and

- is there anything at all peculiar about the way the other boat is being handled?

In judging whether it was "reasonably possible" for a boat to have avoided contact, I'd consider whether the contact could have been avoided given the sailors' best attempts at avoiding or minimizing the impact of the collision, factoring in the amount of warning they had that a give-way boat might not *keep clear* or give *room*, the time they had to consider what their best attempt might be, and the amount and difficulty of the boat and sail handling involved. Also factored in to a much lesser degree would be the competency of the sailors and the condition of their equipment and boat, i.e. their steering gear, cleats and so on. However, the *rules* do not make allowances for poor seamanship, and I would be hesitant to excuse a boat due to poor sailing skills or less than adequately functioning equipment. In other words, in my opinion, "reasonable" is defined in terms of what an average sailor possessing average sailing skills could be expected to do in a similar situation.

ISAF Case 51 concerns a collision where P, a 5-0-5, and S, a Soling, were rounding the same leeward *mark* in opposite directions. Needless to say, the 5-0-5 received most of the damage as the Soling's bow sliced through P's hull and side buoyancy-tank just aft of the mast, the force of the impact knocking P's crew overboard unhurt. The decision reads, "P failed to keep a proper look out and to observe her primary duty to keep clear. She is correctly disqualified under rule 10 (On Opposite Tacks). One purpose of the rules of Part 2 is to avoid contact between boats racing. All boats, whether or not holding right of way, should keep a look out at all times.

"When a boat has the opportunity to avoid a collision she must make a reasonable attempt to do so. When she does not, she breaks rule 14. When the two conflict, rule 14 overrides rule 16 (Changing Course), and when the right-of-way boat finds herself so close that collision cannot be avoided by the action of the give-way boat alone, she is entitled to take such action under rule 14 as best will avoid damage. Since S made no attempt to avoid a collision, and damage, indeed serious damage, resulted, she is disqualified under rule 14." See also US SAILING Appeal 266.

ISAF Case 53 is an illustration of when it was not reasonably possible for a boat to avoid contact. "L, a length to leeward and a length ahead of W, tacked as soon as she reached the starboard lay line. Almost immediately she was hit and holed by W traveling at about ten knots." The Decision states, "When L began to tack, right of way transferred to W which would retain it until L completed her tack in accordance with rule 13. W took no action to avoid collision, but what could she have done? Given her speed and the distance involved, she had perhaps one to two seconds to decide what to do and then do it. It is a long-established underlying principle of the right-of-way rules that a boat becoming burdened by an action of another boat is entitled to sufficient time for response, as rule 15 (Acquiring Right of Way) provides in this situation. Also, while it was obvious that L would have to tack to round the mark, W was under no obligation to anticipate that she would do so in contravention of rule 15."

Another scenario in which it may not be reasonably possible for boats to avoid contact is in light air when boats have very little steerageway and large powerboat waves enter the racing area and toss the boats about.

In conclusion, to penalize a boat under rule 14, two things must be decided. One, was the boat involved in contact that caused "damage;" and two, was it "reasonably possible" for the boat to have avoided the contact? If either there was no "damage," or if it is decided that the boat couldn't have reasonably avoided the contact, then the boat should not be penalized under rule 14. As a juror, I would have to be satisfied from the weight of the evidence submitted (in other words there is no onus) that a boat was negligent or had shown very poor judgment or seamanship before I penalized them. On the other hand, I expect jurors would not be very tolerant of situations where the right-of-way boat intentionally hits the give-way boat to prove the foul, causing any damage as a result.

"If I'm on port tack, and a starboard-tacker hits and damages me, and the damage caused me to get a significantly worse finishing position, I realize that I have to do a '720' because I was on port tack; but can I request redress because of the damage?"

Yes! Rule 62 (Redress) says that you are entitled to request redress when *"your finishing place...has, through no fault of your own, been made significantly worse by...physical damage because of the action of a boat that was breaking a rule of Part 2..."* In the hearing, the protest committee, acting under rule 64.2 (Decisions on Redress) must first decide if S broke rule 14. If so, they must next decide if you contributed to the receiving of damage. That means contributing more than just being in S's way. If you were trying to cross S, and while she was ducking you she hit you causing damage, there is very little you could have done to have prevented that. Finally, the protest committee must decide if the physical damage itself made your finishing place significantly worse.

RULE 15 - ACQUIRING RIGHT OF WAY

When a boat acquires right of way, she shall initially give the other boat *room* to *keep clear*, unless she acquires right of way because of the other boat's actions.

This rule states one of the oldest and most fundamental principles in the rules, and it makes perfect sense. When a boat takes action that gives her the right of way over you, she must give you the chance to respond and *keep clear* of her. For example, you are sailing on a run on *port tack* with another *port-tack* boat just

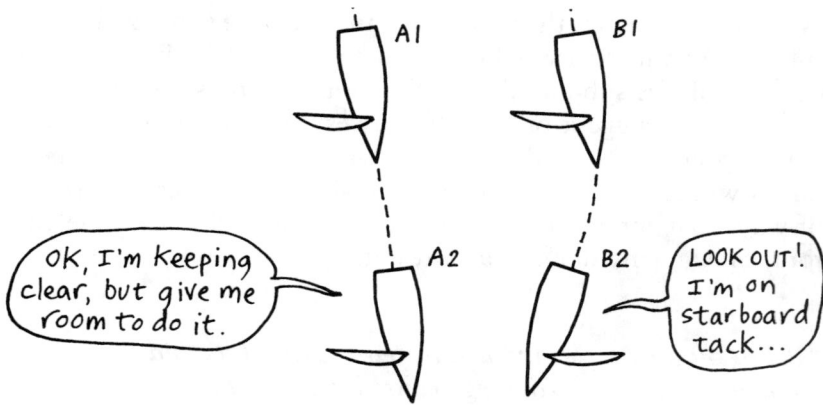

to *windward*. As the *leeward* boat, you have the right-of-way (rule 11, On the Same Tack, Overlapped) and everything is under control. You have the "sword," so to speak, and the *windward* boat must stay out of "its" way. Suddenly, the *windward* boat gybes. Now she is on *starboard tack* and you are on *port tack*. She now has the right-of-way, i.e. she now has the "sword" (rule 10, On Opposite Tacks), but she can't just turn and hit you; her actions are limited by rule 15.

ISAF Case 46 reads, "...it is a general principle in the rules that when the right of way suddenly shifts from one boat to another, the boat with the newly acquired right of way must give the other boat space and time for response and a fair opportunity to keep clear." This principle is loudly echoed in many appeals, including US SAILING Appeals 139 and 221 and ISAF Case 53.

Note that a right-of-way boat does not have to anticipate that she will lose her right of way. ISAF Case 116 is clear on this point: "Adequate time for response, when rights and obligations change between two boats, is necessarily implied in rule 15 by its requirement to allow the newly-obligated boat 'room to keep clear'." Therefore, in the example above, the *leeward* boat need not anticipate her requirement to *keep clear* as a *port-tack* boat **before** the *windward* boat gybes to *starboard*.

However, the use of the word "initially" clearly states that the protection of "*room* to *keep clear*" is not continuing. In the old video game *Deluxe Asteroids*, a tiny rocket ship tries to blast apart large rocks that will blow up the ship if they hit her. When there are just too many rocks about to hit, the player can press a button, putting a protective force shield around the ship. At first, the rocks bounce off the shield, but after a few seconds the shield begins to fade and disappear.

The *room* to respond to a newly acquired obligation to *keep clear* is a "shield" for the new give-way boat. It is very strong initially, but fades in strength as the seconds go by. Also, for you to be entitled to the protection of the 'shield,' you must, at the moment you become the give-way boat, make a prompt and careful attempt to begin to get clear of the right-of-way boat. If you delay at all, you lose the protection of *"room* to *keep clear"* and you run the risk of fouling the right-of-way boat

Let's look at some common situations on the race course where this principle of transition comes into play:

Establishing a leeward overlap from clear astern (common during pre-start maneuvering and when sailing downwind):

Two boats on the same tack are sailing near each other, one *clear astern* (BL) of the other (AW) and catching up. While BL is approaching AW, she must *keep clear*. When she establishes an *overlap* to *leeward* of AW, rule 12 (*clear astern/clear ahead*) ceases to apply and she **instantly** becomes the right-of-way boat

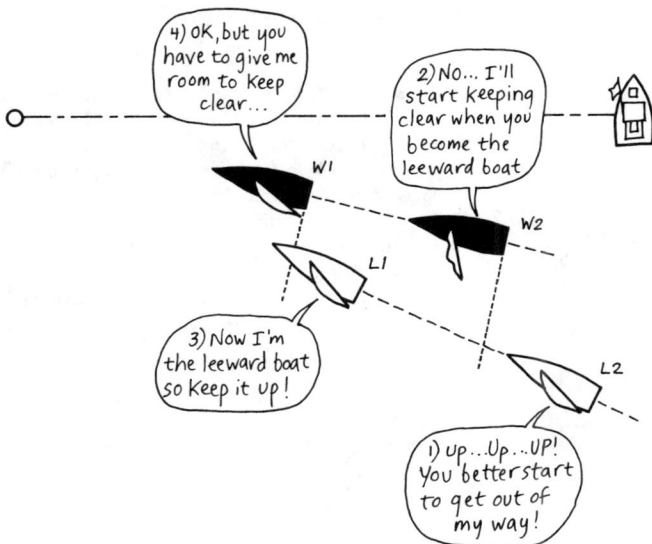

under rule 11 (*windward/leeward*). This is when rule 15 requires her to initially give AW *room* to *keep clear* of her. Remember that AW does not need to anticipate that BL will gain the right of way; therefore she does not need to take any evasive action **before** the *overlap* is established.

Rule 15 does not change the fact that W is required to *keep clear* of L. ISAF Case 116 makes the point that the give-way boat must respond immediately: "Since W at once trimmed sails, headed up, and thereafter kept clear, she fulfilled her obligations under rule 11." ISAF Case 11 states, "...L was bound by rule 15 to allow W room to keep clear, but that obligation is not a continuing one, and in this case the overlap had been in existence for a considerable period during which nothing had obstructed W's room." (See ISAF Case 46.)

Tacking into a right-of-way position to leeward of a right-of-way boat (commonly known as "lee-bowing"):

While a boat is tacking near another boat, rule 13 (While Tacking) requires her to *keep clear* of the other boat from the moment she passes head to wind until on a close-hauled course. But, once she is on a close-hauled course, and if she has become the right-of-way boat, rule 15 applies. For a good analogy (though this may not be the actual highway law), picture yourself coming up the entrance ramp to a three-lane highway. Cars driving down the right-hand lane must stay clear of other cars in

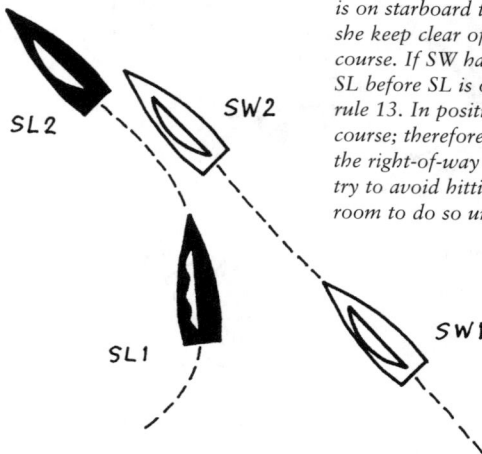

In position 1, SL is past head to wind; therefore she is on starboard tack. However, rule 13 requires that she keep clear of SW until she is on a close-hauled course. If SW has to change course to avoid hitting SL before SL is on a close-hauled course, SL breaks rule 13. In position 2, SL is on a close-hauled course; therefore, as the leeward boat, she is now the right-of-way boat. SW must now immediately try to avoid hitting SL, but SL must initially give her room to do so under rule 15.

the right-hand lane in front of them. While you're on the ramp you cannot interfere with cars driving in the right-hand lane. If, while you are moving across the white line into the right-hand lane, a car hits you or swerves to miss you, you are in the wrong. But once you get **all four wheels** across the line, you are now technically in the right-hand lane yourself and cars coming up from behind have to keep clear of you. However, these cars are not required to begin to avoid you or even to **anticipate** avoiding you until you are completely in the lane. Once you are in the lane they have to try reasonably hard to miss you. If they can't, then you've moved on too close in front of them.

The same is true in sailboats. Let's say I'm on *starboard tack*, you're approaching me on *port tack*, and you want to tack on my lee-bow or in front of me. If I could hit you before you passed head to wind (i.e. before you began to cross the white line), you'd be wrong under rule 10 (*port/starboard*). If I could hit you after you'd passed head to wind but before you were **aiming** on your close-hauled course (i.e. while you were crossing the line), you'd be wrong under rule 13 (a tacking boat must *keep clear*). However, the moment you get to your close-hauled course (i.e. completely in my lane) and you are either *clear ahead* or to *leeward* of me, you have the right of way under either rule 12 (*clear astern/clear ahead*) or rule 11 (*windward/leeward*) and I have to promptly take action to *keep clear* of you. This is when rule 15 requires you to initially give me the *room* I need to *keep clear* of you. Of course, in most situations it will take me only a second or two to react enough to luff or bear away slightly to avoid a collision.

"In protests involving the situation where P tacks very close to leeward of S, it seems that P and S may often disagree on whether P was actually on a close-hauled course before S changed course to avoid her; or whether P, after acquiring right of way, actually gave S room to keep clear. Are there any onuses to help resolve these disagreements?"

No. In resolving these disagreements, most protest committees apply the principle in ISAF Case 113 (see rule 10 discussion),

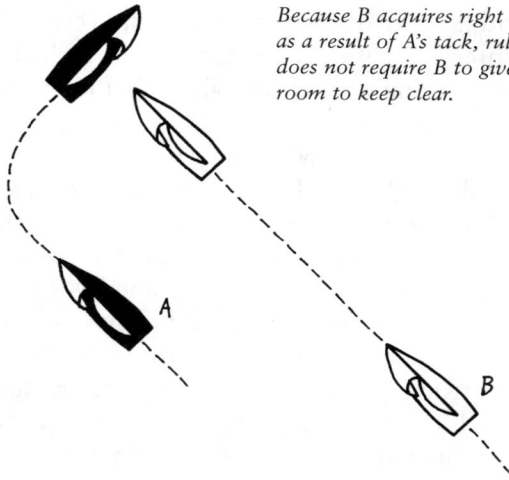

Because B acquires right of way as a result of A's tack, rule 15 does not require B to give A any room to keep clear.

which is that they first put responsibility on S to satisfy the committee that the boats were close together. They then put the responsibility on P to satisfy them that P was on a close-hauled course before S changed her course; and that once she was on a close-hauled course, she gave S *room* to *keep clear*. This responsibility on P is often difficult to win against. Hails to the effect of "My tack is completed-2-3-4, now you're changing course" and a witness are very helpful.

Gybing into a right-of-way position:

The same is true when *gybing*. If two boats are running side by side on *port tack* and the *windward* boat gybes, the **moment** the foot of the mainsail crosses her centerline she is on *starboard tack* and the other boat (P) must promptly maneuver to get clear. However, S must plan to initially give P the *room* she needs to *keep clear*.

Completing penalty turns or starting after being over early:

Again, the principle applies when a boat is completing penalty turns for fouling another boat (rule 44, Penalties for Breaking Rules of Part 2) or touching a mark (rule 31, Touching a Mark). While making her penalty turns, she is required to *keep clear* of boats not doing so (rule 20, Starting Errors; Penalty Turns; Moving Astern). The moment she completes her last "360," she is no longer bound by rule 20. If she suddenly acquires the right of way over a nearby boat, she must give this boat *room* to respond. The same applies when she returns to the correct side of the starting line after rounding an end when rule 30.1 (the "One Minute Rule") is in effect, or when returning to *start* after being on the course side of the starting line at the gun (rule 20).

"What is the reason for the last phrase of the rule, 'unless she acquires right of way because of the other boat's actions?'"

This is to protect boats that suddenly become right-of-way boats because of an action by the other boat. For instance, you are sailing upwind on *starboard tack* just to windward and slightly behind a boat to leeward. Suddenly, the leeward boat tacks and is now directly in front of you on *port tack*! Without the last phrase in rule 15, you would be required to give the boat that tacked *room* to *keep clear* of you, because you have just acquired the right of way! Clearly this would be unacceptable, hence the phrase. Therefore, in the example above, assuming you quickly bore away to avoid contact, the boat that tacked broke rule 10 (*port/starboard*), and rule 15 did not apply to you.

Another situation where this applies is when a boat *clear ahead* (A) bears away and causes a boat *clear astern* (B) to establish a *leeward overlap*. The moment the boats are *overlapped*, B becomes the right-of-way boat under rule 11 (*windward/leeward*). In this case, B was holding her course and it was A's action that gave B the right of way. Therefore rule 15 does not apply to B, and if A were to suddenly luff and strike B's bow with her port stern quarter, A would have broken rule 11 (On the Same Tack, Overlapped).

RULE 16 - CHANGING COURSE

When a right-of-way boat changes course, she shall give the other boat *room* to *keep clear*.

This short, concise rule contains one of the most fundamental principles in the rules. Simply put, before a right-of-way boat changes her course near a give-way boat, she must be aware of the **space** and **time** the give-way boat will need to stay clear of her, assuming the give-way boat reacts and maneuvers promptly in a seamanlike way; and she must be sure to give her that space and time.

Rule 16 represents a major consolidation and simplification of the previous rules, particularly rule 35 (Limitations on Altering Course), rule 38 (Same Tack-Before Clearing the Starting Line) and rule 39 (Same Tack-After Clearing the Starting Line). The rationale for these changes is to greatly simplify and clarify the rules that apply when right-of-way boats change course near other boats, and to eliminate sudden luffing, or any change of course that is so fast that the give-way boat is unable to keep clear.

To help clarify the application of rule 16, here are the major changes in this new rule:

- There are no more exceptions built into the rule; i.e. under previous rule 35 (Limitations on Altering Course), a right-of-way boat could essentially ignore the give-way boat when luffing after *starting* and when assuming a *proper course* to *start* or when rounding a *mark*. This is no longer true.

- *Leeward* boats can no longer luff as they please near *windward* boats; i.e. there is no more sudden luffing, or luffing with no regard for W's ability to keep clear.

- The rule for luffing is now **one and the same** for before-*start* and after-*start* luffing.

- The vague concept of "obstructing the other boat while she is keeping clear," contained in previous rule 35 (Limitations on Altering Course), has been deleted.

- The rule now applies the same whether boats are luffing or bearing away near other boats.

Let's get into this extremely important rule. Rule 16 is clearly talking to right-of-way boats (see ISAF Case 115). When two boats are about to collide, the give-way boat has the obligation to *keep clear*. The only way she can decide how to do this is if she can accurately figure out where the right-of-way boat is going. It would be chaos if just as a *port-tack* boat was reaching by a *starboard-tack* boat, S could suddenly and unexpectedly

S has the right of way over P; but rule 16 requires that S not change her course so close to P that P does not have room to keep clear.

turn and hit P. The purpose of rule 16 is to protect give-way boats from unpredictable changes of course by right-of-way boats which, in essence, prevent the give-way boat from being able to *keep clear.*

"So if I'm on starboard tack near a port-tack boat, rule 10 doesn't allow me to steer any course I want to?"

Absolutely not. That is exactly what rule 16 is designed to prevent. ISAF Case 129 says, "Tactical desires do not relieve a boat from her obligations under the rules. While A (the right-of-way boat in the case) was free to adopt any course she chose to reach the leeward mark, she had no right to luff abruptly into the path of B (the give-way boat). Her extreme and unexpected change of course made it impossible for B to keep clear."

However, rule 16 does not shift the right-of-way between two boats; it is simply a common-sense "limit" on the right-of-way boat requiring her to restrict her course changes when a give-way boat is close by and trying to *keep clear.*

Notice that rule 16 only applies to a "change of course." It in no way applies to a change in a boat's speed or her angle of heel. When P reaches by just to *windward* of S such that S momentarily loses her wind, thereby straightening up and hitting P's mast, P is wrong under rule 10 (On Opposite Tacks). Of course, rule 2 (Fair Sailing) is available to P if she suspects that S deliberately tried to hit her in an unfair manner.

Note also that "course" refers to both "compass" **and** "directional" course. Therefore, when a boat that was moving forward begins to move astern, she has changed "course" (see also rule 20, Starting Errors; Penalty Turns; Moving Astern).

"OK, so if I'm a right-of-way boat and want to change course near another boat, what exactly do I need to give her?"

You need to give her *"room* to *keep clear"* of you. She is *keeping clear* of you when you can sail your course with no need to take action to avoid hitting her, i.e. you have no reasonable apprehension of contact. The *room* you have to give her is the "space" and "time" she needs while getting far enough away from you so that you can sail your course, assuming she acts promptly in a seamanlike way.

Note that "promptly" means "performed readily, quickly, immediately" which builds in the time element for her response. Therefore when a right-of-way boat changes course, rule 16 requires nearby boats to respond "promptly" or risk losing the protection of *room.* However, "seamanlike" means "responsible, prudent, safety conscious." Therefore, you have to be sure that your course change doesn't force the give-way boat to put their or your boat's crew, boat or equipment at risk of injury or damage by the need to make a sudden, hurried or extrem e maneuver. For instance, forcing a *windward* boat to sail head to wind with a spinnaker up in heavy air may be considered "unseamanlike" as it may put the spinnaker in great risk of tearing.

"Well, if I'm the right-of-way boat, how close to the give-way boat can I be and still alter my course without breaking rule 16?"

That's the important question to examine. There are basically two questions the right-of-way boat will need to consider before changing course near another boat:

1) "Will I remain in control of whether or not there will be contact?" and

2) "When I turn toward the give-way boat, will she have enough 'space' and 'time' to get away from me promptly but without having to make an unseamanlike maneuver to avoid me?"

To examine these questions, let's break it down into two scenarios. In both of these, assume there are two boats sailing close-hauled upwind with the *port-tack* boat (P) crossing ahead of the *starboard-tack* boat (S).

1) If S holds her course, P will *keep clear*. When close to P, S changes her course toward P, putting the two boats on a collision course. At that point, there is essentially nothing P can do to avoid the collision (tacking won't help as she's directly in S's path). At the last second, S **chooses** to bear off and pass astern of P because she isn't sure that she gave P enough *room* to *keep clear*. There is no contact. S does not protest P; P protests S for breaking rule 16.

The fact that S **was able to sail her chosen course** with no interference from P means that P *kept clear* and S did not break 16. ISAF Case 52 involves this exact scenario and says, "S being the right-of-way boat was...bound by rule 16 not to change course if by doing so she did not give P room to keep clear. As S altered course again to avoid hitting P, she did not break rule 16."

Note, this is similar to the situation when S and P are converging on a collision course and S then bears away and passes astern of P. Without knowing S's **reason** for altering her course, a protest committee could not determine if P *kept clear* or not. If in a protest hearing it was found that S **voluntarily** allowed P to cross so that P didn't tack on her lee-bow, then P has *kept clear*. If S had borne off **against her preferred choice**, for the sole reason that she needed to avoid a collision, P has not *kept clear*.

Therefore, one question the right-of-way boat needs to consider before changing course is: "Will I remain in control of whether or not there will be contact?" If "yes," then the right-of-way boat, after altering toward the give-way boat, can make any necessary subsequent alteration of course away from the give-way boat necessary to avoid contact. And in the case when the right-of-way boat isn't satisfied that she gave the give-way boat enough *room* to *keep clear*, she simply doesn't protest, indicating that she was able to sail her chosen course.

2) Again, S changes course toward P, putting the two boats on a collision course, and then bears away to avoid contact.

This time, S protests P for breaking rule 10 (On Opposite Tacks) and P protests S for breaking rule 16.

In the hearing, S states that she bore away for the sole reason of avoiding contact with P, i.e. she was **not able to sail her chosen course** because of her need to avoid P. The first job of the protest committee then will be to determine if P actually *kept clear*. If, after determining the facts, they find that there was a reasonable probability that the boats would have hit had S not borne away, then P has not *kept clear*. Their next task then is to decide if, when S altered course, she gave P *"room"* to *keep clear*. If they decide "yes," then P has broken rule 10 (On Opposite Tacks); if they decide "no," then S has broken rule 16.

Therefore, the other important question the right-of-way boat must consider is: "When I turn toward the give-way boat, will she have enough *'room'* (i.e. 'space' and 'time' to get away from me promptly but without having to make an unseamanlike maneuver) to avoid me?"

All the questions must be answered depending on the circumstances at the time.

The major considerations will be:

1. the distance between the boats;

2. the speeds and sizes of the boats;

3. the angles at which they are converging;

4. the visibility and ability to hail and hear between the boats;

5. the amount of alteration by the right-of-way boat;

6. the ability of the give-way boat to predict the alteration, i.e. did the right-of-way boat hail or otherwise attempt to signal;

7. the amount and difficulty of the boat handling required by the give-way boat to *keep clear*; and

8. the reasonableness of the give-way boat's attempt to *keep clear*.

So, back to the question of how close can the right-of-way boat be to the give-way boat and still change her course toward her. Clearly, each incident must be judged on its own, and for that reason it is impossible to project a hypothetical distance apart. Let's look at some common situations when rule 16 will come into play:

When two boats are converging on opposite tacks on a beat:

"On a beat, does rule 16 now allow starboard-tack boats to "hunt" port-tackers; i.e. allow S to turn up towards P when P is committed to crossing S's bow?"

In this crossing situation, rule 16 does not allow S to do anything she was prohibited from doing under previous rule 35 (Limitation on Altering Course). Under old rule 35, S couldn't alter course if it "prevented" P from keeping clear (i.e. made it impossible for P to keep clear). That is clearly the same now. If S turns up and hits P, and there is no way P can *keep clear*, S breaks rule 16.

Also under old rule 35, S couldn't "obstruct" P while she was keeping clear. This vague term was not defined in the rule nor ever clearly interpreted in any appeal. One understanding was that if P altered course to keep clear (e.g. bore off to pass astern of S) and S then altered her course in such a way that P was caused to have to make an **additional** alteration of course to avoid S, S had "obstructed" P. But when P was sailing a straight-line course across S's bow, it was very unclear as to how to apply the term "obstruct." Clearly there was no specific distance prescribed by the rule at which point S was required to hold her course. The convention was that generally S held her course when P was less than two lengths away. But certainly there were times when S altered course closer than that (sometimes bearing away toward P to encourage P to tack sooner; sometimes luffing to discourage P from trying to cross ahead of her) and P was able to easily tack away. If there was a protest, the decision was based on the speed of the boats, the time P had to respond, the difficulty of P's maneuver, etc., etc., just as it is now.

The primary difference and major improvement in the new rule 16 is that now sailors and protest committees have a more tangible test, although a necessarily subjective test, when considering if S changed course too close to P. The test is whether, when S turned toward P, P had enough "*room*," i.e. "space" and "time" to promptly maneuver away from S in a seamanlike way. If P is able to promptly tack in a "seamanlike way," then S has not changed course too close to her; if not, then S has changed course too close. It will obviously depend on all the circumstances; but a conservative and safe rule of thumb is that S should not turn up toward P when less than two lengths away from P unless there is no question that P can easily tack away.

A real life situation might look like this:

P and S are converging on a beat. P will cross S by half a boat-length or so. When about two-lengths apart, S hails "Starboard" and makes a medium fast luff toward P. P, who has been watching S, makes a routine tack to *starboard tack*. S, who would hit P if she holds her course, continues her turn into a tack and sails off on *port tack* with no protest.

When the boats were converging, P was required to *keep clear* under rule 10 (On Opposite Tacks). When S changed her course near P, she was required to give P *room* to *keep clear* under rule 16. As P was able to promptly maneuver in a seamanlike way and S was able to sail her chosen course with no contact, P *kept clear* and S gave her the *room* she needed to do so.

"I assume from all this that if I'm on starboard and get a wind shift on a beat, I can't follow the shift and hit a port-tack boat that is just crossing my bow?"

That's absolutely right. Rule 16 applies to any course change, regardless of the reason. In 1965 the rule read, "A yacht is not misleading or balking another if she alters course by luffing or bearing away to conform to a change in the strength or direction of the wind." But the rule writers realized that (a) it was too difficult for the give-way boat to anticipate how the wind might suddenly shift, and (b) this rule gave the right-of-way boat the ability to misuse the rule too easily. (See ISAF Case 52.)

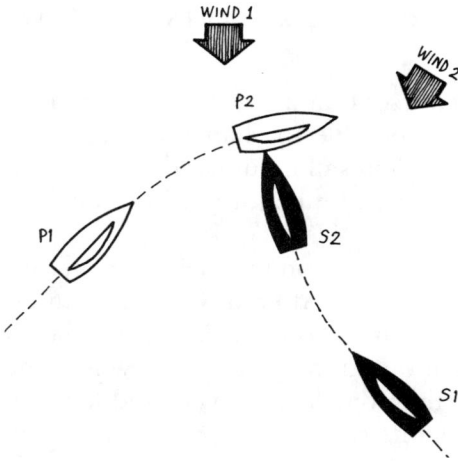

P was safely crossing S. Suddenly the wind shifted to the right giving S a "lift" and P a "header." In following the "lift" S changed course so close to P that P was unable to keep clear. Therefore S broke rule 16.

Therefore, if P is crossing you and you get a favorable wind shift and want to head up and pass close astern of P, but you see that P doesn't have *room* to tack away after you do head up, simply let P know with a hail or a wave that she can continue on across you as you head up toward her.

"If I'm making a smooth turn toward a give-way boat, am I considered to be 'changing my course' if I continue the arc of my turn?"

US SAILING Appeal 172 says, "Yes, it is a change of course for B [right-of-way boat] to continue the established arc of her circle. If B does not bring her helm amidships, she is changing course. She must settle onto a compass course as soon as she gains right of way or risk breaking rule 16."

"Do I have to hail before changing my course?"

The rule does not require a hail. However, a clear hail alerting the give-way boat that you are about to change course is strong evidence that you intend to give her *room* to *keep clear* when you change course, and is therefore strongly recommended in every situation where you are going to change course near another boat.

When two boats are converging on opposite tacks on a down-wind leg:

When sailing downwind on courses that are generally more parallel, *starboard-tack* boats will be able to change course when closer to *port-tack* boats than when sailing upwind. The reason is that it will generally require less of a major course change or maneuver for P to *keep clear* of S.

In ISAF Case 35, S and P are running on parallel courses (with S to P's left) less than one length apart. After about two minutes, S hails and begins to change course toward P, and the boats touch. The Case addresses the question, "Can S sail where she pleases even though P is less than one length away and keeping clear?" and responds, "S...is the starboard-tack right-of-way boat under rule 10, and P as the port-tack give-way boat is bound to keep clear...S may [change course] provided she complies with rule 16."

When two boats are sailing side by side on the same tack

"Does this mean that when a leeward boat luffs, a windward boat can react more slowly under these new rules than before?"

NO! Just as under the previous rules, when W gets near L she must be prepared for L to luff (change course toward her). And when L luffs, W must respond "promptly" (i.e. very quickly; without delay) and make her best effort to get out of L's way. Furthermore, L can luff as quickly as she chooses **provided** she allows W the space and time needed to get out of her way assuming W is responding promptly. So the game hasn't changed that much! The major difference from the previous rules is that L can never luff so suddenly or fast that, despite W's best efforts, W physically cannot *keep clear* of her or is caused to make an unseamanlike maneuver while attempting to *keep clear*.

"If L luffs, then stops luffing to give W more room to respond, is L still bound by rule 16 to give W room to keep clear when L begins luffing again?"

Yes. Rule 16 applies to L whenever she changes her course. The use of the word "initially" in rule 15 (Acquiring Right of Way) makes the requirement in rule 15 a temporary one at the outset of the *overlap*. However, rule 16 does not contain the word "initially." Therefore, each time L stops and then changes her course again, she must give W *room* to *keep clear* once again. W, on the other hand, will put herself at great risk by remaining too close to L over an extended period of time, and should make every effort to get well clear when L first luffs.

"What if, despite the fact that L has given W plenty of room, W allows herself to get so close to L that L can't change course without hitting W?"

The last phrase in the Definition *Keep Clear* tells W that she is not *keeping clear* if she allows herself to get so close to L that L couldn't change course in either direction at that moment without **immediately** making contact with her. (Note: if L couldn't luff without immediate contact but could bear away without immediate contact, the last phrase in this definition doesn't apply because L "could" change course without making immediate contact.) Note also that the second "if" in the definition suggests that L does not need to actually hit W to prove she couldn't change course without contact. If the protest committee decides that L couldn't have changed course without immediately hitting W, then W has broken rule 11 (On the Same Tack, Overlapped) simply by her extreme close proximity to L.

Furthermore, any time L has a reasonable apprehension that contact with W may occur if she holds her course, W fails to *keep clear* and breaks rule 11 (On the Same Tack, Overlapped); and when W allows herself to get that close to L, L will generally be justified in being concerned about the masts touching, the boats being tossed together by waves, etc., etc.

However, when L is luffing and her bow is getting closer to W's stern quarter, there will come a point that, due to the way boats rotate, it will become impossible for W to *keep clear* if L continues her luff. At that point, L must cease her luff and allow W the *room* she needs to move away from L. This acts very much like "mast abeam" did in the old rules, with the difference being that L needn't bear away at this point; she simply needs to hold her course until W once again has *room* to *keep clear* when L continues her luff.

"Is it true that the rules regarding the rate of L's luff are now the same before and after starting?"

Yes. Rule 16 is the rule that deals primarily with the rate of L's luff; and there is absolutely no difference in the application of rule 16 before or after *starting*. This is one of the major simplifications in these rules.

"What if a boat to windward of W, or some other object, restricts her ability to respond to a luff by L?"

This is commonly the situation as boats begin to tightly line-up in the final minutes before a start or as they approach a crowded downwind *mark*. The *room* that rule 16 requires L to give W often must include time for W to wait for boats to *windward* of her to respond, or for W to sail past an object (e.g. something in the water) that prevents her from *keeping clear* of L. A hail by W to the effect, "I am trying to *keep clear* but I have these other boats, or this object, to *windward* of me!" will be useful and is strongly encouraged.

Some real life situations might look like this:

L is sailing along on a reach. W catches up and *overlaps* L to *windward*, but far enough away so that L can change her course toward her (luff) without immediately hitting her. L begins to luff medium fast and W promptly responds and *keeps clear*. No problem so far. At some point during the luff, L gets closer to W (either because W slows down her response rate, or L increases her luffing rate or because of the boats simply get closer as they rotate up) such that if L continues her luff she will immediately hit W. She stops her luff and protests. This protest will be resolved by the protest committee's determination of whether W was maneuvering promptly in a seamanlike way or not. If "yes," then L's protest will be disallowed; if "no," then W will

STARTING LINE

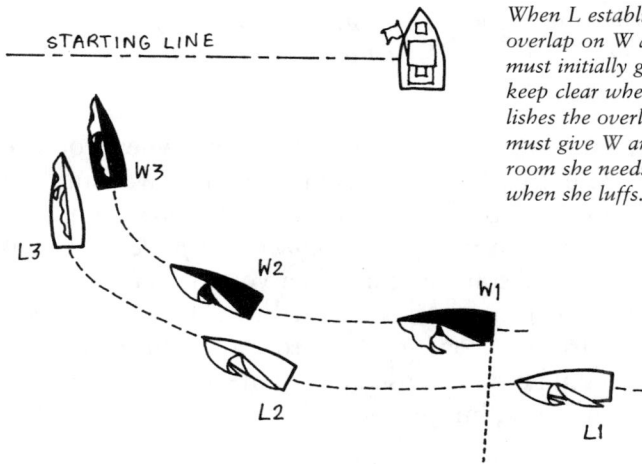

When L establishes a leeward overlap on W and then luffs, L must initially give W room to keep clear when she first establishes the overlap; and then L must give W any additional room she needs to keep clear when she luffs.

be penalized for breaking rule 11 (On the Same Tack, Overlapped).

W is slowly sailing along the starting line about a minute before starting. L catches up from *clear astern* and establishes an *overlap* to *leeward*. Prior to the *overlap*, W, as the boat *clear ahead,* is the right-of-way boat under rule 12 (On the Same Tack, Not Overlapped); therefore she doesn't need to take any action in anticipation of L's *leeward overlap*. When L establishes the *overlap*, L is required by rule 15 (Acquiring Right of Way) to initially give W *room* to *keep clear*. This includes the space and time necessary for W to trim her sails and otherwise get steerageway to get away from L. After W has had *room* to *keep clear,* L may luff provided she gives W any **additional** *room* W needs to *keep clear*. The bottom line is that when *leeward* boats "come in the back door" (i.e. establish *leeward overlaps* from *clear astern* on *windward* boats) and then want to luff, they must plan to be very patient (see ISAF Case 11).

Other situations in which rule 16 will come into play:

"When I'm rounding the windward mark to go onto a run on starboard tack, can't I bear away as fast as I want onto my proper course, even if it means nearby port-tack boats coming upwind don't have room to keep clear of

me; or when the starting gun goes off, can't I luff up to close-hauled even if there's a port-tack boat right in front of me?"

No! Rule 16 contains no exceptions. Therefore, when you are rounding a *mark*, even when you have the right of way and are turning down to your *proper course* to the next *mark*, you have to give give-way boats in your path *room* to *keep clear* of you. The same is true at the starting gun when you are on *starboard tack* and want to head up to close-hauled to *start*. If there is a *port-tack* boat in front of you, you have to wait until she is clear of you before heading up. (You used to be able to do these things under the previous rules, but no longer.)

"Can L ever bear away with no limitation and hit W with her transom?"

No. When L bears away near W, L must comply with rule 16 as well, i.e. not bear away in a way that does not give W *room* to *keep clear*. Normally, if L bears away slowly and with some caution not to swing her stern into W's *leeward* side, L will not break rule 16; and if W has left herself so close to *windward* of

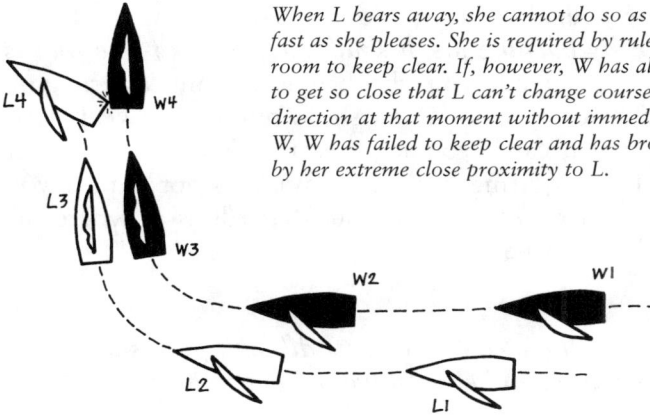

When L bears away, she cannot do so as suddenly and fast as she pleases. She is required by rule 16 to give W room to keep clear. If, however, W has allowed herself to get so close that L can't change course in either direction at that moment without immediately hitting W, W has failed to keep clear and has broken rule 11 by her extreme close proximity to L.

L that L can't luff or bear away at that moment without immediately hitting her, W has failed to *keep clear* under the terms of the definition and has broken rule 11 (On the Same Tack, Overlapped).

"What happens if the boat clear ahead of me suddenly pushes her mainsail out and backs down into me?"

She is in trouble. First off, changing her fore and aft directon is a change of "course" for the boat *clear ahead*; therefore, she must give you *room* to *keep clear* of her. Secondly, rule 20

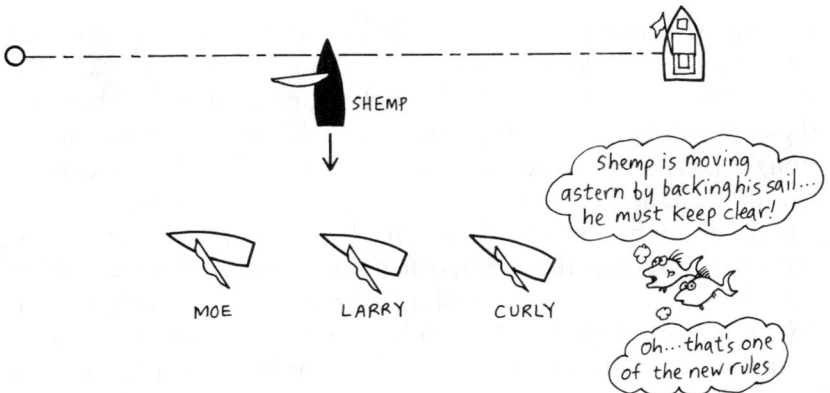

SHEMP

MOE   LARRY   CURLY

Shemp is moving astern by backing his sail... he must keep clear!

oh...that's one of the new rules

(Starting Errors; Penalty Turns; Moving Astern) reads, "*A boat moving astern by backing a sail shall keep clear of one that is not.*" Therefore, the moment she begins moving astern, **you** become the right-of-way boat, and she is required to *keep clear* of you! Note that because you acquired the right of way by **her** actions, rule 15 (Acquiring Right of Way) does not require you to give her *room* to *keep clear* of you. Regardless of where she hits you, she breaks rule 20.

"Sounds like there could be some difficult protests; are there any onuses to help resolve these disputes?"

No. In a dispute over whether W *kept clear* or whether L provided enough *room* to *keep clear*, neither the rules nor the appeals place any "onus" on either boat. The protest committee will have to determine the facts and use its best judgment. However, as in rule 15, a windward boat's right to "room to *keep clear*" is a shield and not a sword for W. Therefore, to be entitled to the protection of *room*, W must respond as promptly as she can in a seamanlike way to get clear. From there it will be up to the protest committee to decide from the weight of the evidence on all the various factors as to whether or not W had "*room* to *keep clear*." Hails by both boats at the time will be very helpful in resolving such conflicts and are strongly encouraged. And to be safe, I would assume that the benefit of the doubt will go to the right-of-way boat.

A surprise!

Finally, be aware of this one situation where the rules produce an unexpected result. L and W are sailing side-by-side dead downwind on *port tack*. Without changing course, L gybes and the end of her boom strikes the end of W's boom. In this situation W has broken rule 10 (On Opposite Tacks)! The reason is: L didn't change course, so rule 16 didn't apply; and L didn't "acquire" right of way when she became the *starboard-tack* boat (because she already had it as the *leeward* boat while on *port tack*; and didn't lose it simply because she gybed), so rule 15 (Acquiring Right of Way) did not apply. Therefore, W (now P) fails to *keep clear* of L (now S). In actuality, it will be difficult for L to gybe without changing course slightly, in which case she will most likely break rule 16. However, W will be smart to move far enough away when L gybes so that L's boom can't hit hers.

RULE 17 - On The Same Tack; Proper Course

Rule 17.1

A boat that establishes a *leeward overlap* from *clear astern* within two of her hull lengths of a *windward* boat shall not sail above her *proper course* during that *overlap* while the boats are less than that distance apart, unless as a result she becomes *clear astern*.

Rule 16 (Changing Course) is about limiting **how fast** a right-of-way boat can turn near a give-way boat; rule 17.1 is about limiting **where** a *leeward* boat can sail when near a give-way boat. Note that rule 17.1 simply puts a "limit" on where a *leeward* boat can sail when near a *windward* boat in certain situations. It does not shift any right-of-way to the *windward* boat. When near each other, W must remember that rule 11 (On the Same Tack, Overlapped) requires her to *keep clear* of L.

Rule 17.1 also represents a major consolidation and simplification of the previous rules, particularly rule 35 (Limitations on Altering Course), rule 38 (Same Tack-Before Clearing the Starting Line), rule 39 (Same Tack-After Clearing the Starting Line) and rule 40 (Other Limitations on a Leeward Yacht). Again, the rationale for these changes is to greatly simplify the rules that apply when boats on the same *tack*, i.e. *windward* and *leeward* boats, sail near each other.

To help clarify the application of rule 17.1, here are the major changes in this new rule:

- The concept of "mast abeam" has been completely removed from the rules!

- *Leeward* boats are now permitted to sail up to head to wind at all times **before** the starting signal.

- When *overlapped* boats *start*, their *overlap* is no longer considered a new *overlap*; now L and W will have to remember how they became *overlapped*, as it will affect L's rights and W's obligations.

The concept in rule 17.1 is simple: either L is "limited" to sailing no higher than her *proper course* or she is free to sail up to head to wind if she pleases; it is always one or the other for L whenever L and W are *overlapped* and within two of L's lengths of each other.

Whether L is "limited" or not depends on the following four factors:

1) whether the boats are *overlapped*;

2) whether the boats are within two of L's hull lengths of each other;

3) whether the *overlap* was established from *clear astern* or not; and

4) whether the starting signal has been made.

(It is important to point out that when boats are passing marks and obstructions, rule 18, Passing Marks and Obstructions, may impose some conflicting obligations or limitations on L, in which case they would override those in rule 17.1. See the explanation of rule 18 for a full discussion.)

A few clarifying points on the four factors listed above:

1) The "limit" in rule 17.1 only applies to boats that are "*overlapped*." The terms *clear ahead*, *clear astern* and *overlap* do not apply to boats on opposite *tacks* (unless they are about to pass a *mark* or *obstruction* and rule 18 applies). So when a *starboard-tack* boat and a *port-tack* boat are half way down a leg and they are sailing side by side, they are not considered *overlapped*; and if P catches up from astern and sails in alongside of S, P has not established a *leeward overlap* from *clear astern* on S.

On the other hand, a boat is always on a *tack*. Therefore, when P and S are converging on a beat and P tacks in front of S, the moment P passes head to wind she is on *starboard tack* (though she still must *keep clear* until she's on a close-hauled course under rule 13, While Tacking). Even when S establishes an *overlap* the moment P passes head to wind, the boats are considered *overlapped*. (See the discussion of Definition *Clear Astern* and *Clear Ahead; Overlap*.)

2) The "limit" only applies when L and W are **within two lengths of each other.** The "two lengths" distance is determined by two of L's hull lengths, i.e. the length of L's hull, and not the additional length of any bowsprits, overhanging mizzen booms, etc. This is particularly important when boats of different sizes are near each other.

3) The only time L is "limited" is when she establishes an *overlap* to *leeward* of W from *clear astern* **within two of her lengths** of W. That's it! The "limit" does not apply when L *overlaps* W when more than two lengths apart, or when W establishes the *overlap* to *windward* of L or when L is to leeward of W on the opposite *tack* and then gybes. Furthermore, once the *overlap* is established with no "limit" on L, there is no way for W to thereafter put the "limit" on during that *overlap*. (Under the previous rules, W could get "mast abeam" and thereby limit L; under these rules, the entire concept of "mast abeam" has been deleted.)

Note that any time a boat that was *clear astern* becomes

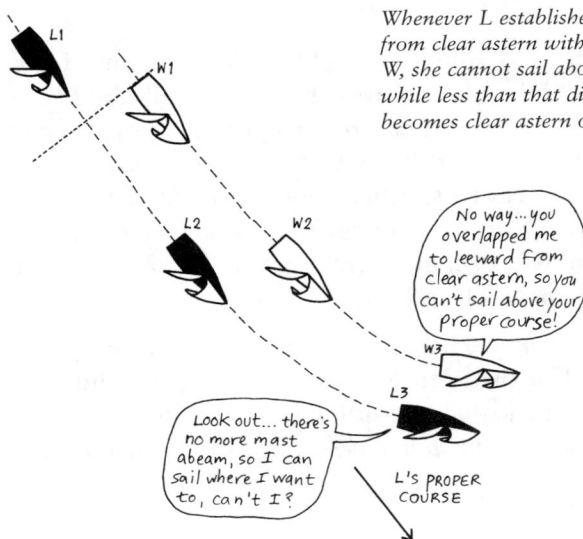

Whenever L establishes a leeward overlap from clear astern within two of her lengths of W, she cannot sail above her proper course while less than that distance apart, unless she becomes clear astern of W.

No way...you overlapped me to leeward from clear astern, so you can't sail above your proper course!

Look out... there's no more mast abeam, so I can sail where I want to, can't I?

L'S PROPER COURSE

overlapped to *leeward* of a boat that was *clear ahead* (i.e. crosses a line perpendicular to the *clear ahead* boat's center-line drawn through the boat's aftermost part in normal position), it is considered that a *leeward overlap* has been "established" by the boat that was *clear astern*, regardless of how that line came to be in front of the boat *clear astern*. In other words, even in the situation where a boat *clear astern* is holding her course and a boat *clear ahead* and to windward turns down and creates an *overlap*, it is considered that the boat *clear astern* "established" the *overlap*. Furthermore, it would be impractical to decide that rule 17.1 was premised on determining the relative speeds and/or turning rates of the two boats that may have created the *overlap* because these factors would generally be extremely difficult to determine and prove.

4) The "limit" in rule 17.1 is that L **cannot sail above her *proper course*.** Because a boat does not have a *proper course* until the starting signal is made, there is never any "limit" on L **before** her starting signal (see the discussion of the Definition *Proper Course*).

"What happens in the situation where L and W are both sailing their proper courses and the two boats are converging; who has to keep clear?"

W must *keep clear* of L under rule 11 (On the Same Tack, Overlapped). Rule 17.1 only requires that L not sail **above** her *proper course*. When L is **on** her *proper course*, W must *keep clear*. Note that the phrase in rule 17.1 "her *proper course*" clarifies that it is L who gets to sail **her** *proper course*. Therefore, when L is sailing on her *proper course*, W must keep clear under rule 11, even when W's *proper course* may be a **lower** course than L's. (See ISAF Cases 11 and 25.)

Remember that a *proper course* is essentially any course a boat chooses to sail in order to get to the next *mark* and ultimately to *finish* as quickly as possible. Therefore it is possible that there may be several *proper courses* at any given moment depending upon the circumstances involved. It is also obvious that two *overlapping* boats sailing for the same *mark* will converge. Note also that a boat's *proper course* is not necessarily a straight-line course. It can change with changes in the breeze, current or waves, or with a change in the boat's strategy. However, whenever L wants to change her course to a new *proper course*, she must give W *room* to *keep clear* under rule 16 (Changing Course). A hail that she intends to change course is strongly recommended. (See the discussion of the Definition *Proper Course*.)

"What happens when L wants to luff two or more boats and one of the middle boats is 'limited' to where she can sail?"

Good question! Let's take the situation where L and W are sailing down a reach about two lengths or so apart. A boat from astern (M) catches up and establishes an *overlap* between them. When M established the *overlap* on W, there was clearly *room* for her to pass between L and W such that she did not break rule 18.5 (Passing a Continuing Obstruction). Now L begins to luff toward M and W. M responds by luffing. W must *keep clear* of M, under rule 11 (On the Same Tack, Overlapped) because in fact M is **not** sailing above her *proper course*.

Here's the reason. Take the two boats involved, M and W. M established a *leeward overlap* on W from *clear astern*. Rule 17.1 requires M, therefore, not to sail above her *proper course*. In determining her *proper course*, the definition of *proper course* instructs us to remove the boats referred to in the rule using the term *proper course*. In this case, rule 17.1 uses the term and refers to the *windward* boat W. As M was sailing a course to *keep clear* of L, she would have been sailing the same course in the absence of W; therefore, M was sailing her *proper course* and not above it.

"What's the purpose of the last phrase in rule 17.1, '...unless as a result she becomes clear astern?'"

This is to close a very subtle, undesirable loophole in the rule. Here's a potential scenario: on a beat to windward, a boat crosses you and tacks just ahead and about half a length to windward of you. With your greater speed you establish an *overlap to leeward* from *clear astern*, but you realize that you won't be able to sail past them enough to get your air clear. You want to tack out of there. Assuming that when sailing upwind your *proper course* is a close-hauled course, without an exception to the rule the question would be: "Could you sail above close-hauled and tack while you're *overlapped* to *leeward* of W; or would you have to wait until you were no longer *overlapped* so you didn't break rule 17.1?" Rule 17.1 clarifies that you can certainly luff provided you become *clear astern*, i.e. you break the *overlap* with W. If you luff and then realize that your bow won't clear W's transom and have to pull your bow back down, you risk breaking rule 17.1.

Rule 17.2

Except on a beat to windward, while a boat is less than two of her hull lengths from a *leeward* boat or a boat *clear astern* steering a course to *leeward* of her, she shall not sail below her *proper course* unless she gybes.

This rule is saying that if you are sailing downwind and there's a boat within two lengths and either *clear ahead* or to *windward* of you, and you are steering a course to leeward of her, she **cannot** sail below her *proper course*. This is only fair, because when you try to pass a boat to *windward*, she can prevent you by luffing. It would give that boat too much of an advantage if, when you tried to pass her to *leeward*, she could bear away on your wind too.

This is possibly the most infringed rule in Part 2, partially because many sailors don't know it and partially because it is very difficult to prove a breach. It is commonly broken as boats near *marks* and the boats ahead try to prevent or discourage the boats behind from getting an inside *overlap*.

Note that this rule does not apply to a boat that is "on a beat to windward." Therefore, on a "beat to windward" it **is** legal to bear off to get closer to a boat to *leeward* or *clear astern* of you, though this is not commonly done except in team racing.

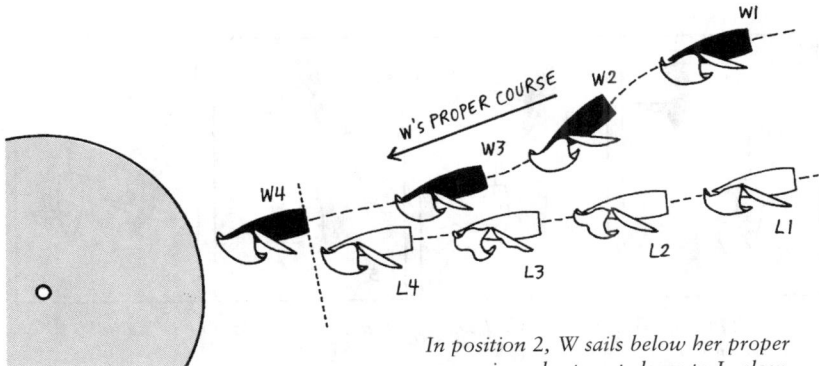

In position 2, W sails below her proper course in order to get closer to L, slow her down and prevent her from maintaining an inside overlap. W would not have borne away in the absence of L. This is a common breach of rule 17.2.

"On a beat to windward" has never been interpreted by an appeal. My opinion is that a boat is "on a beat to windward" if her *proper course* to the next *mark* at the time is to sail close-hauled. All other legs are considered "free legs." Therefore, any leg on which your *proper course* to the next *mark* is below close-hauled is a "free leg" for you, and rule 17.2 can apply. For instance, if you are on a beat sailing close-hauled near the star-board-tack layline and the wind shifts 20 degrees to the right such that now you are "overstanding" (i.e. can get to the *mark* by sailing a lower than close-hauled course), **you** are now on a "free-leg," whereas the boats on the left side of the leg may still be on a "beat to windward." The same logic applies to an off-wind leg. If you can get to the next *mark* by sailing a course lower than close-hauled, it is a "free leg" for you. But if the wind shifts such that you must now sail close-hauled to get there, the leg is now a "beat to windward" for you.

Note the phrase "steering a course to *leeward* of her." In my opinion, a boat *clear astern* is considered to be steering a course to *leeward* of the boat *clear ahead* any time her course will take her to the *leeward* side of the boat *clear ahead*, including when the boat *clear astern* is up to windward of the boat *clear ahead's* wake. An example of a boat *clear astern* **not** "steering a course to *leeward*" is when the boat *clear astern* is aiming at, or to *windward* of, the boat *clear ahead's* transom and is *sailing* a course parallel to or higher than her.

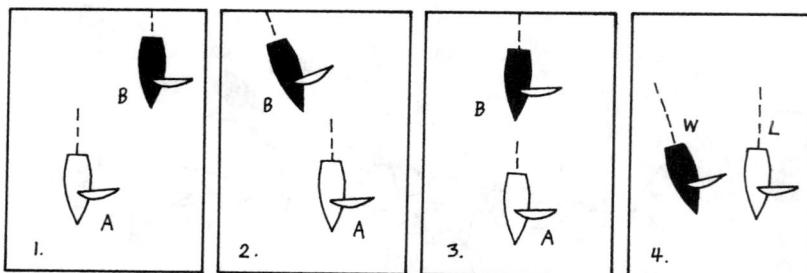

Rule 17.2 applies to A in positions 1 and 2, but not to A in position 3. It applies to W in position 4.

Note also that the rule only applies when boats are within **two** hull lengths of each other. (This is a change from previous rule 39.3 which applied when boats were within three lengths.)

Rule 17.2 contains one exception, ."..unless she gybes." This parallels the exception in rule 17.1. A common scenario is W, sailing downwind and close to L, wants to gybe. Because she is a *windward* boat within two lengths of a *leeward* boat, she technically infringes 17.2 (in the absence of the exception). The rule now clarifies that W can certainly bear away and gybe, provided she doesn't hit L or cause L to take avoiding action, and provided she continues right into her gybe following her bearing away. If she bears away and then realizes her bow won't clear L's transom and has to pull her bow back up, she risks breaking rule 17.2. (Note that she does not need to gybe onto a proper course as she did under the previous rules.)

Section A and B Rules In Action

Now that we've had a thorough explanation, let's look at how the rules in Section A and B work in various common situations on the race course.

AT ANY TIME (i.e. both before and after starting) when a windward boat tries to pass close by to a leeward boat:

Two boats are sailing along with one behind the other. The boat astern catches up to the one ahead and chooses to *overlap* her to *windward*. The *leeward* boat (L) wants to prevent the *windward* boat (W) from passing her. L starts to turn toward W (luff) at a

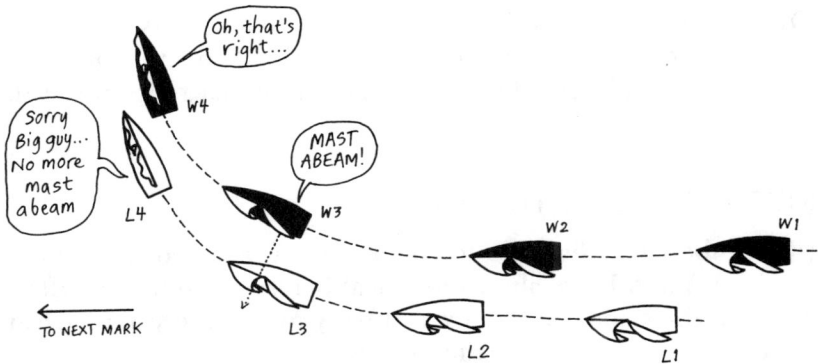

Mast abeam has been removed from the new rules. Therefore, whenever W establishes a windward overlap on L, L can turn all the way up to head to wind for the duration of the overlap, provided she gives W room to keep clear in the process.

medium speed and W *keeps clear*. **For the duration of the *overlap,*** L is permitted to turn all the way up to head to wind if she chooses, provided she gives W *room* to *keep clear*. To clarify, even if L is only *overlapped* with W by two feet, L can sail up to head to wind! (This represents a major change from the previous rules where W could get "mast abeam" and thereby force L to turn back down to her close-hauled course before *starting* or her *proper course* after *starting*.) Therefore, under the 1997-2000 rules *leeward* boats can luff a bit faster before *starting* but will need to luff a bit slower after *starting* than under the previous rules; and *windward* boats must keep a bit farther away when passing close by *leeward* boats (perhaps another half a length or so to allow for the fact that the *leeward* boat can rotate all the way up to head to wind) but will have a bit more time to respond than before.

US SAILING Appeal 102 says, "A boat is head to wind when her bow is facing the wind, and the centerline of her hull is parallel to it, irrespective of the position of her sails." This clarification is helpful because often when a boat is head to wind her sails will blow momentarily to the other side giving the **illusion** that she is past head to wind and therefore tacking.

Remember that when L is head to wind, it is quite possible that W will be required to go **beyond** head to wind (i.e. tack) in order to *keep clear* under rule 11 (On the Same Tack,

Overlapped). If this is the case, W must do so. If it's not possible for W to *keep clear* without fouling other boats to *windward* of her, W should clearly alert L that she needs more *room* to *keep clear.*

STARTING LINE SITUATIONS

(Remember that the rules for maneuvering near other boats in Sections A and B are almost identical before the start and after; and that the same rules apply with very minor exceptions when the boats are near the starting *marks*.)

BEFORE the starting signal - how far L can turn:

L and W are *overlapped* on the starting line before the starting signal is made. Regardless of how the boats became *overlapped*, and regardless of the relative positions of the two boats, L has no "limit," i.e. L can sail up to head to wind if she chooses and W must *keep clear*. To clarify, even if L is only *overlapped* with W by two feet, L can sail up to head to wind. (This represents a major change from the previous rules where L could only sail up to close-hauled when W was "mast abeam.")

AFTER the starting signal - how far L can turn:

L and W are *overlapped* and it is after the starting signal. If L has established the *leeward overlap* from *clear astern* within two lengths of W (even if the *overlap* was established before the starting signal), then L is "limited," i.e. she is not permitted to sail above her *proper course*. On an upwind start, her *proper course* will most likely be a close-hauled course. On a downwind start, L's *proper course* will be more variable and subjective, depending on many factors including: the course to the first *mark*, the breeze direction and strength, the current direction and strength, the type of boats, the sails in use, the position of other nearby boats, etc., etc. If the *overlap* has been established in any other way (W sailing in to *windward* of L, L tacking under W, L closing from more than two lengths away, etc.), then L has no "limit" and she can sail up to head to wind if she pleases.

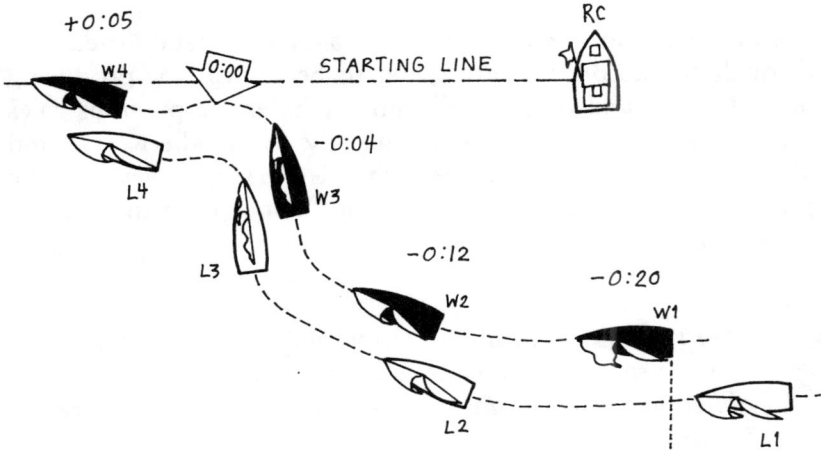

Before the starting signal, when L establishes a leeward overlap from clear astern she is permitted to sail up to head to wind provided she gives W room to keep clear. However, after the starting signal, L may not sail above her proper course which, when sailing to windward, is normally close-hauled.

Note that this applies regardless of whether the boats have actually *started*, i.e. have crossed the starting line after the starting signal. The determining point is the starting signal; not where the boats are relative to the starting line.

"So it appears that under these new rules the starting signal now becomes a deciding factor in determining how far L can turn when near W, correct?"

Exactly right. Before the starting signal, L is not "limited" in any way, i.e. she can sail head to wind if she pleases; after the starting signal, L is "limited" to sailing no higher than her *proper course* if she originally established the leeward *overlap* from *clear astern*. The advantage of having L's limitation begin after the starting signal is that it is a precise and predictable moment in time.

Note that the moment the starting signal is made, L instantly gets a *proper course* (see the Definition *Proper Course*). Now it becomes critical for L and W to remember **how** they became *overlapped*! Hails when the *overlap* is first established and throughout the *overlap* are going to be critical for producing orderly starts and reducing disputes! (Under the previous rules this was much less of an issue because the *overlap* between L and W was considered a "new one" when L *started*; however, in the process of simplification this concept has not been included in the new rules.)

"Do I have to bear away to my proper course before the starting signal is made; i.e. do I have to anticipate my obligation not to sail above my proper course after the starting signal?"

No. You do not have a *proper course* before the starting signal, and therefore you are not "limited" as to where you can sail. When the starting signal is made, and if you are now "limited" because you originally established the *leeward overlap* from *clear astern*, you are required to sail no higher than your *proper course*. The course you will sail to *finish* as quickly as possible will include the course you are on at the moment the starting signal is made. If you must then bear away to a lower course to get to the next *mark* and ultimately the finishing line as quickly as possible, you must do so immediately.

STARTING MARK SITUATIONS

(For the purposes of these following explanations, it will be assumed that the starting *mark* is surrounded by navigable water, and that the boats are approaching the starting *mark* to *start*. For a full explanation of the rules at starting *marks*, see the discussion of rule 18.1(a), Passing Marks and Obstructions, When This Rule Applies.)

UPWIND STARTS (including a discussion on "Barging")

When boats are on their final approach to *start*, rule 18 (Passing Marks and Obstructions) does not apply (rule 18.1(a)), meaning that a *leeward*/outside boat (LO) does **not** have to give a *windward*/inside boat (WI) *room* to pass to *leeward* of the starting

STARTING LINE (10 secs. BEFORE start)

BARGER

I can't believe he's going in there... he's BARGING!

Don't go in there... you're BARGING!

If Barger tries to squeeze in between the race committee boat and L, and hits L or causes L to bear off to avoid a collision, Barger breaks rule 11.

mark (say a race committee boat). If W tries to squeeze between L and the *mark* and hits L or forces L to bear away to avoid a collision, W has broken rule 11 (On the Same Tack, Overlapped). This is what we call "barging."

(Note: the term "barging" applies to action at the starting *mark*. If, halfway down the line, a *windward* boat bears off on a *leeward* boat in an attempt not to be over the line early, the *windward* boat has not "barged" on the *leeward* boat. She has simply broken rule 11, On the Same Tack, Overlapped.)

"I understand that when I'm the windward boat, a lee-ward boat does not have to give me room to pass to lee-ward of the race committee boat; but does that mean she can do anything she pleases to 'shut the door' on me?"

Absolutely not. As we've discussed above, the rules in Sections A and B apply. There are no other special rules that apply at this starting *mark*. Therefore, L must behave in exactly the same way that she must behave anywhere else on the race course. Rule 11 (On the Same Tack, Overlapped) gives L the right of way; and L can sail up to head to wind if she pleases, even when only *over-lapped* with W by two feet.

However, rule 16 (Changing Course) tells L when and how fast she can luff near other boats, i.e. she must give them *room* to *keep clear* whenever she changes course near them. Consider

L and W approaching the race committee boat. If L holds her course W will be able to pass between L and the committee boat without touching either. Just as W sticks her bow in behind the race committee boat, L luffs slowly, but W is unable to *keep clear* due to her proximity to the race committee boat and hits both it and L. L has broken rule 16 by changing course (luffing) without giving W *room* to *keep clear*. If L wants to prevent W from passing between her and the committee boat, she must put herself on a course to "shut the door" before W gets her bow stuck in to *leeward* of the committee boat.

So the answer to the question is "no," L may not do anything she pleases to "shut the door;" she must comply with the rules of Section A and B fully.

"Now, what about after the starting signal?"

If L is not "limited," then she can continue to sail where she pleases. She is under **no obligation** to turn down to her *proper course* (close-hauled course) at the starting signal. (Under the previous rules, there was an exception in the *mark* rounding rules that required this of L, but that exception is not included in rule 18, Passing Marks and Obstructions.) Therefore, L can sail head to wind after the gun, even if it forces W onto the wrong side of the race committee boat, before turning down to *start* herself!

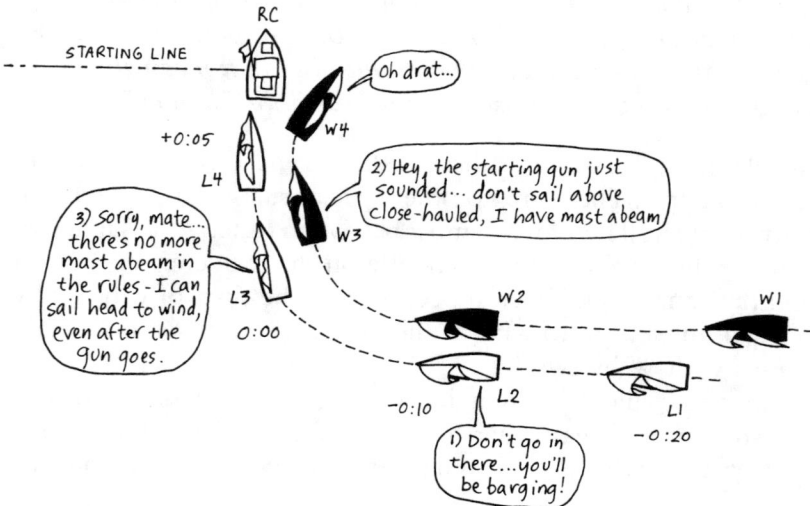

RC

STARTING LINE

+0:05

L4

W4

Oh drat...

2) Hey, the starting gun just sounded... don't sail above close-hauled, I have mast abeam

W3

3) Sorry, mate... there's no more mast abeam in the rules - I can sail head to wind, even after the gun goes.

L3

0:00

W2

W1

L2

−0:10

1) Don't go in there...you'll be barging!

L1

−0:20

If L is "limited," then she must not sail above her *proper course* (normaly close-hauled course) after the starting signal. Therefore, if she is "limited," and sailing above close-hauled before the starting signal, she must immediately turn down to her close-hauled course when the starting signal is made. Again, she does not have to anticipate this obligation; she need only react when the signal is made. However, if LO is sailing on a *proper course* and there is no *room* for WI to squeeze in between her and the committee boat, WI is not allowed to go in there. (See US SAILING Appeal 47.)

"Anything special I should know when I'm starting near the leeward end of the starting line?"

Well one thing that often happens at the leeward end of the starting line is that L gets into a position where she cannot make it around the starting *mark* after the gun goes off without sailing above close-hauled. Remember that in this situation, sailing above close-hauled to get around the *mark* can certainly be considered L's *proper course*, and W must *keep clear* regardless of how the *overlap* was established. (This is also a change from the previous rules where L could not sail above close-hauled if W was "mast abeam.") However, L has to remember that her luff

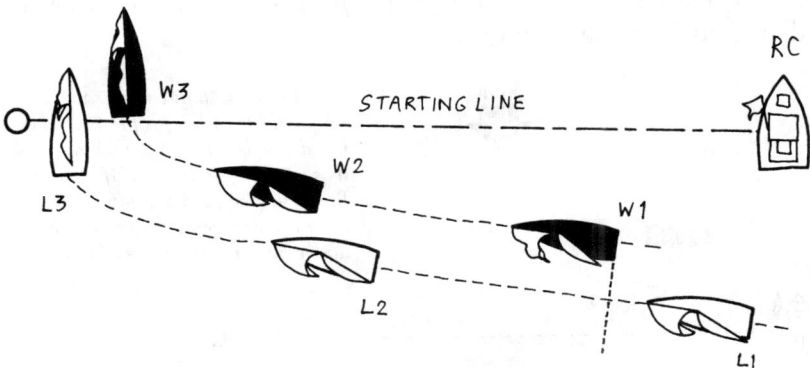

L establishes a leeward overlap from clear astern on W. Before the starting signal she may sail up to head to wind whenever she pleases. After the starting signal she cannot sail above her proper course, which, when sailing to windward, is normally close-hauled. However, in order to pass the starting mark L's proper course may be to momentarily luff up to head to wind. In this case W must keep clear but L must give her room to do so.

is limited by rule 16 (Changing Course) in that she must give W *room* to *keep clear* when she changes her course. This may be difficult when W is close by or when there is a pack of boats to *windward*.

DOWNWIND STARTS

On downwind starts, it is especially critical that boats remember how they became *overlapped*! If L is **not** "limited," she may sail where she pleases; i.e. she is under **no obligation** to head for the first *mark* or sail her *proper course* at the gun. W must beware, especially before setting her spinnaker if L has not set her spinnaker yet!

As *overlapped* boats approach one of the starting *marks* (which can include the race committee boat) and the starting gun goes off, remember that L is under **no obligation** to give W *room* at the starting *mark*! If L is not "limited," then L can force W onto the wrong side of the *mark* before turning down to *start* herself. And if L **is** "limited," then she need only turn down to her *proper course* (not to the compass course to the first *mark* as she was required to do under the previous rules). As *proper course* is so subjective, especially around a starting line, *windward* boats will be well advised to try and avoid becoming *overlapped* to *windward* of *leeward* boats near the starting *marks*. If ever W feels L is sailing above her *proper course*, she is well advised to *keep clear* and protest.

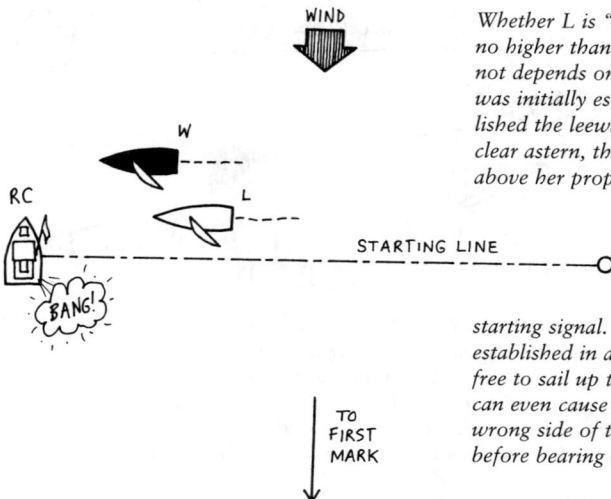

Whether L is "limited" to sailing no higher than her proper course or not depends on how the overlap was initially established. If L established the leeward overlap from clear astern, then she cannot sail above her proper course after the starting signal. If the overlap was established in any other way, L is free to sail up to head to wind, and can even cause W to pass on the wrong side of the committee boat before bearing away to start.

WIND · W · RC · L · STARTING LINE · BANG! · TO FIRST MARK

ON UPWIND LEGS ("Beats")

Again, coming off the starting line it will be essential that L and W remember how they became *overlapped*. If L originally established the *overlap* from *clear astern*, then she is "limited" and cannot sail above her *proper course* (most likely close-hauled). If she is not "limited," she can turn all the way to head to wind and W must *keep clear*.

A common situation on beats is when a *port-tack* boat (PL) tacks on the lee-bow of a *starboard-tack* boat (SW). Because PL did not establish the *overlap* from *clear astern*, she is not "limited" and therefore can luff up to head to wind at any time during the *overlap*, even when only *overlapped* with SW by a couple of feet (i.e. there is no more "mast abeam" to force

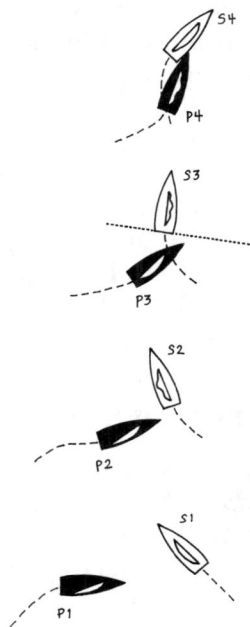

THE SLAM DUNK

Position 1: P has borne away to pass astern of S. The moment P is steering a course to clear S's transom, S luffs. As long as when she luffs, S gives P room to keep clear, S does not break rule 16.

Position 2: S is not past head to wind and is therefore still on starboard tack; P must still keep clear of her under rule 10.

Position 3: S has just passed head to wind. She is now on port tack (i.e. the same tack as P) and P is clear astern. S must keep clear of P under rule 13 until she is close-hauled, and then under rule 11 as the windward boat. P, now the right-of-way boat, does not need to give S room to keep clear under rule 15 if she maintains her straight-line course because she acquired the right of way by

S's actions. However, if P changes course toward S, she is required by rule 16 to give S room to keep clear (i.e. not to prevent S from being able to keep clear or cause her to make an unseamanlike maneuver to do so). Furthermore, under rule 17.1, when P becomes overlapped to leeward of S, she is "limited" to sailing no higher than her proper course (most likely a close-hauled course) for the duration of the overlap because she established the leeward overlap from clear astern.

Position 4: P luffs above her proper course thereby breaking rule 17.1. Whether or not she also broke rule 16 will be decided by the protest committee based on their determination of whether P gave S enough space and time to turn away from P in a sea-

manlike way. (In this case, this would be a moot point because a boat can only be penalized once in an incident regardless of how many rules she may have broken.) The protest committee will have to decide if it was "reasonably possible" for either boat to have avoided the contact; if so, that boat has broken rule 14. However, P can be penalized only if the collision causes damage.

NOTE: If, in position 3, P and S **were** overlapped the moment S passed head to wind, then P would **not** be "limited" under rule 17.1, and would be permitted to sail up to head to wind provided she gave S room to keep clear under rule 16. Again rule 15 wouldn't apply to P, but rule 14 would.

leeward boats down to close-hauled!). *Windward* boats will have to be a bit more cautious when rolling over *leeward* boats in this situation, though *leeward* boats will need to remember that they must initially give W *room* to *keep clear* under rule 15 (Acquiring Right of Way).

If P tacks in front of S, and S chooses to *overlap* her to *leeward*, then S must comply with rule 15 and furthermore must not sail above her *proper course* during the *overlap* unless she chooses to luff and pass *clear astern* (rule 17.1). See the illustration for a detailed analysis of the aggressive maneuver called "The Slam Dunk."

ON DOWNWIND LEGS (Reaches & Runs)

L and W are sailing down a reach. L did not establish the *overlap* from *clear astern* and therefore L is free to sail where she pleases, subject to rule 16 (Changing Course). W begins to pass L and L luffs to prevent her from doing so. W turns more quickly and "breaks" the *overlap*. W then turns back down, thereby

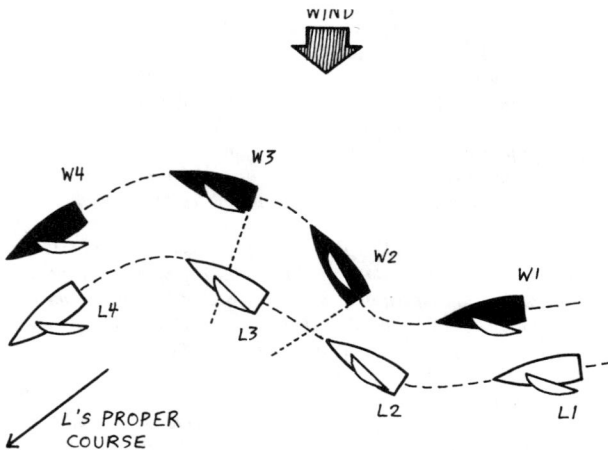

In this situation it is W's luffing that breaks the overlap and her bearing away that causes the overlap to be re-established. When L acquires the right of way at position 3, she does not need to give W room to keep clear because she acquires right of way as a result of W's actions. However, rule 17.1 is not concerned with how the overlap is established. Therefore, because L establishes the overlap from clear astern, she must immediately bear away and continue to sail no higher than her proper course during the overlap.

creating an *overlap* once again (being sure to *keep clear* under rule 11, On the Same Tack, Overlapped, and remembering that her actions have given L the right of way such that rule 15, Acquiring Right of Way, does not require L to "give" W *room* to *keep clear*!). Now, L has established a *leeward overlap* from *clear astern* and therefore is required to immediately comply with her new "limitation" and turn back down to her *proper course*, which includes gybing when that is necessary for L to sail her *proper course* to the next *mark*.

Anytime a boat establishes a *leeward overlap* from *clear astern* within two of her lengths of a *windward* boat, she is not permitted to sail above her *proper course*. However, prior to establishing the *overlap*, L is free to sail where she pleases. Therefore, the moment the *overlap* is established, the course she will sail to *finish* as quickly as possible will include the course she is on at that moment. If she must then bear away to a lower course to get to the next *mark* and ultimately the finishing line as quickly as possible, she must do so immediately; and when L acquires the right of way by her own actions, rule 15 (Acquiring Right of Way) builds in a cushion to protect W while L is bearing away.

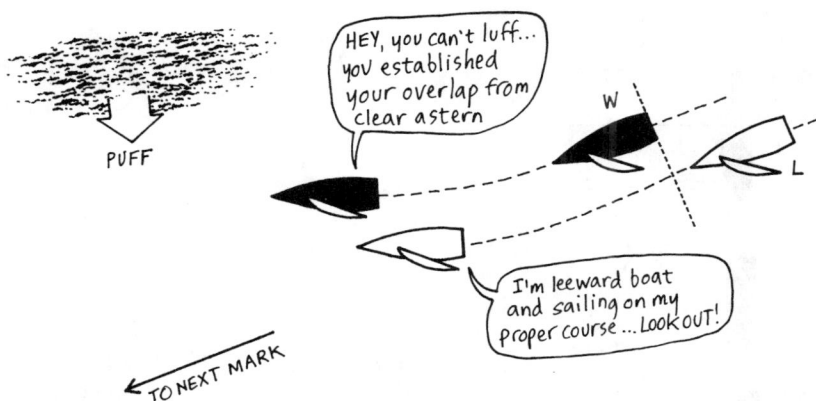

L is slowly luffing up to a new proper course in order to get to a puff of wind sooner. Because she is not sailing above her proper course, she is not breaking rule 17.1; and because she is giving W room to keep clear, she is not breaking rule 16. W must keep clear under rule 11.

Here are three common situations where a boat can catch up from astern and sail in to leeward of a boat ahead and have the right to sail up to head to wind if she chooses, subject to rules 15 (Acquiring Right of Way) and 16 (Changing Course):

1) The boat behind (BL) *overlaps* the boat ahead (AW) more than two of her lengths to *leeward* of AW. Rule 17.1 does not apply because the *overlap* was not established within two of her lengths of AW. Now BL turns toward AW and maintains her *overlap* as she gets within two lengths. BL is not "limited" and can sail up to head to wind, even when she may be *overlapped* with AW by just two feet. As a defense, AW can "break" the *overlap* by heading up just before BL comes within two lengths of her; and then "create it" again by bearing off thereby causing BL to "establish" the *leeward overlap* within two lengths of AW.

2) BL *overlaps* AW to *leeward* within two of her lengths. At that point BL is "limited" to sailing no higher than her *proper course*. BL then gybes and gybes right back, maintaining her "overlap" throughout the maneuver. Now, BL is not "limited" and can sail up to head to wind, even when she may be *overlapped* with AW by just two feet. The reason is that when BL

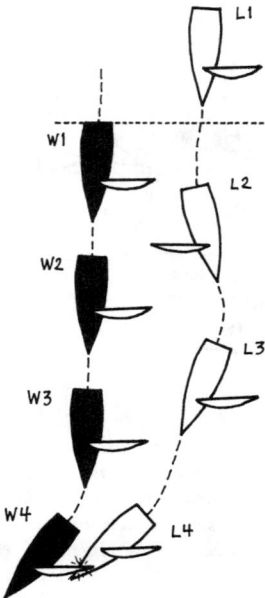

In position 1, L is clear astern of W. When L establishes an overlap on W she is "limited" under rule 17.1 to sailing no higher than her proper course. In position 2, L gybes so that the two boats are on opposite tacks and rule 17.1 no longer applies. In position 3, L gybes back, establishing a new overlap on W, this time not from clear astern; therefore L is not "limited" and can sail up to head to wind if she pleases. In position 4, L luffs, giving W room to keep clear. W fails to keep clear thereby breaking rule 11.

gybed the first time, she became on opposite *tacks* with AW and therefore the term *"overlap"* did not apply (see the Definition *Clear Astern* and *Clear Ahead; Overlap*). When she gybed back onto the same *tack* as AW, she was at that moment *overlapped*, i.e. she did not establish the *leeward overlap* from *clear astern*. Therefore she was not "limited" by rule 17.1. However, BL did acquire the right of way by her own actions, so she must initially give AW *room* to *keep clear* under rule 15 (Acquiring Right of Way); and when she changes her course toward AW, she must give AW **additional** *room* to *keep clear* under rule 16 (Changing Course).

3) Halfway down a run, a *port-tack* boat (PL) is converging with a *starboard-tack* boat (SW). PL, after passing very close astern of SW, turns down thereby creating an "overlap" on SW's *leeward* side (note the terms *clear ahead, clear astern* and *overlap* do not apply because SW and PL are on opposite *tacks* and not near a *mark*). Maintaining her "overlap," PL gybes. When her boom crosses her centerline and she is on the same *tack* as SW, the two boats are *overlapped*. Therefore PL is not "limited" and can sail up to head to wind, even when she may be *overlapped* with SW by just two feet. However, the same "limitations" under rules 15 and 16 apply to PL as in the example above; and SW can employ the same tactic as in #1 above of breaking the *overlap* with PL just as PL is about to gybe and then re-establishing it the moment PL gybes.

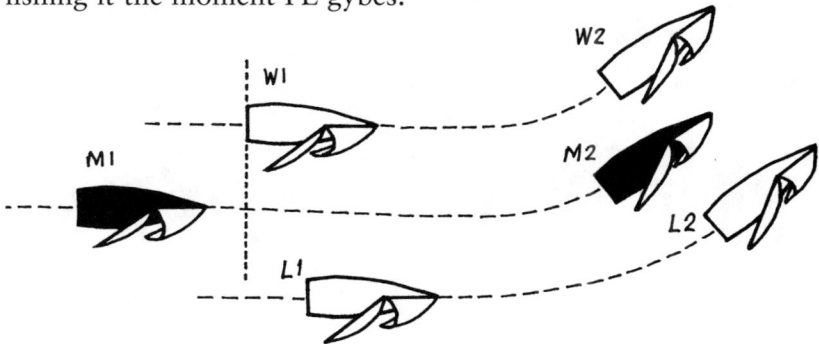

Because M establishes a leeward overlap on W from clear astern, she is "limited" to sailing no higher than her proper course. When L luffs, M is required to keep clear of her under rule 11. Even in the absence of W, M would luff to keep clear of L. Therefore, M is not sailing above her proper course and W must keep clear of M under rule 11.

8

WHEN BOATS MEET AT MARKS AND OBSTRUCTIONS

PART 2 - SECTION C

Section C contains the rules that apply when boats are passing *marks* and *obstructions* on the race course (rules 18 and 19). The purpose of these rules is to allow for safe and orderly sailing when boats converge at *marks* and *obstructions*. In order for that to happen, there are times when a right-of-way boat may find herself with a **limit** on her right of way or a **temporary requirement** to give *room* to a give-way boat. An example is when a *leeward* boat is on the outside of a *windward* boat while passing a *mark*; the *leeward*/outside boat may have to give that *windward*/inside boat *room* to pass the *mark* (rule 18.2(a), Giving Room; Keeping Clear). Another example is when a *starboard-tack* or *leeward* boat is on the inside at a *mark*, and she must gybe to sail her *proper course*, she cannot pass any farther from the *mark* than needed to sail that course (rule 18.4, Gybing). Finally, there are times when a boat may need to tack to avoid hitting an *obstruction*, but other boats are too close by for her to tack without fouling them. Rule 19 (Room to Tack at an Obstruction) gives **special permission** in certain circumstances that permit the boat to tack.

135

Preamble to Section C

When a Section C rule applies, the rules in Sections A and B continue to apply unless the Section C rule modifies them or states that they do not apply.

Part 2 is clearly constructed so that in the event one rule conflicts with another it is easy to know which one takes precedence. When a Section C rule is not in conflict with a Section A or B rule, then the A and B rules continue to apply along with the C rule. However, when a Section C rule explicitly provides a requirement that conflicts with a requirement in a rule in Section A or B, the C rule "modifies" the A or B rule and takes precedence. Also, some Section C rules simply state that some A or B rules do not apply while the C rule does.

For instance, a *leeward* boat (L) and a *windward* boat (W) on *port tack* are approaching a *mark* to be left to port. When twenty boat-lengths from the *mark*, the boats are not yet "about to pass" the *mark*, and therefore rule 18 (Passing Marks and Obstructions) in Section C is not yet in effect. W must *keep clear* of L under rule 11 (On the Same Tack, Overlapped) which is in Section A. When the boats are within two lengths of the *mark*, they are now "about to pass" it and rule 18 (in Section C) now applies. Rule 18.2(a) (Giving Room; Keeping Clear) requires L, as the outside boat, to give W *room* to pass the *mark* because she's the inside boat. This requirement clearly modifies rule 11 (in Section A) and therefore it takes precedence for as long as it applies.

RULE 18 - PASSING MARKS AND OBSTRUCTIONS

Rule 18.1 - When This Rule Applies

Rule 18 applies at a mark or obstruction to be left on the same side when boats are about to pass it until they have passed it...

This is the rule that governs boats when they are passing *marks* or *obstructions*. It is commonly called the "buoy room" rule, but that is only half right. Rule 18 applies whether you are passing a racing *mark*, a breakwater, a right-of-way boat in your race such as a *starboard-tack* boat or even an iceberg that has floated onto the course. (See ISAF Cases 20 and 91 and US SAILING Appeals 44, 46 and 192.)

Though rule 18 is the longest rule in Part 2, it is very clearly written and fits very sensibly with the basic right-of-way rules in Section A. Again, the key to understanding it is not to try to memorize its every detail, but to stand back and see how the rule is trying to create orderly sailing when boats converge at *marks* and *obstructions*.

Rule 18 is broken into the following four distinct sections:

18.2(a) .... when the boats are *overlapped* at the *mark* or *obstruction*.

18.2(b).......... when the boats are not *overlapped* at the *mark* or *obstruction*.

18.3 & 18.4.. when the boats tack or gybe at the *mark* or *obstruction*.

18.5.............. when the *obstruction* is a continuing one.

"I notice that in rule 18, there is no more use of the term 'rounding;' does this omission represent any change to the previous rule?"

No. Keeping in mind that one of the goals of the rule writers was to shorten the rules, they looked for places where redundant language could be removed. Previous rule 42 (Rounding or Passing Marks and Obstructions) used the phrase "round or pass" throughout. A *mark* is "passed" when a boat sails alongside it; it is "rounded" when the boat turns around it. In either event, the boat sails alongside the *mark* for some period of time; therefore the term "pass" encompasses the term "round."

The significance to the term "round" is that rule 28.1 (Sailing the Course) reads, "A boat shall *start,* pass each *mark* on the required side in the correct order, and *finish,* so that a string representing her wake after *starting* and until *finishing* would, when drawn taut, lie on the required side of each *mark* and **touch each rounding *mark*** (emphasis added)." Therefore, in order to sail the course correctly, you must know which *marks* you actually have to "round" as opposed to merely "pass;" you will normally find that information contained in the sailing instructions for the race or series.

"How do I know on which side the mark or obstruction is to be left?"

Good question. First of all, "side" in rule 18.1 refers to the boat's side, not the *mark's* or *obstruction's* side. Therefore, when two boats are passing a *mark* going in the opposite direction (as they might when they are in different races using the same *mark* but leaving it on opposite sides as in ISAF Case 51), or are passing an *obstruction* going in the opposite direction (as they might when they are circling around a race committee boat or spectator boat during pre-start maneuvering), rule 18 does **not** apply, and the rules of Section A and B apply.

As for which way to "leave" a *mark*, the sailing instructions must indicate that (Definition *Mark* and rule M2.1(4), Sailing Instruction Contents). As for which way an *obstruction* will be "left," that will become increasingly more evident by the courses of the boats as they approach the *obstruction* at the time of the incident.

"To whom is rule 18 talking?"

Rule 18 is "talking" to all the boats involved in the passing maneuver, but fundamentally it is talking to the outside or *clear astern* boats. As boats get closer to a *mark* or *obstruction*, the "force" of Rule 18 begins to reach out to them. Outside and *clear astern* boats, whether on *port tack* or *starboard tack* and whether *leeward* or *windward* boats, must start preparing for their upcoming obligations to the inside or *clear ahead* boats.

Remember, rule 18 is a rule of exception. In some situations at *marks* and *obstructions*, an outside boat otherwise holding right of way must nonetheless yield to an inside give-way boat and even alter course to move far enough away from the *mark* or *obstruction* to give the give-way inside boat the *room* she needs to pass it. A *starboard-tack* boat with a *port-tack* boat inside and a *leeward* boat with a *windward* boat inside are examples of this sort of situation which put a "limit" on the right-of-way boat. So, even though you are the right-of-way

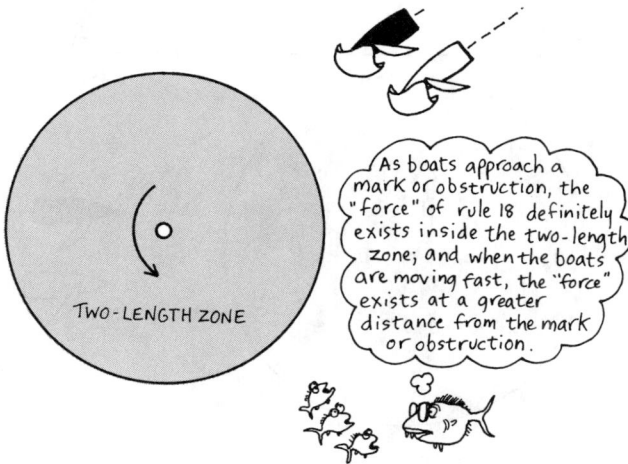

As boats approach a mark or obstruction, the "force" of rule 18 definitely exists inside the two-length zone; and when the boats are moving fast, the "force" exists at a greater distance from the mark or obstruction.

TWO-LENGTH ZONE

boat approaching a *mark* or *obstruction*, when the "force" of rule 18 begins to reach you, your right of way may be temporarily "limited."

"As I approach a mark or obstruction, when does the 'force' of rule 18 begin to apply to me?"

The "force" of rule 18 begins to apply when you are "about to pass" the *mark* or *obstruction*. ISAF Case 163 reads, "The phrase 'about to pass' has never been defined precisely, nor can it be. In approaching a mark, there is no exact point at which a boat becomes 'about to pass it.' Almost always, a boat two hull lengths from a mark is about to pass it, but this is sometimes so at a greater distance too. Not only is the distance from the mark a factor, but the boat's speed is also important, and other factors such as the conditions of wind and current and the amount of sail handling required before or during the rounding may also be relevant. Moreover, the nearer the boat is to the mark the more definitely she is about to pass it. The answer to the question depends upon the particular circumstances of each situation."

So the "force" of rule 18 is "on you" when you are two of your hull lengths from the *mark* or *obstruction, and at times even farther away, e.g.,* if you are on a catamaran going 20 miles per hour or on an offshore boat with a huge spinnaker to get down. Remember, before you are "about to pass," you have

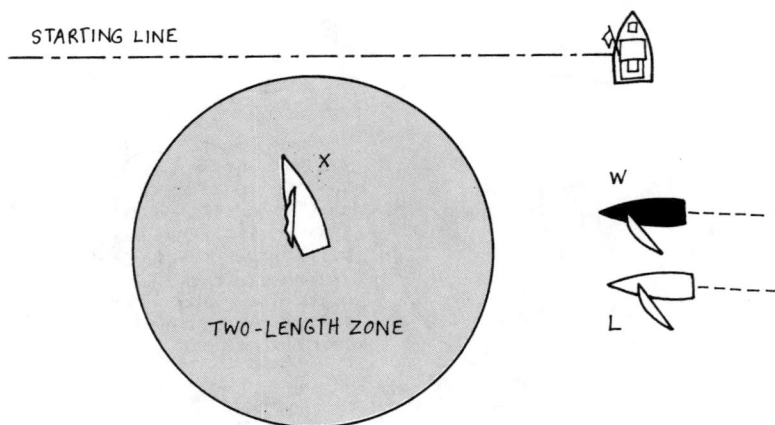

X is clear ahead of both L and W; therefore, as a right-of-way boat, she is an obstruction to both. The "force" of rule 18 exists within the two-length zone around X, but it is L who gets to choose on which side of X she will pass. If she chooses to pass to leeward of X, rule 18.2(a) requires her to give W room to do likewise if W also wants to pass to leeward of X.

your basic right-of-way rights; i.e. if you are a *leeward* boat, a *windward* boat must *keep clear*, etc.

Though a boat is "about to pass" an **obstruction** when two lengths away, the "force" of rule 18 does not grow strong until it is evident on which side of the *obstruction* the right-of-way boat chooses to go. So on a starting line for example, as two *overlapped* boats approach a boat *clear ahead* (an *obstruction*), rule 18 begins to apply when the first boat gets to two of her lengths from the *obstruction*. At that point the boats need to be *overlapped* in order for either one to be entitled to *room* to pass the *obstruction*. But the *leeward* boat, as right-of-way boat, gets to **choose** on which side she wants to pass the *obstruction*. The moment it's evident that L will pass to *leeward* of the *obstruction*, the full force of rule 18 is on and W is entitled to *room* to pass to *leeward* also, if she chooses. (See US SAILING Appeal 46, 192 and ISAF Case 91.)

WHEN THE BOATS ARE OVERLAPPED

"When the 'force' is on the boats, what rights and requirements do the inside and outside boats have?"

That's the key question, and it's covered in rule 18.2(a). Let's get into it.

Rule 18.2(a) - Giving Room; Keeping Clear

When boats are overlapped before one of them reaches the two-length zone, if the outside boat has right of way she shall give the inside boat room to pass the mark or obstruction, or if the inside boat has right of way the outside boat shall keep clear. If they are still overlapped when one of them reaches the two-length zone, the outside boat's obligation continues even if the overlap is broken later. This rule does not apply if the outside boat is unable to give room when the overlap begins.

To possibly make it easier to understand the various rights and requirements contained in this rule, I have broken it out below.

The rule is "talking" only to overlapped boats:

Rule 18.2(a) starts off, *"When boats are **overlapped**..."* Therefore, rule 18.2(a) deals with boats that are ***overlapped**.* (Rule 18.2(b) deals with boats that are not *overlapped*.)

Remember, a boat is *overlapped* with another if her bow is on or across a line drawn abeam through the aftermost point of the other boat's hull and equipment in normal position. Also, two boats that otherwise are not *overlapped* suddenly become *overlapped* when a boat **in between them** *overlaps* both of them. So if you are approaching a *mark* to be left to port and are just *overlapped* on the port transom of the boat ahead of you, and she is just *overlapped* on the port transom of the boat ahead of her, you are technically *overlapped* with the boat ahead of her. Therefore you are entitled to the rights in 18.2(a) if you are *overlapped* when the **farthest boat ahead** arrives at the *two-length zone*.

Also remember that, by definition, two boats *overlap* when the bow of one is over the line drawn through the aftermost part

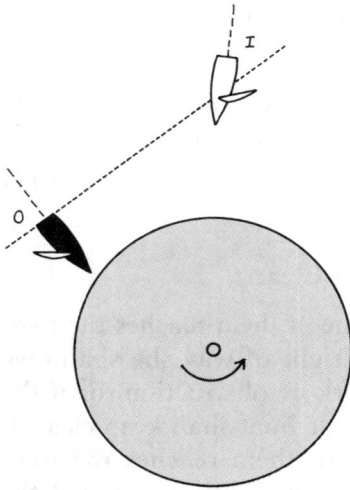

Above: *Even though I is well behind O, I has an inside overlap when O reaches the two-length zone; therefore O must keep clear of I until both boats have passed the mark.*

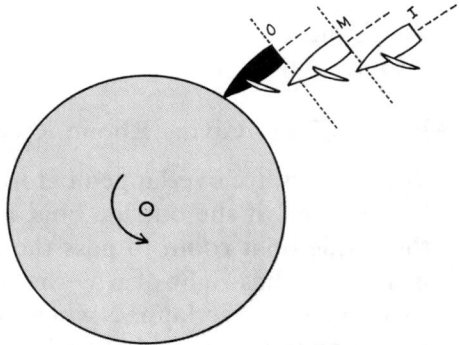

Above: *M is in between O and I and overlaps both of them; therefore, I is technically overlapped with O when O reaches the two-length zone. O and M must keep clear of I until all three boats have passed the mark.*

of the other, even when the boats are a quarter of a mile apart; and that when rule 18 applies, the boats are considered *overlapped* even when they are on opposite *tacks*. This becomes important as boats approach the leeward *mark* on opposite *tacks* and widely differing angles. (See Definition *Clear Astern* and *Clear Ahead*; *Overlap*.)

"Are there any limitations on establishing an overlap and becoming entitled to the rights in rule 18.2(a)?"

Yes, there are two:
1) the *overlap* must be established before one of the boats reaches the *two-length zone*;
2) the outside boat must be physically able to give the inside boat *room*.

Up to 1965, a boat *clear astern* could get a legal inside *overlap* as long as it was (a) in time to enable the outside boat(s) to give *room*; (b) before the boat ahead altered her course in the act of rounding; and (c) before any part of the boat ahead came abreast of the *mark* or *obstruction*. Things were often a tad out of control as boats came barreling up from astern yelling for "buoy room" at the last second.

In 1965 the rule writers took a creative step. Realizing that there ought to be some cutoff "point" after which a boat *clear astern* could not establish an inside *overlap*, they devised the "two boat-length circle," known now as the *two-length zone*, which has proved to work very effectively. And because the "point" can be in any direction from the *mark* or *obstruction*, the *two-length zone* is an imaginary circle with the *mark* or *obstruction* in the center and having a radius of two of the **nearer boat's hull lengths**; for instance, 48 feet in a J/24 (see the Definition *Two-Length Zone*). Note the fact that it is the nearer boat's hull lengths. This becomes important when the boats are different sizes.

Rule 18.2(a) starts off, "*When boats are* **overlapped** *before one of them reaches the* **two-length zone**..." So the game ends at the *two-length zone*. In order to be entitled to the rights in rule 18.2(a), you must have an inside *overlap* at the moment the first of the *overlapped* boats arrives at the *two-length zone*. If you do, then you are entitled to the rights in rule 18.2(a). If you are catching up from *clear astern* but don't have the *overlap* before the other boat gets to two of her hull lengths from the *mark*, then you are not entitled to the rights in rule 18.2(a) and must *keep clear* of her under rule 18.2(b).

"What if I physically can't give room to the boat that just established the inside overlap on me?"

That's the second limitation in rule 18.2(a). When a boat establishes an inside *overlap* from *clear astern*, the boat ahead has a "protective shield" if she needs it. When a boat gets *overlap* at the zero-moment before you enter the *two-length zone*, she becomes entitled to the rights in rule 18.2(a) as an inside boat. However, you are not required to anticipate her arrival. There are times when you may be physically unable to give her the *room* she needs to pass the *mark* based on your situation at that moment.

Rule 18.2(a) says, *"This rule does not apply if the outside boat is unable to give **room** when the **overlap** begins."* In this situation, she is not entitled to *room* and must *keep clear* under the applicable Section A rule.

One example of where this situation might occur is a tightly packed *mark* rounding in light air where a boat astern gets an inside *overlap* on a boat that is two and a half boat-lengths from the *mark*, but there's just no way the outside boat can get everyone else outside of her to move away from the *mark* in time to create *room* for the new inside boat. Another example is when two boats are going so fast that by the time the outside boat can react to her new obligation and make the *room*, the inside boat is already past the *mark* on the wrong side. Twelve knots of boat-speed equals about 20 feet per second, so on a windy reach a Hobie 18 will chew up two boat-lengths in less than two seconds!

When the inside boat has the right of way, the outside boat must simply "keep clear":

The rule goes on to say *"...if the inside boat has the right of way, the outside boat shall **keep clear**."* As this requirement does not "modify" any rules in Section A, the Section A rules apply. Therefore, when a *leeward* and a *windward* boat are passing a *mark* or *obstruction* with L on the inside, L (as the right-of-way boat) does not need an exception to the rules to get the *space* she needs from W to sail around the *mark* or *obstruction*; rule 11 (On the Same Tack, Overlapped) is sufficient.

"I understand that when the inside boat also has the right of way, the outside boat must 'keep clear' of her; but does that mean that the inside boat can sail wherever she pleases?"

No. It means that the inside right-of-way boat can sail her course without the need to avoid the outside boat, subject to either of the two "limits" she may have on sailing above her *proper course*. Let's look at those two "limits."

- One such "limit" is in rule 17.1 (On the Same Tack; Proper Course) which limits L to sailing no higher than her *proper course* when she establishes the *leeward overlap* from *clear astern*. Therefore, at a windward *mark*, if LI (*leeward/inside*) establishes an inside *overlap* on a boat that has just tacked in front of her, LI must sail her *proper course* around the *mark*. Note that, in this situation, her *proper course* may be to sail head to wind momentarily to get up and around the *mark*.

- The other "limit" is in rule 18.4 (Passing Marks and Obstructions, Gybing) which essentially says that if the boats are *overlapped* when the first one reaches the *two-length zone*, and an inside boat must gybe to continue sailing her *proper course* to the next *mark*, she is required to gybe onto her *proper course*; i.e. she can't continue on straight past the *mark* or luff away from the *mark* if that takes her farther from the *mark* than necessary to sail her *proper course*. (For a full discussion see the explanation of rule 18.4.) This "limit" commonly arises at offwind *marks* whenever L or S is on the inside and her *proper course* is to gybe around the *mark*.

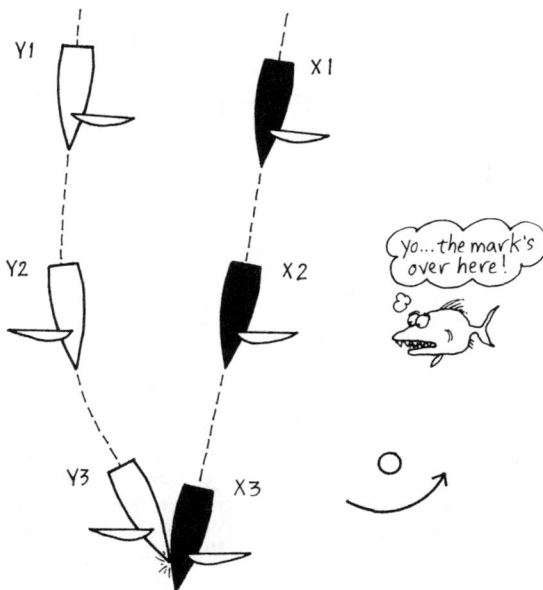

When boats are about to pass a mark, the term "overlap" applies to boats on opposite tacks. Therefore, X and Y are "overlapped" at the mark. When the inside boat has the right of way and when she must gybe to sail her proper course, rule 18.4 requires her not to sail any farther from the mark than needed to sail her proper course. By not gybing, X breaks rule 18.4.

In fact, when passing a *mark*, the only time an inside right-of-way boat can sail higher than her *proper course* is when she is a *leeward* boat passing a *mark* that she **doesn't** have to gybe around to sail her *proper course* (typically a windward *mark* or a "gybe" *mark* going onto a very broad reach or run) and she did not establish the *leeward*/inside *overlap* from *clear astern* within two boat-lengths of WO (the *windward*/outside boat).

But because inside right-of-way boats **always** have the right to at least sail their *proper courses* when passing *marks*, and outside boats must *keep clear* of them, inside right-of-way boats can therefore make a "**tactical rounding,**" i.e. they can swing wide on their approach into the *mark* and then cut the *mark* as close as possible on their exit, and outside boats must give them the space needed to do so.

When the inside boat is the give-way boat, the outside boat need only give her "room" to pass the mark or obstruction:

The rule also states, "...*if the outside boat has right of way she shall give the inside boat* **room** *to pass the* **mark** *or* **obstruction**..." In other words, when the inside boat does **not** have the right of way (i.e. she's the give-way boat as either a *port-tack* or a *windward* boat), the outside right-of-way boat is required to give the inside boat only the *room* she needs to pass

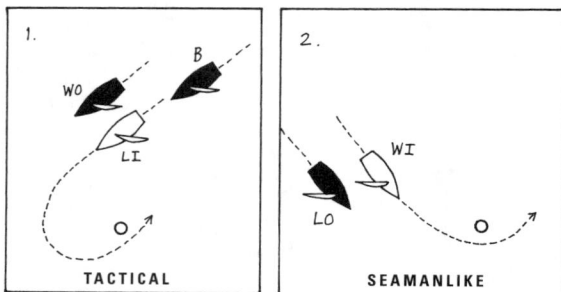

When overlapped boats are passing a mark or obstruction, the inside boat will either have the right or way or not; when not overlapped, the boat clear ahead will have the right of way. When the inside or clear ahead boat has the right of way, the other boat is required to "keep clear" during the passing maneuver; therefore the inside or clear ahead boat can make a "tactical (swing wide-cut close) rounding." When the inside boat does not have the right of way, the outside boat is required to give only "room," i.e. only the space the inside boat needs to make a "seamanlike (approximately equal distance on either side of the mark) rounding."

the *mark* or *obstruction*. As this requirement does "modify" rule 10 (On Opposite Tacks) and rule 11 (On the Same Tack, Overlapped) in Section A, it takes precedence for as long as rule 18.2(a) applies. Therefore, when a *leeward* and a *windward* boat are passing a *mark* with W on the inside, L has a "temporary requirement" to give W *room* until the boats have passed the *mark*; at that point S and L will get their full rights back under rules 10 or 11.

Note that rule 18.2(a) does not shift the right of way from the *leeward*/outside boat to the *windward*/inside boat. Approaching the *mark* or *obstruction*, W must keep clear of L under rule 11. When they are "about to pass" the *mark* or *obstruction*, L becomes required to provide W *room* under rule 18.2(a) **only if W needs the *room*.** ISAF Case 145 reads, "In this incident rule 11 did not cease to apply; it continued to obligate W to keep clear of L unless she was prevented from doing so by L's failure to give her sufficient room. Although rule 18 applied because the boats were 'about to pass' the mark, and rule 18.2(a) gave W the right to the room she needed to pass it, the fact was that she already had this room before and at the time of contact. The boats were within the two-length zone but this did not give W any additional rights. She therefore broke rule 11 by failing to keep clear of L."

"When inside boats do need 'room' and are entitled to have it, how much 'room' can they have?"

Room is defined as *"the space a boat needs in the existing conditions while manoeuvring promptly in a seamanlike way."* (See the discussion of the Definition *Room*, including the excerpt from ISAF Case 40 which gives the definitive interpretation of *room*.) Therefore, if the inside boat is a give-way boat, she can make only a **"seamanlike rounding"** (i.e. pass the *mark* at roughly equal distances on either side). The reason is that inside give-way boats must confine their rounding to the *room* the outside boats are required to give them under rule 18.2(a).

In essence, *room* is the space needed to pass between the *mark* and the outside boat in a safe and seamanlike way, which includes *room* to tack or gybe when either is necessary to sail that course. *Room* does not include all the space the inside boat might like to take to make a tactically desirable "swing wide-cut close" type rounding, though in actual practice most outside boats are a little more forgiving. Note therefore that the courses inside boats are permitted to sail around a *mark* differ depending on whether they are a right-of-way boat or a give-way boat.

When a give-way boat sails farther from the *mark* than allowed under *room*, the rules of Section C no longer apply to her and she is subject to the rules in Sections A and B (see US SAILING Appeal 119). For instance, when a *windward*/inside boat is slow in coming up to close-hauled around a *mark* and contact occurs between her and a *leeward*/outside boat, and it is found that she took more *room* than was needed to pass the *mark*, the Section A and B rules apply and WI breaks rule 11 (On the Same Tack, Overlapped).

"What happens when I've established my inside overlap before reaching the two-length zone, but once inside the zone the outside boat pulls clear ahead of me?"

You are still entitled to your rights as inside boat. Rule 18.2(a) reads, *"If they are still **overlapped** when one of the them reaches the **two-length zone**, the outside boat's obligation continues even if the **overlap** is broken later."* This is called the "lock-in" provision of rule 18.2(a). In other words, as long as you've established your *overlap* in compliance with 18.2(a), your rights under that rule are "locked in" until the rule no longer applies.

WI is the windward/inside boat. Because she does not have right of way over LO, she is entitled only to enough "room" to pass the mark in a safe and seamanlike way, as opposed to all the room she might like in order to make a tactical "swing wide-cut close" type of rounding. WI is taking too much room, and by hitting the leeward boat she breaks rule 11.

"What happens when boats on the outside that are keeping clear of overlapped boats on the inside never get to the two-length zone until after they've turned and begun heading for the mark; now can a boat that was well clear astern suddenly claim room?"

Yes! ISAF Case 127 clarifies this very common situation at crowded *marks*:

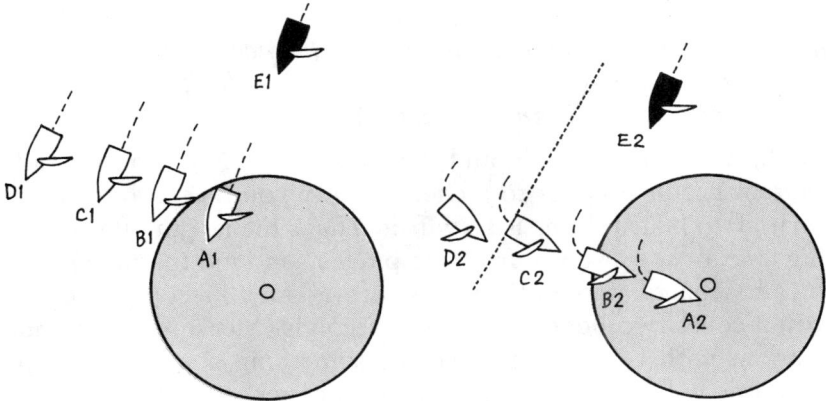

A, B, C and D are in a bunch at a mark. D is keeping clear of the three boats inside her, and as a result is outside the two-length zone. E is well astern. In position 2, the four boats gybe and line up to pass the mark one behind the other. The position of A and B make it obvious that C and D are outside the two-length zone. Because E is overlapped on their inside, C and D must keep clear of her until they have all passed the mark.

"QUESTION: Five boats are approaching a leeward mark dead before the wind. Four of them are overlapped in line with A nearest the mark. The fifth boat, E, is clear astern of A, B, C and D when A and B reach the two-length zone. When the four front boats reach the mark and turn to round it, the change of bearing of C and D, relative to E, results in E becoming overlapped inside them while each of them is outside the two-length zone. E rounds the mark behind A and B but inside C and D, both of which are able to give room to E. Is E entitled to room under rule 18.2(a) from C and D?

"ANSWER: Since E is astern of A and B when they reach the two-length zone, she is required by Rule 18.2(b) to keep clear of them. As between E and the two outside boats, however, a different relationship develops. C and D, in order to leave room for the two inside boats with their booms fully extended, must approach the mark on courses that bring them abreast of it outside the two-length zone. When C and D alter course towards the mark, E obtains an inside overlap while they are outside the two-length zone. Therefore, the conditions of rule 18.2(a) were met, and E is entitled to her rights under rule 18.2(a)."

"I understand now about the significance of the 'two-length zone;' but how do I know where the 'two-length zone' actually is on the water?"

Well, at first it's difficult, and then after you've raced more and more it becomes easier to judge. Let's say you race a thirty-foot boat. Two boat-lengths is sixty feet. That's the length of a bowling lane, or the distance from the pitcher's mound to home plate on a baseball diamond. Doing 6 knots (about 10 feet per second) you'll cover two boat-lengths in 6 seconds. Measure it out and mark it with two orange poles or something at your club so everyone will learn to "guesstimate" it better.

"OK, but what if two boats simply can't agree on whether an overlap was established or broken before reaching the two-length zone?"

Competitors and protest committees should try their hardest to remember and determine the facts. However, realizing that there will be disputes, the rule writers built in some "guidance" for competitors and protest committees to help resolve such disputes. Rule 18.2(c) reads, *"If there is reasonable doubt that a boat established or broke an **overlap** in time, it shall be presumed that she did not."*

In other words, if you come up from behind and claim that you got the inside *overlap* before the outside boat reached the *two-length zone*, but the outside boat disagrees saying that you were still *clear astern* when she arrived at the *two-length zone* and that you subsequently established the *overlap*, rule 18.2(c) states that if there is "reasonable doubt," it shall be presumed by the sailors that the *overlap* was not established in time. Similarly,

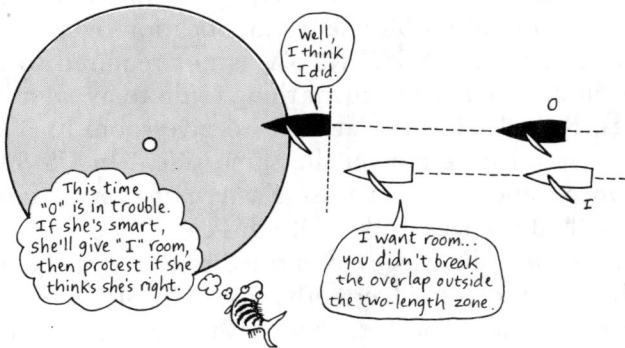

if it goes to protest you will have to satisfy the protest committee that there is no doubt that you established the *overlap* in time.

By the same token, if an outside boat has an *overlap* on you at, say, five and then four boat-lengths away, she will be required to give you rights under rule 18.2(a) unless she pulls *clear ahead* before reaching the *two-length zone*. If she claims to have "broken" the *overlap* just before she reached the *two-length zone*, but you disagree saying that you were still *overlapped* at the *two-length zone*, then again if there is "reasonable doubt," it shall be presumed that she didn't break the *overlap* in time; and in the protest it's her who must satisfy the protest committee that there is no doubt that the *overlap* was broken in time.

Satisfying the protest committee is generally very tough to do as it is usually one word against the other. Hails to each other regarding the *overlap* situation as the boats near the *two-length zone* are very helpful to the point that they are almost expected by good protest committees. Also, witnesses can be very useful, particularly independent witnesses who were positioned exactly at the *two-length zone* and in a position to determine *overlap*s.

"Does the inside boat have to call for 'room?'"

No. When you are on the inside while passing a *mark* or *obstruction*, you are not required to call for *room*. ISAF Case 91 reads, "QUESTION: Does BW have to claim room to pass to leeward of A, or would BL risk disqualification by not automatically giving room? ANSWER: BW is not required to hail for room, although that is a prudent thing to do to avoid misunderstandings. Rule 18.2(a) requires BL to give room to BW when they pass the obstruction on the same side." In US SAILING Appeal 46, SL and SW were passing astern of another *starboard-tacker* that had been *clear ahead*. In this case SW didn't know SL was there or that she was even entitled to *room* at the *obstruction*. She bore off inadvertently and hit SL. The Appeals Committee stated, "The fact that [SW] was unaware of [SL's] presence in no way altered [SL's] obligation under the rules or justified her in not giving [SW] room to clear the obstruction." Clearly, outside boats must be aware at all times to be sure they give each inside boat enough *room* or they *keep clear* when required to.

"What should I do in the situation where I'm entitled to room but when I'm about a boat-length away from the mark it becomes obvious that the outside boat isn't leaving me enough space to fit between her and the mark?"

At the moment it becomes clear that the outside boat is not going to give you *room*, rule 14 (Avoiding Contact) requires you to avoid hitting her if reasonably possible. This may result in you not being able to pass the *mark* on that approach, and cause you to circle around and try again. Though the outside boat's rule breach caused you to pass on the wrong side of the *mark* on that approach, it hasn't prevented you from ultimately passing the *mark* correctly as required by rule 28.1 (Sailing the Course), i.e. she didn't compel you to break rule 28.1. Therefore you are not entitled to exoneration under rule 64.1(b) (Penalties and Exoneration). You should certainly win your protest against the outside boat, but there is nothing the protest committee can do to compensate you for the distance/places lost while making a second try to pass the *mark*.

Of course, if you do choose to hit the outside boat and force your way in between the outside boat and the *mark*, you can be penalized only if the contact causes damage. Remember, however, that you have to successfully protest the outside boat to be exonerated from touching the *mark* (rule 31.3, Touching a Mark).

"How long does the force of Rule 18 last?"

Rule 18.1 reads, *"Rule 18 applies at a mark or obstruction...when boats are about to pass it until they have passed it."* This last phrase is new wording intended to clarify when the requirements and obligations in rule 18 cease to apply. Notice the word "they." In other words, the requirements in rule 18 continue to apply until the latter of a pair or group of boats subject to rule 18 have passed the *mark*. In my opinion, once a boat leaves the *mark* or *obstruction* astern and is no longer in danger of touching it, she has "passed" it; i.e. once she is no longer "overlapping" it she has "passed" it.

Remember that the primary purpose of rule 18 is to allow boats to pass a *mark* or *obstruction* without the inside boats getting wedged in between the outside boats and the *mark* or *obstruction*, or getting forced onto the wrong side of the *mark*. As discussed above, sometimes these outside boats are going to otherwise have the right of way. The "force" of rule 18 requires them to give only enough *room* for the inside boat to pass the *mark* or *obstruction*. The moment the inside boat has completed her passing maneuver, the purpose of rule 18 has been served and the "force" shuts off. At that moment the outside/right-of-way boat gets her full rights back, and the inside/give-way boat must *keep clear*. As a reminder, if the outside/right-of-way boat wants to then turn toward the inside/give-way boat, she must give her *room* to *keep clear* under rule 16 (Changing Course).

For example, let's say that two *overlapped* boats on *port tack* are rounding the leeward *mark* onto a beat. The *leeward*/outside boat (LO) is allowing just enough *room* for the *windward*/inside boat (WI) to pass the *mark*, but LO is trying to keep her bow just ahead of WI. As WI comes up to close-hauled and her transom just passes the *mark*, LO luffs at a medium rate. WI responds by luffing and tacking onto *starboard tack*. She *keeps clear* of LO and does not hit the *mark* or tack too close to any boat about to pass the *mark*. No foul. LO gave WI just enough *room* to pass the *mark*, and when LO changed course WI was able to *keep clear* without hitting the *mark*. Note that the circumstances will weigh heavily in determining exactly when the outside boat can assert her rights. If there are a lot of boats near the *mark* such that WI could not tack without fouling them under rule 15 (Acquiring Right of Way), LO will have to be careful to allow WI the *room* needed to *keep clear* without tacking. If there is current or strong wind or waves, LO will again have to wait until WI can *keep clear* without risk of losing speed and being pushed back into the *mark*.

Another example is when two close-hauled *port-tack*ers are ducking a *starboard-tack*er. The *leeward*/outside boat can "luff" the *windward*/inside boat the moment WI's transom has passed S, assuming that WI can respond to the luff without hitting the *obstruction* (S).

The same principle arises when two *overlapped starboard-tack-ers* are rounding a windward *mark* to go onto a run, with O just to windward of I. As I is bearing away around the *mark*, O must *keep clear*, **even if I gybes**. When O's transom leaves the *mark* astern, the boats are now fully subject to the rules in Sections A and B, and I must then be careful if she wants to gybe. (See ISAF Case 50 and 132 and US SAILING Appeal 12.)

"What if a boat sails into the two-length zone and then back out; when they re-enter, do they retain their original rights or is it a whole new ball game?"

It's a whole new ball game. Whenever a boat sails beyond the point where they are "about to pass" the *mark* or *obstruction* (and remember, that could be farther than two lengths away), whether intentionally or accidentally, rule 18 ceases to apply. Rule 18.1 says, "Rule 18 applies at a *mark* or *obstruction*...**when** (emphasis added) boats are about to pass it..." When boats are **not** "about to pass it," the rule does not apply. When boats get close enough again to be considered "about to pass it," they are required to give *room* or otherwise *keep clear* of any boat *overlapped* on their inside. (See US SAILING Appeal 221.)

WHEN THE BOATS ARE NOT OVERLAPPED

"OK, I've got it so far; now how about when the boats are not overlapped when they get to the two-length zone?"

Rule 18.2(b) covers the situation where the boats are not *overlapped* when the boat *clear ahead* reaches the *two-length zone*.

Rule 18.2(b) - Giving Room; Keeping Clear
If a boat is *clear ahead* when she reaches the *two-length zone*, the boat *clear astern* shall *keep clear* even if an *overlap* is established later. Rule 10 does not apply. If the boat *clear ahead* tacks, rule 13 applies and this rule no longer does.

Remember that rule 18 applies until the latter of a pair or group of boats subject to rule 18 passes the *mark*. So if you are *clear astern* when the boat *clear ahead* arrives at the *two-length zone*, then you must stay clear of that boat until **you** have passed the *mark* or *obstruction*, provided the boat *clear ahead* stays on the same tack or gybes. Notice that, in my opinion, a boat has "passed" the *mark* when her transom leaves it astern. Prior to that, the boat astern must *keep clear*, even when the boat ahead gybes around the *mark*. However, once you have left the *mark* astern, the "force" of rule 18 shuts off and the boats are subject to the rules in Sections A and B. At that point a boat ahead must be careful if she then chooses to gybe. (See ISAF Case 132.)

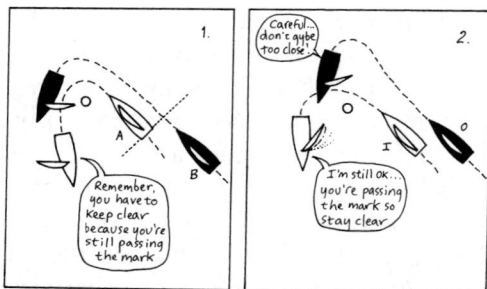

In both situations 1 and 2, rule 18.2 requires the black boat to keep clear of the white boat, including when the white boat gybes, until the black boat has passed the mark.

An example is when two boats are rounding a *windward mark* onto a run. As long as the boat behind (B) remains "overlapped" with the *mark*, she must *keep clear* of the boat ahead (A). This will permit A to make an immediate gybe around the *mark* if she so chooses.

Another example is when two boats on opposite *tacks* are approaching the leeward *mark*, with S astern of P. S calls, "Starboard tack, get out of my way!" If P is not yet "about to pass the *mark*," she is not yet within the "force-field" of rule 18, and the rules of Section A apply. In this case S has the right-of-way under rule 10 (On Opposite Tacks). However, if P is "about to pass the *mark*," then rule 18 applies, meaning that the terms *clear ahead* and *clear astern* now apply to boats on opposite *tacks*. Therefore, when P reaches the *two-length zone clear ahead*, she becomes the right-of-way boat because rule 18.2(b)

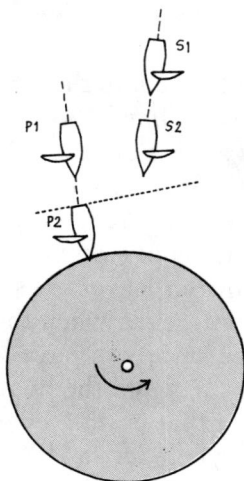

Before reaching the two-length zone, S has right of way over P under rule 10. However, the moment P reaches the two-length zone clear ahead of S, rule 18.2(b) requires S to keep clear of P until both boats have passed the mark.

requires S to *keep clear* of her during her passing maneuver. The rule itself reminds S of this by stating, "*Rule 10 does not apply.*"

ISAF Case 68 discusses an interesting case where a line of boats were running downwind on *starboard tack* as close to the shore as possible to get out of the current. The leading boat (P) gybed to *port tack* but was still sailing as close to the shore as possible. The boat immediately astern (S), still on starboard, then came up and hit the *port tack* boat. The Appeals Committee decided, "Rule 18.2(b) applies throughout this incident. That rule explicitly states that rule 10 does not apply and requires B to keep clear of A whether or not A gybes."

Note that rule 18.2(b) also has a "lock-in" provision ("...even if an *overlap* is established later") similar to that in rule 18.2(a). Therefore, if you are *clear ahead* when you reached the *two-length zone*, the boat(s) *clear astern* of you must *keep clear* of you even if they *overlap* you later during your passing maneuver.

"*What if the boat ahead wants to tack around the mark or obstruction?*"

She must be very careful! A boat *clear ahead* that tacks around a *mark* gets no protection from rule 18.2(b) whatsoever. The rule says, "*If the boat clear ahead tacks, rule 13 applies and this rule no longer does.*" In simple terms, the moment the boat ahead passes head to wind, she is subject to the rules in Sections A and B, beginning with rule 13 (While Tacking).

Technically, when the boat ahead begins to tack, i.e. sail above close-hauled, rule 18.2(b) shuts off. However, she continues to hold the right of way under rule 12 (as the boat *clear ahead*) or rule 11 (as the *leeward* boat) if the boats become *overlapped* during her luff. The moment she passes head to wind, she loses her right of way (rule 13).

Notice also that the boat *clear astern* can now sail above close-hauled to make it more difficult for the boat *clear ahead* to tack. (Under the previous rules, the boat astern was not allowed to sail above close-hauled to prevent the boat ahead from tacking.)

Let's say you (A) and another boat (B) are sailing close-hauled on *port tack* into the windward *mark*, not *overlapped*. The *mark* is to be left to port. You thought you were allowed to just tack around the *mark*. After you had passed head to wind but before you were close-hauled, B had to bear away to miss your transom. You have broken rule 13. In this situation, tactically speaking for a moment, your best move is to luff to head to wind, glide up to the *mark*, then tack around making it difficult for a boat close astern to prevent you from tacking. (See US SAILING Appeal 138.)

Note that if you two had been *overlapped* with you on the inside, then the outside boat would have had to give you *room* to tack because you needed to tack to continue sailing your *proper course* around the *mark* (rule 18.2(a)).

ISAF Case 159 discusses the situation where two boats, A and B, close reach on *starboard tack* into a windward *mark* to be left to starboard. A enters the *two-length zone clear ahead* and to leeward of B, then proceeds to tack to *port tack* in order to round the *mark*. B (still on *starboard tack*), collides with A (now on *port tack*), causing no damage. The Appeals Committee said, "Rule 18 applies when two boats on the same tack are about to pass a mark, whether or not they are on a beat. Therefore, rule 18.2(b) applied, beginning when A reached the two-length zone clear ahead of B on the same tack. Rule 18.2(b) requires a boat clear astern to keep clear of a boat clear ahead which remains on the same tack or gybes to pass the mark. When the boat clear ahead begins to tack, rule 18.2(b) ceases to apply and she is subject to rule 13 (While Tacking) while tacking and rule 10 (On Opposite Tacks) after satisfying rule 13. From the time A tacked on to port tack, she was subject to rules 13 and 10."

"Now I understand when I can and cannot be entitled to 'room,' but what if an outside boat leaves enough space between her and the mark; is it a foul to sneak in there?"

Absolutely not, as long as you don't hit the *mark* or the outside boat or force the outside boat to change course to avoid hitting you. US SAILING Appeal 38 is clear: "When a boat voluntarily or unintentionally makes room available to another boat that, under the rules, has no right to that room and makes no claim to it, that other boat may take advantage, at her own risk, of the room so given."

"I heard once that it is legal to force someone onto the wrong side of a mark once you are in the two-length zone; is it?"

No! There used to be a provision for this under the rules, but that was removed in 1989. In actuality, the occasion to do so rarely presented itself in fleet racing, and only slightly more so in team or match racing. However, provided the boats never get so close to the *mark* that rule 18 begins to apply, a *leeward* boat that is not "limited" (i.e. with the right to sail above her *proper course*) can still hold a *windward* boat to windward of the rhumb line, and in fact can "carry" that *windward* boat right on past the *mark*. Clearly, when L gets to the *two-length zone*, rule 18 applies; and it can begin to apply at a farther distance depending on the circumstances (see US SAILING Appeal 153). Once rule 18 begins to apply, L must begin to allow for W to have *room* at the *mark*.

WHEN ONE OF TWO OPPOSITE TACK BOATS TACKS WITHIN TWO LENGTHS OF THE MARK

Rule 18.3 - Tacking

If two boats were on opposite *tacks* and one of them tacked within the *two-length zone* to pass a *mark* or *obstruction*, rule 18.2 does not apply. The boat that tacked

(a) shall not cause the other boat to sail above close-hauled to avoid her or prevent the other boat from passing the *mark* or *obstruction*, and

(b) shall *keep clear* if the other boat becomes *overlapped* inside her, in which case rule 15 does not apply.

This new rule produces one of the most significant game changes under the 1997-2000 rules. The concept is to improve the racing by trying to minimize the frustrating and sometimes dangerous congestion that occurs at crowded windward *mark* roundings. It was felt that the problem is often caused by *port-tack* boats approaching on or near the port layline and trying to squeeze in between *starboard-tack* boats on the starboard layline and the *mark*. Too often, these *port-tackers* don't even get to their close-hauled courses before shooting back up to try to make it around the *mark*, or they get hung up on the *mark* itself, or worse---they fall back onto *port tack* directly in front of approaching *starboard-tackers*! Too many otherwise excellent close races have been hurt by these actions; and with the popular trend toward shorter courses and more races, the rule writers have taken this proactive step to improve the game.

In a nutshell, the rule works like this (we'll get into the technicalities below):

A boat that completes a tack within the *two-length zone* in front of another boat that is about to pass the *mark* must do it in a place that allows the other boat to pass the *mark* with no interference, and without ever having to sail above close-hauled to avoid hitting the boat that tacked.

If the boat that tacks causes the other boat to sail above close-hauled to keep from hitting her or prevents the other boat from being able to pass the *mark*, the boat that tacked has broken rule 18.3(a).

If the other boat gets an inside *overlap* on the boat that tacked at any time during her rounding, the boat that tacked must *keep clear* of the inside boat; and the inside boat does not initially need to give her *room* to *keep clear* (i.e. the boat that tacked becomes more or less a "sitting duck" for the *leeward*/inside boat).

"OK, I'm ready to have you lead me through this rule!"

Well, first the two boats must be approaching each other on opposite *tacks*, as they would be at a windward *mark*. Remember that rule 18 doesn't apply at all yet (rule 18.1(b), When This Rule Applies).

Next, the boat that tacks must be tacking "to pass a *mark* or *obstruction*." If, at a windward *mark* to be left to port, a *star-*

board-tack boat is not quite making the *mark* and tacks to *port tack* one length from the *mark*, rule 18.3 does not apply because she is not yet tacking to pass the *mark*. Therefore, she is subject to the rules in Section A and B. But when she tacks back to *starboard tack* on the layline **to pass the *mark***, rule 18.3 applies to her at that point.

Finally, if any part of a boat's tack occurs within the *two-length zone*, rule 18.3 applies. Remember that a boat is tacking throughout her entire maneuver while changing *tacks*. Therefore, in order for this rule not to apply, a boat must complete her tack, i.e. be on a close-hauled course, **before** she is within the *two-length zone*. It will be argued that it is difficult to know exactly where the *two-length zone* is, but that is the case when applying the *two-length zone* in any *mark* or *obstruction* passing situation. Sailors approaching port-hand windward *marks* on *port tack* will be well advised to be conservative when the *mark* area is congested and to complete their tack clearly outside the *two-length zone*.

In interpreting and applying rule 18.3(a), it can be viewed as one obligation on the boat that tacks not to do either of two things; i.e. she breaks rule 18.3(a) if either:

1) she causes the other boat to sail above close-hauled to avoid hitting her, or

2) she prevents the other boat from passing the mark or obstruction.

In my opinion, "causes" means "is the primary and reasonable reason for;" "avoid" means "avoid contact with;" and "prevents" means "physically prevent," as opposed to prevent as a result of disturbing the air and water, etc.

Let me make a brief comment on interpreting words used in rules. When there is some latitude in the interpretation of the word, it is my opinion that one should use the meaning that most reasonably fits the intent and meaning of the rule in order to avoid a strained interpretation that results in an undesirable result for the sport. Interpreting the word "causes" is a good example. One can argue that, in the situation where P tacks just ahead of S such that S needs to either sail above close-hauled or bear away to avoid hitting P, S can't claim that she was "caused" to sail above close-hauled because she could have borne away. This argument would conclude that S is only "caused" to sail above close-hauled when she has no other option by which to avoid hitting P.

In my opinion, this is not a reasonable interpretation of "causes." Clearly, a boat astern has many options other than to sail above close-hauled. She can bear away even if that means she can't make the *mark*, back her sails and stop (in a dinghy) or even drag her feet in the water to slow the boat down. I do not think these are reasonable expectations for racing sailors. If my house burns down and I choose to re-build it, I can accurately say that my house burning down "caused" me to re-build it, although I had other options (buy a new home with my own money, live in a tent, etc.). The event of my house burning down clearly was the primary reason I needed to re-build it, and it was a reasonable reason for doing so. Therefore it is accurate to say I was "caused" to re-build it.

The reason for this discussion is that interpreting the word "causes" is central to the interpretation and application of rule 18.3(a). I interpret rule 18.3(a) to say that P "causes" S to sail above close-hauled when either that is the only way S can avoid hitting her, or if bearing off in that situation would not be reasonable. Certainly, bearing off into a position where S is then prevented from passing the *mark* is unreasonable to me. However, if S can clearly bear off and pass the *mark*, then I would not say she was "caused" to sail above close-hauled.

Notice that rule 18.3(b) states that rule 15 (Acquiring Right of Way) does not apply. Therefore, whenever a boat *clear astern* establishes a *leeward/*inside *overlap* at any point in the passing maneuver of the boat that tacked, the boat that tacked must immediately *keep clear* of her, and the inside *overlapping* boat does not need to give the boat that tacked any *room* to *keep clear* of her whatsoever.

Let's look at some scenarios that will involve rule 18.3.

P approaches S at a port-hand windward mark, and tacks within the two-length zone just to leeward of S (i.e. on her lee-bow):

First of all, if S is caused to alter her course **at all** to avoid P while P is still on *port tack*, or during the time that P was past

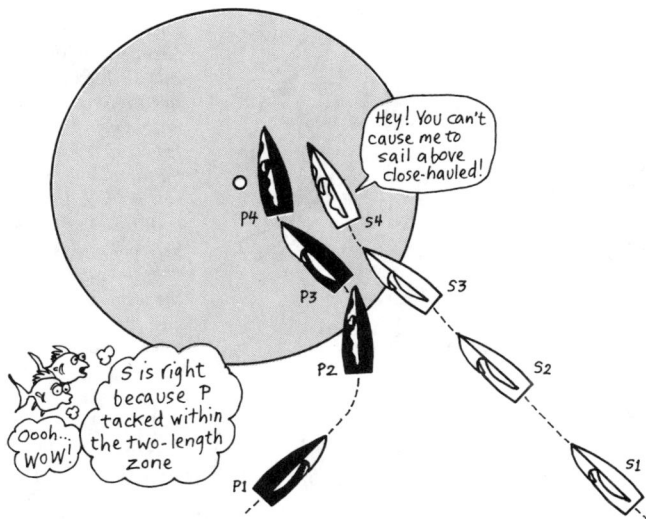

head to wind but not yet close-hauled, then P has broken either rule 10 (On Opposite Tacks) or rule 13 (While Tacking). Let's say that P gets to close-hauled without requiring any alteration of course by S, and the boats are now a boat-length from the *mark*. As P (now the *leeward*/inside boat) approaches the *mark*, she realizes she won't make the *mark* unless she luffs above close-hauled. She does so, thereby clearing the *mark*, but as a result of her luff, S is caused to sail above close-hauled to avoid hitting her. P has broken rule 18.3(a). Note that even though she's an inside/right-of-way boat, P is not entitled to rights under rule 18.2 because rule 18.3 specifically states so. The same would be true if S had to sail above close-hauled to avoid P's transom as she bore off around the *mark*.

Had S been able to pass the *mark* without needing to sail above close-hauled to avoid P, then P would not have broken rule 18.3(a), and S would be required to *keep clear* under rule 11 (On the Same Tack, Overlapped).

At a port-hand windward mark, P tacks within the two-length zone directly ahead of S; once P is close-hauled, S must alter course either up or down to avoid colliding with her:

First of all, once P gets to a close-hauled course *clear ahead* of S, S is required to *keep clear* of her under rule 12 (On the Same

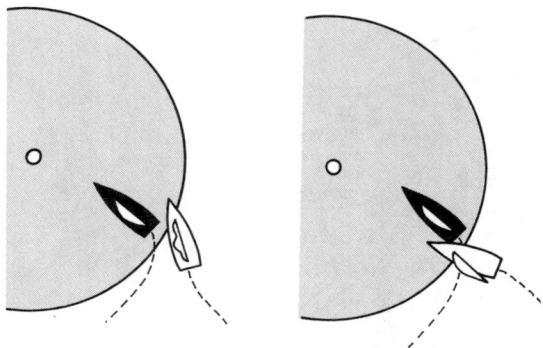

When a boat completes a tack within the two-length zone to pass a mark, she breaks new rule 18.3 if she causes a boat to sail above close-hauled to avoid hitting her or prevents a boat from passing the mark. Furthermore, she breaks the rule if she fails to keep clear if a boat becomes overlapped inside her; and in this case, rule 15 does not apply meaning that the inside boat does not need to give the boat that tacked room to keep clear of her.

Tack, Not Overlapped). If, despite her best efforts to avoid P beginning the moment P is close-hauled, S is unable to do so and she hits P on the transom, P has "tacked too close" and broken rule 15 (Acquiring Right of Way). If S does have *room* to *keep clear* of P but hits P on the transom anyway, then S breaks rule 12 as well as rule 14 (Avoiding Contact).

If, when P gets to a close-hauled course, she has left S a way to pass the *mark* with no interference, and without having to sail above close-hauled to avoid hitting her, P has not broken rule 18.3(a).

But if S is faced with the choice of *overlapping* P to *leeward* and probably not being able to pass the *mark* or sailing above close-hauled, and S chooses to sail above close-hauled, then P has broken rule 18.3(a) by causing S to sail above close-hauled to avoid her, because **it isn't reasonable to expect S to bear away and not make the *mark*.**

Note that in congested roundings S may have boats to *windward* of her making it impossible to sail above close-hauled. In this case her only option may be to *overlap* P to *leeward*. If she does so, but once there finds that she can't pass the *mark* due to P's physical presence, even when she luffs up to head to wind, P has "prevented" S from passing the *mark* thereby breaking rule 18.3(a). (Note that S is not allowed to sail past head to wind as she would be tacking onto *port tack* and required to give-way first under rule 13, While Tacking, and then under rule 10, On Opposite Tacks.) If S had **not** been able to pass the *mark* even before P's tack, then P has not "prevented" S from making the *mark*.

Now if P tacks far enough to windward of the layline such that S can clearly *overlap* P to *leeward* and pass the *mark*, then P has not caused S to sail above close-hauled to avoid her because it would be reasonable to expect S to bear away and pass the *mark*. However, if S chooses to sail above close-hauled and protest, it will be the **protest committee** who decides whether S would have been "prevented" from passing the *mark* had she chosen to *overlap* P to *leeward* (and my guess is, they will give S the benefit of the doubt). So P's will want to be very conservative with where they choose to tack in the *two-length zone* near opposite tack boats!

Finally, if S is on the layline and P tacks sufficiently far ahead of her that S is not required to take **any** action to avoid hitting P after the tack, but then S fails to make the *mark* due to the disturbed air and water caused by P, P has not "prevented" S from passing the *mark* due to her physical presence.

At a port-hand windward mark, P tacks within the two-length zone and one length later, as P is preparing to bear off around the mark, S sails in to leeward telling P to keep clear of her:

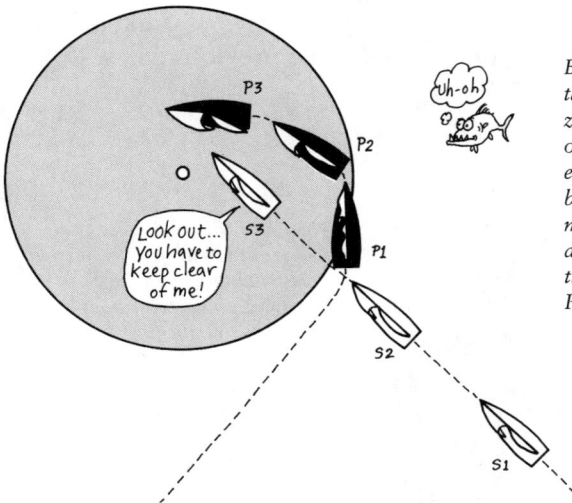

Because P completed her tack within the two-length zone, she must keep clear of S at any time S establishes an inside overlap until both boats have passed the mark; furthermore, rule 15 does not apply meaning that S does not need to give P room to keep clear of her.

Once P tacks within the *two-length zone*, **then for the duration of her passing maneuver** a *clear astern* boat (S) is allowed to establish a *leeward/inside overlap* on P and P must *keep clear* of her! To make life even tougher on P, rule 18.3(b) "shuts off" rule 15 (Acquiring Right of Way), such that when S does establish the *leeward* inside *overlap*, S does not have to give P any *room* to *keep clear* whatsoever!

As an example, P tacks within the *two-length zone clear ahead* of S. One length later, S chooses to *overlap* P to *leeward*. The moment S sticks her bow in to *leeward* of P, P must *keep clear*. If S makes contact with P, or if S is unable to sail her course because she would hit P, then P has not *kept clear* and has broken rule 18.3(b). If P can stay out of S's way such that S is not prevented from sailing her course around the *mark*, then P has not broken rule 18.3(b).

"It sounds like this rule will eliminate the port-tack layline and a port-tacker's tactic of lee-bowing a starboard tacker right at the mark!"

I don't think the rule will dramatically change the way the top of the beat is sailed. If you are doing well in the race, the windward *mark* rounding won't be that congested, and you will probably approach it as you did under the previous rules. If you

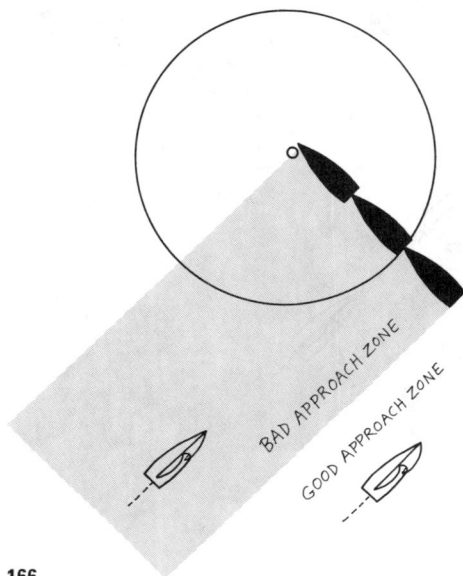

New rule 18.3 will cause port-tackers approaching a congested port-hand windward mark to approach about three boat-lengths below the port-tack layline so that they can complete their tack when clearly outside the two-length zone.

BAD APPROACH ZONE

GOOD APPROACH ZONE

are farther down in the pack (out of the top ten, let's say), coming in right on the *port-tack* layline isn't a great look anyway. For at least some of the time, you are sailing more slowly in the disturbed air and water of the boats going down the reach, or trying to pick your way through the *starboard-tack* boats as they turn and go down the run. Under the previous rules, when you arrived at the *mark* and tacked near the incoming *starboard-tackers*, you had to turn all the way to a close-hauled course before you gained any rights, which meant you needed to approach at least one length below the actual *port-tack* layline anyway. Now you will want to approach at least three lengths below, which means the new rule merely moves the approach down two lengths.

I agree that the most significant effect of this rule will be on the decision the *port-tacker* makes on whether to duck the nearby *starboard-tackers* and tack safely up to windward of them or to lee-bow them (i.e. tack just to *leeward* of them) and hope to make the *mark* from there. My personal experience (and I've been there myself!) is that too often sailors choose the (dare I say) "greedier" choice, and end up not only not making the *mark*, but causing a real mess for others at the *mark*. I think the net effect of the rule, once sailors get used to it, will be to have fewer *port-tackers* tacking right at the *mark* in crowds, which should be a welcome improvement for all.

WHEN AN INSIDE RIGHT-OF-WAY BOAT NEEDS TO GYBE TO SAIL HER PROPER COURSE AROUND A MARK

Rule 18.4 - Gybing

When rule 18.2(a) applies and an inside overlapped right-of-way boat must gybe at the mark or obstruction to sail her proper course, she shall pass no farther from the mark or obstruction than needed to sail that course.

First of all, rule 18.4 puts a "limit" on inside right-of-way boats, i.e. *leeward* boats and *starboard-tack* boats. Essentially, that "limit" is that whenever their *proper course* is to gybe at a *mark*, they must do so. Actually, the instruction in the rule is that the

Remember, you have to continue sailing your proper course, which means gybe at the mark

WO

I do... even if I have luffing rights?

LI

yup... that's one of the New rules.

L'S PROPER COURSE TO NEXT MARK

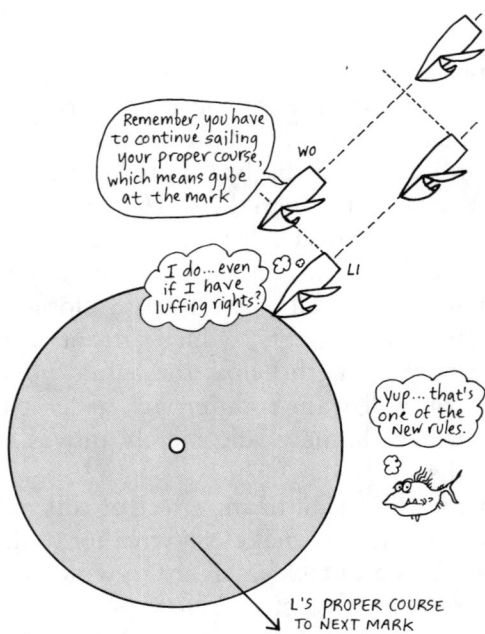

right-of-way boat "shall pass no farther from the *mark* or *obstruction* than needed to sail [her *proper course*]." This means that not only does she have to gybe when it is her *proper course* to do so, but she can't luff (turn) away from the *mark* or *obstruction* if that takes her farther from it than necessary to sail her *proper course*, even when the outside *windward* boat initially established the *overlap* to *windward* such that L would otherwise have the right to sail above her *proper course*.

(This is a change from the previous rules where L could sail past the *mark* or even luff when she had "luffing rights." The rationale is that the rules should keep the boats moving around the *marks*; and that it is less dangerous and much simpler if all inside boats have to gybe at the *marks* as opposed to giving right-of-way boats the option of not gybing as the previous rules did.)

The situation will commonly arise at gybe *marks* when the *leeward*/inside boat will be required to gybe around the *mark*, and at leeward *marks* to be left to port when the *starboard tack*/inside boat will be required to gybe in order to round the *mark*. Notice that a boat's *proper course* is the course she feels will get her to the finish line as quickly as possible. Therefore she can certainly make a "tactical" (swing wide-cut close) rounding.

Note that rule 18.4 applies only when rule 18.2(a) (Giving Room; Keeping Clear) applies. For rule 18.2(a) to apply, the boats need to be *overlapped* before one of them reaches the *two-length zone*. Therefore, if the boats are not *overlapped* when the boat ahead enters the *two-length zone*, then rule 18.4 does not apply, even if the boat astern establishes an outside *overlap* later.

This will enable team racers to continue setting "mark traps" whereby they enter the *two-length zone clear ahead* and then stop their boats. "Enemy boats" astern must now *keep clear* of them. They can't *overlap* them on the inside because of rule 18.2(b); and if they *overlap* the boat ahead on the outside, the boat ahead can luff or otherwise sail them past the *mark*, meanwhile letting teammates pass the *mark* on the inside. Note also that the Team Racing Rules (Appendix D) have modified rule 18.4 slightly such that it applies only when L has established the *overlap* from *clear astern*; i.e. when the boats are *overlapped* when they enter the *two-length zone* and originally W had established the *overlap* to *windward* of L, then L can sail straight past the *mark* or luff as she could under the previous rules (rule D1.1(b), Team Racing Rules). (See ISAF Case 151.)

Note also that if the boats are *overlapped* when one of them reaches the *two-length zone*, rule 18.4 applies throughout the passing maneuver, even if the *overlap* is broken later by either boat. This is because the inside right-of-way boat **was** *overlapped* when the boats reached the *two-length zone*.

Finally, note that rule 18.4 applies only when the inside right-of-way boat **must** gybe to sail her *proper course*. Therefore, at a windward *mark* going onto a run, when either *tack* can be a *proper course* (i.e. she'll be on a *proper course* whether she stays on the same *tack* or gybes), the inside right-of-way boat needs to gybe only when she decides it is her *proper course* to do so.

WHEN PASSING A CONTINUING OBSTRUCTION

Rule 18.5 - Passing a Continuing Obstruction

At a continuing obstruction, rule 18.2 is modified so that while boats are passing the obstruction an outside boat's obligation

ends if the overlap is broken, and a boat clear astern may establish an inside overlap provided there is room at that time to pass
between the other boat and the obstruction. If she does so, her
obligation under rule 18.2(b) ends.

First of all, we need to discuss what a "continuing *obstruction*"
is. It is an *obstruction* that a boat "continues" to sail next to, as
opposed to one that is passed in a matter of seconds. For
instance, a breakwater that a boat is sailing along is a "continuing *obstruction*," whereas a small spectator boat that gets sailed
by in a few seconds is not a "continuing *obstruction*." When a
windward boat is sailing parallel to a *leeward* boat for a few
boat-lengths, the *leeward* boat, as a right-of-way boat, is an
obstruction by definition, and a "continuing" one, as the two
boats are sailing side by side for several lengths. However, when
a *port-tack*er converges with a *starboard-tack*er upwind, S is not
a "continuing *obstruction*," as P won't be sailing near her for
more than a few seconds. Rule 18.5 modifies rule 18.2 (Giving
Room; Keeping Clear) to clarify when the rights and obligations
of the inside and outside boats begin and end.

ISAF Case 67 reads in part, "rule 18.5 makes an exception to
rule 18.2(b) which states that 'a boat clear astern may establish
an inside overlap provided there is room at that time to pass
between the other boat and the obstruction.' L clearly was an
obstruction to W, as she was to M as well, because she was not
required to keep clear or give room to either of them. Was she
also a continuing obstruction? Once W overhauled L, the two
boats sailed overlapped at least six lengths towards the finishing
line. That was easily long enough to qualify L as a continuing
obstruction."

ISAF Case 76 interprets the situation where boats are sailing by
the very end of a long breakwater protruding from shore as follows, "...the two boats, still overlapped, are outside the two-
length zone of an obstruction, the end of the breakwater. PL, the
outside boat, is required by rule 18.2(a) to give PW, inside, room
to pass the obstruction. While the breakwater is a continuous
structure from the shore to its outer end, it does not rank as a
continuing obstruction, since the boats are concerned only with
the very end."

"So when can a boat come up from clear astern and establish an inside overlap and be entitled to room at a continuing obstruction?"

The answer is: A boat *clear astern* (B) can establish an inside *overlap* on the boat *clear ahead* (A) only when, **at the moment the overlap is established,** there is enough *room* for B to pass completely between A and the *obstruction* without touching either. In other words, imagine that the moment the *overlap* on A is made, you could "freeze" the motion of A and the *obstruction*. If there is enough physical space for B to sail through between them in a seamanlike way without touching either, then the *overlap* is legal and A must give B *room* for as long as they are *overlapped* and B needs the *room* to keep from touching the *obstruction*; i.e. hitting the wall, running aground, hitting the right-of-way boat, etc. If B loses the *overlap* on A, then A ceases to be required to give *room* until B reestablishes another legal *overlap* and again needs *room*. (See US SAILING Appeal 257.)

One sensitive situation occurs when A is sailing as close as she dares to shore but it's not obvious how close a boat of her class can really go without running aground. Boat B comes up and wants to establish an inside *overlap*. The question becomes, "How do you determine if there is *room* for her to pass inside of A?"

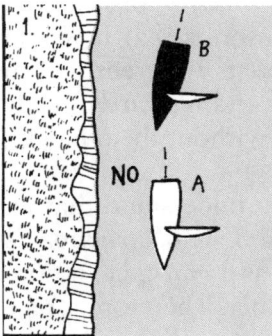

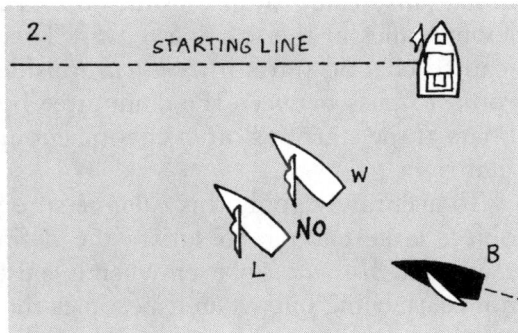

In situation 1, there is not room for B to sail between A and the shoreline without hitting one or the other. Therefore, she is not allowed to establish an overlap between them and become entitled to the rights in rule 18.2(a). The same principle applies in situation 2.

US SAILING Appeal 257 answers: "The determinative of 'room' is whether, under the conditions existing, the inside boat can navigate between the outside boat and the obstruction without undue risk." When she does decide to risk it, US SAILING Appeal 257 continues, "If the inside boat, after establishing her inside overlap, promptly runs aground, she has demonstrated that there was not room for her to pass...After she has sailed inside for two boat-lengths or so, however, any question of the failure of the outside boat to give sufficient room is to be answered by the facts found by the protest committee."

TWO EXCEPTIONS

"I notice there seem to be two exceptions to rule 18 listed as rules 18.1(a) and (b); could you go over those please?"

You bet. There are two very narrow situations when boats are passing *marks* and *obstructions* in which rule 18 does not apply at all. They are listed as rules 18.1(a) and 18.1(b).

Rule 18.1(a)

Rule 18...does not apply at a starting mark or its anchor line surrounded by navigable water from the time the boats are approaching them to start until they have passed them...

Essentially, rule 18.1(a) "shuts off" the "buoy / *obstruction* room" rules at the starting *marks*. The reason is that it would lead to chaotic starts if *windward*/inside boats were entitled to *room* to pass between the committee boat and *leeward*/outside boats at the start (it's often chaotic enough without them having that right!).

To accurately apply this rule, be sure you understand that an object large enough to satisfy the definition of *obstruction* is always an *obstruction*, even when it is used as a *mark*; i.e. it does not cease being one when it becomes the other. Therefore a race committee boat used as one end of the starting line is **both** a starting *mark* and an *obstruction* at the same time.

Now, having said that rule 18.1(a) "shuts off" rule 18 (Passing Marks and Obstructions), there are in fact two narrow

STARTING LINE

No I'm not... This starting mark isn't surrounded by navigable water, so you must let me in!

Don't go in there... you're BARGING!!

situations when, for reasons of safety, the rules do entitle a *windward*/inside boat to *room* at a starting *mark* under rule 18.2(a) (Giving Room; Keeping Clear) from a *leeward*/outside boat. Let's look at those first.

1) AT A STARTING MARK NOT SURROUNDED BY NAVIGABLE WATER

Though this situation is not common, it will arise when one end of the starting line is the end of a dock or breakwater, or is a bell buoy that marks some shallow rocks or sandbars. Rule 18 always applies at starting *marks* **not** surrounded by navigable water, i.e. enough water so that the inside boat can sail around the *mark* without running aground or hitting a dock or other object. Therefore, an inside boat is entitled to *room* at such a *mark* under rule 18.2(a) (Giving Room; Keeping Clear) from any outside boat provided her inside *overlap* was established in proper time; i.e. before the boats reached the *two-length zone* or, if the starting *mark* is a continuing *obstruction*, then when there was *room* at the time of the *overlap* to pass between the outside boat and the *obstruction* (rules 18.2(a) and 18.5, Passing a Continuing Obstruction).

2) AT A STARTING MARK WHEN THE BOATS ARE NOT APPROACHING THEM TO START

If the boats are **not** approaching the starting *mark* to start, an inside boat is entitled to *room* at a starting *mark* from any outside boat provided her *overlap* was established in proper time. Notice that this applies whether the starting *mark* is a buoy or large boat (*obstruction*). This is for safety purposes as boats are sailing past the *marks* well before starting.

So, if say at three minutes before the starting signal you were sailing along to *leeward* of W and were about to sail to leeward of the race committee boat, and for whatever reason W wanted to pass to leeward of it also, you would have to give her *room* to do so under rule 18.2(a), provided she had her inside *overlap* before the *two-length zone*. Now to play this out, because the *mark* doesn't have a "required" side yet (rule 28.2, Sailing the Course), you two can pass it on either side. You, as the *leeward* boat, have the right to sail where you please (rule 11, On the Same Tack, Overlapped), provided you make no sudden, fast course changes (rule 16, Changing Course); therefore, you can choose to luff and pass to windward of the committee boat. If, however, you choose to pass to leeward of the committee boat and fail to provide enough *room* for W to do likewise, you have broken rule 18.2(a).

Note that when you break a rule before the starting signal, you can make your 720 Turns Penalty immediately; i.e. you do not have to wait until your starting signal to do so (rule 44.1, Penalties for Breaking Rules of Part 2). If W happens to hit the

mark because you didn't give her enough *room*, she is exonerated by your "720" (or her successful protest against you) from breaking rule 31.1 under rule 31.3 (see rule 31, Touching a Mark).

"When is a boat considered to be 'approaching a starting mark to start?'"

Though this question has never been discussed in an appeal, I would develop my opinion as follows. What is the purpose of the rule? Rule 18.1(a) is preventing the situation where *wind-ward*/inside boats can reach in and demand *room* at the starting *mark* from *leeward*/outside boats that are trying to *start* there. And "when approaching the starting *mark* to *start*" is establishing the period of time during which these *windward*/inside boats know that they are not entitled to any *room*. Before LO is "approaching the starting *mark* to *start*," WI is entitled to *room* at the *mark*; and the rules are consistently clear in providing predictable and specific times when a boat's rights change. To me, this is no exception. When LO is clearly on her final approach toward the line with the intention of *starting*, i.e. crossing the line after the gun, it will be obvious to WI and she will know to *keep clear*. Furthermore, a boat that is "approaching the starting *mark* to *start*" and is close enough to the starting *mark* to shut out a *windward* boat, will clearly be *starting* in close proximity distance-wise to the starting *mark*.

Therefore, in my opinion, a boat that in fifteen knots of breeze goes reaching full-speed by the committee boat with one and a half minutes to go before the starting signal, and ends up *starting* halfway down the starting line, was in no way "approaching the starting *mark* to start" at the moment she went by the starting *mark*. But a boat that is passing the starting *mark* with ten seconds to go certainly is on her final approach to *start* very near to the starting *mark*. In addition, I feel that a boat that in light air sits nearly wayless behind the race committee boat may be approaching the line to *start* at one minute to go, and it will be more obvious and predictable that she plans to start near the *mark*, and the *windward*/inside boats can see this and *keep clear* accordingly.

This is a distinction that in general has caused very few problems, and in general has been very liberally interpreted in the *lee-ward*/outside boat's favor. But until it is officially interpreted, the safe move on LO's part would be to allow WI *room* up to one minute before the starting signal; and the safe move for WI would be not to try to force *room* with much less than two minutes to go. Both boats have the option to protest, and the protest committee can then decide whether LO was "approaching the starting *mark* to start" in the particular circumstances.

There are no other times that rule 18 applies at a starting *mark*; therefore, at all other times, boats are subject to the rules in Sections A and B. For a complete explanation of how these rules work when *starting* near starting *marks*, see "The Section A and B Rules in Action" section at the end of Chapter 7.

Rule 18.1(b)

Rule 18...does not apply between boats on opposite tacks when they are on a beat to windward or when the proper course for one of them to pass a mark or obstruction is to tack.

"Does rule 18.1(b) mean that 'buoy room' doesn't apply at the windward mark?"

No; rule 18.1(b) means that if two boats are coming into a windward *mark* on **opposite** *tacks*, rule 18 (Passing Marks and Obstructions) doesn't apply. But if the boats are coming into the windward *mark* on the **same** *tack*, then rule 18 applies just like at any other *mark*.

Though the phrase "a beat to windward" has never been interpreted by an appeal, my opinion is that a boat is on a "beat to windward" if her *proper course* to the *mark* is to sail close-hauled. However, the second phrase in rule 18.1(b) takes the pressure off deciding whether boats are on a beat to windward. Anytime one of two boats on opposite *tacks* will have to tack at a *mark* or *obstruction* in order to continue sailing their *proper course*, rule 18.1(b) "shuts down" rule 18.2(a) (Giving Room; Keeping Clear).

Picture a windward *mark* to be left to port. It would be chaos if suddenly a *port-tack* boat could come in and call for *room* from a *starboard-tack* boat while still on *port tack*. While the boats are on opposite *tacks*, rule 10 (*port/starboard*) applies; and if the *port-tack* boat (PI) wants to tack to *leeward* of the *starboard-tack* boat (SO), rules 13 (changing *tacks*) and 15 (acquiring right of way) apply. Once the *port-tack* boat has borne away to a close-hauled course without breaking rule 13 or 15, she is on the same *tack* as SO and the *leeward* boat.

If she has tacked outside the *two-length zone* (i.e. passed head to wind outside the *two-length zone*), then she is "doubly protected" to sail around the *mark*. PI, as the *leeward* boat, is free to sail where she pleases, i.e. she's not "limited." Therefore she can luff head to wind if she pleases, which she may need to do to pass the *mark*. SO, as the *windward* boat, is required to *keep clear* under rule 11 (On the Same Tack, Overlapped). Furthermore, as an outside *overlapped* boat, SO is required to *keep clear* of PI under rule 18.2(a).

If she has tacked within the *two-length zone*, she is subject to rule 18.3 (Passing Marks and Obstructions, Tacking).

Notice that the exception in rule 18.1(b) applies only at a *mark* that one of the boats needs to tack around. The reasoning is that at all the other *mark*s, even though the boats may be on opposite *tacks*, they are going in the same direction, or at least generally converging at much smaller angles. Therefore, at leeward *mark*s, inside/*port-tack* boats are entitled to *room* under rule 18.2(a) from outside/*starboard-tack* boats.

The same exception applies when passing an *obstruction*. When two boats on a beat to windward are on opposite *tacks*, the inside boat cannot ask for *room* to pass an *obstruction*. Therefore, if in a narrow harbor you are sailing close-hauled on *port tack* as close to the shore or a dock as you can get, you cannot call for *room* from a converging close-hauled *starboard-tack* boat. Rule 10 (On Opposite Tacks) applies and you must slow down or bear off and take their stern. (See ISAF Cases 17 and 93.)

We've discussed thoroughly how rule 18 applies slightly differently at a windward *mark* and at a starting *mark*. These are its only two exceptions. The rules for "buoy room" are exactly the same at every other *mark* on the course, **including the finishing mark**s.

"Cool; does this mean that I now know everything there is to know about the rules at marks and obstructions?"

Almost!

RULE 19 - ROOM TO TACK AT AN OBSTRUCTION

Rule 19.1

When safety requires a close-hauled boat to make a substantial course change to avoid an obstruction and she intends to tack, but cannot tack and avoid another boat on the same tack, she shall hail for room to do so. Before tacking she shall give the hailed boat time to respond...

This is the rule that is used when calling for "sea-room" at a shore, breakwater or dock; however, it is also commonly used when two *port-tack* boats are sailing side by side up a beat and are converging with a *starboard-tack*er. The purpose of the rule is to permit a close-hauled boat caught between another boat on the same *tack* and an *obstruction* to avoid the *obstruction* without loss of distance when a substantial alteration of course is required to clear it.

Notice that rule 19.1 does not apply to boats on opposite *tacks*. ISAF Case 93 describes a situation where a *port-tack* boat (P) is sailing close-hauled as close to shore as possible. A *port-tack* boat to leeward tacks to *starboard tack* onto a collision course with P. S hails "Starboard" and P hails for "sea-room." In ISAF Case 93, the Appeals Committee said, "In accordance with rule

Uh-oh... the black boat is in BIG trouble. On a beat, a boat on the opposite tack can't call for room.

I need room to stay clear of the shore.

No way... you'd better go behind me.

18.1(b), which makes rule 18 inapplicable, S establishes rights over P when she tacks onto starboard under rule 10 and reaches her new close-hauled course, provided that she observes rules 13 and 15, which she does by not tacking so close that P has to begin to keep clear before she reaches her close-hauled course. P is now subject to rule 10 and must keep clear." P is not entitled to hail for *room* since rule 19.1 applies to two boats on the "same" *tack* approaching an *obstruction*. So, in this situation P must slow down or bear away and pass astern of S.

When all the conditions in rule 19.1 are met, a *leeward* boat or one *clear ahead* will be able to call for "*room* to tack at the *obstruction*" when nearby *windward* boats are otherwise preventing her from tacking.

Here is how rule 19.1 works:

1) Two boats must be on the **same** *tack* and approaching an *obstruction*, and the *leeward* boat (L) or the boat *clear ahead* (A) must be sailing **close-hauled**.

2) Rule 19.1 is intended for the use of L or A when she is about to hit, or be hit by, an *obstruction*, e.g. a sandbar, a dock, a fishing boat, a *starboard-tack* boat or the like. When there is any doubt as to whether L or A actually is in imminent danger of colliding with an *obstruction*, ISAF Case 117 is clear: "Unless the facts found by [the protest committee] prove oth

STARTING LINE

1. Don't tack

4. No, I'm not close-hauled

W

L

3. Now I'm close-hauled. I need room to tack!

2. OK

L is RIGHT. Only L must be close-hauled to call for room to tack

cool

erwise . . . the judgment of the *leeward* boat [or the boat *clear ahead*] is conclusive."

3. Rule 19.1 can be used only when L or A must make a "**substantial alteration of course**" to avoid the *obstruction*. Here, the alteration is simply that needed not to hit the *obstruction*. In this case, as my general guideline, a course change of less than 10 degrees is not very "substantial." That's only 3 feet, 6 inches, in a twenty-foot boat. Therefore, in a twenty-foot boat, if you can bear away and miss an *obstruction* that you would otherwise hit only 3 feet from its edge, you are not entitled to use rule 19.1; but if you need to tack to avoid the last 3 feet, then that's "substantial."

US SAILING Appeal 81 reads, "If [L] had approached the police launch sufficiently close to its leeward end so that, with only a slight alteration of course when within one of her hull lengths of it, she could have safely passed to leeward of it, she should have done so. This was not the case here. As is clear in the diagram, L's course brought her close to the windward end of the police launch. She not only had to tack to pass it to windward but she would have had to bear away substantially below her actual course to pass it to leeward. Inasmuch as she was required to change course substantially to clear the obstruction whichever side she passed it, she had a right under rule 19.1 to hail W for room to tack." (See also ISAF Case 20.) Notice that even when an *obstruction* is surrounded by open water, L or A can use rule 19.1 (see US SAILING Appeal 81).

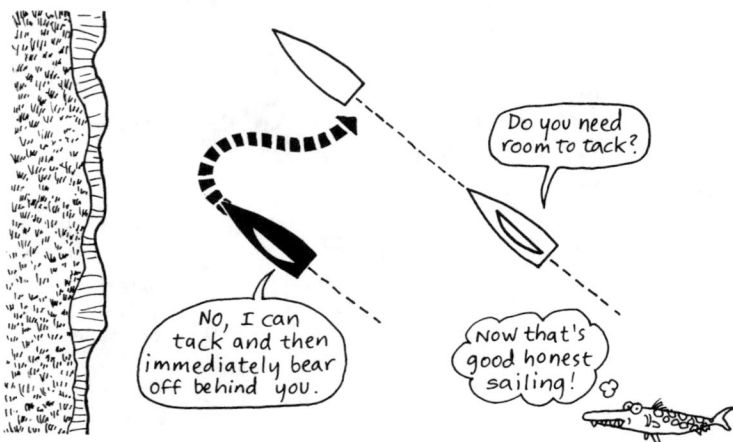

4. When there is a *windward* boat (W) or a boat *clear astern* (B) that is very close by, L or A can hail for *"room* to tack" to avoid the *obstruction* only when she can't tack and avoid a collision with W or B. If the course of L or A is sufficiently to *leeward* of W's or B's course such that, after tacking onto *port tack* she has *room* to bear away and pass astern, she is required to do so, since she then is able to tack and avoid the other boat. This means that if L or A can tack and immediately bear away sharply and miss W or B, she must do so and cannot use rule 19.1. (See ISAF Case 80.)

5. When L or A is approaching an *obstruction*, and safety requires her to make a substantial course change to avoid the *obstruction*, and when L or A intends to tack but cannot tack and avoid a collision with W or B, she **shall hail** W or B for *"room* to tack."

Notice four things about the hail:

a) L or A is **required** to hail; i.e. the hail is mandatory! If a boat does not hail, she cannot claim that she intended to tack. Therefore, if a boat does not hail, rule 19.1 does not apply.

b) L or A's hail must be **adequate**, which implies that it must be loud enough for W or B to hear it above the wind and noise of the boats, and it must be absolutely clear as to what the hail means. I personally try to turn my head toward the other boat, use their helmsman's name if I know it, and say to the effect, "I have a dock or a *starboard-tack*er coming up; I need *room* to tack."

ISAF Case 117 reads, "The failure of a boat to hear an adequate hail does not relieve her of her obligations under rule 19...Rule 19.1 provides that after hailing the hailing boat shall give the other boat time to respond. The purpose of that is to provide time for the specific response called for under rules 19.1(a) and (b) (to tack or reply 'You tack'). In either case, the hailing boat shall tack after the appropriate response from the hailed boat. Therefore the leeward boat must not sail into a position, before hailing, where she cannot allow sufficient time for a response.

"Failure of a windward boat to hear a properly made hail would not necessarily relieve her of her obligations to a leeward boat. Where, however, the leeward boat...observed no response after her hail, a second and more vigorous hail would be required to constitute proper notice of her intention to tack."

c) After hailing, L or A must give the hailed boat **time to respond**; i.e. she cannot hail and tack simultaneously. US SAILING Appeal 246 reads, "Since L hailed and tacked simultaneously, she also broke rule 19.1." This is intended to require L or A to keep a good lookout so she is not "surprised" by an *obstruction*.

d) She must adequately hail **in time** for W or B to respond so that both boats can clear the *obstruction*. This will obviously require more time if W or B will have to subsequently hail a boat or boats to *windward* of them. Also, US SAILING Appeal 246 reads, "[The finding] that W should have been aware of the presence of S and should have been prepared to respond is unwarranted." Therefore W or B does not have to anticipate that L or A might be approaching an *obstruction*. If L or A does not adequately hail in time and subsequently runs aground or fouls a *starboard-tack* boat, she cannot blame W or B. (See ISAF Case 117.)

"I thought that when two port-tack boats were approaching a starboard-tacker, it was whoever hailed first that got to tell the other what to do."

No. The applicable phrase in rule 19.1 is, "and she intends to tack." So when L or A will have to make a substantial alteration of course to bear away and pass astern of an *obstruction*, it is **her choice** whether to duck or tack. When two *port-tack* boats (PW and PL) are approaching a *starboard-tack* boat (S), US SAILING Appeal 131 says, "Therefore, when PL chose not to bear off, PW was not entitled to room to pass the obstruction." If PL chooses to pass astern of S and PW wants to pass astern of S also, then ISAF Case 20 reminds PL that, as an outside boat passing an *obstruction*, "under rule 18.2(a) PW is entitled to room to pass between PL and the stern of S." But if PL chooses to tack, PW must comply even when she'd rather duck. This is reinforced by the last sentence in rule 19.2, *"When rule 19.1 applies, rule 18 does not."*

When L or A adequately hails, rule 19.1 tells W or B how to respond.

Rule 19.1 (continued)

The hailed boat shall either

(a) tack as soon as possible, in which case the hailing boat shall also tack as soon as possible, or

(b) immediately reply 'You tack', in which case the hailing boat shall immediately tack and the hailed boat shall give *room*, and rules 10 and 13 do not apply.

So when L or A adequately hails, W or B has only **two** choices for a response: either tack as soon as possible or **immediately** reply "You tack." W or B does not have the option of disputing L or A's judgment about her need to hail. When W or B feels L or A's hail is not proper (e.g. she is not really near an *obstruction* or she will not have to make a substantial course change to go around an *obstruction*) she nevertheless must respond. She can then protest claiming she was improperly forced to take avoiding action under rule 19.1. (See ISAF Case 117.)

Notice that if you choose to reply "You tack," you must make that hail **immediately**, i.e. without delay. (Note that in the previous rules you needed to hail only at the "earliest possible moment.") Note also that you must use those exact two words in your hail.

However, if you choose to respond by tacking, you need only do that "as soon as possible." The reason is that often it will not be possible for W or B to respond by tacking immediately after hearing a hail. Examples would include: (a) when there are several boats to *windward* of W or B which need to be hailed; (b) when coming in on *port tack* to a windward *mark* where the boats already going down the first reach are so close that tacking is impossible or (c) when some object in the water such as a log or *mark* momentarily restricts her ability to respond. When it is not possible for W or B to respond by tacking immediately, it is good seamanship for them to inform L or A.

Notice also that it makes no difference whether the hailed boat (W or B) can clear the *obstruction* herself (unless it is also

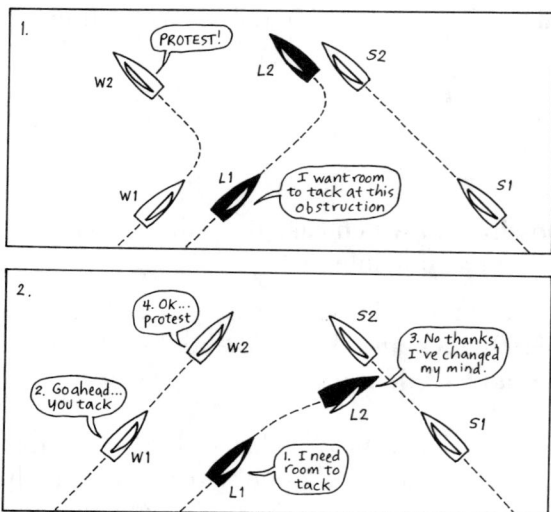

In situation 1, L breaks rule 19.1(a) by delaying her tack to starboard. After W tacks in response to L's hail, L must tack as soon as possible. In situation 2, L breaks rule 19.1(b) by not immediately tacking after W replies "You tack."

a *mark*; see rule 19.2). If the hailing boat (L or A) cannot clear it without tacking or bearing away sharply, she is entitled to hail and to get a response, regardless of whether the hailed boat can clear the *obstruction.*

Now let's say that you are L and have hailed W for *room* to tack because of a converging *starboard-tack*er. Upon hearing your hail, W tacks. You must begin your tack (i.e. pass head to wind) as soon as you can without hitting W. In other words, you must put your helm down within a couple of seconds after W puts hers down. You break rule 19.1(a) if you continue another couple of boat-lengths before tacking.

If W responds to your hail with the reply "You tack," again you must immediately put your helm down and tack. If you don't, you break rule 19.1(b). Once W hails "You tack" she assumes all the obligation to give you *room* to tack and clear her; so if you hear her reply and immediately put your helm down and hit her, she is wrong. And if you decide to stop your tack or otherwise alter course before completing your tack in order to avoid her, she is wrong as well. Notice that while you are tacking and clearing her, rules 10 (On Opposite Tacks) and 13 (While Tacking) don't apply. Clearly, once you have tacked and cleared her, you are subject to those rules again.

"Could you discuss the situation where two port-tackers (PW and PL) are sailing close-hauled side by side on a converging course with a starboard-tacker (S). PL hails PW for 'room to tack,' gets no response, and ultimately S must alter course to avoid hitting PL. Who should be penalized?"

The answer will depend on the protest committee's judgment as to whether PL hailed adequately and gave the hailed boat enough time to respond.

ISAF Case 6 states, "Having hailed three times, PL was entitled to expect that PW would respond and give her room to tack. She was not obliged either to anticipate PW's failure to comply with rule 19.1 or to bear away astern of the obstruction S. PL is exonerated as the innocent victim of another boat's breach of a rule, under the provisions of rule 64.1(b) (Penalties and Exoneration)."

US SAILING Appeal 116 is another good example of how PL fulfilled her obligation to adequately hail, but then was forced to foul S by PW's failure to respond. "FACTS: [PW and PL] were close-hauled on port tack. S, which was to leeward and ahead of both PW and PL, tacked to starboard. S completed her tack in compliance with rule 15 (Acquiring Right of Way). PL thereupon twice hailed PW to tack, so she also could tack and avoid S. By the time it was clear that PW would not respond, it was too late for PL to make any alternative maneuver without interfering with the oncoming S. PL called to S that she could not respond, whereupon S tacked back to port to avoid a collision.

"DECISION: Inasmuch as PL would have had to make a substantial course change to pass astern of S, even had she borne away instantly when S tacked to starboard, she had the right to hail PW as she did. By the time it was clear that PW would not respond, it was too late for PL to clear S by bearing away. PW broke rule 19.1...Since PL was compelled to break a rule as a consequence of PW's failure to meet her requirements under rule 19.1, PL is exonerated."

However, there will be times when L or A simply wait too long before hailing. Though deleted for other reasons, US SAILING

Appeal 142 contained an excellent summation of this situation. "The situation developed slowly with rights and obligations established at some distance from the point of convergence. In fact PL acknowledged recognizing the problem a minute before S hailed her. Had she taken timely action then, either by hailing PW for room to tack under rule 19.1 or by bearing away and passing astern of S, she could have avoided S. Under the circumstances, the failure of her late reliance on rule 19.1 does not entitle her to exoneration as an innocent victim, her principal obligation having been to keep clear of S under rule 10."

The key to all this is that L or A must keep a good lookout and begin hailing in time for W or B to hear and understand the hail and then respond. If L or A waits until the last second to hail, and then immediately fouls S, she cannot blame W or B. But if after two clear hails W or B does not respond, L or A must make a reasonable effort to *keep clear* of S. If she cannot *keep clear* she should be exonerated under rule 64.1(b), and W or B should be penalized for breaking rule 19.1. If, however, L or A did have enough time and space to *keep clear* of S after getting no response from W or B but failed to make an effort to use it, she should also be penalized under rule 10 (On Opposite Tacks).

This situation commonly occurs at the windward *mark*. Note that when PW and PL are within the *two-length zone*, PW is entitled to "buoy *room*" from PL under rule 18.2(a) (Giving Room; Keeping Clear). However, the *room* will not be given until the boats reach the *mark*. If PL wants to tack to avoid a converging S, she can hail PW for "*room* to tack," and as long as it is possible for PW to respond, PW must do so. (See US SAILING Appeal 11.)

"What about when the obstruction is also a mark; can I still call for room to tack?"

Good question. The answer is in rule 19.2.

Rule 19.2

Rule 19.1 does not apply at a starting mark or its anchor line surrounded by navigable water from the time boats are

approaching them to start until they have passed them or at a mark that the hailed boat can fetch. When rule 19.1 applies, rule 18 does not.

Notice that, once she is approaching it to *start*, a boat can never call for "*room* to tack" at an *obstruction* that is also a starting *mark*, including the *mark's* anchor line. (For a full discussion on the phrase "approaching a starting *mark* to *start*," see the discussion of rule 18.1(a), Passing Marks and Obstructions, When This Rule Applies.) This situation usually develops when there is a race committee boat anchored as the port or "leeward" end of the starting line. A *leeward* boat is truly in "coffin corner" if she sails into a position where she can neither tack without fouling the *windward* boat nor bear away and pass astern of the race committee boat.

But if a *mark* is a boat or other object large enough to qualify as an *obstruction*, then L or A is allowed to call for "*room* to tack" unless W or B can "fetch" it (i.e. pass the *mark* without tacking. Note that this exception applies only at *obstructions* that are **also** *marks*.

Let's say you are approaching a *mark/obstruction* and cannot pass it on its required side without tacking, and that you want to tack but can't without colliding with the boat just to *wind-*

ward of you (W). First you must hail W for *"room* to tack" under rule 19.1. If W cannot "fetch" it herself, then she must respond under rule 19.1(a) or (b), i.e. tack or reply "You tack." But if she can "fetch" it, she does **not** have to respond at all (though it is good seamanship for her to do so). In this case you are going to have to gybe or bear away and tack around to try it again. Of course, if after telling you that she is "fetching" she does not "fetch" it on that tack due to a miscalculation or a wind shift, etc., she breaks rule 19.1 by not responding to your hail.

"What happens when I'm the leeward hailing boat and by the time I learn that the windward hailed boat is fetching the mark/obstruction, it's too late for me to bear away without hitting the mark/obstruction?"

Well, it's not a pretty picture! You should begin hailing soon enough so that, if W doesn't respond, you still have the option to bear away before it's too late. However, if you do get stuck, a quick hail to W will usually be enough to encourage them to give you *room* to clear the *mark/obstruction*, realizing that you would then do your "720" Turns Penalty.

It's also possible in this situation that a competitor might calculate that they will actually lose fewer places by forcing the *windward* boat to give them *room* to pass the *mark* and then doing a "720," rather than gybing around and making a second run at the *mark*, particularly at a crowded windward *mark*. This doesn't work, however. Rule 44.1 (Penalties for Breaking Rules of Part 2) reads, *"However, if she...gained a significant advantage in the race or series by her breach she shall retire."*

Finally, notice the last sentence of rule 19.2. This clarifies that when L and W are about to pass an *obstruction* and all the conditions in rule 19.1 are met, including the fact that L intends to tack, rule 19.1 takes precedence over rule 18 (Passing Marks and Obstructions) by stating that rule 18 doesn't apply. Therefore W, which may prefer to pass on the other side of the *obstruction*, is nevertheless governed by L's choice of action. Also notice that when L intends to tack, rule 19.1 requires her to hail for *room* to do so. Therefore, as far as W is concerned, rule 19.1 begins to apply the moment L hails for "*room* to tack."

"Now do I know everything there is to know about room at marks and obstructions?"

Yes!

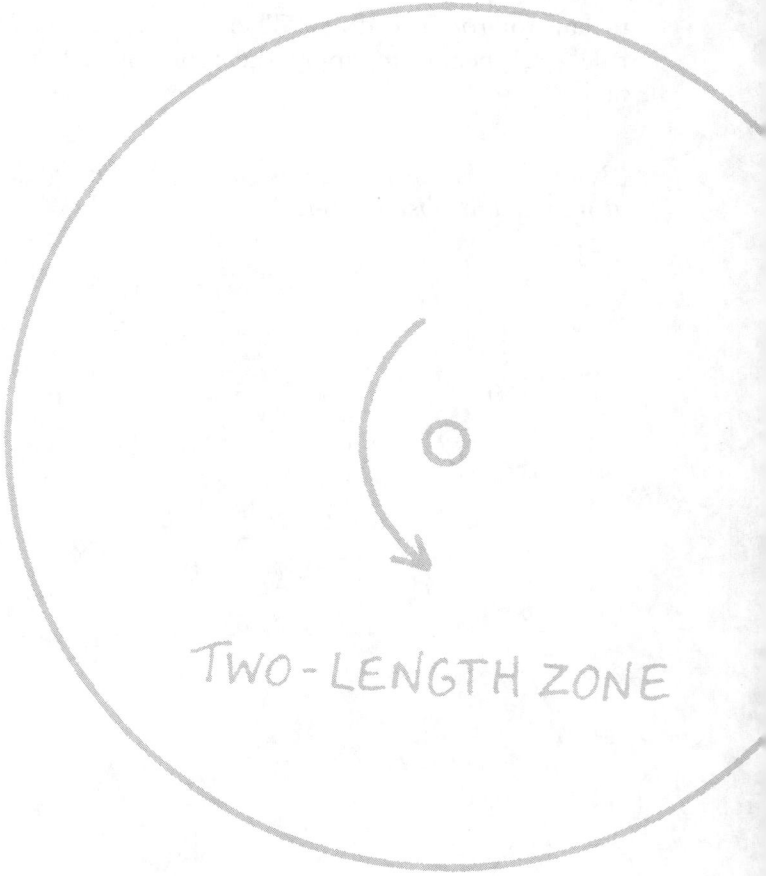

TWO-LENGTH ZONE

9

WHEN BOATS MEET OTHER RULES

PART 2 - SECTION D

Section D contains rules that apply in special situations that arise on the race course (rules 20-22). Again, these rules contain times when a right-of-way boat may find herself with a **temporary requirement** to *keep clear* of, or otherwise avoid, a give-way boat. An example is if you are on *port tack* shortly after the start and a *starboard-tack* boat is sailing back to the line because she was over early, rule 20 (Starting Line Errors; Penalty Turns; Moving Astern) requires her to *keep clear* of you because you have started correctly, even though she is on *starboard tack* and you are on *port tack*. In this case you become the right-of-way boat and she the give-way boat for as long as the rule requires her to *keep clear*. Another example is that all boats are required to avoid a boat that is capsized, whether holding right of way over her or not (rule 21, Capsized, Anchored or Aground; Rescuing).

Preamble to Section D

When rule 20 or 21 applies between two boats, Section A rules do not.

This preamble clarifies that whenever rule 20 (Starting Errors; Penalty Turns; Moving Astern) or rule 21 (Capsized, Anchored or Aground; Rescuing) applies, it takes precedence over the basic right-of-way rules in Section A. Note, however, that the rules of Section B still apply, which most significantly means that rule 16 (Changing Course) applies to a boat given the right of way in rule 20.

Rule 20 - Starting Errors; Penalty Turns; Moving Astern

A boat sailing towards the pre-start side of the starting line or its extensions to comply with rule 29.1 or rule 30.1 shall keep clear of a boat not doing so until she is completely on the pre-start side. A boat making penalty turns shall keep clear of one that is not. A boat moving astern by backing a sail shall keep clear of one that is not.

Rule 20 is a consolidation of three previous rules: rule 44 (On the Course Side of the Starting Line), rule 45 (Keeping Clear After Touching a Mark) and Appendix B1.1.1 (Alternative Penalties for Infringing a Rule of Part IV). Rule 20 also adds a rule about sailing backward, previously contained only in the Sailboard Racing Rules (Appendix B4.4.3(c)). Let's take them one at a time.

1) *A boat sailing towards the pre-start side of the starting line or its extensions to comply with rule 29.1 or rule 30.1 shall keep clear of a boat not doing so until she is completely on the pre-start side.*

Rule 29.1 (On the Course Side at the Start) reads, "*When at her starting signal any part of a boat's hull, crew or equipment is on the course side of the starting line, the boat shall sail completely to the pre-start side of the line before starting.*" If you aren't completely behind the starting line at the starting signal, you are considered to be "on the course side" of the line (OCS). However, even when you and everyone else knows you are OCS, you keep all your right of way until you are sailing back **toward** the pre-start side of the starting line or its extensions, i.e. are converging with them. This means that you continue to have rights even while slowing down or luffing in order to get clear enough to turn back. When it is obvious that you are sailing back toward the starting line, you must then *keep clear* of all boats that have *started* properly or are on the pre-start side of the starting line.

Notice that when the "one minute rule" (rule 30.1, I Flag Rule) is in effect, this same requirement applies when you have been on the course side of the starting line in the final minute before your starting signal and are sailing toward either end of the starting line to comply with rule 30.1 **at any time during the minute before your starting signal** as well as after it!

Once you are completely on the pre-start side of the starting line or its extensions, you are instantly subject to the Section A rules again; however, remember that if you acquire the right of way over another boat, you have to initially give her *room* to *keep clear* of you under rule 15 (Acquiring Right of Way).

Between two or more OCS boats sailing toward the pre-start side of the line, the Section A rules apply in the usual way.

"I realize that if another boat fouls me and forces me over the starting line just before the gun I'm OCS, but do I have to go back and restart?"

I'm afraid you do. Rule 29.1 requires that, when you are OCS, you sail completely to the pre-start side of the line before *starting*. If you don't, then you haven't *started* the race and have broken rule 29.1. You can only be exonerated from breaking a rule when another boat "compels" you to break a rule (rule 64.1(b), Penalties and Exoneration). In your case, the other boat may have forced you over the line, and you certainly should win your *protest* against her, but she hasn't prevented you from returning to the pre-start side and *starting*. Therefore no exoneration is available.

This is similar to the situation when an outside boat wrongfully fails to give you enough *room* at a *mark* and forces you on the wrong side of it. Though you were clearly fouled, you still must round the *mark* on the correct side. Notice that rule 31 (Touching a Mark) builds in its own exoneration clause which allows a boat that has been wrongfully compelled to touch a *mark* to be exonerated by either the culprit acknowledging fault or by successfully protesting the culprit (rule 31.3). These are two examples of situations where you can be right under the rules but have your finishing place seriously hurt by a give-way boat with no way for a protest committee to compensate you.

At these times I'm reminded of the old saying, "He had the right of way as he sped along; but he's just as dead as though he were wrong!"

2) A boat making penalty turns shall keep clear of one that is not.

This rule talks to boats that are either doing a 360-degree turn penalty for touching a *mark* under rule 31.2 (Touching a Mark) or a 720-degree Turns Penalty for possibly breaking a rule of Part 2 under rule 44.2 (720-degree Turns Penalty). It clearly tells them that, while they are making their penalty turns, they have to *keep clear* of other boats, which makes sense.

Notice that when you hit a *mark* or possibly break a rule of Part 2, you still have all your rights as long as you continue sailing the course and while you are sailing well clear of the other boats preparatory to doing your penalty turns. But the moment it is obvious to other boats that you are clearly beginning to make your penalty turns, you must then *keep clear* of other boats in the race. You get your rights back when you have completed your last turn; but remember that if you acquire the right of way over another boat, you must initially give her *room* to *keep clear* of you under rule 15 (Acquiring Right of Way).

Note that if you touch a starting *mark* or possibly break a rule of Part 2 before the starting signal, you can make your turns immediately, as opposed to waiting for the starting signal before doing them. And when two boats are making penalty turns, as between them the Section A rules apply in the usual way, as does rule 22.2 (Interfering with Another Boat).

3) A boat moving astern by backing a sail shall keep clear of one that is not.

This is a new rule to all segments of the sport except boardsailing (which have their own version of this rule that I will also explain below). It covers the situation where a boat actually backs its sail (i.e. holds the sail against the wind) and thereby causes the boat to move backward through the water. When a boat does this, she must *keep clear* of any other boat that is not doing likewise. Furthermore, she must remember that when she begins sailing backward, her action gives the right of way to boats astern; therefore they do not have to give her any *room* to *keep clear* of them under rule 15 (Acquiring Right of Way).

Note that if a boat begins to move backward due to the backing of her sail, she continues to be subject to this rule for as long as she is moving backward, even if she lets her boom come amidships. However, if a boat simply begins to move backward because she has lost her headway, rule 20 does not apply to her.

Notice that the rule is somewhat different for boardsailors. Rule B2.1 reads, "*A sailboard moving astern shall keep clear of other sailboards and boats.*" Therefore, **anytime** a sailboard is moving backward, she must *keep clear* of other sailboards and boats.

Rule 21 - Capsized, Anchored or Aground; Rescuing

If possible, a boat shall avoid a boat that is capsized or has not regained control after capsizing, is anchored or aground, or is trying to help a person or vessel in danger. A boat is capsized when her masthead is in the water.

SPECIAL SAILBOARD DEFINITIONS AND RULES

Rule B1 - Definitions:

Capsized A sailboard is capsized when her sail or the competitor's body is in the water.

Recovering A sailboard is recovering from the time her sail or, when water-starting, the competitor's body is out of the water until she has steerage way.

Rule B2.2 - Add to Section D:

Rule 23 - Sail Out of the Water When Starting

When approaching the starting line to start, a sailboard shall have her sail out of the water and in a normal position, except when accidentally capsized.

Rule 24 - Recovering

A sailboard recovering shall avoid a sailboard or boat under way.

Rule 21 is a common sense rule of safety, and as such it complements rule 1 (Safety). These two rules place the safety of sailors and their boats well above the importance of any race they may be in. The rationale for rule 21 is clear: if a boat is anchored, aground or capsized it cannot very well "move" to get out of another boat's way, and it may be in peril; and if one boat is in the act of rescuing another boat or person, no other boat should hinder the rescue in any way.

Note that rule 21 requires you to "avoid" the boats described in the rule. In my opinion, this means not only avoid contact but keep away from them as well. However, the rule's opening phrase ("If possible...") clarifies that if for whatever reasonable reason it is not possible for you to avoid them, you should not be penalized. This further emphasizes the safety principle in that if you are attempting to assist a boat that otherwise has right-of-way over you, you should not be penalized.

Note that a sailboard is "capsized" when any part of its sail is in the water; but for sailboats, it is the location of the masthead that determines when the boat is "capsized." Given that it is possible to "capsize" a boat without the very top of the mast ever touching the water, I interpret "masthead" to include the top few feet of the mast. Note also that rule 21 offers protection to a sailboat while she is regaining control after capsizing, whereas a sailboard must avoid other sailboards and boats once her sail or the competitor's body is lifted from the water.

Rule 22 - Interfering with Another Boat

Rule 22 states two situations in which a boat cannot interfere with other boats.

Rule 22.1

If reasonably possible, a boat not racing shall not interfere with a boat that is racing.

Rule 22.1 makes it clear that before you begin *racing* and once you are no longer *racing*, you cannot interfere with boats that are *racing*. "Interfere" means that you have adversely affected a boat's forward progress or maneuverability. The principle of the rule is that a boat that is not *racing* should not adversely affect a boat that is *racing*.

Note that there is no qualifier on "interfere with." (In the previous rules, rule 30 (Hindering Another Yacht) read, "...a yacht shall not seriously hinder a yacht that is *racing*.") Rule 22.1, therefore, is stricter in the sense that **any** "interference" will potentially break this rule. Particularly after *finishing*, boats need to be very careful where they sail so that their windshadow and physical presence do not hurt boats still *racing*. However, the rule's opening phrase ("If reasonably possible...") means that boats do not need to go to unreasonable measures to avoid interfering. If they are careful, they should have no problems.

Rule 22.2

A boat shall not deliberately interfere with a boat making penalty turns to delay her.

Rule 22.2 is intended to provide some protection to boats while they exonerate themselves. Notice there is no reference to a boat's *proper course* in the rule. Simply put, a boat can never intentionally interfere with another boat with the intent to delay her doing her turns, even if she can "justify" it by claiming she was sailing her *proper course*.

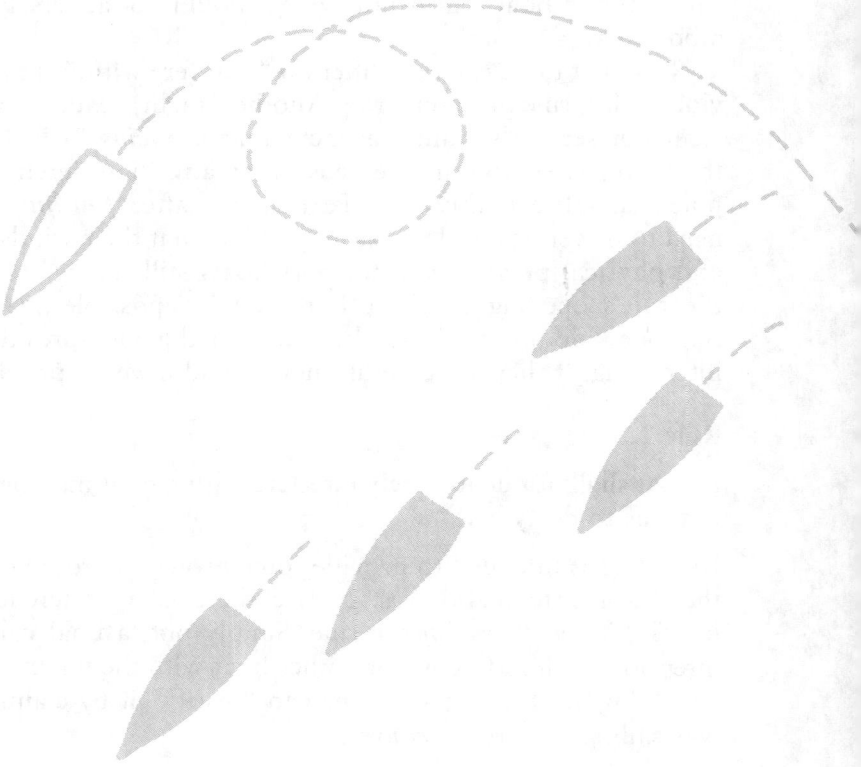

White got clear of
other boats, then
immediately did her
circle, so she's
exonerated for
touching the
mark.

10

CONDUCT OF A RACE
OTHER REQUIREMENTS
WHEN RACING
PART 3 - PART 4

Part 3 contains the rules that govern the conduct of a race (rules 25-36). Part 4 contains other rules that govern us while we are *racing* (rules 40-42). Most of the rules are straightforward and simple to understand. I'll focus on the four for which an explanation might be helpful: rule 31 (Touching a Mark), rule 42 (Propulsion), rule 44 (Penalties for Breaking Rules of Part 2) and rule 50 (Setting and Sheeting Sails).

RULE 31 - TOUCHING A MARK

Rule 31.1

While racing, a boat shall not touch a starting mark before starting, a mark that begins, bounds or ends the leg of the course on which she is sailing, or a finishing mark after finishing.

Rule 31.2

A boat that has broken rule 31.1 may, after getting well clear of other boats as soon as possible, take a penalty by promptly making one complete 360o turn including one tack and one gybe. When a boat takes the penalty after touching a finishing mark, she shall return completely to the course side of the line before finishing. However, if a boat has gained a significant advantage in the race or series by touching the mark she shall retire.

Rule 31.3

When a boat is wrongfully compelled by another boat to break rule 31.1, she shall be exonerated

(a) if the other boat acknowledges breaking a rule of Part 2 by taking a penalty or retiring immediately, or

(b) under rule 64.1(b), after successfully protesting another boat involved in the same incident.

Prior to the 1969-73 rules, if you touched a *mark* and it was your fault, you had to drop out of the race. In the 1968 Olympics in Mexico, the late Carl Van Duyne, sailing the Finn for the United States, saw the leech of his main touch the windward *mark* as he rounded it in first place. Despite the claims of the race officer at the *mark* who insisted that Carl did not touch the *mark*, Carl withdrew from the race. From this example and others, the rule writers saw the obvious over-severity of this penalty for the infraction, and changed the rule to permit sailors to take a penalty when they accidentally touch a *mark*.

Notice that the rule applies only while you are *racing*, which is the time from your preparatory signal until you have *finished* and cleared the finishing line and finishing *marks*. Also, if the starting line is set to leeward of the leeward *mark* on the first leg or the finishing line is set to windward of the windward *mark* on the last leg, that leeward or windward *mark* does not begin, bound or end that leg so there is no penalty for touching it. Otherwise, when you touch a starting or finishing *mark*, or any *mark* that begins, bounds or ends a leg on which you are sailing, you have broken rule 31.1.

When you've broken rule 31.1 and want to take a penalty, here's how the penalty works. You must first get well clear of other boats **as soon as possible** after touching the *mark* (not

White got clear of other boats, then immediately did her circle, so she's exonerated for touching the mark.

halfway down the leg!). Then, once clear you must **promptly** (i.e. without delay) make a 360-degree turn including one tack and one gybe. While you are making your turn, you have to *keep clear* of other boats (rule 20, Starting Errors; Penalty Turns; Moving Astern). Once you have completed your turn, you have completed your penalty and the rules of Section A apply to you again. Remember, if you acquire right of way over another boat after your turn, you have to initially give her *room* to *keep clear* under rule 15 (Acquiring Right of Way).

"If I hit one of the starting marks after the preparatory signal but well before the starting signal, when can I make my penalty turn?"

As soon as possible! The rule does not require you to wait until the starting signal. The rationale is that the penalty should fit the crime. Touching the *mark* three minutes before your start probably has little effect on anyone's race; likewise your penalty turn will be of little adverse consequence to you. However, touching it ten seconds from the start means that you are probably somewhere you shouldn't be and are likely adversely affecting the start for others; by the same token, making a penalty turn while others are *starting* will be of more negative consequence to you.

*"What do I do if I accidentally hit the finishing mark
after I've finished but before I've cleared the mark?"*

If you touch a finishing *mark* before you have cleared the finishing line and *marks* (i.e. while you are still *racing*), you can
make your penalty turn anywhere, but you then have to cross
the finishing line again from the course side of the line. The second time you cross will be your finishing place or time.

Notice the last sentence in rule 31.2, *"However, if a boat has
gained a significant advantage in the race or series by touching
the mark she shall retire."* This is clearly intended to deter boats
from sailing into situations where they calculate that they can hit
the *mark*, do a quick 360-degree turn and still come out well
ahead of where they would be had they not done so. One example is at a crowded windward *mark* with a long line of *starboard-tackers*, where there is just enough space for a *port-tacker* (P) to tack in to *leeward* of the *starboard-tackers* without
fouling them, but not enough space to also make it around the
mark without hitting it. P could probably come out ahead by
hitting the *mark* and doing a quick "360" as opposed to ducking the long line of *starboard-tackers*, but this wouldn't be fair;
hence the rule against it in 31.2.

It is possible that if a boat that has unfairly passed six boats
were to subsequently slow down and let those six boats pass her
by, she wouldn't be found later by a protest committee to have
broken this rule.

*"What happens when I'm forced to touch a mark by
another boat that was required to keep clear of me or give
me room?"*

Whenever you touch a *mark*, you have two options:

1) If you think it was your own fault that you touched the *mark*,
you can get clear of other boats and take your penalty as
described in rule 31.2; or

2) If you believe another boat wrongfully compelled you to hit
the *mark*, you do not have to take a penalty. But you must
protest the other boat by hailing and flying your flag at the first
reasonable opportunity and lodging a valid written protest,

unless the other boat acknowledges breaking a rule of Part 2 by taking a voluntary penalty ("720" or Scoring Penalty, etc. under rule 44, Penalties for Breaking Rules of Part 2) or **immediately** retiring from the race. Notice that if you don't protest and the other boat continues in the race without taking a penalty, and then decides to retire, you are not exonerated! To be safe, always immediately hail "Protest" and fly your flag; you can always take it down if the other boat correctly acknowledges fault.

If you do protest and the protest committee decides that in fact it was the other boat's Part 2 rule breach that compelled you to touch the *mark*, they will DSQ the other boat and exonerate you under rule 64.1(b) (Penalties and Exoneration).

"Does it count if just my head brushes against the mark?"

Absolutely yes. In fact, if you have a late spinnaker take-down and your spinnaker sheet trails behind the boat and rubs against the mark after you're already around and a boat-length away from it, you still have to take your penalty. ISAF Case 153 sums it up, "A boat touches a mark within the meaning of rule 31 when any part of her hull, crew or equipment comes in contact with the mark. The fact that her equipment touches the mark because she has maneuvering or sail-handling difficulties does not excuse her breach."

"If I get the mark's anchor line caught on my centerboard but quickly raise my board and clear the line before I touch the mark, have I hit the mark? What happens when I'm not so quick and the mark is dragged in and touches my boat?"

Remember that the anchor line of a *mark* is **not** part of the *mark* (see the Definition *Mark*). So on a race committee boat with a high bow, where fifteen feet of anchor line may be above the water, the *mark* begins at the bow of the boat. The same is true when a *mark's* anchor line is partially or wholly submerged. In both cases, there is no penalty for touching the line. However, if touching its anchor line causes the *mark* to be drawn against your boat, you have touched the *mark* and must do a 360-degree turn penalty or protest. US SAILING Appeal 59 reads, "If, however, fouling its anchor line causes the mark to be drawn against a boat, the mark has been touched."

"What if I foul another boat and hit a mark in the same incident?"

Good question. Rule 44.4(a) (Penalties for Breaking Rules of Part 2, Limits on Penalties) says, *"When a boat intends to take a penalty as provided in rule 44.1 and in the same incident has touched a **mark**, she need not take the penalty provided in rule 31.2."* Therefore, when a 720-degree Turns Penalty or a Scoring Penalty under rule 44 is available, and you choose to accept that penalty, you do not have to also do a 360-degree turn penalty for hitting the *mark*.

SPECIAL SAILBOARD RULE

(Rule B3, Conduct of a Race)

Rule 31 is changed to: 'A competitor shall not hold on to a starting mark.'

Notice that, other than the prohibition against holding onto the starting *mark*, there is no rule 31 for boardsailing. This means that when sailboard racing, it is legal to touch the *marks*! Just remember that you still must leave them on the correct side (rule 28.1, Sailing the Course).

RULE 42 PROPULSION

Rule 42.1 - Basic Rule

Except when permitted in rule 42.3 or rule 45, a boat shall compete by using only the wind and water to increase, maintain or decrease her speed. Her crew may adjust the trim of sails and hull, and perform other acts of seamanship, but shall not otherwise move their bodies to propel the boat.

Rule 42 is the "pumping, rocking, ooching, sculling" rule. The rule specifically tells sailors how they can, and cannot, propel their boats in a sailboat race. The principle behind rule 42 is simple: the rule writers (and most sailors themselves) want people to race their sailboats by sailing them (i.e. using the natural wind) as opposed to by propelling or slowing them in other ways. If you are a bit too early for a start, it is more of a sport if you have to slow down using your sails and rudder than if you could just stick your arms in the water and backpaddle; just as it's more challenging and fun to try to ride the waves on a windy reach as opposed to handing all the sheets to Igor and telling him to "pump" nonstop to the leeward *mark*.

Compliance with this rule continues to be a major problem facing the sport. In my opinion, the rule clearly states what is permitted and what is prohibited. After an explanation of the rule, I will discuss the more central issue of competitor self-control and self-policing.

Rule 42.1 clearly states the basic premise: *"A boat shall compete by using only the wind and water to increase, maintain or decrease her speed. Her crew may adjust the trim of sails and hull, and perform other acts of seamanship, but shall not otherwise move their bodies to propel the boat."* This is the way sailboats are to be raced; i.e. they can be powered only by the natural action of the wind and water. The last phrase in the rule serves to prohibit any crew action that **in and of itself** propels the boat (paddling is an obvious example), and serves to prohibit any newly discovered kinetic technique not listed in rule 42.2. Note that the term "crew" refers to **all sailors on board**, including the helmsman.

Notice that it is just as illegal to slow yourself down ("decrease speed") unnaturally as it is to propel yourself. So if you're early for a start or trapped on the outside of a crowd at a *mark*, you can't stick your leg in the water to slow down. Likewise, if you luff a boat before the start and hit them, you can't hang onto them to slow yourself down so you're not early. However, there are legal ways to slow yourself down using the natural action of the wind and water. One is to physically hold the boom out so the wind pushes against the sail; another is to turn the rudder hard over against the flow of the water provided it is not done repeatedly back and forth (see the discussion of "sculling" in rule 42.2(d)). (See US SAILING Appeal 132.)

Note also that a boat can be penalized for breaking rule 42 only while she is *racing* (see preamble to Part 4). ISAF Case 144 says, "During the period in which the...boat was racing she was using wind and water as sources of power as required by rule 42.1. Her motion resulted from momentum created by engine power that propelled her before she began racing. Nothing in the rule requires that a boat be in any particular state of motion or non-motion when she begins racing." Likewise, in light air and adverse current, a boat can just get its bow across the finish line (thereby *finishing*), drift backward, and, when clear of the finishing line and finishing *marks* (i.e., no longer *racing*), turn on her engine and power out of the course area.

There are some common sense exceptions built into rule 42 for safety reasons.

Rule 42.3(c) Any means of propulsion may be used to help a person or another vessel in danger.

Rule 42.3(d) To get clear after grounding or colliding with another boat or object, a boat may use force applied by the crew of either boat and any equipment other than a propulsion engine.

These reinforce the overriding safety principle that you should get to a boat or person's rescue as fast as you can using any means available, including paddling, rocking or an engine when you have one. Obviously, this is not intended to be misused as a deceitful way to advance along the race course. ISAF Case 38 and the discussion of rule 1.1 (Safety, Helping Those in Danger) are clear as to the responsibility all racing sailors have, and when and how a boat that renders assistance should be compensated.

Also, when you go aground or hit another boat, you may use whatever means of force is necessary to clear yourself, except that you can't use your engine to propel yourself. Note that you can use the power from your engine to run a winch or windlass, etc. if necessary.

"Can I anchor?"

Yes. Rule 45 (Hauling Out; Making Fast; Anchoring) states, "*[A boat] may anchor or the crew may stand on the bottom.*" Rule 42.1 specifically permits the actions described in rule 45. Generally boats anchor either as a safety measure or to decrease the speed at which they are moving away from their destination (as in adverse current). Note that a means of anchoring is the crew standing on the bottom. Of course if that crew starts walking the boat around, rule 42 is infringed.

ISAF Case 9 says, "Recovering an anchor, whether it was lowered or thrown forward, so as to gather way over the ground breaks rule 42.1." The point is clear: anchoring should be a means of keeping you where you are, and not a means of advancing yourself along the race course. Clearly, if you throw your anchor forward and then recover the anchor, you will be "pulling yourself" forward past where you were when you threw out the anchor. Therefore, when *racing* the anchor must be dropped **straight down** to be safe. Likewise, when you pull the anchor back up, you can't generate momentum that will cause the boat to move **past** the point where the anchor was on the ground, i.e. where it was dropped.

"Now what about the actions listed in rule 42.2; are they always prohibited, or only when they are actually capable of propelling the boat?"

Rule 42.2 lists five specific types of actions which are always prohibited, regardless of whether they are capable of propelling the boat or not. This makes it easier for sailors to know what they can't do, and for judges to administer the rule on the water and in protest hearings. The five are the major "offenses" and are listed in order of perceived frequency of use (or abuse!).

Rule 42.2 - Prohibited Actions

Without limiting the application of rule 42.1, these actions are prohibited:

(a) **pumping: repeated fanning of any sail either by trimming and releasing the sail or by vertical or athwartships body movement;**

(b) rocking: repeated rolling of the boat, induced either by body movement or adjustment of the sails or centreboard, that does not facilitate steering;

(c) ooching: sudden forward body movement, stopped abruptly;

(d) sculling: repeated movement of the helm not necessary for steering;

(e) repeated tacks or gybes unrelated to changes in the wind or to tactical considerations.

Let me reemphasize: if you do **any** of these above-listed actions, you have broken rule 42.2. It does not matter whether the action actually propelled the boat, or even if it was capable of propelling the boat! Therefore, it applies to boats of all sizes. Note that class rules and sailing instructions can change rule 42, including some of the prohibitions in rule 42.2 (see rule 86, Rule Changes).

To understand these descriptions, notice the use of the word "repeated" throughout, indicating that for the actions to be illegal they must continue nonstop for an extended period of time or for more than just one movement. "Ooching" is the only action that involves a singular movement.

(a) PUMPING: for a sail to be "pumped," it must be trimmed and then released. When a sail is pumped "repeatedly" in short succession, it will look like the sail is being "fanned." This is illegal. This can be done using the sheets, or by using body motions. Bouncing up and down on the rail is an example of "vertical" movement; and crossing the boat quickly from side to side is "athwartships" movement. In a small boat with a flexible mast, bouncing can "pump" the top of the sail. Likewise, movement side to side will commonly cause the angle of heel to change, which in turn can act to "pump" the sail. These means of "pumping" are also illegal. Rule 42.3(b) allows limited "pumping" in certain conditions.

This rule is not designed to inhibit good sailing techniques. On a puffy windy day, the mainsail can be played in and out constantly to keep the boat flat, provided it doesn't become a "fanning" action. Similarly, downwind, the spinnaker sheet can be constantly played in response to changes in apparent wind.

(b) ROCKING: Your boat is "rocking" when it is rolling back and forth. You may be intentionally doing it with your body, or you may have simply encouraged it by pulling your centerboard up, letting your boom way out, and then starting the action like a pendulum. It doesn't matter whether your body is moving. If your boat is rhythmically rolling back and forth, it's "rocking," and that is illegal at all times. Obviously, waves themselves will cause the boat to toss about. You do not have to run all over the boat counteracting every wave action. If you've ever watched a fleet of boats on a broad reach or run, you know that they all are being tossed in a similar way. If one boat is being intentionally "rocked," she will stand out instantly as being different from the others.

Notice that the rule permits "rolling" the boat to facilitate steering. For instance, going down a wavy reach it is legal to heel the boat to leeward to head up over a wave, then heel it to windward to steer down the backside, etc. Notice also that on a run most boats sail faster when heeled to windward, and the crew can position their weight to do this, provided the boat doesn't start "rocking" back and forth as a result.

(c) OOCHING: "Ooching" is a "sudden forward body movement, stopped abruptly." The key to "ooching" is that it is forward motion, it is sudden, and it is stopped abruptly. Even just one "ooch" is illegal. Pushing or pulling on the mast or shrouds (forward hand movements), slamming forward on the front of the cockpit, mast shrouds or forestay, and subtle abrupt forward motions with the rear or feet are all examples of "ooching" and are illegal at all times.

(d) SCULLING: "Sculling" is "repeated movement of the helm not necessary for steering." Notice there is no reference to "forceful" or to "crossing the centerline." Simply put, you can not "wiggle" your tiller unless you are attempting to steer the boat.

There are two common situations in which repeated movement of the helm is often required to help steer a boat. One is when you are trying to bear off on a broad reach in heavy air when about to broach and forcefully moving the helm back and forth can help prevent the rudder from "stalling," thereby increasing steerageway; and the second is in very light winds in order just to turn the boat.

(e) REPEATED TACKS OR GYBES UNRELATED TO CHANGES IN THE WIND OR TO TACTICAL CONSIDERATIONS: You cannot repeatedly tack or gybe back and forth in quick succession unless you can justify your maneuvers based on changes in the wind (windshifts, etc.) or tactical considerations (covering another boat, etc.). Notice, you can tack or gybe for any reason you want; you just can't do it "repeatedly" without the specific reasons listed in this rule.

"Are there any exceptions to the prohibitions in rule 42.2?"

Yes. They are in rule 42.3, Exceptions

42.3 - Exceptions

(a) A boat's crew may move their bodies to exaggerate the rolling that facilitates steering the boat through a tack or a gybe, provided that, just after the tack or gybe is completed, the boat's speed is not greater than it would have been in the absence of the tack or gybe.

(b) Except on a beat to windward, when surfing (rapidly accelerating down the leeward side of a wave) or planing is possible, the boat's crew may pull the sheet and the guy controlling any sail in order to initiate surfing or planing, but only once for each wave or gust of wind.

"So it is legal to roll-tack?"

Absolutely yes. Rule 42.3(a) specifically permits you to exaggerate the rolling provided it helps you steer the boat onto the new *tack*, and provided you don't come out of your tack going faster than just before you began it. Therefore, you can begin with a heel to *leeward* to begin the boat heading up. Then, as the boat is at or near head to wind, you can roll the boat hard to the new *leeward* side to help "pivot" the boat onto its new close-hauled course. Finally, you can bring the boat upright to its close-hauled course.

The most important thing is that once the boat is brought up from its roll, the mast cannot make a major dip to *leeward* and back up again. This second "pump," which serves to accelerate the boat rather than steer it, is illegal.

"Does rule 42.3(b) permit one pump of each sail per wave?"

Rule 42.3(b) permits "pumping" to initiate surfing or planing. The rule permits one "pump" for each sail (main, spinnaker and jib if desired, though pumping the jib is generally slow) to try to catch a wave or hop up on a plane. However, if the "pump" on the main gets the boat surfing, a subsequent "pump" on the spinnaker sheet would not be legal. If the main and spinnaker were "pumped" simultaneously, there would be no problem.

Notice that you must be just ready to launch down the leeward face of the wave. You can't "pump" up the windward side of the wave claiming it will get you over the top and down the leeward side faster. A "planing" boat will be lifted partly out of the water by its own bow wave, and its stern wave will disappear. Visually it will look like the boat is skimming across the surface of the water. The phrase "except on a beat to windward" prohibits you from "pumping" upwind at all for any reason.

Notice also that you can only "pump" using the sheet or guy controlling the sail. You cannot therefore "pump" using the vang or a special "pumping" line.

"Is it true I can never ooch?"

That's right. Rule 42.3 makes no exception for ooching.

"Why is rule 42.3(b) so restrictive, and can the rule ever be made more permissive?"

The rule writers have taken this step to reduce the strength factor required to race sailboats successfully, and to ensure that the sport remains a sailing contest. Notice that the class rules or sailing instructions can make this rule more permissive by modifying it with a specific reference to it (rule 86, Rule Changes). Therefore a class can permit more than one pump per wave or ooching, etc. This is an issue all the members of each class should thoroughly discuss.

"I heard that a protest committee can throw me out under rule 42 without a hearing; and that a DSQ under rule 42 can't be used as a 'throwout' race; is this true?"

Rule 67 (Rule 42 and Hearing Requirement) states, *"When so stated in the sailing instructions, the protest committee may penalize without a hearing a boat that has broken rule 42, provided that a member of the committee or its designated observer has seen the incident. A boat so penalized shall be informed by notification in the race results."* Notice that the protest committee can only DSQ you without a hearing **if the sailing instructions give them that permission.** Also, if you are DSQ'd without a hearing and feel you did not break rule 42, you can request redress under rule 62.1(a) (Redress) which entitles you to a hearing under rule 63.1 (Hearings, Requirement for a Hearing).

Furthermore, rule A1.3 (Scores Not Discardable) prevents a boat from "dropping" a DSQ under rule 42 when the protest committee, acting under rule 67, has penalized the boat without a hearing. Note, however, that the US SAILING prescription to this rule states that this does not apply in the U.S.

"Now I understand what rule 42 allows and doesn't allow; but what do I do when another competitor starts to rock or pump by me?"

Most active racers believe that the rule itself is clear enough and is not the cause of the problem. The real problem is the enforcement of the rule. There are several extreme positions, and there have been many creative attempts made at resolving this issue. Some say the enforcement should be left completely up to judges around the course; i.e. flood the course with referees. Others argue that it is impractical to put that many judges on the course, and that because competitors will never police themselves, the rule itself should be abolished altogether and the race committees given the authority to proclaim before a race that either "anything" or "nothing" goes.

Fortunately, the majority of us believe that the racing is best when the sailors themselves have the responsibility to sail within the rules. We have seen too many regattas with either too few judges or poorly qualified ones. More to the point, we like the concept of competitor-enforced rules which makes our sport unique from almost all others.

But it takes only a few people in each fleet to ruin it for the rest. If some decide that doing well in the race by cheating is okay, and they start pumping and sculling off the starting line and rocking downwind, it puts the other sailors in a very awkward position. Either they can join in, or warn and then protest the other boat, or do nothing. To join in, they have to admit that the problem is not worth their effort to fight it. To do nothing is frustrating because those sailors will feel that not only are they being left behind, but that nothing is being done to enforce the rule.

I strongly recommend these three steps when a boat near you is illegally propelling herself: 1) first warn the other boat; 2) then get the attention of some other boats nearby with the hopes that they'll say something too; and 3) then protest if the illegal actions continue. You are not being the "bad guy" for simply doing what you'd do if a *port-tacker* hit you when you were on *starboard-tack*. It is destructive to the racing when people feel they can get away with cheating; and they will continue to only get worse if no one calls them on it.

In the hearing the protest committee should (a) find out exactly what the wind and wave conditions were; (b) discuss what the sailing characteristics of the boat are from their shared experiences, competitors' testimony and expert witnesses when useful; and (c) determine what the exact actions of the protestee were. Witnesses are useful to everyone and are desired. Remember, it is permissible for members of the protest committee to also be the protestor, but they must be sure to give their entire testimony with evidence while all the *parties* to the hearing are present and able to ask questions and otherwise respond. (See rule 60, Right to Protest and Request Redress; rule 63.3, Right to be Present; and rule 63.6, Taking Evidence and Finding Facts.)

The bottom line to the rule 42 issue is that everyone who

races should make the effort to understand exactly what the rule does and does not allow, and then sail within the rule's limits. The rule is not that complex to understand, and my guess is that most sailors who have studied it have a good sense of what is right and wrong. Where it breaks down is when sailors intentionally ignore the rule for their own personal gratification. All fleets of sailors should talk about this issue.

SPECIAL SAILBOARD RULE RELATING TO RULE 42

Rule B4.1 - Part 4-Other Requirements When Racing

Rule 42 is changed to: 'A sailboard shall be propelled only by the action of the wind on the sail, by the action of the water on the hull and by the unassisted actions of the competitor.'

For sailboard racing, the rule writers have removed any prohibition on how the sailors use their bodies to propel their sailboards. This is a "black and white" step that removes any need to worry about what is "natural sailing motion" and what is "illegal kinetics."

Remember that rule B3 (Part 3-Conduct of a Race) does not permit sailboard sailors to hold onto starting *marks*.

Rule 44 - PENALTIES FOR BREAKING RULES OF PART 2

Rule 44.1 - Taking a Penalty

A boat that may have broken a rule of Part 2 while racing may take a penalty at the time of the incident. Her penalty shall be a 720 Turns Penalty unless the sailing instructions specify the use of the Scoring Penalty or some other penalty. However, if she caused serious damage or gained a significant advantage in the race or series by her breach she shall retire.

Rule 44.1 states that if you think you may have broken a rule of Part 2 while *racing*, you can **always** take a voluntary penalty at the time of the incident. This is sensible. Mistakes happen, and there should be a consequence for breaking a rule; but forcing sailors to retire and sail in for a minor infraction is not in balance with the great effort, time and expense that goes into participating in a race.

Rule 44.1 states that the voluntary penalty is the "720" (described below) unless the sailing instructions specify the use of some other penalty. Another common penalty is the Scoring Penalty, often known as the "percentage penalty." This is clearly described in rule 44.3 (Scoring Penalty) and won't be described in this book.

Note that even a right-of-way boat can need to take a penalty. If a right-of-way boat fails to avoid contact with another boat when it was reasonably possible for her to do so, she breaks rule 14 (Avoiding Contact). If damage results from the contact, she is liable to being penalized and can do a "720" to absolve herself.

Notice, however, that if any boat causes "serious damage" or gains a "significant advantage" in the race or series by her breach, **she must retire**; i.e. she cannot absolve herself by taking a voluntary penalty. This is a clear reminder to all competitors, whether holding the right of way or not, to be careful and sportsmanlike.

"Before going on, could you discuss the term 'serious damage?'"

Sure. Understand, however, that this is one of those terms that is impossible to define. I will discuss what, in my opinion, are the important considerations based on the rule, the appeals, the dictionary and my interpretation.

The dictionary offers the following definitions:

"serious:"   having significant or dangerous possible consequences, not trifling or inconsequential.

"damage:"   harm or injury impairing the value or usefulness of something, or the health or normal function of a person.

The three primary considerations are:
1) what was the extent of the damage; i.e. how much damage or injury was done, did the damage or injury require immediate repair or medical attention to prevent further damage or injury, what was the cost of the repair or medical attention, and what affect did the damage or injury have on the boat in future races.

2) was it feasible or prudent for the boat to continue in the race; and

3) did the damage markedly affect the boat's speed, performance or maneuverability; i.e. did the damage materially prejudice her finishing place in the race?

Certainly, if the damage causes the boat to discontinue the race, it is "serious," including when the "damage" is an injury to a person on board. If the boat can safely continue in the race and loses no finishing places as a direct result of the damage, and the nature and cost of any necessary repair isn't too high, the damage is not "serious." (Note that it is most impossible to put a price tag on "serious"; that will have to be decided by the protest committee after considering all the relevant factors.)

If the damage is a deep scratch that penetrates the fiberglass, thereby requiring immediate repair after the race so that further damage doesn't result or so that the future speed, performance or maneuverability of the boat isn't affected, that damage would begin to fall into the "serious" category. If the extent of the repair were such that it could be handled that evening by the sailors involved with a minimum of hassle and expense, I would be inclined to rule it not "serious." But if the repair required more professional work and became a more costly and time-consuming affair, I would be more inclined to rule it "serious." If, however, the damage is a twelve-inch surface scratch in the gelcoat, which does not affect the overall speed, performance or maneuverability of the boat, I would not be as inclined to rule it "serious."

If the damage is a broken boom near the finish and the boat loses no places but cannot repair or replace the boom before the second race of that day, I'd consider the damage to be "serious"; but if the damage was to something that could normally be repaired or replaced on the water, such as a bent guyhook, the damage would not be "serious."

"Thanks! Now how do I take a "720" Turns Penalty?"

Rule 44.2 - 720° Turns Penalty
After getting well clear of other boats as soon after the incident

as possible, a boat takes a 720° Turns Penalty by promptly making two complete 360° turns (720°) in the same direction, including two tacks and two gybes. When a boat takes the penalty at or near the finishing line, she shall return completely to the course side of the line before *finishing*.

When you want to do a "720," you must first get well clear of other boats **as soon as possible** after the incident (not halfway down the leg!). Remember that while you are getting clear you still have all your Section A rights; i.e. your penalty does not begin until you clearly begin making your turns (rule 20, Starting Errors; Penalty Turns; Moving Astern).

Once you are clear, you must **promptly** (i.e. without delay) make two complete 360-degree turns in the same direction, including one tack and one gybe. Notice that you have to do one turn immediately after the other, though it is generally acceptable to build enough speed after the first circle to be able to sail efficiently through the second one. While you are making your turns, you have to *keep clear* of other boats (rule 20).

Once you have completed your turns, you have completed your penalty and the rules of Section A apply to you again. Remember, if you acquire right of way over another boat after your second turn, you have to initially give her *room* to *keep clear* under rule 15 (Acquiring Right of Way).

Note that if you break a rule before the starting signal, you can do your "720" immediately; i.e. you don't have to wait until after the starting signal. As in touching a *mark*, the rationale is that the penalty should fit the crime. Breaking a rule three minutes before your start probably has little effect on anyone's race; likewise your "720" will be of little adverse consequence to you. However, breaking a rule ten seconds from the start means that you are probably somewhere you shouldn't be and are likely adversely affecting the start for others; by the same token, doing a "720" while others are *starting* will be of more negative consequence to you.

If you break a rule near the finishing line, you can do your "720" anywhere, but you then have to cross the finishing line again from the course side of the line. The second time you cross will be your finishing place or time.

Rule 44.4 - Limits on Penalties

(a) When a boat intends to take a penalty as provided in rule 44.1 and in the same incident has touched a *mark*, she need not take the penalty provided in rule 31.2.

(b) A boat that takes a penalty shall not be penalized further with respect to the same incident unless she failed to retire when rule 44.1 required her to do so.

These limits are very straightforward. In rule 44.4(a), the rule writers are being compassionate saying, "You know you got yourself in trouble; do your two circles for fouling the other boat but there's no need to do a third circle!"

Rule 44.4(b) states that a boat can only be penalized once per incident, regardless of how many rules she may have broken in that incident. Therefore, when a give-way boat breaks rule 10 (On Opposite Tacks) and fails to avoid a collision, thereby breaking rule 14 (Avoiding Contact), she need only do one "720." US SAILING Appeal 295 discusses the question of when two occurrences are considered one or two incidents, saying in essence that the test is whether the second occurrence was the inevitable result of the first.

"If I'm not sure who's right, can I do a '720' and still protest the other boat, or am I admitting guilt by doing my '720?'"

Excellent question. You can definitely protest the other boat and your "720" is not an admission of guilt. Rule 44.1 carefully says, "A boat that **may** (emphasis added) have broken a rule...may take a penalty." Furthermore, the US SAILING prescription to rule 68 (Damages) says, "*A boat that...accepts a penalty does not, by that action alone, admit liability for damages.*" Let's say you do a "720" and protest and that the other boat did neither. If the protest committee finds that the other boat was wrong in your incident, she will be disqualified. If the protest committee decides that you actually were wrong, you can't be further penalized because you already took a voluntary penalty (rule 44.4(b)). Therefore, you can view your "720" as "insurance" against further penalty in an incident where you're not 100% certain how the protest committee will decide it.

RULE 50   SETTING AND SHEETING SAILS

Rule 50.1- Changing Sails
When headsails or spinnakers are being changed, a replacing sail may be fully set and trimmed before the replaced sail is lowered. However, only one mainsail and, except when changing, only one spinnaker shall be carried set at a time.

Rule 50.2 - Spinnaker Poles, Whisker Poles
Only one spinnaker pole or whisker pole shall be used at a time except when gybing. When in use, it shall be attached to the foremost mast.

Rule 50.3 - Use of Outriggers
(a) No sail shall be sheeted over or through an outrigger, except as permitted in rule 50.3(b). An outrigger is any fitting or other device so placed that it could exert outward pressure on a sheet or sail at a point from which, with the boat upright, a vertical line would fall outside the hull or deck planking. For the purpose of this rule, bulwarks, rails and rubbing strakes are not part of the hull or deck planking and the following are not outriggers: a bowsprit used to secure the tack of a working sail, a bumkin used to sheet the boom of a working sail, or a boom of a boomed headsail that requires no adjustment when tacking.

(b) (1) Any sail may be sheeted to or led above a boom that is regularly used for a working sail and is permanently attached to the mast from which the head of the working sail is set.

(2) A headsail may be sheeted or attached at its clew to a spinnaker pole or whisker pole, provided that a spinnaker is not set.

50.4 - Headsails

The difference between a headsail and a spinnaker is that the mid-girth of a headsail, measured from the mid-points of its luff and leech, does not exceed 50% of the length of its foot, and no other intermediate girth exceeds a percentage similarly proportional to its distance from the head of the sail. A sail tacked down behind the foremost mast is not a headsail.

Note that this rule does not require that a spinnaker pole be used at all when flying a spinnaker! The only pole requirements are in rule 50.2. In other words, you can only use one pole at a time (except that you can use two when gybing); and when it is "in use," i.e. projecting the spinnaker or headsail outboard, it must be attached to the mast.

With no requirement to use a pole, boats are free to do "gybe-sets" and "floater-drops." In both of these maneuvers, the spinnaker is set and drawing with no pole attached. In other words, a boat can legally gybe around the windward *mark*, set her spinnaker, fill it, and sail on down the leg with no pole. And likewise, when coming into a leeward *mark*, a boat can legally remove her pole and sail for as long as she chooses before lowering her spinnaker. However, when the pole is down, note that rule 49.2 (Crew Position) forbids competitors from leaning their torsos out over the lifelines "except briefly to perform a necessary task." Though a judgment call by the protest committee, crews leaning out to hold the guy away from the boat when the pole has been lowered in the final approach to the leeward *mark* should be OK as this is normally a brief time period and it is necessary to do in order to keep the guy away from the boat. (See US SAILING Appeal 306.)

Also note that there is no requirement that the tack of the spinnaker be in "close proximity" to the outboard end of the spinnaker pole. The rationale is that it is generally faster to have the tack close to the outboard end, such that why penalize a boat if she chooses not to do so.

Note that rule 86.1(c) (Rule Changes) permits class rules to alter this rule.

"I see a lot of boats flying asymmetrical spinnakers from bowsprits; I assume this is legal?"

Yes. Rule 50.3(a) specifically states, "For the purpose of this rule...the following are not outriggers: a bowsprit used to secure the tack of a working sail..." ISAF Case 164 says that rule 50.3 is not broken "...assuming that the bowsprit is used to secure the tack (the windward corner) of the spinnaker or as a lead for a line attached to the tack. Rule 50.3 prohibits sheeting a spinnaker with an outrigger; e.g. controlling the clew (the leeward corner) with a sheet led through a bowsprit, because a bowsprit is an outrigger."

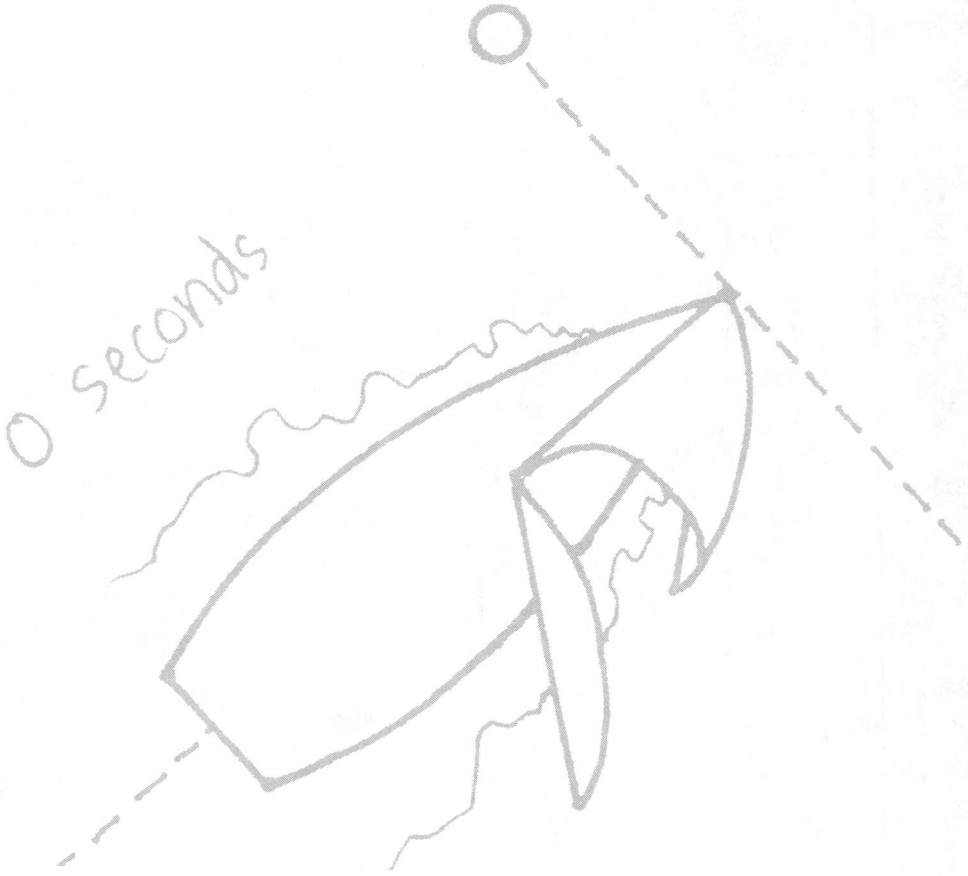

0 seconds

11

PROTESTS, HEARINGS, MISCONDUCT AND APPEALS

PART 5

Part 5 contains all the rules governing who can protest, how to protest, how to ask for redress, how and when a protest hearing should be run, what penalties can be applied and how to appeal (rules 60-71). It is divided into four sections: Section A, Protests; Section B, Hearings and Decisions; Section C, Gross Misconduct; and Section D, Appeals. I will focus on the Section A rules governing *protests* by boats.

Remember that a *protest* is defined as *"An allegation by a boat, a race committee or a protest committee that a boat has broken a **rule**."* A *protest*, therefore, is merely a means of bringing a *rules* issue to a hearing after the race where the sailors involved and the members of the protest committee can review the incident and decide how the *rules* apply. Our sport is premised on competitors doing just that when there is an incident in which neither boat acknowledges being in the wrong. *Protests* that are the result of honest differences of opinions on the *rules* or observations of the incident should never have a negative taint to them. Competitor enforcement of the *rules* is the tradition of our sport, and when the *rules* are not followed, or their application is in question, we owe it to our fellow competitors, for the quality and fairness of the racing, to protest.

Section A - PROTESTS

Rule 60 - RIGHT TO PROTEST AND REQUEST REDRESS

Rule 60.1

A boat may

(a) **protest another boat, but not for an alleged breach of a rule of Part 2 unless she was involved in or saw the incident; or**

(b) **request redress.**

Any boat that thinks another boat may have broken a *rule* can protest. This can occur during a race, or before or after a race; and it can involve a boat in the same race or one in a different race. Note, however, that the use of the word "may" in rule 60.1 clarifies that it is a boat's **choice** as to whether or not she protests. A boat cannot be penalized for choosing not to protest.

If you want to protest another boat for breaking a rule of Part 2 (When Boats Meet), you must have been directly involved in the incident or have seen it happen yourself. A *protest* involving a Part 2 rule cannot be initiated by you when you learn about the incident from a "report" by someone else.

"I heard that there are no more 'third-party protests' allowed; is this true?"

NO! If you witness an incident in which you think that at least one of the boats broke a rule of Part 2, you can protest. It doesn't matter if they have contact or not. In this case you are the "third party." What is different is that under the previous rule 33 (Contact between Yachts Racing), the protest committee would be forced to disqualify both of the boats in the incident if they had contact and neither took a penalty or protested. That rule has been deleted. Now, the protest committee will simply call a hearing based on your *protest*, find the facts about what happened in the incident, and penalize just the boat that broke a rule, if any. In other words, under the previous rules a right-of-way boat could be disqualified in an incident in which she had contact and neither boat took a penalty or protested; under these rules, she cannot be.

Rule 61 - PROTEST REQUIREMENTS

Rule 61.1 - Informing the Protestee

(a) A boat intending to protest because of an incident occurring in the racing area that she is aware of shall hail 'Protest' and conspicuously display a red flag at the first reasonable opportunity for each. She shall display the flag either until she finishes or retires, or, if the incident occurs near the finishing line, until the race committee acknowledges seeing her flag. In all other cases she shall inform the other boat as soon as reasonably possible.

When you are aware of an incident as it occurs in the racing area and you want to protest, you have to do two things. If you do not correctly do these two things, your *protest* will not be valid and no hearing on the incident should occur. You must hail the word "Protest" and conspicuously display a red flag at the first reasonable opportunity **for each**.

THE HAIL

Note that you must use the actual word "Protest." Telling another boat to "do your '720!'" does not satisfy this rule. The purpose of the requirement is to be sure that the other boat clearly knows you intend to protest her. As with other mandatory hails in the rules, the hail should be loud and clear, and it should be unambiguous as to which boat is being protested. When there could be confusion, I strongly suggest including in the hail the boat's number or name, or the person's name if you know it.

The hail must be made at the first reasonable opportunity after you become aware of the incident. Though some may exist, it is very difficult to imagine a situation in which the first reasonable opportunity to say the word "Protest" isn't **immediately**. Remember that you can always decide not to go through with a protest, including for the reasons that you just aren't sure the other boat broke a rule or who it was that fouled you. But if you don't say the word "Protest" at the time of the incident, you lose the opportunity to protest that incident. Therefore, it is always prudent to simply say "Protest" immediately. (See US SAILING Appeal 286.)

If you intend to protest because of an incident that either occurred in the racing area without you being aware of it, or did not occur in the racing area, you do not need to say the word "Protest," but you do need to inform the other boat of your intent to protest as soon as is reasonably possible after becoming aware of the incident. The purpose of this rule is to be sure that boats intending to protest make every prompt and reasonable effort to go tell the other boat that a *protest* will be lodged so that all the boats involved can be prepared and present for the hearing.

THE FLAG

Now let's look at the flag requirements. When you are aware of an incident as it occurs in the racing area and want to protest because of it, you must conspicuously display a red flag at the first reasonable opportunity. Again, the purpose of the requirement is to provide a visual signal to the other boat that you intend to protest her. The Appeals are loud and clear throughout that if you are required to fly a flag and do not, then the protest committee cannot accept your *protest*. Notice that even if the incident involves a breach of a class rule or sailing instructions, etc., you must display your flag. (See rule 63.5, Validity of the Protest, ISAF Cases 88 and 168 and US SAILING Appeal 298.)

On the other hand, if you intend to protest because of an incident that either occurred in the racing area without you being aware of it, or did not occur in the racing area, you do not need to display a flag. Remember that you do need to inform the competitor that you intend to protest as soon as reasonably possible after becoming aware of the incident.

Note that Sailboard sailors are not required to display a flag at all, but they must hail "Protest" at the time of the incident and tell the race committee of their intention to protest when they finish (rule B5). Similarly, the Inter-Collegiate Yacht Racing

Association (ICYRA) waives the flag requirement and simply requires hailing the word "Protest" in intercollegiate racing (see the ICYRA Procedural Rules).

"Just how quickly do I need to get my flag up?"

Rule 61.1(a) requires that it be displayed "at the first reasonable opportunity." My best advice is that the "first reasonable opportunity" is normally **immediately** after the incident. Remember that the purpose of the rule is to provide a visual signal to the other boat, and to any other boats in the incident or vicinity, that you intend to protest because of **that** incident. Any delay at all only raises the likelihood that the boat being protested won't be aware of that fact, or that it won't be clear for which incident your flag is being displayed.

The timeliness of the flag issue is the cause of some acrimony in our sport, generally arising when a boat's protest is refused because the protest committee decides that her flag was not displayed soon enough after the incident. Often it is suggested that the flag requirement is less important when the other boat is fully aware of the protesting boat's intent to protest, e.g. after a collision and an immediate hail of "Protest." I agree that it is frustrating when a *protest* is refused on a technicality rather than resolving the rules issue contained in the *protest*. But the *rules* are carefully worded to provide safe and fair racing, and that purpose would be seriously undermined if protest and appeals committees were permitted to overlook the requirements in *rules* when they decide that the "intent" of the rule was satisfied.

With a little attention and preparation, each boat can prepare a couple of flags (why not have a spare aboard?) that is easily displayed (Velcro is wonderful!), and find a reasonable and convenient place to store their flag during a race so that members of the crew know where it is, and so that it can be displayed very quickly after an incident with a minimum of hassle (when all else fails put it in your windsuit pocket). No one is suggesting the flag be "put in stops" on the shroud before the start. I am simply strongly recommending that you put your flag up immediately after an incident; if you do, you will not have your protest refused for that reason.

As for examples of when it might be reasonable to delay the display of the flag for a brief time, in my opinion it would be reasonable to delay the display of the flag after a big collision until just after you and your crew finish checking to be sure things were OK; or when setting the spinnaker, when all hands were no longer involved putting it up. However, if after the collision or during the spinnaker set, at least one crew member is not doing anything, it is reasonable to expect that he or she can display the flag. Delaying because the flag is in the ditty bag, which is up in the bow under the anchor, is not reasonable to me. (See US SAILING Appeal 298.)

"Can I just fly anything red and call it a protest flag?"

Absolutely not. ISAF Case 147 reads, "QUESTION: What is the test of whether an object can be considered as a flag within the meaning of rule 61.1(a)? ANSWER: In the context of rule 61.1(a), a flag is used as a signal to visually communicate the message 'I intend to protest' or the equivalent. Only if the object used as a flag communicates that message, with little or no possibility of causing confusion on the part of persons on competing boats, will the object qualify as a flag. A flag must be seen primarily to be a flag."

As part of a question to them, the US SAILING Appeals Committee was asked if a pair of red shorts was acceptable as a "flag," to which they answered "No" because a pair of shorts was not a flag. They went on to say that a pair of shorts will be perceived by most observers to be a pair of shorts rather than a symbol or signaling device.

The bottom line is that whatever you display must be RED, and it must be reasonably obvious that it's a flag, and not a telltale, baseball-type cap or piece of clothing.

"Does the flag have to be flown on the starboard shroud?"

No. The flag must simply be "conspicuously displayed." There is no requirement in the rule that the flag need be put anywhere in particular. For one thing, many boats don't have shrouds. More importantly, the flag should initially be highly visible to the protested boat. In many cases the starboard side of the boat may be the worst (least conspicuous) place to display it. Notice also, that the flag is displayed just by holding it up and waving it at the other boat, which you can do as you head for the location where you will attach it.

Note also that "conspicuous" applies not only to the location of the display but to the actual size of the flag. In US SAILING Appeal 297, the Appeals Committee decided that a 2" by 8" flag on a 40-foot boat was not of sufficient size or of suitable proportions to be considered "conspicuously displayed."

Also notice that you must keep your flag displayed until you *finish* or retire. If your flag blows off your shroud before you've *finished*, you can't protest. Again, devise a good system and carry a spare. If your incident occurs so close to the finishing line that the first reasonable opportunity to display the flag doesn't occur until after you've *finished*, then you simply display it until the race committee acknowledges seeing it.

"Is it true that singlehanded sailors now have to keep their protest flags displayed during the entire race?"

Yes! The rule now is the same for all sailors. So singlehanded sailors will need to develop a convenient place and way to keep their flag displayed throughout the race.

Rule 61.2 - Protest Contents
A *protest* shall be in writing and identify

(a) the protestor and protestee;
(b) the incident, including where and when it occurred;
(c) any *rule* the protestor believes was broken; and
(d) the name of the protestor's representative.

Provided the written *protest* identifies the incident, other details may be corrected before or during the hearing.

Rule 61.2 clearly lists the details about the *protest*. Notice that the *protest* must be **in writing**. Also notice that the only detail that cannot be corrected once the time limit for lodging *protests* is past is an omission of a **description of the incident** itself. Therefore, be sure you clearly identify the incident, including where and when it occurred. (See ISAF Case 158.)

Rule 61.3 - Protest Time Limit

A *protest* by a boat, or by the race committee or protest committee about an incident the committee observes in the racing area, shall be delivered to the race office no later than the time limit stated in the sailing instructions. If none is stated, the time limit is two hours after the last boat in the race *finishes*. Other race committee or protest committee *protests* shall be delivered to the race office within two hours after the committee receives the relevant information. The protest committee shall extend the time if there is good reason to do so.

Notice that the first place to look for the time limit for lodging a *protest* is the sailing instructions. If the sailing instructions are silent, then the default time limit in rule 61.3 is "two hours after the last boat in the race *finishes*."

Also notice that the protest committee **must** extend the time limit if there is a good reason to do so. This may be useful to you if you have made every reasonable effort to lodge your protest in time but were unable to do so for good reason.

A

APPENDIX A
THE MOST SIGNIFICANT CHANGES IN THE 1997-2000 RACING RULES OF SAILING
BY DAVE PERRY

NOTE: US SAILING and the author grant specific permission to reprint this Appendix A for educational and informational use, but not for commercial use. Each reprint is to contain the following wording:

"The Most Significant Changes in the 1997-2000 Racing Rules of Sailing is excerpted from *Understanding the Racing Rules of Sailing Through 2000* by Dave Perry. This comprehensive explanation and discussion of *The Racing Rules of Sailing* is available from US SAILING; call 1-800-US-SAIL-1."

The following is a summary of the significant changes in the 1997-2000 *Racing Rules of Sailing* (RRS). There are additional smaller changes that are not described here. These summaries do not intend to be actual representations of the rules themselves; they are intended to give a sense of where the new rules differ from the old rules. For this discussion, the 1997-00 rules will be referred to as the 'new' rules and the 1993-96 rules will be referred to as the 'old' rules.

Keep in mind that two of the rule writers' goals were to (1) simplify the rules and to (2) focus the racing more on tactical and strategic positioning relative to the other boats and all the elements of nature, and less on using the rules as a 'sword' with which to attack other boats. At the heart of the second goal was the effort to send the message that 'sailing is not a contact sport,' in acknowledgment that collisions are often dangerous, ruinous to a race and intimidating; and their repair can be expensive, time consuming and troublesome—none of which improve the game or help the sport to grow.

NEW LINGO...

As part of the effort to simplify, improve and shorten the rules, some of the terminology used in the rules has been changed.

Under the old rules, we said:	Under the new rules, we say:
alter course or alter a rule	change course or change a rule
Appendix B2, 1.3 (Ties)	rule A2.3 (Ties)
assist (assistance)	help
Code flag	flag
infringe a rule	break a rule
infringement	breach
International Yacht Racing Union (IYRU)	International Sailing Federation (ISAF)
lodging a protest	delivering a protest
party to a protest	party to a hearing
PMS (Premature Starter)	OCS (On the Course Side)
round or pass	pass
two boat-length circle	two-length zone
yacht	boat

THEY'RE HISTORY...

Again, as part of the process to simplify, improve and shorten the rules, many definitions and rules have been deleted because they were considered to be either well understood, unnecessary or undesirable. Here are the major deletions; there are additional smaller deletions not listed here.

Definitions and Terminology: Some previously defined terms are no longer used in the rules and therefore have been deleted, e.g., "Bearing Away," "Luffing" and "Mast Abeam." Other terms are used in their everyday, well understood dictionary meaning; therefore it was felt that they needed no special definition. These include: the old Introduction's explanation that "shall" is mandatory and "can/may" is permissive; the definitions "Close-hauled," "Gybing" and "Tacking" and words such as "above" and "below" referring to a boat sailing relative to its proper course in rules 17.1 and 17.2.

Rule 33 (Contact between Yachts Racing): This was commonly known as the 'third party' rule. Under this rule, if a boat saw two other boats hit and neither do a '720' or protest, the third boat could protest and both the colliding boats would be disqualified regardless of which one was actually wrong. The intent of the rule, which was introduced in the 70's, was to address the unhealthy rise in the number of collisions after which neither boat took their penalty or protested. Many felt that when a boat receives no penalty after fouling, she gains an advantage over all the boats in the race, not just the one she fouled. By introducing the rule, right-of-way boats in collisions became much more inclined to protest, and as a result more give-way boats began doing their '720.' However, a counter sentiment grew claiming that boats should not be penalized for deciding not to protest in minor contact situations, and that it was just a matter between the two boats. The rule has now been deleted.

Note, however, that this does not represent any change in how an incident can be brought to a protest committee for their consideration. A third boat can still protest any incident she sees (whether it involves contact or not!) under rule 60.1(a) (Right to Protest and Request Redress). The difference is that now the protest committee can only penalize the boat(s) in the wrong, if any. Note also that new rule 14 (Avoiding Contact) is much stricter on avoiding contact such that right-of-way boats run a much higher risk of penalty when they have contact with another boat. See discussion of rule 14.

Rule 34 (Retention of Rights): This rule merely stated that while a boat is racing she was entitled to all her rights under the rules.

It addressed the question, 'If a boat fouls me in an earlier incident, do I have to keep out of their way in a subsequent incident?' The answer, of course, is 'yes;' but as no rule suggests otherwise, it was considered unnecessary to have an entire rule that merely restates rule 3(a) (Acceptance of the Rules) and the preamble to Part 2 (When Boats Meet).

Rule 35(a) and 35(b) (exceptions to Limitations on Altering Course): Deleting these exceptions simplifies the rules. Furthermore, two of these exceptions (sudden luffing and turning around a mark) allowed the right-of-way boat to make major changes in course with no regard for a give-way boat's ability to keep clear, and were therefore considered potentially dangerous. The deletion of these exceptions means that there are virtually no more times when a right-of-way boat can change course with no regard to other boats nearby. See the discussion of new rule 16 (Changing Course).

Rule 40.2 (Safety Limitation): This rule gave windward boats a hail that required leeward boats to stop turning toward them when windward boats couldn't avoid them due to something to windward of them. This principle of safety is now built into new rule 16 (Changing Course); furthermore, it was felt that leeward boats don't need a mandatory hail to tell them what common sense already tells them, and hails are generally undesirable in international rules.

Rule 41.3 and 43.2(b)(iii): These two specific "onuses" have been removed from the rules, as has the word "onus" altogether. An "onus" meant that the accused boat had the responsibility of satisfying the protest committee that she did not break a rule. Rule 43.2(b)(iii), which came into play when boats were tacking to clear an obstruction, seldom was used. Rule 41.3, which applied after a boat tacked into a right-of-way position near another boat, was commonly misapplied to the actions of the tacking boat before she completed her tack; and was also used by boats on a tack to put the tacking boat in an unfair defensive position in a protest.

In addition, it was felt that these "onuses" were contrary to the premise of our protest system wherein, to quote the preamble to Appendix P (Recommendations for Protest Committees), "no boat or competitor is guilty until a breach of a rule has been established to the satisfaction of the protest committee." The deletion sends a strong message to PC's to work hard at finding sufficient facts to make a decision based on the facts alone.

Note, however, that rule 18.2(c) (Passing Marks and Obstructions) essentially acts as the previous "onus" rules did regarding establishing and breaking overlaps near the two boat-length circle (old rules 42.1(c) and (d)), in that it gives strong guidance to competitors at the time and to protest committees in a hearing when it is not possible to decide exactly when overlaps were established or broken.

Rule 61.2 (Clothing and Equipment): The deletion of this rule bans weight jackets from the sport for safety and general health reasons. See the discussion of rule 43.1 (Competitor Clothing and Equipment).

Rule 68.3(c)(iii) (Protest Flag Requirements): The deletion of this exception simplifies the rules. It means that when single-handed sailors (Optimists, Lasers, Sunfish, Finns, etc.) intend to protest, they must keep their protest flags flying throughout the entire race, which many already do using simple, convenient devices.

AND THE SIGNIFICANT CHANGES ARE...

Definition of Clear Astern and Clear Ahead; Overlap: An overlap between two boats is no longer considered a 'new' overlap when the leeward boat starts. Also, the concept of an overlap only existing when L and W are within two lengths of each other for the purposes of 'limiting' L's course is now built into rule 17.1 (On the Same Tack; Proper Course).

Definition of Keep Clear: This new definition states what is meant by the phrase "keep clear" used throughout the Part 2 rules. It works in conjunction with the new preamble to Part 2, Section A (Right of Way) which says, "A boat has right of way when another boat is required to keep clear of her." It clarifies that when a boat can sail her 'chosen' course without the need to avoid the other boat, the other boat has "kept clear." This permits starboard-tack boats to voluntarily wave port-tack boats across on beats for tactical purposes and to bear off astern of them without worry that they are causing P to break rule 10 (On Opposite Tacks). Also, if a windward boat gets so close to a leeward boat that L can't turn in either direction at that moment without immediately making contact with W, W has not kept clear merely by her extreme close proximity to L.

Definition of Leeward and Windward: A boat is on starboard or port tack corresponding to her windward side. A boat's windward side is now the side the wind is blowing over or, when head to wind, was blowing over. This eliminates the question about which tack a boat is on when she is backing her sail. When a boat is sailing dead downwind or by the lee, her windward side is still the side opposite the side where the boom is pushed by the wind.

Definition of Obstruction: The definition now clarifies that when three or more boats sail near each other, only the boat holding the right of way, or entitled to room under rule 18.2(a), over all the others can be considered an "obstruction."

Definition of Room: The definition has added the words "while" and "promptly," building in a time element to the test of "room." In other words, when one boat is required to give the other boat "room," the other boat must act "promptly" (i.e. without delay) to avoid losing the protection of "room;" and she is only entitled to space "while" she is making her maneuver (e.g. her maneuver to keep clear or pass a mark, etc.).

Definition of Tack, Starboard or Port: In the old rules, a boat could be in four 'states:' on port or starboard tack, or changing tacks by tacking or gybing. Under the new rules, there is no more 'state' of "tacking" or "gybing;" i.e. a boat is now always on one tack or the other. In other words, when a port-tack boat tacks, she is on port tack up to head to wind and then instantly on starboard tack when she passes head to wind. However, there is no game change here (see rule 13, While Tacking).

Definition of Two-Length Zone: This is a streamlined packaging of the concept of the "two boat-length circle" used in the rules regarding passing marks and obstructions. It acknowledges the fact that the space is not a true circle, particularly around obstructions.

Rule 2 (Fair Sailing): A boat can now be penalized under this rule even when other rules may apply to the incident.

Rule 13 (While Tacking): This new rule contains no game change. Under the new definition "Tack, Starboard or Port" a boat changes her tack the moment she passes head to wind. However, under rule 13 she still has no rights until she is on a close-hauled course (as under old rule 41.1, Changing Tacks, Basic Rule); and when she then acquires right of way over another boat, rule 15 (Acquiring Right of Way) requires her to initially give that boat "room to keep clear" (as under old rule 41.2, Transitional). Rule 13 also covers the situation when two boats are tacking at the same time (as under old rule 41.4, Tacking or Gybing at the Same Time). Only the "onus" in old rule 41.3 (Onus) has been deleted. What has been deleted from old rule 41.1 is any mention of "gybing." The rationale is that the action of gybing is momentary; and rule 15 adequately covers the situation when a boat gybes into a right-of-way position.

Rule 14 (Avoiding Contact): This new rule is much stricter than previous rules regarding contact. New rule 14 says that a boat (including when she has right of way) breaks this rule anytime she has contact with another boat if it was reasonably possible for her to avoid doing so. Therefore, a boat that intentionally hits another to prove the other failed to keep clear has broken this rule. It goes on to say that a r-o-w boat can be penalized for breaking this rule whenever the contact causes any damage whatsoever! (Under old rule 32, the test was "serious" damage.) Two related changes: a r-o-w boat that breaks this rule can now do a '720' to absolve herself (rule 44.1, Taking a Penalty); and a give-way boat can now seek redress if she is physically damaged by a r-o-w boat in a way that significantly worsens her finishing place (rule 62.1(b), Redress).

Rule 15 (Acquiring Right of Way): This is not so much a new rule but a clear statement of the principle previously contained in many separate rules that any time a boat takes action that gives her the right of way, she has to initially give nearby boats some space and time to react and keep clear. This covers when boats establish leeward overlaps from clear astern (old rule 37.3, Establishing an Overlap), when boats tack or gybe into r-o-w positions (old rule 41.2, Transitional) and when boats finish their penalty turns or return to start correctly (old rule 44, On the Course Side of the Starting Line, and rule 45, Keeping Clear after Touching a Mark). The rule also tells r-o-w boats that if they acquire their right of way because of the actions of the other boat, they do not have to give them any room to keep clear. An example would be when two starboard-tack boats are sailing upwind near each other, and the one to leeward suddenly tacks onto port tack (P) directly in the path of the other (S). Because S acquired right-of-way by P's action of tacking, S does not have to give P any room to keep clear whatsoever.

Rule 16 (Changing Course): Rule 16 represents a major consolidation and simplification of the previous rules, particularly rule 35 (Limitations on Altering Course), rule 38 (Same Tack-Before Clearing the Starting Line) and rule 39 (Same Tack-After Clearing the Starting Line). The rationale for these changes is to simplify and clarify the rules that apply when right-of-way boats change course near other boats; and to eliminate sudden luffing (i.e. a leeward boat's right to 'luff as she pleases') or any change of course by a r-o-w boat that is so fast that the give-way boat is unable to keep clear.

One major change is that there are no more exceptions built into the rule (under previous rule 35, a right-of-way boat could essentially ignore the give-way boat when luffing after she had started and when assuming a proper course to start or when rounding a mark). Another is that now the rule governing the rate of a leeward boat's luff is one and the same for before-start and after-start luffing; and applies equally whether L is luffing or bearing away. The final major change is the elimination of the old rule 35 concept of 'obstructing' the other boat while she is keeping clear, a vague concept that was never clearly defined in either the rule or any appeal.

Now, anytime a r-o-w boat changes course near another boat, rule 16 provides a tangible, though necessarily subjective, test as to whether she did so too close or too quickly. The test is that she must give the other boat "room to keep clear." The "room" the r-o-w boat must give is the 'space' the other boat needs while getting far enough away so that the r-o-w boat can sail her course, assuming the other boat acts promptly and in a seamanlike way. "Promptly" means 'without delay;' "seamanlike" means 'responsible, prudent, safety conscious.' Therefore, the give-way boat must respond immediately to the r-o-w boat's course change; but the r-o-w boat can't force the give-way boat to put either boat's crew, boat or equipment at risk of injury or damage by the need to make a sudden, hurried or extreme maneuver (e.g. a 'crash-tack' at the last second before contact).

In the situation where a port-tack boat is attempting to cross a starboard-tack boat on a beat, there is no change from old rule 35, except that the test of 'obstruct' has been replaced by "room to keep clear." No rule ever required S to hold her course when two lengths from P; S could always change course provided she didn't "prevent" P from keeping clear or "obstruct" her while she was doing so. The major change is when P changes course to avoid S. If S then changes her course and causes P to have to make an additional change of course to avoid hitting S, but P can avoid hitting S while acting in a seamanlike way, S has not broken rule 16.

Rule 17.1 (On the Same Tack; Proper Course): Rule 17.1 also represents a major consolidation and simplification of the previous rules, particularly rule 35 (Limitations on Altering Course), rule 38 (Same Tack-Before Clearing the Starting Line), rule 39 (Same Tack-After Clearing the Starting Line) and rule 40 (Other Limitations on a Leeward Yacht). Again, the rationale for these changes is to greatly simplify the rules that apply when boats on the same tack (i.e. windward and leeward boats) sail near each other.

One major change is that the concept of "mast abeam" has been completely removed from the rules! "Mast abeam" was a relative position windward boats could get to and thereby limit where nearby leeward boats could sail. The concept was complex because the limits it put on L were different before and after starting, the position itself was based on a hypothetical relationship between L and W whenever W was sailing higher than L, and it commonly relied on a hail (which is not desirable in international rules) by W's helmsman in "normal position" (subjective and commonly misused).

The new concept is simple. Before the starting signal the rule does not apply at all because there is no "proper course" yet.

Therefore, L is always 'free' to sail up to head to wind if she pleases, even when overlapped with W by only a couple of feet. After the starting signal (a predictable moment in time), L is either 'limited' (to sailing no higher than her proper course) or she is 'free' (to sail up to head to wind if she pleases, again even when overlapped with W by only a couple of feet); it is always one or the other.

L is 'limited' or 'free' depending on how the overlap was first established. If L established the leeward overlap from clear astern, L is 'limited' to not sailing above her proper course for the duration of that overlap (as she was under old rule 39.1, Same Tack, Sailing above a Proper Course). If the overlap was established in any other way (e.g., W established the windward overlap from astern, L tacked or gybed in to leeward of W, L and W were more than two lengths apart or were on opposite tacks when the overlap was established, etc.) then rule 17.1 does not apply and L is 'free' to sail up to head to wind if she pleases.

Note, the definition "Clear Astern and Clear Ahead; Overlap" has been changed such that an overlap that exists when the leeward boat starts is not a new overlap (as it was under the old definition); therefore, when nearing the starting signal, boats will need to remember how they became over-lapped! For windward starts, a boat's proper course is normally close-hauled; for downwind starts, a boat's proper course will depend on many factors (e.g. type of boat, wind and current speed and direction, sails in use, other nearby boats, etc.).

This change has a major effect on starting near the windward end of the starting line (usually a race committee boat). If, at the starting signal, L is not 'limited,' she can continue sailing up to head to wind if she pleases, even if W is thereby forced to sail to the wrong side of the starting mark; if she is 'limited,' she must sail no higher than her proper course. For windward starts this is normally close-hauled, so the rule is similar to old 42(a)(ii) (Rounding or Passing Marks and Obstructions); but for down-wind starts, this is a major change because old rule 42(a)(i) required L to sail no higher than her "compass course" to the next mark.

Keeping in mind that rule 11 (On the Same Tack, Overlapped) requires W to keep clear of L, the combined effect of new rules 16 and 17 on L and W when they are sailing near each other will work very much like the previous rules did, without the complexity of the previous rules. When L establishes a leeward overlap on W, L can't sail above her proper course for the duration of the overlap. When W is approaching L and when she first establishes an overlap to windward of L, L will generally be able to luff quite rapidly toward the wind and still give W room to keep clear of her. However, as W moves further ahead alongside L, L's ability to luff will progressively decrease because she must allow space for W's stern to swing down as W luffs away from her. Therefore, L can sail higher than she could under the old rules, but she must do it in a more controlled way with an awareness of W's ability to keep clear of her.

Rule 17.2 (On the Same Tack; Proper Course): The distance at which the rule comes into effect has been reduced from three lengths to two lengths. Also, W does not need to gybe onto a "proper course" as she was required to do under old rule 39.3 (Sailing Below a Proper Course).

Rule 18 (Passing Marks and Obstructions): This rule is old rule 42; it is 135 words or about 20% shorter. As part of the shortening effort, the term "rounding" has been deleted throughout. This represents no game change; a mark or obstruction that has been "rounded" has been "passed" in the process.

Rule 18.1 (When This Rule Applies): Rule 18 no longer only applies when passing a mark on the same "required" side; therefore, before boats are "approaching the starting line to start," outside boats must give inside overlapping boats room to pass any starting mark.

Rule 18 now has a tangible 'shut-off' point; it ceases to apply when all the boats subject to rule 18 together have passed the mark. A boat has passed a mark when she is no longer alongside it. Therefore, when two overlapped boats are rounding a windward mark onto a run with the outside boat farther behind in the turn, the outside boat must stay clear of the inside boat until the outside boat passes the mark, even when the inside boat gybes directly in front of her (under old rule 42.1(a), When Overlapped, the inside boat was permitted room to gybe only when it was an integral part of her rounding maneuver).

Rule 18.1(a) (When This Rule Applies): When starting near the starting mark, there are no longer any requirements for L not to deprive W of room at the mark after the starting signal by sailing either above close-hauled or the compass course to the next mark. See the discussion of rule 17.1 (On the Same Tack; Proper Course).

Rule 18.2(a) (Giving Room; Keeping Clear): New rule 18.2(a) contains the limitations on establishing an overlap previously listed in old rule 42.3 (Limitations); the limitations remain the same.

Rule 18.2(b) (Giving Room; Keeping Clear): When approaching a windward mark clear astern of another boat, the boat astern can now sail above close-hauled to make it more difficult for the boat ahead to tack around the mark (old rule 42.2(b), When Not Overlapped, prohibited this).

Rule 18.3 (Tacking): This new rule is a major change. It is intended to improve the game by trying to minimize the frustrating and sometimes dangerous congestion that occurs at crowded windward mark roundings caused by port-tack boats approaching on or near the port layline and trying to squeeze in between starboard-tack boats and the mark.

Essentially, the rule says that when two boats are approaching a windward mark on opposite tacks, and one of the boats completes her tack within the two-length zone, she must do it in a place that allows the other boat to pass the mark with no interference, and without ever having to sail above close-hauled to avoid hitting the boat that tacked. If the boat that tacks causes the other boat to sail above close-hauled to keep from hitting her or prevents the other boat from being able to pass the mark, the boat that tacked has broken rule 18.3(a). If the other boat gets an inside overlap on the boat that tacked at any time during her rounding, the boat that tacked must keep clear of the inside boat; and the inside boat does not initially need to give her room to keep clear (i.e. the boat that tacked becomes more or less a 'sitting duck' for the leeward/inside boat).

Rule 18.4 (Gybing): Rule 18.4 is similar to old rule 42.1(e), but its limitation is broader. Rule 18.4 puts a 'limit' on all inside right-of-way boats (i.e. leeward and starboard-tack boats).

Essentially, that 'limit' is that whenever their proper course is to gybe at a mark, they must do so. This means that not only do they have to gybe when it is their proper course to do so, but they can't sail above their proper course at all while they are still passing it, even when the outside windward boat initially established the overlap to windward such that L would otherwise have the right to sail above her proper course.

This is a change from the previous rules where L could sail past the mark or even luff when she had 'luffing rights.' The rationale is that the rules should keep the boats moving around the marks; and that it is much less dangerous and more simple if all inside boats have to gybe at the marks as opposed to giving some leeward boats the option of not gybing, and even luffing, as the previous rules did.

Rule 18.5 (Passing a Continuing Obstruction): Under new rule 18.5, the determination of whether there is room to pass between the obstruction and the other boat is made at the moment the boat astern overlaps the other boat. Under old rule 42.3(b), the moment of truth was the moment the overlap was established "between" the other boat and the obstruction.

Rule 19.1 and 19.2 (Room to Tack at an Obstruction): The only change from old rule 43 (Cloe-hauled, Hailing for Room to Tack at Obstructions) is that when a boat is hailed for room to tack at an obstruction and wants to respond "You tack," rule 19.1(b) requires that she make that response "immediately" or lose the opportunity. If she wants to tack in response to the hail, she simply has to tack as soon as possible (as under old rule 43.2(a), Responding). Under rule 19.2, when a boat that is hailed for room to tack at an obstruction that is also a mark is fetching that mark, she is no longer required to hail that fact to the hailing boat. Again, required hails are undesirable in international rules, and common sense suggests that the hailed boat will let the hailing boat know the situation.

Rule 20 (Starting Errors; Penalty Turns; Moving Astern): Rule 20 now requires boats that are intentionally backing down to keep clear of other boats. Also, when rule 30.1 (the 'One Minute Rule') is in effect and when sailing around an end of the starting line, a boat must keep clear of other boats until completely on the pre-start side of the starting line extension.

Rule 31.2 (Touching a Mark): If a boat gains a "significant advantage" by touching a mark, she cannot absolve herself with a 360-degree penalty turn; she must retire from the race (or let enough boats pass her by to 'give back' the advantage she gained). This is aimed at boats that, for instance, choose to tack inside a long line of starboard-tackers at a crowded windward mark and figure they can come out ahead by not fouling a boat but hitting the mark and doing a quick '360' instead, as opposed to ducking astern of the long line of starboard-tackers.

Rule 43 (Competitor Clothing and Equipment): Weight jackets have been banned from the sport (old rule 61.2, Clothing and Equipment, has been deleted); and class rules cannot legalize them (rule 86.1(c) does not permit classes to change rule 43). Also, the overall maximum weight of all clothing has been reduced, though classes can modify that somewhat.

Rule 44 (Penalties for Breaking Rules of Part 2): Now the '720' rule is automatically in effect unless the sailing instructions specify some other penalty. Also, rule 44.1 (Taking a Penalty) requires that a boat retire when she causes "serious damage" or gains a "significant advantage" in a race or series by her breach. This shifts more responsibility on the boat to self-penalize herself than under the old rules.

Rule 49.2 (Crew Position): New rule 49.2 requires that all life-lines (upper and lower) be taut. Sailors can still lean their torsos out over the lifelines to perform a necessary task (e.g. clear kelp or hold a spinnaker guy away from the boat after the pole is removed), but only "briefly." As the modifier in old rule 62(b) (Increasing Stability) was "temporarily," the new rule is a bit stricter.

Rule 50 (Setting and Sheeting Sails): Rule 50.2 now permits a boat to use two spinnaker poles when gybing. Rule 50.3(a) clarifies that it is legal for bowsprits to control the tack of a sail such as an asymmetrical spinnaker.

Rule 61.1(a), (b) and (c) (Informing the Protestee): A boat intending to protest must hail the word "Protest;" no other word or phrase will do. Single-handed sailors must now keep their protest flag displayed throughout the entire race. A race or protest committee member intending to protest an incident it saw must tell the protested boat(s) within the time limit for delivering protests.

Rule 63.1 (Requirement for a Hearing): Now, when a written protest has been delivered, the protestor can ask to withdraw the protest and the protest committee can allow it at their discretion.

Rule 69.1(b) (Allegations of Gross Misconduct, Action by a Protest Committee): When a protest committee decides that a competitor has committed the alleged misconduct, they can now give that competitor a warning, and they are not required to report that incident to the national authority.

B

APPENDIX B
WHERE HAVE ALL THE OLD
RULES GONE?

Rules Conversion Table developed by Tom Farquhar US SAIL-
ING Senior Certified Judge and member of the US SAILING
Appeals Committee

The following table lists all the 1993-96 International Yacht
Racing Rules (IYRR) and US SAILING prescriptions, along with
their titles or subject, and indicates where that rule or U.S. prescription appears in the 1997-2000 *Racing Rules of Sailing*
(RRS).

You will notice that some of the 1993-96 rules do not appear in
the 1997-00 RRS. In addition, there are new 1997-00 rules that
previously did not appear in the 1993-96 IYRR; these, however,
are not the subject of this table and therefore are not listed.

The symbol "Rx" indicates a US SAILING prescription.

Old Rule Number	Old Rule Name	New Rule Number(s)
Old Rule Number	Old Rule Name	New Rule Number(s)
Part I	"Fundamental Rules, Definitions and Alterations"	Part 1; Definitions
FR A	Rendering Assistance	1.1
FR B	Competitors' Responsibilities	4
FR B(i)	Governed by rules	3(a)
FR B(ii)	Rules are final determination	3(b)
FR B(iii)	No courts	3(c)
FR C	Fair Sailing	2
FR D	Accepting Penalties	Sportsmanship
Definition	Definitions	Definitions
Definition	Abandonment	Abandon
Definition	Bearing Away	
Definition	Clear Astern and Clear Ahead; Overlap	Clear Astern and Clear Ahead; Overlap
Definition	Close-hauled	
Definition	Finishing	Finish
Definition	Gybing	
Definition	Interested Party	Interested Party
		Keep Clear
Definition	Leeward and Windward	Leeward and Windward
Definition	Luffing	
Definition	Mark	Mark
Definition	Mast Abeam	
Definition	Obstruction	Obstruction
Definition	On a Tack; Starboard Tack; Port Tack	"Tack, Starboard or Port"
Definition	Overlap	Overlap
Definition	Parties to a Protest	Party
Parties(a)	Yachts	Party
Parties(b)	Redress	Party
Parties(c)	Race Committee	Party
Parties(d)	Competitor	Party
Definition	Postponement	Postpone
Definition	Proper Course	Proper Course
Definition	Protest	Protest
Definition	Protest Committee	89
Definition	Racing	Racing
Definition	Room	Room
Definition	Rules	Rule
Rules(a)	IYRR	Rule(a)
Rules(b)	Prescriptions	Rule(b)
Rules(c)	SIs	Rule(c)
Rules(d)	Class Rules	Rule(d)

Old Rule Number	Old Rule Name	New Rule Number(s)
Rules(e)	Other Conditions	Rule(e)
Definition	Sailing	42.1
Definition	Starting	Start
Definition	Tacking	13
Definition	Windward	Windward
Alteration	Alterations	"Introduction: Appendices, Changes to the Rules"
Part II	Organisation and Management	Part 3; Part 7
1	"Organising, Conducting and Judging Races"	85
1.1	Governing Rules	25; 85
1.2	Organising Authority	87.1; 87.2
1.2(a)	IYRU	87.1(a)
1.2(b)	Member National Authority	87.1(b)
1.2(c)	Club or regatta committee	87.1(c)
1.2(d)	Class association & club	87.1(d)
1.2(e)	Unaffiliated body	87.1(e)
1.3	Race Committee	88.1; 88.2(a); 88.3; Terminology
1.4	Protest Committee	89
1.4(a)	Race Committee	89(a)
1.4(b)	RC subcommittee	89(a)
1.4(c)	Jury	89(b)
1.4(d)	International Jury	89(c)
1.5	Right of Appeal	70.1
1.5(a)	None from International Jury	70.4
1.5(b)	Right can be denied in NOR & SI:	70.4
1.5(b)(i)	from qualifying event	70.4(a)
1.5(b)(ii)	when prescribed by National Authority	70.4(b); 70.4(c)
1.6	EXCLUSION OF YACHTS AND COMPETITORS	76
2	Notice of Race	M1
2(a)	Mandatory:	M1.1
2(a)(i)	"title, place & dates; organizing authority"	M1.1(1)
2(a)(ii)	"governed by IYRR, prescriptions, etc."	M1.1(2)
2(a)(iii)	classes and restrictions	M1.1(3)
2(a)(iv)	times of registration & practice	M1.1(4)
2(b)	When appropriate:	M1.2
2(b)(i)	eligibility requirements	M1.2(1)
2(b)(ii)	Appendix A3 category	M1.2(2)
2(b)(iii)	scoring system	M1.2(12)
2(b)(iv)	SI availability	M1.2(6)
2(b)(v)	IYRR alterations	M1.2(7)
2(b)(vi)	class rule alterations	M1.2(8)

Old Rule Number	Old Rule Name	New Rule Number(s)
2(b)(vii)	registration procedures & fees	M1.2(3)
2(b)(viii)	measurement procedures	M1.2(5)
2(b)(ix)	courses	M1.2(9)
2(b)(x)	alternative penalties	M1.2(10)
2(b)(xi)	prizes	M1.2(13)
2(b)(xii)	denial of right of appeal	M1.2(11)
2(b)(xiii)	entry form & acceptance of rules	M1.2(4)
3	Sailing Instructions	86; M2
3.1	STATUS	86
3.1(a)	IYRR Alterations	86.1(b)
3.1(b)	Not alterable:	86.1(a); 86.1(b)
3.1(b)(i)	Parts I and IV	86.1(a)
3.1(b)(ii)	"IYRR 1, 2, 3, 16, 17, 18, 51.1(a) & 61"	86.1(a)
3.1(b)(iii)	"Part VI, Sections C and D"	86.1(b)
3.1(b)(iv)	Group A Appendices	86.1(a)
3.1(b)(v)	Code flag 'B'	
3.1(b)(vi)	Appendices altering 3.1(b)	86.1(a)
3.1(c)	STATUS	86.2
3.2	CONTENTS	M2
3.2(a)	Mandatory:	M2.1
3.2(a)(i)	IYRR & other rules	M2.1(1)
3.2(a)(ii)	schedule & classes	M2.1(2)
3.2(a)(iii)	courses	M2.1(3); M2.1(4)
3.2(a)(iv)	starting & finishing lines	M2.1(5)
3.2(a)(v)	time limit	M2.1(6)
3.2(a)(vi)	scoring system	M2.1(7)
3.2(b)	When appropriate:	M2.2
3.2(b)(i)	eligibility	M2.2(1)
3.2(b)(ii)	Appendix A3 category	M2.2(2)
3.2(b)(iii)	IYRR alterations	M2.2(4)
3.2(b)(iv)	class rule alterations	M2.2(5)
3.2(b)(v)	registration procedure	M2.2(7)
3.2(b)(vi)	official notice board(s) location	M2.2(9)
3.2(b)(vii)	SI change procedure	M2.2(10)
3.2(b)(viii)	restrictions on altering supplied yachts	M2.2(6)
3.2(b)(ix)	signals made ashore	M2.2(13)
3.2(b)(x)	class flags	M2.2(18)
3.2(b)(xi)	racing area (chart)	M2.2(14)
3.2(b)(xii)	starting area	M2.2(19)
3.2(b)(xiii)	course signals	M2.1(3)
3.2(b)(xiv)	course length; windward leg length	M2.2(15)

Old Rule Number	Old Rule Name	New Rule Number(s)
3.2(b)(xv)	tides and currents	M2.2(32)
3.2(b)(xvi)	recall signals	M2.2(20)
3.2(b)(xvii)	shortened course procedures	M2.2(23)
3.2(b)(xviii)	mark or lead boats	M2.2(21)
3.2(b)(xix)	change of course signals	M2.2(22)
3.2(b)(xx)	time limit for all yachts	M2.2(16)
3.2(b)(xxi)	re-sailing schedule	M2.2(31)
3.2(b)(xxii)	number of races required	M2.1(7); A2.1
3.2(b)(xxiii)	safety requirements & procedures	M2.2(11)
3.2(b)(xxiv)	measurement or inspection procedures	M2.2(8)
3.2(b)(xxv)	alternative penalties	M2.2(25)
3.2(b)(xxvi)	declarations	M2.2(12)
3.2(b)(xxvii)	protest & hearing procedures	M2.2(26)
3.2(b)(xxviii)	"other restrictions, e.g. radios"	M2.2(24)
3.2(b)(xxix)	substitutes	M2.2(29)
3.2(b)(xxx)	prizes	M2.2(32)
3.2(b)(xxxi)	time allowances	M2.2(17)
3.2(b)(xxxii)	COLREGS applicability	M2.2(3)
3.2(b)(xxxiii)	yacht appearing alone	M2.2(30)
3.2(b)(xxxiv)	denial of right of appeal	M2.2(27)
3.2(b)(xxxv)	other RC commitments & obligations of yachts	M2.2(34)
		M2.2(28)
3.3	DISTRIBUTION	25
3.4	CHANGES	88.2(c)
3.4(a)	Posting	88.2(c)
3.4(b)	On the water	88.2(c)
4	Race Committee Signals	Race Signals
4.1	VISUAL SIGNALS	Race Signals
4.1'AP'	Answering Pennant-Postponement Signal	AP
4.1'AP'(a)	Answering Pennant-Postponement Signal	AP
4.1'AP'(b)	Answering Pennant over Numeral Pennants 1 to 9	AP over numeral pennant 1-6
4.1'AP'(c)	Answering Pennant over 'A'	AP over A
4.1'AP'(d)	Answering Pennant over 'H'	AP over H
4.1'C'	Change of Course While Racing	C
4.1'I'	Round-the-Ends Starting Rule	I
4.1'L'	Notification Signal	L
4.1'L'(a)	Notification-Displayed Ashore	L
4.1'L'(b)	Notification-Displayed Afloat	L
4.1'M'	Mark Signal	M
4.1'N'	Abandonment Signal	N
4.1'N'(a)	Abandonment Signal	N

Old Rule Number	Old Rule Name	New Rule Number(s)
4.1'N'(b)	Abandonment over 'H'	N over H
4.1'P'	Preparatory Signal	P
4.1'S'	Shorten Course Signal	S
4.1'S'(a)	Shorten Course-Before the Warning	S
4.1'S'(b)	Shorten Course-At the Finish	S
4.1'S'(b)(i)	At the finish line	S
4.1'S'(b)(ii)	Per Sailing Instructions	
4.1'S'(c)	Shorten Course-At a Rounding Mark	S
4.1'X'	Individual Recall	X
4.1'Y'	Life Jacket Signal	Y
4.1'First Sub'	General Recall Signal	First Substitute
		Black flag; 30.3
4.1'Red'	Leave Marks to Port	
		Red: Starting signal in System 2
4.1'Green'	Leave Marks to Starboard	
4.1'Blue'	Finishing Signal	Blue
		Blue: Prep. signal in System 2
		Yellow: Warning signal in System 2
4.2	CALLING ATTENTION TO VISUAL SIGNALS	Race Signals
4.2(a)	Three Sounds	Race Signals
4.2(b)	Two Sounds	Race Signals
4.2(c)	Repetitive Sounds	Race Signals
4.2(d)	One Sound	Race Signals
4.3	VISUAL SIGNALS FOR STARTING RACES	26.1
4.3(a)	VISUAL SIGNALS FOR STARTING RACES	26.1
4.3(a)System 1	Starting System 1	26.1; 26.2
4.3(a)System 2	Starting System 2	26.1
4.3(a)System 2-Ten	System 2-Ten Minute Intervals	26.3
4.3(a)System 2-Five	System 2-Five Minute Intervals	26.3
4.3(b)	Warning Signal	
4.4	VISUAL STARTING SIGNALS TO GOVERN	26.1
5	"Designating the Course, Altering the Course or Race"	27.1
5.1	Before the Warning	27.1
5.1(a)	Designate the course	27.1
5.1(b)	Change the course designation	27.1
5.2	Before the Prep: Adjust the starting marks	27.2
5.3	Before the Start:	27.3
5.3(a)	Postpone	27.3
5.3(b)	Postpone to another day	27.3
5.3(c)	Abandon	27.3
5.4	After the Start:	32

Old Rule Number	Old Rule Name	New Rule Number(s)
5.4(a)	General Recall	29.3
5.4(b)	Abandon and resail	32(a)
5.4(c)	"Change the course, if in SIs"	33
5.4(d)	Abandon or shorten:	32
5.4(d)(i)	Foul weather	32(b)
5.4(d)(ii)	Unlikely to finish within time limit	32(c)
5.4(d)(iii)	Mark missing or moved	32(d)
5.4(d)(iv)	Safety or fairness	32(e)
5.5	Limitation on abandonment	32
6	Start of a Race	
6.1	STARTING AREA	
6.2	TIMING THE START	26.1; A1.6
7	Recalls	29
7.1	INDIVIDUAL RECALL	29.2
7.2	GENERAL RECALL	29.3
7.2(a)	Definition	29.3
7.2(b)	Ignoring rule infringements	36
8	Marks	35
8.1	MARK MISSING	34
8.2	MARK UNSEEN	
9	Finishing Within a Time Limit	35
10	Ties	A1.4
11	Races to be Re-sailed	80
11(a)	Yachts from original race	80
11(b)	New entries	80
11(c)	Previous infringements ignored	36
11(d)	Notification required	80
Part III	General Requirements	Part 6 - Entry and Qualification
Preamble	Part III Preamble	75.1
16	Competitors' Eligibility	75.1
17	Banned Substances and Banned Methods	5
17.1(a)	IYRU Medical List	5
17.1(b)	Refusal to be Tested	L1.2
17.1(c)	IYRU Doping Control Procedure	L4
17.2	Not grounds for protest	5
17.3	IYRU or NGB Permission Required	L1.1
18	Advertising and Event Categories	79
19	Entries	75.1
20	Measurement or Rating Certificates	78
20.1	Certificate Required	75.1; 78.1
20.2	Maintaining Yacht in Conformance with Certificate	78.1

Old Rule Number	Old Rule Name	New Rule Number(s)
20.3(a)	Promise to Produce Certificate	78.2
20.3(b)	Deposit to Ensure Production	
21	Ownership of Yachts	46
21.1	Club membership	75.1
21.2	Multiple Yachts	
21.3	Owner on Another Yacht	
22	Member on Board	46
23	Shifting Ballast	51
23.1	GENERAL RESTRICTIONS	51
23.2	"SHIPPING, UNSHIPPING OR SHIFTING BALLAST; WATER"	51
24	Life-saving Equipment	1.2
25	"Identification-Class Insignia, National Letters an"	77
25.1	"Class Insignia, National Letters and Numbers"	77
25.2	Penalty limitation	H4
26	Forestays and Jib Tacks	54
Part IV	Right-of-Way Rules	Part 2 - When Boats Meet
Preamble	Part IV Preamble	Part 2 - Preamble
		Section A - Right of Way
SECTION A	Obligations and Penalties	
30	Hindering Another Yacht	22
30.1	Not racing	22.1
30.2	While exonerating herself	22.2
31	Penalty Limitations	Part 2 - Preamble
32	Serious Damage	14(b)
33	Contact Between Yachts Racing	
33(a)	Not applicable if valid protest	
33(b)	Not applicable if one exonerates	
34	Retention of Rights	
SECTION B	Basic Right-of-Way Rules and their Limitations	
Preamble	SECTION B Preamble	
35	Limitations of Altering Course	16
35(a)	Not Applicable: When luffing under 39.2	
35(b)(i)	Not Applicable: To Starboard when starting	
35(b)(ii)	Not Applicable: at marks	
36	Opposite Tacks-Basic Rule	10
37	Same Tack-Basic Rule	
37.1	OVERLAPPED	11
37.2	NOT OVERLAPPED	12
37.3	ESTABLISHING AN OVERLAP	15
38	Same Tack-Before Clearing the Starting Line	
38.1	SAILING ABOVE A CLOSE-HAULED COURSE	17.1

Old Rule Number	Old Rule Name	New Rule Number(s)
38.2	LUFFING	
39	Same Tack-After Clearing the Starting Line	
39.1	SAILING ABOVE A PROPER COURSE	17.1
39.2	LUFFING	
39.3	SAILING BELOW A PROPER COURSE	17.2
40	Other Limitations on a Leeward Yacht	
40.1	DOUBT ABOUT MAST ABEAM	
40.2	SAFETY LIMITATION	18.2(a)
40.3	LUFFING TWO OR MORE YACHTS	
41	Changing Tacks-Tacking and Gybing	
41.1	BASIC RULE	13
41.2	TRANSITIONAL	15
41.3	ONUS	
41.4	TACKING OR GYBING AT THE SAME TIME	13
SECTION C	Rules that Apply at Marks and Obstructions and Oth	
Preamble	SECTION C Preamble	Section C - Preamble
42	Rounding or Passing Marks and Obstructions	18.1
42(a)	Starting Mark	18.1(a)
42(a)(i)	Leeward cannot sail above mark	
42(a)(ii)	Leeward cannot sail above close-hauled	
42(b)	Not applicable to opposite tacks:	18.1(b)
42(b)(i)	On a beat	18.1(b)
42(b)(ii)	Tacking at marks and obstructions	18.1(b)
42.1	WHEN OVERLAPPED	18.2
42.1(a)	Outside: Giving room	18.2(a)
42.1(b)	Outside: Overlap broken	18.2(a)
42.1(c)	Outside: Onus	18.2(c)
42.1(d)	Inside: Onus	18.2(c)
42.1(e)	Inside; Gybing	18.4
42.2	WHEN NOT OVERLAPPED	18.2(b)
42.2(a)	Clear Astern: Keep clear	18.2(b)
42.2(b)	Clear Astern: Limitation on Luffing	18.2(b)
42.3	LIMITATIONS	
42.3(a)	Limitations of Establishing an Overlap	18.3(b)
42.3(a)(i)	Able to give room	
42.3(a)(ii)	From clear astern	
42.3(b)	Continuing Obstruction: Safety	18.5
43	"Close-hauled, Hailing for Room to Tack at Obstruct"	19
43.1	HAILING	19.1
43.2	RESPONDING	19.1
43.2(a)	By tacking	19.1(a)

Old Rule Number	Old Rule Name	New Rule Number(s)
43.2(b)	"By hailing ""You tack"""	19.1(b)
43.2(b)(i)	Tacking	19.1(b)
43.2(b)(ii)	Room to Tack	19.1(b)
43.2(b)(iii)	Onus	
43.3	WHEN AN OBSTRUCTION IS ALSO A MARK	19.2
43.3(a)	Starting Mark	19.2
43.3(b)	Other Marks	19.2
		Section D
		Section D - Preamble
44	On the Course Side of the Starting Line	20
45	Keeping Clear after Touching a Mark	20
46	"Person Overboard; Yachts Anchored, Aground or Caps"	21
46.1	Keeping Clear of:	21
46.1(a)	Person Overboard	21
46.1(b)	"Anchored, Aground or Capsized"	21
46.2	Exoneration	21
46.3	Def. of Capsized	21
46.4	Informing Other Yachts	
Part V	Other Sailing Rules	
Preamble	Part V Preamble	
51	Sailing the Course	
51.1(a)	Start and Finish	28.1
51.1(b)	PMS	29.1
51.1(c)	Around-the-Ends Rule	30.1
51.1(d)	Failure to hear or see signal	
51.2	String rule	28.1
51.3	Required side of marks	28.2
51.4	Finishing	
51.5	No RC at finish (Rx)	
52	Touching a Mark	31
52.1(a)	touch:	31.1
52.1(a)(i)	starting mark	31.1
52.1(a)(ii)	marks of a leg she is on	31.1
52.1(a)(iii)	finishing mark	31.1
52.1(b)	cause a mark to shift	
52.2(a)	exoneration; 360-degree turn	31.2
52.2(b)	finishing after touching a mark	31.2
52.3	wrongfully compelled to touch a mark	31.3
52.3(a)	other yacht acknowledges fault	31.3(a)
52.3(b)	lodges a valid protest	31.3(b)
53	"Anchoring, Making Fast and Hauling Out"	45

Old Rule Number	Old Rule Name	New Rule Number(s)
53.1	LIMITATIONS ON MAKING FAST AND HAULING OUT	45
53.2	MEANS OF ANCHORING	45
54	Propulsion	42
54.1	BASIC RULE	42.1; 42.3(c); 42.3(d)
54.2	PROHIBITED ACTIONS	42.2
54.2(a)	pumping	42.2(a)
54.2(b)	rocking	42.2(b)
54.2(c)	ooching	42.2(c)
54.2(d)	sculling	42.2(d)
54.2(e)	repeated tacks or gybes	42.2(e)
54.3	EXCEPTIONS	42.3
54.3(a)	roll tacking or gybing	42.3(a)
54.3(b)	pumping on a free leg	42.3(b)
54.4	CLASS RULES	
55	Aground or Foul of an Obstruction	41
56	Manual and Stored Power	52
57	Boarding	41
58	"Leaving, Crew Overboard"	47.2
59	Outside Assistance	41
60	Personal Buoyancy	40
60.1	Personal responsibility; wetsuits	1.2; 40
60.2	Code flag 'Y'	'Y'; 40
61	Clothing and Equipment	43
61.1(a)	no clothing to increase weight	43.1(a)
61.1(b)	total clothing weight cannot exceed 15kg.	43.1(b)
61.2	Class rules can approve weight jackets	
61.2(a)	permanently buoyant	
61.2(b)	height limitation	
61.2(c)	worn outside all other clothing & equipment	
61.2(d)	can be removed in under 10 seconds	
61.3	All equipment available for measurement	
61.4	Exclusion for cruiser-racer yachts	43.2
62	Increasing Stability	49
62(a)	"No trapezes, etc. unless class rules approve"	49.1
62(b)	Torsos inside lifelines	49.2
63	Skin Friction	53
63(a)	No release of substances	53
63(b)	No special surface textures	53
64	Setting and Sheeting Sails	50
64.1	CHANGING SAILS	50.1
64.2	SPINNAKER POLES AND WHISKER POLES	50.2

Old Rule Number	Old Rule Name	New Rule Number(s)
64.3	USE OF OUTRIGGERS	50.3
64.3(a)	general prohibition; definitions	50.3(a)
64.3(b)(i)	exception for ordinary booms	50.3(b)(1)
64.3(b)(ii)	exception when spinnaker not in use	50.3(b)(2)
64.4	HEADSAILS	50.4
64.5	CLASS RULES	
65	Fog Signals and Lights	48
66	Flags (Rx)	
Part VI	"Protests, Penalties and Appeals"	"Part 5 - Protests, Hearings,
Misconduct"		
SECTION A	Initiation of Action	60
68	Protests by Yachts	60.1
68.1	RIGHT TO PROTEST	60.1
68.2	INFORMING THE PROTESTED YACHT	61.1
68.3	PROTEST FLAG REQUIREMENTS	61.1(a)
68.3(a)	During a race	61.1(a)
68.3(b)	First reasonable opportunity	61.1(a)
68.3(c)(i)	How long displayed	61.1(a)
68.3(c)(ii)	Singlehanded	
68.3(d)	Yacht retires	61.1(a)
68.4	EXCEPTION TO PROTEST REQUIREMENTS	61.1(a)
68.4(a)	No knowledge until finished	61.1(a)
68.4(b)	Witness not involved	
68.5	PARTICULARS TO BE INCLUDED	61.2
68.5(a)	Identity	61.2(a)
68.5(b)	"Date, time and location"	61.2(b)
68.5(c)	Rules infringed	61.2(c)
68.5(d)	Description of the incident	61.2(b)
68.5(e)	Diagram	
68.6	TIME LIMIT	61.3
68.6(a)	Within two hours	61.3
68.6(b)	Not finished	
68.7	REMEDYING DEFECTS IN THE PROTEST	61.2
68.8	WITHDRAWING A PROTEST	63.1
68.9	BETWEEN EVENT RATING CERTIFICATE REVIEWS	
69	Requests for Redress	60.1; 62
69(a)	Improper RC or PC action	62.1(a)
69(b)	Rendering assistance	62.1(c)
69(c)	Physically damaged	62.1(b)
69(d)	FR C or 75	62.1(d)
70	Action by Race or Protest Committee	

Old Rule Number	Old Rule Name	New Rule Number(s)
70.1	WITHOUT A HEARING	
70.1(a)	Failure to start or finish	A1.1
70.1(b)	Propulsion	67
70.1(c)	Notification	67
70.2	WITH A HEARING	60.2; 60.3
70.2(a)	Sees an infringement	
70.2(b)	Learns directly:	
70.2(b)(i)	from infringer	
70.2(b)(ii)	from infringer's invalid protest	
70.2(c)	Serious damage	
70.2(d)	Receives report	
70.2(e)	Valid protest	
70.2	Deadline for notification:	61.1(b)
70.2(i)	after finish of race	61.1(b)
70.2(ii)	after receipt of relevant information	
70.2(iii)	after hearing of the protest	
70.3	YACHT MATERIALLY PREJUDICED	60.2(b); 60.3(b)
70.4	MEASURER'S RESPONSIBILITY	78.3
70.4(a)	Before a race	78.3
70.4(b)	After a race	78.3
SECTION B	Protest Procedure	Section B - Hearings & Decisions
71	Procedural Requirements	63
71.1	REQUIREMENT FOR A HEARING	63.1
71.2	INTERESTED PARTIES	63.4
71.2(a)	Not permitted on protest committee	63.4
71.2(b)	Deadline for making objections	63.4
71.3	PROTESTS BETWEEN YACHTS IN SEPARATE RACES	63.7
72	Notification of Parties	63.2
73	Hearings	63
73.1	RIGHT TO BE PRESENT	63.3
73.2	ACCEPTANCE OR REFUSAL OF A PROTEST	63.5
73.3	TAKING OF EVIDENCE	63.3(a)
73.4	EVIDENCE OF COMMITTEE MEMBER	63.6
73.5	FAILURE TO ATTEND	63.3(b)
73.6	REOPENING A HEARING	66
73.6(a)	Reasons; deadlines to request reopening	66
73.6(b)	Protest committee composition	66
74	Decisions and Penalties	64
74.1	FINDING OF FACTS	63.6
74.2	CONSIDERATION OF REDRESS	64.2
74.2(a)	material prejudice; no fault of her own	

Old Rule Number	Old Rule Name	New Rule Number(s)
74.2(b)	must consider all relevant facts and consequences	64.2
74.2(c)	equitable solution for all yachts	64.2
74.3	MEASUREMENT PROTESTS	64.3
74.3(a)	"referral to qualified authority, if in doubt"	64.3(b)
74.3(b)	notification of prior measurer	65.3
74.3(c)	"if appealed, can continue to compete"	64.3(c)
74.4	PENALTIES AND EXONERATION	64.1
74.4(a)	DSQ and exoneration	64.1(a)
74.4(a)(i)	yacht infringes	64.1(a)
74.4(a)(ii)	yacht compels another to infringe	64.1(b)
74.4(b)	Yacht infringes while not racing	64.1(c)
74.5	SCORING	A1
74.5(a)	definition of competing yacht	
74.5(b)	yachts below DSQ not moved up	A1.2
74.5(c)	yacht removed from series	A1.7
74.5(d)	not excluding FR C or D DSQ	A1.3
74.6	THE DECISION	65
74.6(a)	Promptly communicate to parties:	65.1
74.6(a)(i)	facts	65.1
74.6(a)(ii)	rules applicable	65.1
74.6(a)(iii)	decision and grounds	65.1
74.6(a)(iv)	yacht penalized	65.1
74.6(a)(v)	penalty or redress	65.1
74.6(b)	Requesting a written decision	65.2
SECTION C	Special Rules	
75	Gross Infringement of Rules or Misconduct	Section C - Gross Misconduct
75.1	PENALTIES BY THE RACE OR PROTEST COMMITTEE	69.1
75.1(a)	Hearing for gross infringement or misconduct	69.1(a)
75.1(b)	Penalties and reporting to NA	69.1(b); 69.1(c)
75.1(c)	Written allegations required	69.1(a); 69.1(b)
75.2	PENALTIES BY THE NATIONAL AUTHORITY	69.2
75.2(a)	NA penalties	69.2(a)
75.2(a)(i)	suspension of eligibility	69.2(a)
75.2(a)(ii)	suspension of IYRU eligibility	69.2(a)
		69.2(b)
75.2(b)	reporting penalties to IYRU	69.2(c)
75.3	PENALTIES BY THE IYRU	69.3
76	Liability	
76.1	DAMAGES	68
76.2	MEASUREMENT EXPENSES	64.3(d)
SECTION D	Appeals	Part 5 - Section D

Old Rule Number	Old Rule Name	New Rule Number(s)
77	Right of Appeal and Decisions	70; 71
77.1	RIGHT OF APPEAL	70.1
77.2	RIGHT OF REFERENCE	70.2
77.3	QUESTIONS OF INTERPRETATION	70.3
77.4	INTERPRETATION OF RULES	70.1; F8(c)
77.5	INTERESTED PARTIES	71.1; F8(a)
77.6	DECISIONS	71
77.6(a)	"AC may uphold, alter or reverse"	71.2
77.6(b)	AC must penalize infringing yachts	71.3
77.6(c)	AC decision if final	71.4
78	Appeal Procedures	Appendix F
78.1	APPELLANT'S RESPONSIBILITIES	F2
78.1(a)	Time limit and contents	F2.1
78.1(b)	Other required documents:	F2.2
78.1(b)(i)	protest	F2.2(a)
78.1(b)(ii)	diagram	F2.2(b)
78.1(b)(iii)	"NOR, SI & other conditions"	F2.2(c)
78.1(b)(iv)	written statements from parties	
78.1(b)(v)	additional relevant documents	F2.2(d)
78.1(b)(vi)	parties' names & addresses	F2.2(e)
78.2	NOTIFICATION OF THE PC AND AAC	F3
78.3	PROTEST COMMITTEE'S RESPONSIBILITIES	F4
78.4	AAC'S OR USSA'S RESPONSIBILITIES	F5; F6
78.5	COMMENTS	F7
78.6	FEE	F2.1; F2.3
78.7	WITHDRAWING AN APPEAL	
APPENDICES	APPENDICES	Appendices
Preamble	Preamble to Appendices	Introduction-Appendices
App. A1	Competitors' Eligibility Code	Appendix K
App. A1A	Definitions for Competitor Eligibility	
App. A2	Banned Substances and Banned Methods	Appendix L
App. A3	Advertising and Event Categories	Appendix G
App. A4	Weighing of Wet Clothing	Appendix J
App. A5	International Juries	Appendix Q
App. B1	Alternative Penalties for Infringing a Rule of Par	44
App. B2	Scoring Systems	Appendix A
App. B2A	Alternative Scoring System for Long Series	
App. B3	"Identification-Class Insignia, National Letters an"	Appendix H
App. B4	Sailboard Racing Rules	Appendix B
App. B5	Team Racing Rules	Appendix D

Old Rule Number	Old Rule Name	New Rule Number(s)
App. B6	Match Racing Rules	Appendix C
App. B8	Performance Handicap Racing Fleet Rules	
App. B9	IMS and IOR Rating Certificate Reviews	
App. B10	Sound-Signal Starting System	
App. C1	Protest Committee Procedures	Appendix P
App. C2	Sailing Instruction Guide	Appendix N
App. C2A	Notice of Race Guide	
App. C3	Guide for Principal Events	
App. C4	Protest Form	Protest Form

THE RACING RULES OF SAILING

1997–2000

Including US SAILING *Prescriptions*

15 Maritime Drive   Post Office Box 1260   Portsmouth, RI 02871

A NOTE FROM US SAILING'S PRESIDENT

Here it is—after years of talking about simplifying the rules, more years of work to write and test them, after approval by the International Sailing Federation (ISAF) and US SAILING, we now have this exciting new rule book for our game of racing sailboats.

These rules are written in plain language and simple form that you and I can understand. We can read the rule and have a pretty good understanding of how it applies to our racing, how it governs the game. The order of the rules within the book makes sense as well. The most important stuff is right up front, you don't have to plow through pages of procedural matters to get to the right-of-way rules. A third major feature is that, for the first time, there is a comprehensive index (in the back of the book), that will quickly lead you to the information you need without leafing through page after page to find what you know is in there somewhere.

This little rule book, remarkably brief, is the result on an incredible volunteer effort, as well as significant investment by ISAF and US SAILING. All members of US SAILING may be justifiably proud of the contributions by our Racing Rules Committee, and in particular Dick Rose and Bill Bentsen, members of the ISAF Working Party on the new rules.

The volunteers and staff of US SAILING recognize that meeting your needs as a sailor is our mission. US SAILING strives to provide you with a comprehensive array of services, including these racing rules, management of various handicapping rules, appeals systems, sailing championships, safety development and promotion, training programs at every level, race management training and development, and a host of other services for sailors and their local sailing organizations.

In return, US SAILING needs the help of all of you in persuading your friends and crew mates that they also should be members and help shoulder the cost of these services. A membership application is bound into the back of the book for your use.

The game we know and love will change only modestly under these new simplified rules, and such change will definitely be for the better. In particular, those newly discovering competitive sailing will fast track to rule understanding, making the game better for all.

So, here they are, the first truly new rules in decades. Read at least the first few pages, then go out on the water and have great fun sailing fair and fast.

David H. Irish, President

© 1997 International Sailing Federation
Reprinted by permission of the International Sailing Federation
Foreword and Prescriptions Copyright © 1997
United States Sailing Association all rights reserved

ISBN 1-882502-43-4

CONTENTS

FOREWORD

On April 1, 1997, the Racing Rules of Sailing for 1997-2000 replace the 1993-1996 International Yacht Racing Rules. Every four years, after the Olympic Games, the International Sailing Federation (formerly called the International Yacht Racing Union) revises the racing rules. This edition of the racing rules is the result of the most thorough review and revision of the rules of our sport that has taken place since the 1940's. The new rules are about half the length of the old rules, and efforts have been made to organize them in a manner that will be helpful to competitors and to express them in simple, modern English. Virtually every rule has been rewritten and assigned a new rule number. Readers will find the new Index helpful for locating the rules that cover a particular topic.

Competitors in club or local races should pay particular attention to the rules in Parts 1-7. The appendices treat special topics that are primarily of interest to race officials and competitors in international and other high-profile events.

Judges and members of protest committees will find Appendix P helpful. Those who write sailing instructions can obtain excellent guidance from Appendices M and N. Time spent well before a regatta studying the appendices that relate to your duties will be time well spent.

The rules that apply when boats meet are in Part 2. The most significant changes in those rules are in Section B of Part 2, and they warrant close study. In addition, rule 18.3 is an important new constraint on boats approaching a windward mark. Outside of Part 2, the substantive changes in the rules are no more extensive than those that were made in 1989 and 1993. Other rules worthy of careful study include: 13, 20, 26.1, 30.2, 30.3, 31.2, 33, 40, 42.1, 42.3(d), 43, 44, 46, 49, 50.3(a), 51, 60.2, 61, 63.1, 69.1(b)(1), 69.2(a), 86.1, and the definitions *keep clear*, *room*, and *obstruction*.

This book contains the international rules of our sport and additional rules adopted by US SAILING. The added rules, called 'prescriptions', appear in bold italics. If a competitor takes this rule book to a regatta in another national authority's waters, he need only study the prescriptions in that national authority's rule book. Appendices AA, R, S and T have been added by US SAILING.

Many rule changes are the result of ideas proposed by competitors and race officials. Suggestions for improving the rules are welcomed by US SAILING's Racing Rules Committee. Please mail your ideas to: US SAILING Racing Rules Committee, 15 Maritime Drive, Portsmouth, RI 02871-6015, fax them to (401) 683-0840, or e-mail them to 75530.502@compuserve.com.

Dick Rose, Outgoing Chairman,
Rob Overton, Incoming Chairman,
US SAILING Racing Rules Committee

INTRODUCTION

The Racing Rules of Sailing includes two main sections. The first, Parts 1–7, contains rules that affect all competitors. The second section contains appendices that provide details of rules, rules that apply to particular kinds of racing, and rules that affect only a small number of competitors or officials.

The racing rules are revised and published every four years by the International Sailing Federation (ISAF), the international authority for the sport. This edition becomes effective on 1 April 1997. No changes are contemplated before 2001, but changes determined by the ISAF to be urgent will be made as needed and announced through national authorities.

Terminology A term used in the sense stated in the Definitions is printed in italics or, in preambles, in bold italics (for example, *racing* and ***racing***). Other words and terms are used in the sense ordinarily understood in nautical or general use. 'Race committee' includes any person or committee performing a race committee function. 'Class rules' includes rules of handicapping and rating systems.

Appendices When the rules of an appendix apply, they take precedence over any conflicting rules in Parts 1–7. A reference to a rule of an appendix will contain the letter of the appendix and the rule number; for example, 'rule A1.1'. (There is no Appendix I or Appendix O.)

Changes to the Rules The prescriptions of a national authority, class rules or the sailing instructions may change a racing rule only as permitted in rule 86.

US SAILING prescriptions are printed in bold italics.

SPORTSMANSHIP AND THE RULES

COMPETITORS IN THE SPORT OF SAILING ARE GOVERNED BY
A BODY OF RULES THAT THEY ARE EXPECTED TO FOLLOW
AND ENFORCE. A FUNDAMENTAL PRINCIPLE OF SPORTSMANSHIP
IS THAT WHEN COMPETITORS BREAK A RULE THEY WILL
PROMPTLY TAKE A PENALTY OR RETIRE.

PART 1 - FUNDAMENTAL RULES

1   SAFETY

1.1   **Helping Those in Danger**

A boat or competitor shall give all possible help to any person or vessel in danger.

1.2   **Life-saving Equipment and Personal Buoyancy**

A boat shall carry adequate life-saving equipment for all persons on board, including one item ready for immediate use, unless her class rules make some other provision. Each competitor is individually responsible for wearing personal buoyancy adequate for the conditions.

2   **FAIR SAILING**

A boat and her owner shall compete in compliance with recognized principles of sportsmanship and fair play. A boat may be penalized under this rule only if it is clearly established that these principles have been violated.

3   **ACCEPTANCE OF THE RULES**

By participating in a race conducted under these racing rules, each competitor and boat owner agrees

(a) to be governed by the *rules*;

(b) to accept the penalties imposed and other action taken under the *rules*, subject to the appeal and review procedures provided in them, as the final determination of any matter arising under the *rules*; and

(c) with respect to such determination, not to resort to any court or other tribunal not provided by the *rules*.

4 DECISION TO RACE

A boat is solely responsible for deciding whether or not to *start* or to continue *racing*.

5 DRUGS

A competitor shall neither take a substance nor use a method banned by Appendix L. An alleged breach of this rule shall not be grounds for a *protest*, and rule 63.1 does not apply.

PART 2 – WHEN BOATS MEET

*The rules of Part 2 apply between boats that are sailing in or near the racing area and intend to **race**, are **racing**, or have been **racing**. However, a boat not **racing** shall not be penalized for breaking one of these rules, except rule 22.1. The International Regulations for Preventing Collisions at Sea or government right-of-way rules apply between a boat sailing under these rules and a vessel that is not, and they replace these rules if the sailing instructions so state.*

Section A – Right of Way

*A boat has right of way when another boat is required to **keep clear** of her. However, some rules in Sections B and C limit the actions of a right-of-way boat.*

10 ON OPPOSITE TACKS

When boats are on opposite *tacks*, a *port-tack* boat shall *keep clear* of a *starboard-tack* boat.

11 ON THE SAME TACK, OVERLAPPED

When boats are on the same *tack* and *overlapped*, a *windward* boat shall *keep clear* of a *leeward* boat.

12 ON THE SAME TACK, NOT OVERLAPPED

When boats are on the same *tack* and not *overlapped*, a boat *clear astern* shall *keep clear* of a boat *clear ahead*.

13 WHILE TACKING

After a boat passes head to wind, she shall *keep clear* of other boats until she is on a close-hauled course. During that time rules 10, 11 and 12 do not apply. If two boats are subject to this rule at the same time, the one on the other's port side shall *keep clear*.

Section B – General Limitations

14   AVOIDING CONTACT

A boat shall avoid contact with another boat if reasonably possible. However, a right-of-way boat or one entitled to *room*

(a) need not act to avoid contact until it is clear that the other boat is not *keeping clear* or giving *room,* and

(b) shall not be penalized unless there is contact that causes damage.

15   ACQUIRING RIGHT OF WAY

When a boat acquires right of way, she shall initially give the other boat *room* to *keep clear,* unless she acquires right of way because of the other boat's actions.

16   CHANGING COURSE

When a right-of-way boat changes course, she shall give the other boat *room* to *keep clear.*

17   ON THE SAME TACK; PROPER COURSE

17.1   A boat that establishes a *leeward overlap* from *clear astern* within two of her hull lengths of a *windward* boat shall not sail above her *proper course* during that *overlap* while the boats are less than that distance apart, unless as a result she becomes *clear astern.*

17.2   Except on a beat to windward, while a boat is less than two of her hull lengths from a *leeward* boat or a boat *clear astern* steering a course to *leeward* of her, she shall not sail below her *proper course* unless she gybes.

Section C – At Marks and Obstructions

When a Section C rule applies, the rules in Sections A and B continue to apply unless the Section C rule modifies them or states that they do not apply.

18   PASSING MARKS AND OBSTRUCTIONS

18.1 When this Rule Applies

Rule 18 applies at a *mark* or *obstruction* to be left on the same side when boats are about to pass it until they have passed it. However, it does not apply

(a) at a starting *mark* or its anchor line surrounded by navigable water from the time the boats are approaching them to *start* until they have passed them, or

(b) between boats on opposite *tacks* when they are on a beat to windward or when the *proper course* for one of them to pass the *mark* or *obstruction* is to tack.

18.2 Giving Room; Keeping Clear

(a) When boats are *overlapped* before one of them reaches the *two-length zone*, if the outside boat has right of way she shall give the inside boat *room* to pass the *mark* or *obstruction*, or if the inside boat has right of way the outside boat shall *keep clear*. If they are still *overlapped* when one of them reaches the *two-length zone*, the outside boat's obligation continues even if the *overlap* is broken later. This rule does not apply if the outside boat is unable to give *room* when the *overlap* begins.

(b) If a boat is *clear ahead* when she reaches the *two-length zone*, the boat *clear astern* shall *keep clear* even if an *overlap* is established later. Rule 10 does not apply. If the boat *clear ahead* tacks, rule 13 applies and this rule no longer does.

(c) If there is reasonable doubt that a boat established or broke an *overlap* in time, it shall be presumed that she did not.

7

18.3 Tacking

If two boats were on opposite *tacks* and one of them tacked within the *two-length zone* to pass a *mark* or *obstruction*, rule 18.2 does not apply. The boat that tacked

(a) shall not cause the other boat to sail above close-hauled to avoid her or prevent the other boat from passing the *mark* or *obstruction*, and

(b) shall *keep clear* if the other boat becomes *overlapped* inside her, in which case rule 15 does not apply.

18.4 Gybing

When rule 18.2(a) applies and an inside *overlapped* right-of-way boat must gybe at the *mark* or *obstruction* to sail her *proper course*, she shall pass no farther from the *mark* or *obstruction* than needed to sail that course.

18.5 Passing a Continuing Obstruction

At a continuing *obstruction*, rule 18.2 is modified so that while boats are passing the *obstruction* an outside boat's obligation ends if the *overlap* is broken, and a boat *clear astern* may establish an inside *overlap* provided there is *room* at that time to pass between the other boat and the *obstruction*. If she does so, her obligation under rule 18.2(b) ends.

19 ROOM TO TACK AT AN OBSTRUCTION

19.1

When safety requires a close-hauled boat to make a substantial course change to avoid an *obstruction* and she intends to tack, but cannot tack and avoid another boat on the same *tack*, she shall hail for *room* to do so. Before tacking she shall give the hailed boat time to respond. The hailed boat shall either

(a) tack as soon as possible, in which case the hailing boat shall also tack as soon as possible, or

(b) immediately reply 'You tack', in which case the hailing boat shall immediately tack and the hailed boat shall give *room*, and rules 10 and 13 do not apply.

19.2

Rule 19.1 does not apply at a starting *mark* or its anchor line surrounded by navigable water from the time boats are approaching them to *start* until they have passed them or at a *mark* that the hailed boat can fetch. When rule 19.1 applies, rule 18 does not.

Section D – Other Rules

When rule 20 or 21 applies between two boats, Section A rules do not.

20 **STARTING ERRORS; PENALTY TURNS; MOVING ASTERN**

A boat sailing towards the pre-start side of the starting line or its extensions to comply with rule 29.1 or rule 30.1 shall *keep clear* of a boat not doing so until she is completely on the pre-start side. A boat making penalty turns shall *keep clear* of one that is not. A boat moving astern by backing a sail shall *keep clear* of one that is not.

21 **CAPSIZED, ANCHORED OR AGROUND; RESCUING**

If possible, a boat shall avoid a boat that is capsized or has not regained control after capsizing, is anchored or aground, or is trying to help a person or vessel in danger. A boat is capsized when her masthead is in the water.

22 **INTERFERING WITH ANOTHER BOAT**

22.1 If reasonably possible, a boat not *racing* shall not interfere with a boat that is *racing*.

22.2 A boat shall not deliberately interfere with a boat making penalty turns to delay her.

PART 3 – CONDUCT OF A RACE

25   SAILING INSTRUCTIONS AND SIGNALS

Sailing instructions shall be made available to each boat before a race begins. The race committee shall conduct the race using the visual and sound signals defined in the Race Signals and any other signals included in the sailing instructions.

26   STARTING SYSTEMS 1 AND 2

26.1   A race shall be started by using either System 1 or System 2. Signals shall be made at five-minute intervals. Times shall be taken from the visual signals; the failure of a sound signal shall be disregarded. Signals shall be as follows (flags of a single colour may be replaced by shapes of the same colour):

Signal	System 1	System 2
Warning	Class flag; 1 sound	Yellow flag; 1 sound
Preparatory	Flag P; 1 sound	Blue flag; 1 sound
Starting	Flags removed; 1 sound	Red flag; 1 sound

26.2   In System 1, when classes are started at ten-minute intervals, the warning signal for each succeeding class shall be displayed at the starting signal of the preceding class. When five-minute intervals are used, flag P shall be left displayed until the last class starts and the warning signal for each succeeding class shall be displayed at the time of the preparatory signal of the preceding class. If there is a general recall, the warning and preparatory signals of any succeeding classes shall be removed immediately after the general recall has been signalled.

26.3   In System 2, each signal shall be removed one minute before the next is made. When classes are started at ten-minute intervals, the starting signal for each class shall be the warning signal for the next. When classes are started at five-minute intervals, the preparatory signal for each class shall be the warning signal for the next. When class flags are used, they shall be displayed before or with the preparatory signal for the class.

27 OTHER RACE COMMITTEE ACTIONS BEFORE THE STARTING SIGNAL

27.1 No later than the warning signal, the race committee shall signal or otherwise designate the course to be sailed if the sailing instructions have not stated the course, and it may replace one course signal with another, signal that a designated short course will be used (flag S), and apply rule 40 (flag Y).

27.2 No later than the preparatory signal, the race committee may move a starting *mark* and may apply rule 30.

27.3 Before the starting signal, the race committee may *postpone* (flag AP) or *abandon* the race (flag N over H or A) for any reason.

28 SAILING THE COURSE

28.1 A boat shall *start,* pass each *mark* on the required side in the correct order, and *finish,* so that a string representing her wake after *starting* and until *finishing* would, when drawn taut, lie on the required side of each *mark* and touch each rounding *mark*. She may correct any errors to comply with this rule, provided she has not already *finished*. After *finishing,* a boat need not cross the finishing line completely.

28.2 A *mark* has a required side for a boat only when she is on a leg that the *mark* begins, bounds or ends, except that a starting *mark* begins to have a required side when she is approaching the starting line from its pre-start side to *start*.

29 STARTING; RECALLS

29.1 On the Course Side at the Start

When at her starting signal any part of a boat's hull, crew or equipment is on the course side of the starting line, the boat shall sail completely to the pre-start side of the line before *starting*.

29.2 Individual Recall

When at her starting signal a boat must comply with rule 29.1 or rule 30.1, the race committee shall promptly display flag X. The signal shall be displayed until all such boats are completely on the pre-start side of the starting line or its extensions and have complied with rule 30.1 if it applies, but not later than four minutes after the starting signal or one minute before any later starting signal, whichever is earlier.

29.3 General Recall

When at the starting signal several unidentified boats are on the course side of the starting line or there has been an error in the starting procedure, the race committee may signal a general recall (flag First Substitute). The preparatory signal for a new start for the recalled class shall be made one minute after the First Substitute is lowered, and the starts for any succeeding classes shall follow the new start.

30 STARTING PENALTIES

30.1 I Flag Rule

If flag I has been displayed before or with her preparatory signal, and any part of a boat's hull, crew or equipment is on the course side of the starting line or its extensions during the minute before her starting signal, she shall sail to the pre-start side of the line around either end before *starting*.

30.2 Z Flag Rule

If flag Z has been displayed before or with her preparatory signal, and any part of a boat's hull, crew or equipment is identified within the triangle formed by the ends of the starting line and the first *mark* during the minute before her starting signal and a general recall is then signalled, she shall, without a hearing, be given a 20% scoring penalty calculated as stated in rule 44.3(c). If the race is restarted, resailed or rescheduled, she shall still be given the penalty.

30.3 Black Flag Rule

If a black flag has been displayed before or with her preparatory signal, and any part of a boat's hull, crew or equipment is identified within the triangle formed by the ends of the starting line and the first *mark* during the minute before her starting signal, the boat will be disqualified without a hearing. If the race is restarted, resailed or rescheduled, she is not entitled to compete in it. If a general recall is signalled or the race is *abandoned*, the race committee shall display her sail number.

The prescription to 30.3 is deleted by action of the United States Sailing Association Board of Directors on March 23, 1997.

31 TOUCHING A MARK

31.1 While *racing*, a boat shall not touch a starting *mark* before *starting*, a *mark* that begins, bounds or ends the leg of the course on which she is sailing, or a finishing *mark* after *finishing*.

31.2 A boat that has broken rule 31.1 may, after getting well clear of other boats as soon as possible, take a penalty by promptly making one complete 360° turn including one tack and one gybe. When a boat takes the penalty after touching a finishing *mark,* she shall return completely to the course side of the line before *finishing*. However, if a boat has gained a significant advantage in the race or series by touching the *mark* she shall retire.

31.3 When a boat is wrongfully compelled by another boat to break rule 31.1, she shall be exonerated

    (a) if the other boat acknowledges breaking a rule of Part 2 by taking a penalty or retiring immediately, or

    (b) under rule 64.1(b), after successfully protesting another boat involved in the same incident.

32 SHORTENING OR ABANDONING AFTER THE START

After the starting signal, the race committee may *abandon* the race (flag N or flag N over H or A) or shorten the course (flag S), as appropriate,

    (a) because of an error in the starting procedure,

    (b) because of foul weather,

13

(c) because of insufficient wind making it unlikely that any boat will *finish* within the time limit,

(d) because a *mark* is missing or out of position, or

(e) for any other reason directly affecting the safety or fairness of the competition.

However, after one boat has sailed the course and *finished* within the time limit, if any, the race committee shall not *abandon* the race without considering the consequences for all boats in the race or series.

33   CHANGING THE COURSE AFTER THE START

At any rounding *mark* the race committee may signal a change of the direction of the next leg of the course by displaying flag C and the compass bearing of that leg before any boat begins it. The race committee may change the length of the next leg by displaying flag C and a '–' if the leg will be shortened or a '+' if the leg will be lengthened.

34   MARK MISSING; *RACE COMMITTEE ABSENT*

When a *mark* is missing or out of position, the race committee shall, if possible,

(a) replace it in its correct position, or

(b) substitute one of similar appearance, or a buoy or vessel displaying flag M.

US SAILING prescribes that, in the absence of the race committee, a boat shall take her own finishing time and report it to the race committee as soon as possible. If there is no longer an established finishing line, it shall be a line extending from the required side of the finishing mark at right angles to the course from the last mark and of the shortest practicable length.

35 **TIME LIMIT**

If one boat sails the course as required in rule 28.1 and *finishes* within the time limit, if any, all boats shall be scored unless the race is *abandoned*. If no boat *finishes* within the time limit, the race committee shall *abandon* the race.

36 **RACES TO BE RESTARTED OR RESAILED**

If a race is restarted or resailed, a breach of a *rule*, other than rule 30.3, in the original race shall not prohibit a boat from competing or, except under rule 30.2, 30.3 or 69, cause her to be penalized.

PART 4 – OTHER REQUIREMENTS WHEN RACING

Part 4 rules apply only to boats **racing**.

40   **PERSONAL BUOYANCY;** *LIFE-SAVING EQUIPMENT*

When flag Y is displayed before or with the warning signal, competitors shall wear life-jackets or other adequate personal buoyancy. Wet suits and dry suits are not adequate personal buoyancy.

US SAILING **prescribes that every boat shall carry life-saving equipment conforming to government regulations.**

41   **OUTSIDE HELP**

A boat may receive outside help as provided for in rule 1. Otherwise, she shall not receive help except for an ill or injured crew member or, after a collision, from the crew of the other boat.

42   **PROPULSION**

42.1   **Basic Rule**

Except when permitted in rule 42.3 or rule 45, a boat shall compete by using only the wind and water to increase, maintain or decrease her speed. Her crew may adjust the trim of sails and hull, and perform other acts of seamanship, but shall not otherwise move their bodies to propel the boat.

42.2   **Prohibited Actions**

Without limiting the application of rule 42.1, these actions are prohibited:

(a) pumping: repeated fanning of any sail either by trimming and releasing the sail or by vertical or athwartships body movement;

(b) rocking: repeated rolling of the boat, induced either by body movement or adjustment of the sails or centreboard, that does not facilitate steering;

(c) ooching: sudden forward body movement, stopped abruptly;

(d) sculling: repeated movement of the helm not necessary for steering;

(e) repeated tacks or gybes unrelated to changes in the wind or to tactical considerations.

42.3 Exceptions

(a) A boat's crew may move their bodies to exaggerate the rolling that facilitates steering the boat through a tack or a gybe, provided that, just after the tack or gybe is completed, the boat's speed is not greater than it would have been in the absence of the tack or gybe.

(b) Except on a beat to windward, when surfing (rapidly accelerating down the leeward side of a wave) or planing is possible, the boat's crew may pull the sheet and the guy controlling any sail in order to initiate surfing or planing, but only once for each wave or gust of wind.

(c) Any means of propulsion may be used to help a person or another vessel in danger.

(d) To get clear after grounding or colliding with another boat or object, a boat may use force applied by the crew of either boat and any equipment other than a propulsion engine.

43 COMPETITOR CLOTHING AND EQUIPMENT

43.1 (a) Competitors shall not wear or carry clothing or equipment for the purpose of increasing their weight.

(b) Furthermore, a competitor's clothing and equipment shall not weigh more than 8 kilograms, excluding a hiking or trapeze harness and clothing (including footwear) worn only below the knee. Class rules or sailing instructions may specify a lower weight or a higher weight up to 10 kilograms. Class rules may include footwear and other clothing worn below the knee within that weight. A hiking or trapeze harness shall have positive buoyancy and shall not weigh more than 2 kilograms, except that class rules may specify a higher weight up to 4 kilograms. Weights shall be determined as required by Appendix J.

(c) When a measurer in charge of weighing clothing and equipment believes a competitor may have broken rule 43.1(a) or rule 43.1(b) he shall report the matter in writing to the protest committee.

43.2 Rule 43.1(b) does not apply to boats required to be equipped with lifelines.

44 PENALTIES FOR BREAKING RULES OF PART 2

44.1 Taking a Penalty

A boat that may have broken a rule of Part 2 while *racing* may take a penalty at the time of the incident. Her penalty shall be a 720° Turns Penalty unless the sailing instructions specify the use of the Scoring Penalty or some other penalty. However, if she caused serious damage or gained a significant advantage in the race or series by her breach she shall retire.

44.2 720° Turns Penalty

After getting well clear of other boats as soon after the incident as possible, a boat takes a 720° Turns Penalty by promptly making two complete 360° turns (720°) in the same direction, including two tacks and two gybes. When a boat takes the penalty at or near the finishing line, she shall return completely to the course side of the line before *finishing*.

44.3 Scoring Penalty

(a) A boat takes a Scoring Penalty by displaying a yellow flag at the first reasonable opportunity after the incident, keeping it displayed until *finishing,* and calling the race committee's attention to it at the finishing line. At that time she shall also inform the race committee of the identity of the other boat involved in the incident. If this is impracticable, she shall do so at the first reasonable opportunity within the time limit for *protests.*

(b) If a boat displays a yellow flag, she shall also comply with the other parts of rule 44.3(a).

(c) The boat's penalty score shall be the score for the place worse than her actual finishing place by the number of places stated in the sailing instructions, except that she shall not be scored worse than Did Not Finish. When the sailing instructions do not state the number of places, the number shall be the whole number (rounding 0.5 upward) nearest to 20% of the number of boats entered. The scores of other boats shall not be changed; therefore two boats may receive the same score.

44.4   Limits on Penalties

(a) When a boat intends to take a penalty as provided in rule 44.1 and in the same incident has touched a *mark*, she need not take the penalty provided in rule 31.2.

(b) A boat that takes a penalty shall not be penalized further with respect to the same incident unless she failed to retire when rule 44.1 required her to do so.

45   HAULING OUT; MAKING FAST; ANCHORING

A boat shall be afloat and off moorings at her preparatory signal. Thereafter, she may not be hauled out or made fast except to bail out, reef sails, or make repairs. She may anchor or the crew may stand on the bottom. She shall recover the anchor before continuing in the race unless she is unable to do so.

46   PERSON IN CHARGE

A boat shall have on board a person in charge designated by the member or organization that entered the boat. See rule 75.

47   LIMITATIONS ON EQUIPMENT AND CREW

**47.1   **A boat shall use only the equipment on board at her preparatory signal.

**47.2   **No person on board shall leave, unless ill or injured or to help a person or vessel in danger. However, a person leaving the boat by accident or to swim shall be back on board before the boat continues in the race.

48   FOG SIGNALS AND LIGHTS

When safety requires, a boat shall sound fog signals and show lights as required by the International Regulations for Preventing Collisions at Sea or applicable government rules.

US SAILING prescribes that the use of additional special purpose lights such as masthead, spreader and jib-luff lights shall not constitute a breach of this rule.

49   CREW POSITION

49.1   A boat shall use no device other than hiking straps to project a competitor's body outboard.

49.2   When lifelines are required by the class rules or the sailing instructions they shall be taut, and competitors shall not position any part of their torsos outside them, except briefly to perform a necessary task. On boats equipped with upper and lower lifelines of wire, a competitor sitting on the deck facing outboard with his waist inside the lower lifeline may have the upper part of his body outside the upper lifeline.

50   SETTING AND SHEETING SAILS

50.1   **Changing Sails**

When headsails or spinnakers are being changed, a replacing sail may be fully set and trimmed before the replaced sail is lowered. However, only one mainsail and, except when changing, only one spinnaker shall be carried set at a time.

50.2   **Spinnaker Poles, Whisker Poles**

Only one spinnaker pole or whisker pole shall be used at a time except when gybing. When in use, it shall be attached to the foremost mast.

50.3   **Use of Outriggers**

(a)   No sail shall be sheeted over or through an outrigger, except as permitted in rule 50.3(b). An outrigger is any fitting or other device so placed that it could exert outward pressure on a sheet or sail at a point from which, with the boat upright, a vertical line would fall outside the hull or deck planking. For the purpose of this rule, bulwarks, rails and rubbing strakes are not part of the hull or deck planking and the following are not outriggers: a bowsprit used to secure the tack of a working sail, a bumkin used to sheet the boom of a working sail, or a boom of a boomed headsail that requires no adjustment when tacking.

(b) (1) Any sail may be sheeted to or led above a boom that is regularly used for a working sail and is permanently attached to the mast from which the head of the working sail is set.

(2) A headsail may be sheeted or attached at its clew to a spinnaker pole or whisker pole, provided that a spinnaker is not set.

50.4 Headsails

The difference between a headsail and a spinnaker is that the mid-girth of a headsail, measured from the mid-points of its luff and leech, does not exceed 50% of the length of its foot, and no other intermediate girth exceeds a percentage similarly proportional to its distance from the head of the sail. A sail tacked down behind the foremost mast is not a headsail.

51 MOVING BALLAST

All movable ballast shall be properly stowed, and water, dead weight or ballast shall not be moved for the purpose of changing trim or stability. Floorboards, bulkheads, doors, stairs and water tanks shall be left in place and all cabin fixtures kept on board.

52 MANUAL POWER

A boat's standing rigging, running rigging, spars and movable hull appendages shall be adjusted and operated only by manual power.

53 SKIN FRICTION

A boat shall not eject or release a substance, such as a polymer, or have specially textured surfaces that could improve the character of the flow of water inside the boundary layer.

54   FORESTAYS AND HEADSAIL TACKS

Forestays and headsail tacks, except those of spinnaker staysails when the boat is not close-hauled, shall be attached approximately on a boat's centre-line.

55   FLAGS

US SAILING prescribes that a boat shall not display flags except for signaling.   A boat shall not be penalized for breaking this rule without prior warning and opportunity to make correction.

PART 5 – PROTESTS, HEARINGS, MISCONDUCT AND APPEALS

Section A – Protests

60   RIGHT TO PROTEST AND REQUEST REDRESS

60.1   A boat may

(a) protest another boat, but not for an alleged breach of a rule of Part 2 unless she was involved in or saw the incident; or

(b) request redress.

60.2   A race committee may

(a) protest a boat, but not as a result of a report by a competitor from another boat or other *interested party* or of information in an invalid *protest*;

(b) request the protest committee to consider giving redress; or

(c) report to the protest committee requesting action under rule 69.1(a).

60.3   A protest committee may

(a) protest a boat, but not as a result of a report by a competitor from another boat or other *interested party*, except under rule 61.1(c), nor as a result of information in an invalid *protest*;

(b) consider giving redress; or

(c) act under rule 69.1(a).

61   PROTEST REQUIREMENTS

61.1   Informing the Protestee

(a) A boat intending to protest because of an incident occurring in the racing area that she is aware of shall hail 'Protest' and conspicuously display a red flag at the first reasonable opportunity for each. She shall display the flag either until she *finishes* or retires, or, if the incident occurs near the finishing line, until the race committee acknowledges seeing her flag. In all other cases she shall inform the other boat as soon as reasonably possible.

(b) A race committee or protest committee intending to protest a boat under rule 60.2(a) or rule 60.3(a) because of an incident it observes in the racing area shall inform her after the race within the time limit determined by rule 61.3. In all other cases it shall inform her as soon as reasonably possible.

(c) During the hearing of a valid *protest,* if the protest committee decides to protest a boat that was involved in the incident but is not a *party* to that hearing, it shall inform the boat as soon as reasonably possible of its intention and of the time and place of the hearing.

61.2 Protest Contents

A *protest* shall be in writing and identify

(a) the protestor and protestee;

(b) the incident, including where and when it occurred;

(c) any *rule* the protestor believes was broken; and

(d) the name of the protestor's representative.

Provided the written *protest* identifies the incident, other details may be corrected before or during the hearing.

61.3 Protest Time Limit

A *protest* by a boat, or by the race committee or protest committee about an incident the committee observes in the racing area, shall be delivered to the race office no later than the time limit stated in the sailing instructions. If none is stated, the time limit is two hours after the last boat in the race *finishes.* Other race committee or protest committee *protests* shall be delivered to the race office within two hours after the committee receives the relevant information. The protest committee shall extend the time if there is good reason to do so.

62   REDRESS

62.1 A request for redress shall be based on a claim that a boat's finishing place in a race or series has, through no fault of her own, been made significantly worse by

(a) an improper action or omission of the race committee or protest committee,

(b) physical damage because of the action of a boat that was breaking a rule of Part 2 or of a vessel not *racing* that was required to keep clear,

(c) giving help (except to herself or her crew) in compliance with rule 1.1, or

(d) a boat against which a penalty has been imposed under rule 2 or disciplinary action has been taken under rule 69.1(b).

62.2 The request shall be made in writing within the time limit of rule 61.3 or within two hours of the relevant incident, whichever is later. No protest flag is required.

US SAILING prescribes that a request for redress claiming that a boat's finishing place was made significantly worse by an action or omission of a protest committee shall be delivered before 1800 on the day following the protest committee's action or omission or its decision, or later if there is good reason to extend this time limit.

Section B – Hearings and Decisions

63   HEARINGS

63.1   Requirement for a Hearing

A boat or competitor shall not be penalized without a hearing, except as provided in rules 30.2, 30.3, 67 and A1.1. A decision on redress shall not be made without a hearing. The protest committee shall hear all *protests* that have been delivered to the race office unless it approves a protestor's request to withdraw the *protest*.

63.2 Time and Place of the Hearing

All *parties* to the hearing shall be notified of the time and place of the hearing, the *protest* or redress information shall be made available to them, and they shall be allowed reasonable time to prepare for the hearing.

63.3 Right to Be Present

(a) The *parties* to the hearing, or a representative of each, have the right to be present throughout the hearing of all the evidence. When the *protest* claims a breach of a rule of Part 2, Part 3 or Part 4, the representatives of boats shall have been on board at the time of the incident, unless there is good reason for the protest committee to rule otherwise. Any witness, other than a member of the protest committee, shall be excluded except when giving evidence.

(b) If a *party* to the hearing does not come to the hearing, the protest committee may nevertheless decide the *protest*. If the *party* was unavoidably absent, the committee may reopen the hearing.

63.4 Interested Party

A member of a protest committee who is an *interested party* shall not take any further part in the hearing but may appear as a witness. A *party* to the hearing who believes a member of the protest committee is an *interested party* shall object as soon as possible.

63.5 Validity of the Protest

At the beginning of the hearing the protest committee shall decide whether all requirements for the *protest* have been met, after first taking any evidence it considers necessary. If all requirements have been met, the *protest* is valid and the hearing shall be continued. If not, it shall be closed.

63.6 Taking Evidence and Finding Facts

The protest committee shall take the evidence of the *parties* to the hearing and of their witnesses and other evidence it considers necessary. A member of the protest committee who saw the incident may give evidence. A *party* to the hearing may question any person who gives evidence. The committee shall then find the facts and base its decision on them.

63.7 Protests Between Boats in Different Races

A *protest* between boats sailing in different races conducted by different organizing authorities shall be heard by a protest committee acceptable to those authorities.

64 PROTEST DECISIONS

64.1 Penalties and Exoneration

(a) When the protest committee decides that a boat that is a *party* to the hearing has broken a *rule,* she shall be disqualified unless some other penalty applies. A penalty shall be imposed whether or not the applicable *rule* was mentioned in the *protest.*

(b) When as a consequence of breaking a *rule* a boat has compelled another boat to break a *rule,* rule 64.1(a) does not apply to the other boat and she shall be exonerated.

(c) If a boat has broken a *rule* when not *racing,* her penalty shall apply to the race sailed nearest in time to that of the incident.

64.2 Decisions on Redress

When the protest committee decides that a boat is entitled to redress under rule 62, it shall make as fair an arrangement as possible for all boats affected, whether or not they asked for redress. This may be to adjust the scoring (see rule A4 for some examples) or finishing times of boats, to *abandon* the race, to let the results stand or to make some other arrangement. When in doubt about the facts or probable results of any arrangement for the race or series, especially before *abandoning* the race, the protest committee shall take evidence from appropriate sources.

64.3 Decisions on Measurement Protests

(a) When the protest committee finds that deviations in excess of tolerances specified in the class rules were caused by damage or normal wear and do not improve the performance of the boat, it shall not penalize her. However, the boat shall not *race* again until the deviations have been corrected, except when the protest committee decides there is or has been no reasonable opportunity to do so.

(b) When the protest committee is in doubt about the meaning of a measurement rule, it shall refer its questions, together with the relevant facts, to an authority responsible for interpreting the rule. In making its decision, the committee shall be bound by the reply of the authority.

US SAILING prescribes that the authority responsible for intepreting the International Measurement System rules or the International Offshore Rule is the US SAILING Offshore Director.

(c) When a boat disqualified under a measurement rule states in writing that she intends to appeal, she may compete in subsequent races without changes to the boat, but will be disqualified if she fails to appeal or the appeal is decided against her.

(d) Measurement costs arising from a *protest* involving a measurement rule shall be paid by the unsuccessful *party* unless the protest committee decides otherwise.

64.4 DECISIONS ON PROTESTS INVOLVING APPENDIX R

US SAILING prescribes that when the protest committee is in doubt about the meaning of a rule of Appendix R, it shall refer its questions, together with the relevant facts, to the US SAILING Eligibility Committee. In making its decision, the protest committee shall be bound by the Eligibility Committee's reply.

65 INFORMING THE PARTIES AND OTHERS

65.1 After making its decision, the protest committee shall promptly inform the *parties* to the hearing of the facts found, the applicable *rules,* the decision, the reasons for it, and any penalties imposed or redress given.

65.2 A *party* to the hearing is entitled to receive the above information in writing, provided she asks for it in writing from the protest committee within seven days of being informed of the decision. The committee shall then promptly provide the information, including, when relevant, a diagram of the incident prepared or endorsed by the committee.

65.3 When the protest committee penalizes a boat under a measurement rule, it shall send the above information to the relevant measurement authorities.

66 REOPENING A HEARING

The protest committee may reopen a hearing when it decides that it may have made a significant error, or when significant new evidence becomes available within a reasonable time. It shall reopen a hearing when required by the national authority under rule F5. A *party* to the hearing may ask for a reopening no later than 24 hours after being informed of the decision. When a hearing is reopened, a majority of the members of the protest committee shall, if possible, be members of the original protest committee.

67 RULE 42 AND HEARING REQUIREMENT

When so stated in the sailing instructions, the protest committee may penalize without a hearing a boat that has broken rule 42, provided that a member of the committee or its designated observer has seen the incident. A boat so penalized shall be informed by notification in the race results.

68 DAMAGES

The question of damages arising from a breach of any *rule* shall be governed by the prescriptions, if any, of the national authority.

US SAILING prescribes that:

(a) *A boat that retires from a race or accepts a penalty does not, by that action alone, admit liability for damages.*

(b) *A protest committee shall find facts and make decisions only in compliance with the rules. No protest committee or US SAILING appeal authority shall adjudicate any claim for damages. Such a claim is subject to the jurisdiction of the courts.*

(c) *A basic purpose of the rules is to prevent contact between boats. By participating in an event governed by the rules, a boat agrees that responsibility for damages arising from any breach of the rules shall be based on fault as determined by application of the rules, and that she shall not be governed by the legal doctrine of 'assumption of risk' for monetary damages resulting from contact with other boats.*

29

Section C – Gross Misconduct

69   **ALLEGATIONS OF GROSS MISCONDUCT**

69.1   **Action by a Protest Committee**

(a)   When a protest committee, from its own observation or a report received, believes that a competitor may have committed a gross breach of a *rule* or of good manners or sportsmanship, or may have brought the sport into disrepute, it may call a hearing. The protest committee shall promptly inform the competitor in writing of the alleged misconduct and of the time and place of the hearing.

(b)   A protest committee of at least three members shall conduct the hearing, following rules 63.2, 63.3, 63.4 and 63.6. If it decides that the competitor committed the alleged misconduct it shall either
(1)   warn the competitor or
(2)   impose a penalty by excluding the competitor, and a boat when appropriate, from a race, or the remaining races of a series or the entire series, or by taking other action within its jurisdiction.

(c)   The protest committee shall promptly report a penalty, but not a warning, to the national authorities of the venue, of the competitor and of the boat owner.

(d)   If the competitor has left the venue and cannot be notified or fails to attend the hearing, the protest committee shall collect all available evidence and, when the allegation seems justified, make a report to the relevant national authorities.

(e)   When the protest committee has left the event and a report alleging misconduct is received, the race committee or organizing authority may appoint a new protest committee to proceed under this rule.

69.2   **Action by a National Authority**

(a)   When a national authority receives a report required in rule 69.1(c) or rule 69.1(d), or a report alleging a gross breach of a *rule* or of good manners or sportsmanship or conduct that brought the sport into disrepute, it may conduct an investigation and, when appropriate, shall conduct a hearing. It may then take any disciplinary action within its jurisdiction it considers appropriate against the competitor or boat, or other person involved, including suspending eligibility, permanently or for a specified period of time, to compete in any event held within its jurisdiction, and suspending ISAF eligibility under rule K3.1(a).

(b) The national authority of a competitor shall also suspend the ISAF eligibility of the competitor as required in rule K3.1(a).

(c) The national authority shall promptly report a suspension of eligibility under rule 69.2(a) to the ISAF, and to the national authorities of the person or the owner of the boat suspended if they are not members of the suspending national authority.

69.3   Action by the ISAF

Upon receipt of a report required by rules 69.2(c) and K4.1, the ISAF shall inform all national authorities, which may also suspend eligibility for events held within their jurisdiction. The ISAF Executive Committee shall suspend the competitor's ISAF eligibility as required in rule K3.1(a) if the competitor's national authority does not do so.

Section D – Appeals

70 RIGHT OF APPEAL AND REQUESTS FOR INTERPRETATIONS

70.1 Provided that the right of appeal has not been denied under rule 70.4, a protest committee's interpretation of a *rule* or its procedures, but not the facts in its decision, may be appealed to the national authority of the venue by

(a) a boat or competitor that is a *party* to a hearing, or

(b) a race committee that is a *party* to a hearing, provided the protest committee is a jury.

70.2 A protest committee may request confirmation or correction of its decision.

70.3 A club or other organization affiliated to a national authority may request an interpretation of the *rules,* provided no *protest* that may be appealed is involved.

70.4 There shall be no appeal from the decisions of an international jury constituted in compliance with Appendix Q. Furthermore, if the notice of race and the sailing instructions so state, the right of appeal may be denied provided that

(a) it is essential to determine promptly the result of a race that will qualify a boat to compete in a later stage of an event or a subsequent event (a national authority may prescribe that its approval is required for such a procedure),

(b) a national authority so approves for a particular event open only to entrants under its own jurisdiction, or

(c) a national authority after consultation with the ISAF so approves for a particular event, provided the jury is constituted as required by Appendix Q, except that only two members of the jury need be International Judges.

70.5 Appeals and requests shall conform to Appendix F.

71 APPEAL DECISIONS

71.1 No *interested party* or member of the protest committee shall take any part in the discussion or decision on an appeal or a request for confirmation or correction.

71.2 The national authority may uphold, change or reverse a protest committee's decision, declare the *protest* invalid, or return the *protest* for a new hearing and decision by the same or a different protest committee.

71.3 When from the facts found by the protest committee the national authority decides that a boat that was a *party* to the hearing broke a *rule,* it shall penalize her, whether or not that boat or that *rule* was mentioned in the protest committee's decision.

71.4 The decision of the national authority shall be final. The national authority shall send its decision in writing to all *parties* to the hearing and the protest committee, who shall be bound by the decision.

PART 6 – ENTRY AND QUALIFICATION

75   ENTERING A RACE

75.1   To enter a race, a boat shall comply with the requirements of the organizing authority of the race. She shall be entered by

(a)   a member of a club or other organization affiliated to a national authority,

(b)   such a club or organization, or

(c)   a member of a national authority.

75.2   Competitors shall comply with Appendix K, if applicable.

76   EXCLUSION OF BOATS OR COMPETITORS

76.1   The organizing authority or the race committee may reject or cancel the entry of a boat or exclude a competitor, subject to rule 76.2, provided it does so before the start of the first race and states the reason for doing so.

76.2   At world and continental championships no entry within stated quotas shall be rejected or cancelled without first obtaining the approval of the relevant international class association (or the Offshore Racing Council) or the ISAF.

76.3   *US SAILING prescribes that, when a reason for excluding a competitor is related to an eligibility rule, the competitor shall be entitled to a hearing.*

77   IDENTIFICATION ON SAILS

A boat shall comply with the requirements of Appendix H governing class insignia, national letters and numbers on sails.

78   COMPLIANCE WITH CLASS RULES; CERTIFICATES

78.1   A boat's owner and any other person in charge shall ensure that the boat is maintained to comply with her class rules and that her measurement or rating certificate, if any, remains valid.

78.2   When a *rule* requires a certificate to be produced before a boat *races,* and it is not produced, the boat may *race* provided that the race committee receives a statement signed by the person in charge that the valid certificate exists and that it will be given to the race committee before the end of the event. If the certificate is not received in time, the boat's scores shall be removed from the event results.

78.3   When a measurer for an event concludes that a boat does not comply with her class rules, he shall report the matter in writing to the race committee, which shall protest the boat.

78.4   *US SAILING prescribes that Performance Handicap Racing Fleet races shall be governed by Appendix S.*

79   ADVERTISING

A boat and her crew shall comply with Appendix G.

80   RESCHEDULED RACES

When a race has been rescheduled, rule 36 applies and all boats entered in the original race shall be notified and, unless disqualified under rule 30.3, be entitled to sail the rescheduled race. New entries that meet the entry requirements of the original race may be accepted at the discretion of the race committee.

PART 7 – RACE ORGANIZATION

85   **GOVERNING RULES**

The organizing authority, race committee and protest committee shall be governed by the *rules* in the conduct and judging of races.

86   **RULE CHANGES**

86.1   A racing rule may not be changed unless permitted in the rule itself or as follows:

(a) Prescriptions of a national authority may change a racing rule, but not the Definitions; a rule in the Introduction; Sportsmanship and the Rules; Part 1, 2 or 7; rule 43.1, 43.2, 69, 70, 71, 75, 76.2 or 79; a rule of an appendix that changes one of these rules; or Appendix G, J, K, L or Q.

(b) Sailing instructions may change a racing rule by referring specifically to it and stating the change, but not rule 76.1, Appendix F, or a rule listed in rule 86.1(a).

US SAILING prescribes that sailing instructions shall not change rule 76.3, Appendix R, or its prescriptions to rules 40 and 68.

(c) Class rules may change only rules 42, 49, 50, 51, 52, 53 and 54.

86.2   If a national authority so prescribes, these restrictions do not apply if rules are changed to develop or test proposed rules in local races. The national authority may prescribe that its approval is required for such changes.

US SAILING prescribes that proposed rules may be tested in local races and that its approval is not required for such tests.

87   **ORGANIZING AUTHORITY; NOTICE OF RACE; COMMITTEE APPOINTMENTS**

87.1   **Organizing Authority**

Races shall be organized by an organizing authority, which shall be

(a) the ISAF;

(b) a member national authority of the ISAF;

(c) a club or other organization affiliated to a national authority;

(d) a class association, either with the approval of a national authority or in conjunction with an affiliated club; or

(e) an unaffiliated body in conjunction with an affiliated club.

87.2   Notice of Race; Committee Appointments

The organizing authority shall publish a notice of race that conforms to rule M1, appoint a race committee and, when appropriate, appoint a jury.

88   RACE COMMITTEE; SAILING INSTRUCTIONS; SCORING

88.1   Race Committee

The race committee shall conduct races as directed by the organizing authority and as required by the *rules*.

88.2   Sailing Instructions

(a) The race committee shall publish written sailing instructions that conform to rule M2.

(b) The sailing instructions for an international event shall include, in English, the applicable prescriptions of the national authority.

(c) Changes to the sailing instructions shall be in writing and posted within the required time on the official notice board or, on the water, communicated to each boat before her warning signal. Oral changes may be given only on the water, and only if the procedure is stated in the sailing instructions.

88.3   Scoring

The race committee shall score a race or series as required in rule A1 and by the scoring system specified in the sailing instructions.

89   PROTEST COMMITTEE

A protest committee shall be

(a) a committee appointed by the race committee;

(b) a jury, which is separate from and independent of the race committee; or

(c) an international jury meeting the requirements of Appendix Q. A national authority may prescribe that its approval is required for the appointment of international juries for races within its jurisdiction, except those of the ISAF.

US SAILING makes no prescription to this rule.

APPENDIX A – SCORING

See rule 88.3.

A1   GENERAL SCORING RULES

These rules apply regardless of the scoring system in effect.

A1.1   Failure to Start or Finish

When the race committee scores a boat as failing to *start* or *finish* it need not protest her.

A1.2   Boat Retiring or Disqualified After Finishing

When a boat retires or is disqualified after *finishing*, each boat that *finished* after her shall be moved up one place.

A1.3   Scores Not Discardable

When a scoring system provides that one or more race scores are to be discarded in calculating a boat's series score, the score for disqualification under rule 2, or rule 42 when rule 67 applies, shall not be discarded.

US SAILING **prescribes that rule A1.3 shall not apply to a disqualification under rule 42.**

A1.4   Unbroken Ties

(a) When boats are tied at the end of a race, the points for the place for which the boats have tied and for the place(s) immediately below shall be added together and divided equally. Boats tied for a prize shall share it or receive equal prizes.

(b) When boats have equal scores at the end of a series and a tie is unbroken by the scoring system, the scores shall remain unchanged in the final results. Boats tied for a prize shall share it or receive equal prizes.

A1.5   Numbering of Races

Races shall be numbered sequentially in the order of completion.

A1.6   A Boat's Starting Time

The time of a boat's starting signal shall be used as her starting time.

A1.7   Scores Removed from All or Part of a Series

When a boat is penalized by having her scores removed from the results of some or all races of a series, no changes shall be made in the race scores of other boats.

A2   SCORING SYSTEMS

The Bonus Point Scoring System and the Low Point Scoring System are the systems most often used. The bonus point system gives extra points for the first six places because it is harder to sail from fourth place into third, for example, than from fourteenth place into thirteenth. It is used for many class championships. The low point system is also suitable for championships, is better for small-fleet racing and is easier to use. Both systems are primarily designed for regattas but may be adapted for other series; see rule A5.

Either system may be made applicable by stating in the sailing instructions that the bonus point or low point system of Appendix A of the racing rules will apply and including the information required in rule A2.1.

A2.1   Number of Races and Series Scores

The number of races scheduled and the number required to constitute a series shall be stated in the sailing instructions. Each boat's series score will be the total of her race scores, discarding her worst score* except when prohibited in rule A1.3. The lowest series score wins.

* More than one score may be required to be discarded or all scores may be required to be counted; in either case the sailing instructions shall so state.

A2.2   Race Scores

Each boat *starting* and *finishing* in a race, and not thereafter retiring or being disqualified, will be scored points as follows:

Finishing place	Bonus point system	Low point system
First	0	1
Second	3	2
Third	5.7	3
Fourth	8	4
Fifth	10	5
Sixth	11.7	6
Seventh	13	7
Each place thereafter	Add 1 point	Add 1 point

All other boats will be scored points for the finishing place one more than the total number of boats entered in the series.

A2.3 Ties

When there is a tie in series points between two or more boats, the tie will be broken in favour of the boat with the most first places, or, if the tie remains, the most second places, or lower places if necessary, using only the scores for each boat that count for her series score. When a tie still remains, it will be broken in favour of the boat with the best score in the last race in which the tied boats *raced* and scored differently, using only the scores for each boat that count for her series score. For these calculations, if a boat has been awarded average points that do not correspond to a place, she shall be considered to have the place closest in points to the points awarded; if a boat has tied for a place, she shall be considered to have that place.

A3 ABBREVIATIONS FOR SCORING RECORDS

These abbreviations are recommended for recording the circumstances that determine a score:

DNC   Did not come to the starting area
DNS   Did not *start*
OCS   On the course side of the starting line and failed to comply with rule 29.1 or rule 30.1

DNF   Did not *finish*
RET   Retired after *finishing*
DSQ   Disqualified
DND   Disqualification not discardable because of rule A1.3
RDG   Redress given
ZPG   Z flag penalty given

A4   REDRESS

If under rule 64.2 the protest committee decides to change a boat's score, it should consider scoring her

(a)   points equal to the average, to the nearest tenth of a point (0.05 to be rounded upward), of her points in all the races in the series except [her worst race and]* the race in question, or

(b)   points equal to the average, to the nearest tenth of a point (0.05 to be rounded upward), of her points in all the races before the race in question, or

(c)   points based on the position of the boat at the time of the incident that justified the redress.

* Delete these words when all scores count for series results, or adjust when more than one race is to be discarded.

A5   WHEN A SERIES IS NOT A REGATTA

In a regatta all boats are expected to compete in all races and the difference between the number of entrants and the number of starters is usually insignificant. However, in a longer series there may be a number of boats that compete in fewer races than others, in which case the following may be substituted for the second paragraph of rule A2.2:

Boats not so scored that came to the starting area will be scored points for the finishing place one more than the number of all boats that came to the starting area. Boats that did not come to the starting area will be scored points for the finishing place one more than the number of boats entered in the series.

APPENDIX AA — ALTERNATIVE SCORING SYSTEM FOR LONG SERIES

US SAILING *prescribes the Low-Point Averaged Scoring System, below, as an alternative to the Appendix A scoring systems. It is appropriate for a long series, such as a season championship spanning several weeks. In the Appendix A systems, each boat receives a score in every race of the series. This feature of the Appendix A systems places a boat that misses some of the races at a disadvantage to another boat that sails more races. In the Low-Point Averaged system, a boat receives a score only for races in which she competes, and therefore, provided she sails in sufficient races to qualify for the series, she is not placed at a disadvantage if she cannot compete in some races.*

The Low-Point Averaged system may be used by including a statement in the sailing instructions such as: 'The Low-Point Averaged Scoring System, Appendix AA of the racing rules, will apply.' If the system is modified as provided in Notes 1 or 2, state the modification completely.

THE LOW-POINT AVERAGED SCORING SYSTEM

AA1   RACES TO COUNT AND MINIMUM REQUIRED

The sailing instructions shall include a schedule of the races that count for the series. To qualify for inclusion in the final series results a boat shall compete in (i.e., come to the starting area for) at least 75 percent* of the races completed.

* The sailing instructions may state that a different percentage of races, or a minimum number of races, will be used.

AA2   RACE SCORES

*Each boat **finishing** a race and not thereafter retiring or being disqualified will be scored as follows:*

Finishing place	*Score*
First	1
Second	2
Third	3
Fourth	4
and so on.	

All other competing boats, including any that **finish** *and thereafter retire or are disqualified, will receive the score for the finishing place one more than the number of competing boats in that race. Boats that do not come to the starting area will not be scored.*

AA3 SERIES SCORES

The series score for each boat will be the sum of her race scores divided by the number of races for which she is scored.* The qualified boat with the lowest series score is the winner, and others are ranked accordingly.

* *When one or more race scores are to be discarded, add ', discarding her ___ worst score(s).' A discarded race counts as a race to qualify a boat for a series score, but not as one of her scored races.*

AA4 TIES

When boats have equal series scores at the end of a series, the tie will be broken in favor of the boat with the most first places, and, when the tie remains, the most second places, and so on. Rule A1.4 also applies.

APPENDIX B – SAILBOARD RACING RULES

Sailboard races shall be sailed under The Racing Rules of Sailing *as changed by this appendix.*

B1   DEFINITIONS

Add the following definitions:

Capsized   A sailboard is *capsized* when her sail or the competitor's body is in the water.

Recovering   A sailboard is *recovering* from the time her sail or, when water-starting, the competitor's body is out of the water until she has steerage way.

B2   PART 2 – WHEN BOATS MEET

B2.1   The last sentence of rule 20 is changed to: 'A sailboard moving astern shall *keep clear* of other sailboards and boats.'

B2.2   Add to Section D:

23   Sail Out of the Water When Starting

When approaching the starting line to *start*, a sailboard shall have her sail out of the water and in a normal position, except when accidentally *capsized*.

24   Recovering

A sailboard *recovering* shall avoid a sailboard or boat under way.

B3   PART 3 – CONDUCT OF A RACE

Rule 31 is changed to: 'A competitor shall not hold on to a starting *mark*.'

B4   PART 4 – OTHER REQUIREMENTS WHEN RACING

B4.1   Rule 42 is changed to: 'A sailboard shall be propelled only by the action of the wind on the sail, by the action of the water on the hull and by the unassisted actions of the competitor.'

B4.2   Rule 43.1(a) is modified to permit a competitor to wear a container for holding beverages. The container shall have a capacity of at least one litre and weigh no more than 1.5 kilograms.

B4.3   In rule 44.2, delete 'including two tacks and two gybes.'

B5   PART 5 – PROTESTS, HEARINGS, MISCONDUCT AND APPEALS

Rule 61.1(a) is changed to:

Informing the Protestee

A sailboard intending to protest because of an incident that occurs in the racing area shall inform the other sailboard by hailing 'Protest' at the first reasonable opportunity and shall inform the race committee as soon as reasonably possible after she *finishes* or retires. In all other cases she shall inform the other sailboard as soon as reasonably possible.

B6   PART 6 – ENTRY AND QUALIFICATION

Add to rule 78.1: 'When so prescribed by the national authority, a numbered and dated device on a sailboard and her daggerboard and sail shall serve as her measurement certificate.'

B7   PART 7 – RACE ORGANIZATION

In rule 88.2(c), the last sentence is changed to: 'Changes to the sailing instructions may be communicated orally, but only if the procedure is stated in the sailing instructions.'

B8   APPENDIX H – IDENTIFICATION ON SAILS

B8.1   Add to rule H1.1(a): 'The insignia shall not refer to anything other than the manufacturer or class and shall not consist of more than two letters and three numbers or an abstract design.'

B8.2   Rules H1.3(a), (c), (d) and (e) are changed to: 'The class insignia shall be displayed once on each side of the sail in the area above a line projected at right angles from a point on the luff of the sail one third of the distance from the head to the wishbone. The national letters and sail numbers shall be in the central third of the sail above the wishbone and clearly separated from any advertising and shall be placed at different heights on the two sides of the sail, those on the starboard side being uppermost.'

APPENDIX C – MATCH RACING RULES

Match races shall be sailed under The Racing Rules of Sailing *as changed by this appendix. Matches shall be umpired unless the notice of race and sailing instructions state otherwise.*

C1   TERMINOLOGY

'Competitor' means the skipper, team or boat as appropriate for the event. 'Flight' means two or more matches started in the same starting sequence.

C2   CHANGES TO THE DEFINITIONS AND THE RULES OF PART 2

C2.1   The definition *Finish* is changed to: 'A boat *finishes* when any part of her hull, or crew or equipment in normal position, crosses the finishing line in the direction of the course from the last *mark* after completing any penalties.'

C2.2   Rule 17.2 is deleted.

C2.3   When rule 19.1 applies, the following arm signals by the helmsman are required in addition to the hails:

(a) for 'Room to tack', repeatedly and clearly pointing to windward; and

(b) for 'You tack', repeatedly and clearly pointing at the other boat and waving to windward.

C2.4   In rule 20 the second sentence is changed to: 'A boat taking a penalty shall *keep clear* of one that is not.'

C2.5   Rule 22.1 is changed to: 'If reasonably possible, a boat not *racing* shall not interfere with a boat that is *racing* or an umpire boat.'

C2.6   Rule 22.2 is changed to: 'Except when sailing a *proper course*, a boat shall not interfere with a boat taking a penalty or sailing on another leg.'

C2.7   A new rule 22.3 is added: 'When boats in different matches meet, any change of course by either boat shall be consistent with complying with a rule and winning her own match.'

C3   RACE SIGNALS AND RELATED RULES

C3.1   Starting Signals

The signals for starting a match shall be as follows. Times shall be taken from the visual signals; the failure of a sound signal shall be disregarded. If more than one match will be sailed, the starting signal for one match shall be the warning signal for the next match.

Time in minutes	Visual signal	Sound signal	Means
10	Flag F displayed	One	Attention signal
6	Flag F removed	None	
5	Numeral pennant displayed*	One	Warning signal
4	Flag P displayed	One signal	Preparatory
2	Blue or yellow flag or both displayed**	One**	End of pre-start entry time
0	Warning and Preparatory signals removed	One	Starting signal

*   Within a flight, numeral pennant 1 means Match 1, pennant 2 means Match 2, etc., unless the sailing instructions state otherwise.

** These signals shall be made only if one or both boats fail to comply with rule C4.2. The flag(s) shall be displayed until the umpires have signalled a penalty or for one minute, whichever is earlier.

C3.2   **Related Rules**

(a) Rule 29.1 is changed to: 'When at her starting signal any part of a boat's hull, crew or equipment is on the course side of the starting line or its extensions, the boat shall sail completely to the pre-start side of the line before *starting*.'

(b) Rule 29.2 is changed to: 'When at her starting signal a boat becomes subject to rule C3.2(a), the race committee shall promptly display a blue or yellow flag or both with one sound signal. Each flag shall be displayed until such boats are completely on the pre-start side of the starting line or its extensions, but not later than two minutes after the starting signal.'

(c) In Race Signals AP and N, the last sentence is changed to: 'The attention (not the warning) or other signal will be made one minute after removal.'

C3.3   **Finishing Line Signals**

The race signal 'Blue flag or shape' shall not be used.

C4   **REQUIREMENTS BEFORE THE START**

C4.1   At her preparatory signal, each boat shall be outside a line that is perpendicular to the starting line through the starting *mark* at her assigned end. In the race schedule pairing list, the boat listed on the left-hand side is assigned the port end and shall display a blue flag at her stern while *racing*. The other boat is assigned the starboard end and shall display a yellow flag at her stern while *racing*.

C4.2   Within the two-minute period following her preparatory signal, a boat shall cross and clear the starting line, the first time from the course side to the pre-start side.

C4.3   When, after one boat has *started,* the umpires are satisfied that the other boat will not *start*, they may signal the boat that did not *start* under rule C10.4 that she is disqualified and the match terminated.

C5   **PROTESTS UNDER RULES OF PART 2 BETWEEN BOATS IN THE SAME MATCH**

C5.1   A boat may protest the other boat in her match under a rule of Part

2, except under rule 14 when damage resulted from contact, by clearly displaying flag Y.

C5.2   After flag Y is displayed, the umpires shall decide whether to penalize either boat. They shall signal their decision by making a single long sound signal and displaying either

(a)   a green and white flag, which means 'No penalty', or

(b)   a blue or yellow flag, which means 'The identified boat shall take a penalty by complying with rule C7 and with rule C8 or rule C9.'

C5.3   The protesting boat shall remove flag Y before or as soon as possible after the umpires' signal.

C6   OTHER PROTESTS AND REQUESTS FOR REDRESS

C6.1   Protest Limitations

(a)   A boat may protest the other boat in her match by complying with the rules of Part 5, Section A, but not under a rule of Part 2, except under rule 14 when damage resulted from contact; rules 31 and 42; or rules C4, C5, C7, C8 and C9.

(b)   A boat may protest a boat in another match but only under a rule of Part 2.

(c)   A boat intending to protest shall keep her red flag displayed until she has so informed the umpires after *finishing* or retiring.

C6.2   Redress

A boat requesting redress because of circumstances that arise before she *finishes* or retires shall display a red flag at the first opportunity after she becomes aware of those circumstances, but not later than five minutes after *finishing* or retiring.

C6.3   Protest Committee Decisions

(a)   While afloat, the protest committee may take evidence in any way it considers appropriate and may communicate its decision orally. When the protest committee decides to conduct a hearing ashore, or to reopen or resume a hearing held on the water, it shall so advise the boats and proceed under the rules of Part 5, except that rule C6.3(b) always applies.

(b) If the protest committee decides that a breach of a *rule* has had no significant effect on the outcome of the match, it may

    (1) impose a penalty of one point or part of one point,

    (2) order a resail, or

    (3) make another arrangement it decides is equitable, which may be to impose no penalty.

C7   PENALTY SYSTEMS

C7.1   Rule Changes

Rules 31.2 and 44 are deleted. The sailing instructions shall state either that rule C8 or that rule C9 will apply.

C7.2   All Penalties (Immediate and Delayed)

(a) In rule 2, a new second sentence is inserted: 'When *racing*, a boat may wait for an umpire's decision before taking a penalty.'

(b) A boat completes a leg of the course when her bow crosses the extension of the line from the previous *mark* through the *mark* she is rounding, or on the last leg when she *finishes*.

(c) A penalized boat shall not be recorded as having *finished* until she takes her penalty and then sails completely to the course side of the line and then *finishes*, unless rule C9 applies and the penalty is cancelled before or after she crosses the finishing line.

(d) A boat taking a penalty that includes a tack shall have the spinnaker head below the mainboom gooseneck from the time she passes head to wind until she is on a close-hauled course.

C8   IMMEDIATE PENALTIES

A penalized boat shall take a penalty as follows:

(a) When signalled before *starting* or while sailing to a windward *mark,* she shall sail clear, gybe and return to a close-hauled course. She shall do so as soon as reasonably possible but not before *starting*.

(b) When signalled while sailing to a leeward *mark* or the finishing line she shall remain on that leg, sail clear, tack and return to a downwind course. She shall do so as soon as reasonably possible unless her spinnaker head is above the main boom gooseneck; in that case she may wait until the spinnaker is lowered, and then take the penalty as soon as possible.

C9   DELAYED PENALTIES

C9.1   A penalized boat may delay taking a penalty within the limitations of rule C9.3 but shall take it as follows, and no part of it may be taken within two of her hull lengths of a rounding *mark*:

(a) When on a leg of the course to a windward *mark*, she shall gybe and return to a close-hauled course.

(b) When on a leg of the course to a leeward *mark* or the finishing line, she shall tack and return to a downwind course.

C9.2   When a boat with a delayed penalty is on a leg to a windward *mark* and gybes, or is on a leg to a leeward *mark* or the finishing line and tacks, she shall be judged to be taking a penalty.

C9.3   If a boat has one delayed penalty, she may take the penalty any time after *starting* and before *finishing*. If a boat has two delayed penalties, she shall take one of them as soon as reasonably possible, but not before *starting*.

C9.4   If a boat has one or two delayed penalties and the other boat in her match is penalized, one penalty for each boat shall be cancelled.

C9.5   If a boat has more than two delayed penalties, the umpires shall signal her disqualification under rule C10.4.

C9.6   The umpire boat for each match shall display coloured shapes, each shape indicating one delayed penalty. When a boat has taken a penalty, or a penalty has been cancelled, one shape shall be removed. Failure of the umpires to display or remove shapes shall not change the number of penalties. The umpires shall make a short sound signal when a boat has taken a penalty.

C10 PENALTIES INITIATED BY UMPIRES

C10.1 Rule Changes

(a) Rules 60.2(a) and 60.3(a) do not apply to *rules* for which penalties may be imposed by umpires.

(b) Rule 64.1(b) is changed so that the provision for exonerating a boat may be applied by the umpires without a hearing, and it takes precedence over any conflicting rule of this appendix.

C10.2 When the umpires decide that a boat has broken rules 31, 42, C4, C5, C7, C8 or C9, she shall be penalized by signalling her under rule C5.2(b).

C10.3 When the umpires decide that a boat has

(a) failed to comply with rules C7, C8 or C9; or

(b) gained an advantage by breaking a *rule* after allowing for a penalty; or

(c) deliberately broken a *rule*; or

(d) committed a breach of sportsmanship;

she shall be penalized under rule C5.2(b) or rule C10.4.

C10.4 When the umpires display a black flag and a boat's identification flag, it means: 'The signalled boat is disqualified, and the match is terminated and awarded to the other boat.'

C10.5 If umpires or protest committee members decide that a boat may have broken a *rule* other than a rule of Part 2, except rule 14 when damage resulted from contact, or a rule for which a penalty is provided in rule C10.2 or C10.3, they shall so inform the protest committee for its action under rule 60.3 and rule C6.3 when appropriate.

C11 REQUESTS FOR REDRESS OR REOPENINGS; APPEALS; OTHER PROCEEDINGS

C11.1 There shall be no request for redress or an appeal from a decision made under rule C5, C6, C7.2, C8, C9 or C10. In rule 66 the third sentence is changed to: 'A *party* to the hearing may not ask for a reopening.'

C11.2   A competitor may not base a request for redress on a claim that an action by an official boat was improper. The protest committee may decide to consider giving redress in such circumstances but only if it believes that the official boat, including an umpire boat, may have seriously interfered with a competing boat.

C11.3   No proceedings of any kind may be taken in relation to any action or non-action by the umpires.

C12   SCORING

C12.1   The winning competitor of each match scores one point (half of one point each for a dead heat); the loser scores no points.

C12.2   When a competitor withdraws from part of an event the results of all completed races shall stand.

C12.3   When multiple round robins are terminated with an incomplete round robin, only one point shall be available for all the matches sailed between any two competitors, as follows:

Number of matches completed between any two competitors	Points for each win
1	One point
2	One-half point
3	One-third point
(etc.)	

C12.4   In a round-robin series,

(a) the highest total score wins;

(b) a competitor who has won a match but is disqualified for breaking a *rule* against a competitor in another match shall lose the point for that match (but the losing competitor shall not be awarded the point); and

(c) the overall position between competitors who have sailed in different groups shall be decided by the total number of wins.

C12.5 In a knock-out series the sailing instructions shall prescribe the minimum number of points required to win a series between two competitors.

C13 TIES

C13.1 General

Ties shall be decided only if a sail-off is not practicable and only if necessary to determine which competitors qualify to compete in a later stage of the event or in a subsequent event. If ties remain, any monetary prizes or ranking points for tied places shall be added together and divided equally among the tied competitors.

C13.2 Round-Robin Series

(a) Ties between two or more competitors in a round-robin series shall be decided in favour of the competitor who has the most points in the matches between the tied competitors.

(b) When the tie remains, it shall be decided in favour of the competitor who has won the match against the competitor (excluding the tied competitors) who has the highest score in the round robin or, if necessary, the second highest score, and so forth until the tie is broken. When the tie is partially resolved, paragraph (a) shall be re-applied to the competitors still tied.

(c) When the tie remains and there have been either fleet races or previous round robins, the tie shall be resolved in favour of the competitor who has won the match against the competitor (excluding the tied competitors) who has the highest score in the most recent series or, if necessary, the second-highest score, and so forth until the tie is broken. When the tie still remains it shall be decided by means of a draw.

(d) Ties from applying rule C12.4(c) shall be decided in favour of the competitor with the highest place in the different groups irrespective of the number of competitors in each group. Remaining ties shall be decided under rule C13.1.

C13.3 Knock-out Series

(a) When a decisive match cannot be sailed to resolve a tie, including those with 0-0 scores, the tie shall be broken in favour

of the competitor placed highest in the most recent round robin
or the combined points from a multiple round robin.

(b) If paragraph (a) does not resolve the tie, it shall be broken in
favour of the winner of the last match completed between the
tied competitors unless there is a 0-0 tie. In that case a draw
shall be used.

(c) Competitors eliminated in one round of a knock-out series
shall be scored as tied unless more matches are sailed to break
such ties.

*Note: A Standard Notice of Race and Standard Sailing Instructions
for match racing are available from the ISAF.*

APPENDIX D – TEAM RACING RULES

Team races shall be sailed under The Racing Rules of Sailing *as changed by this appendix. If umpires or observers will be used the sailing instructions shall so state.*

D1   **CHANGES TO THE RACING RULES**

D1.1   The following rules are changed or added:

(a) Add to rule 16: 'Furthermore, when boats are on a beat to windward and a *port-tack* boat is *keeping clear* of a *starboard-tack* boat, the *starboard-tack* boat shall not change course if that immediately compels the *port-tack* boat to change course.'

(b) Add to rule 18.4: 'This rule applies only if the inside boat established the *overlap* from *clear astern*.'

(c) Add new rule 22.3: 'Except when sailing a *proper course*, a boat shall not interfere with a boat on another leg or lap.'

(d) Add to rule 41: 'A boat that receives help from a team-mate does not break this rule.'

(e) If the sailing instructions so state, rule 17.2 is changed to: 'Except on a beat to windward, while a boat is less than two of her hull lengths from a *leeward* boat, she shall not sail below her *proper course* unless she gybes.'

D1.2   The following additional rules apply:

(a) When boats in different races meet, any change of course by a boat shall be consistent with complying with a rule and winning her own race.

(b) Right of way may be waived between team-mates provided that doing so does not directly affect a boat of the other team adversely.

(c) A boat damaged by a team-mate boat is not eligible for redress based on that damage.

D2 INTENTION TO PROTEST; ACKNOWLEDGEMENT OF BREACHES OF RULES

D2.1 General

(a) A boat intending to protest shall hail the other boat immediately and promptly display a red flag.

(b) A boat that, while *racing*, may have broken a rule of Part 2, except rule 14, or rule D1 may take a penalty as provided by rules 44.1 and 44.2, except that only one turn is required. When an incident occurs at the finishing line or when an umpire's penalty is signalled at or beyond the finishing line, a boat shall not be recorded as having *finished* until she has completed her penalty and returned completely to the course side of the line before *finishing*.

(c) When after displaying a red flag a boat is satisfied that the other boat has taken a penalty in compliance with rule D2.1(b) she shall remove her red flag.

(d) The sailing instructions may state that rule D2.3(g) applies to all *protests*.

D2.2 Races Without Umpires or Observers

A boat that has displayed a red flag and then decides reasonably promptly that she, and not the other boat, was at fault shall immediately remove her flag, take a penalty in compliance with rule D2.1(b), and hail the other boat accordingly.

D2.3 Umpired Races

Races to be umpired shall be identified either in the sailing instructions or by the display of flag U no later than the warning signal.

(a) When a boat protests under a rule of Part 2, except rule 14, or under rule D1, 31.1, 42 or 44, she is not entitled to a hearing. Instead, when the protested boat fails either to acknowledge breaking a *rule* or to take a penalty, the protesting boat may display a yellow flag and request a decision by hailing 'Umpire'.

(b) An umpire shall signal the decision as follows:

(1) a green flag means 'No penalty imposed; incident closed';

(2) a red flag means 'One or more boats are penalized.' The umpire shall hail or signal to identify each boat to be penalized. The protesting boat shall then remove her flag.

(c) A boat penalized by an umpire's decision shall make two 360° turns (720°) in compliance with rule 44.2 as changed by this appendix.

(d) When a boat has gained an advantage by breaking a *rule* or fails to take a penalty when required, an umpire may impose one or more additional 360° turn penalties by hailing her accordingly, or report the incident as provided in rule D2.3(e).

(e) When an incident involves reckless sailing, rule 14, or failure to comply with an umpire's decision, the umpire may report the incident to a protest committee which may further penalize the boat concerned. The umpire shall signal this intention by displaying a black flag and hailing appropriately.

(f) Rules 60.2 and 60.3 do not apply. The protest committee may call a hearing only on receipt of a report from an umpire as provided in rule D2.3(e) or under rule 69.

(g) *Protests* need not be in writing, and the protest committee may take evidence in any way it considers appropriate and communicate its decision orally.

(h) There shall be no requests for redress or to reopen a hearing or appeals by a boat arising from decisions or actions or non-actions by the umpires. The protest committee may decide to consider giving redress when it believes that an official boat may have seriously interfered with a competing boat.

D2.4   Races with Observers

Observers may be appointed by the race committee to observe the racing and give opinions on incidents when requested. If so, rule D2.3 applies except that

(a) a boat need not request an opinion or accept one, in which case any *protest* shall comply with and be decided under the rules of Part 5 as changed by this Appendix;

(b) an observer may display a yellow flag to signal that he has no opinion. If a boat then intends to protest she may do so by complying with the rules of Part 5 as changed by this Appendix.

D3   SCORING A RACE

D3.1   Each boat completing a race, whether or not rules 28.1 and 29.1 have been complied with, shall be scored points equal to her finishing place. All other boats shall be scored points equal to the number of boats entitled to *race*. In addition, a boat's score shall be increased for

Rule broken	*Penalty points*
(a) rule 14, 28.1 or 29.1	10
(b) any other *rule* for which a penalty has not been taken under rule D2.1(b) or D2.3(c)	6

The protest committee may further increase a boat's score when it finds that she gained an advantage from breaking a *rule*. The team with the lowest total points wins. If there is a tie on points, the team having the combination of race scores that does not include a first place wins.

D3.2   When all boats of one team have *finished* or retired, the race committee may stop the race. The other team's boats shall be scored the points they would have received had they *finished*.

D3.3   When all the boats of a team fail to *start* in a race, each shall receive points equal to the number of boats entitled to *race*, and the boats of the other team shall be scored as if they had *finished* in the best positions.

D4   SCORING A SERIES

D4.1   A team racing series shall consist of races or matches. A match shall consist of two races between the same two teams. The team with the lower total points for the race or the match wins.

D4.2   When two or more teams are competing in a series consisting of races or matches, the series winner shall be the team winning the greatest number of races or matches. The other teams shall be ranked in order of number of wins. Tied matches shall count as half a win to each team.

D4.3   When necessary, ties in a series shall be broken by using, in order of precedence,

(a) the total points scored in the series;

(b) the points scored when the tied teams met;

(c) if two teams remain tied after a series of matches, the last race between the teams;

(d) unless otherwise stated in the sailing instructions, a game of chance.

D5   BREAKDOWNS WHEN BOATS ARE SUPPLIED BY THE ORGANIZING AUTHORITY

D5.1   A boat suffering a breakdown shall display a red flag as soon as practicable and, if possible, continue *racing*.

D5.2   When the race committee decides that the boat's finishing position was made significantly worse, that the breakdown was not the fault of the crew, and that in the same circumstances a reasonably competent crew would not have been able to avoid the breakdown, it shall make as equitable a decision as possible, which may be to order the race to be resailed or, when the boat's finishing position was predictable, award her points for that position. In case of doubt about her position when she broke down, the doubt shall be resolved against her.

D5.3   A breakdown caused by defective equipment or a breach of a *rule* by an opponent shall not normally be determined to be the fault of the crew, but one caused by careless handling, capsizing or a breach by a boat of the same team shall be. Any doubt about the fault of the crew shall be resolved in the boat's favour.

APPENDIX E – RADIO-CONTROLLED BOAT RACING RULES

US SAILING has not adopted Appendix E, the Radio-Controlled Boat Racing Rules, which may be obtained from the International Sailing Federation, Ariadne House, Town Quay, Southampton SO14 2AQ, England.

APPENDIX F – APPEALS PROCEDURES

This appendix is a US SAILING prescription that replaces Appendix F as adopted by the International Sailing Federation.

See rules 70 and 71. The US SAILING Appeals Committee acts as the national authority within the meaning of rules 70.1 and 71. This appendix shall not be changed by sailing instructions.

F1   APPEALS COMMITTEES

F1.1   *Appeals of decisions of a protest committee and requests by a protest committee for confirmation or correction of its decisions shall be made to the association appeals committee for the place in which the event was held, except as provided in rule F1.3.*

F1.2   *Appeals of decisions of an association appeals committee, requests by an association appeals committee for confirmation or correction of its decisions, and all requests for interpretations of **rules** shall be made to the US SAILING Appeals Committee.*

F1.3   *Appeals of decisions of a protest committee of a US SAILING national championship and requests by such a committee for confirmation or correction of its decisions shall be made to the US SAILING Appeals Committee.*

F2   APPELLANT'S RESPONSIBILITIES

F2.1   *The appellant shall, within 15 days of receiving the written decision being appealed or a protest committee's decision not to reopen a hearing, send a dated appeal to the appeals committee, with a copy of the decision and the appropriate fee. The appeal shall state why the appellant believes the committee's interpretation of a **rule** or its procedures were incorrect. The fee for appeals to US SAILING is $50 for members and $100 for non-members.*

F2.2   *The appellant shall also send, with the appeal or as soon as possible thereafter, all of the following documents that are available to her:*

   (a) the written protest(s);

   (b) a diagram, prepared or endorsed by the protest committee,

showing the positions and tracks of all boats involved, the course to the next mark and its required side, the force and direction of the wind, and, if relevant, the depth of the water and the direction and speed of any current;

(c) the notice of race, sailing instructions, any other conditions governing the event, and any changes to them;

(d) any additional relevant documents; and

(e) the names and addresses of all parties to the hearing and the protest committee chairman.

F2.3 *A request for confirmation or correction of a committee's decision shall include the decision and all relevant documents. A request for a **rule** interpretation shall include assumed facts. The fee for requests made to US SAILING is $50 for members and $100 for non-members.*

F3 NOTIFICATION OF THE COMMITTEE WHOSE DECISION IS BEING APPEALED

Upon receipt of an appeal, the appeals committee shall send a copy of the appeal to the committee whose decision is being appealed, asking it for the documents in rule F2.2 not supplied by the appellant.

F4 COMMITTEE RESPONSIBILITIES

F4.1 Protest Committee
*A protest committee whose decision is being appealed shall supply any of the documents requested under rule F3 and any facts or information requested under rule F5 and, if directed to do so by the appeals committee, shall conduct a hearing or re-hearing of the **protest.***

F4.2 Association Appeals Committee

*(a) The association appeals committee shall send to all **parties** to the hearing, and to the committee whose decision is being appealed or reviewed, copies of all documents and comments it has received, except those supplied by that **party** or committee.*

(b) *An association appeals committee shall consider an appeal it has refused to decide if directed to do so by the US SAILING Appeals Committee.*

F5   ADDITIONAL INFORMATION

The appeals committee shall accept the protest committee's finding of facts except when it decides they are inadequate, in which case it may require the protest committee to provide additional facts or other information, or to reopen the hearing and report any new finding of facts.

F6   US SAILING APPEALS COMMITTEE'S RESPONSIBILITIES

*The US SAILING Appeals Committee shall send to all **parties** to the hearing, to the protest committee and to the association appeals committee whose decision is being appealed or reviewed, copies of all relevant documents and comments it has received, except those supplied by that **party** or committee.*

F7   COMMENTS

*An appeals committee shall consider written comments on the appeal or request from **parties** to the hearing, the protest committee, and, if relevant, from the association appeals committee, provided that such comments are sent to the appeals committee within 15 days of the **party's** or committee's receipt of the appeal and, if possible, to all **parties** to the hearing and all committees involved.*

F8   OTHER PROVISIONS

In addition to the provisions of rule 71:

(a) *An association appeals committee acting under the rules of this appendix may take any of the actions permitted by the national authority in rules 71.2 and 71.3, subject to further appeal as provided in rule F1.2.*

(b) No member of the association appeals committee shall take part in the discussion or decision on an appeal or a request for confirmation or correction to the US SAILING Appeals Committee.

(c) The appeals committee may direct a protest committee to conduct a hearing or re-hearing of the protest.

(d) The US SAILING Appeals Committee may direct an association appeals committee to consider an appeal it has refused to decide.

APPENDIX G – ADVERTISING

See rule 79. This appendix shall not be changed by sailing instructions or prescriptions of national authorities. When governmental requirements conflict with parts of it, those requirements apply.

G1   DEFINITION OF ADVERTISING

For the purposes of this appendix, advertising is the name, logo, slogan, description, depiction, a variation or distortion thereof, or any other form of communication that promotes an organization, person, product, service, brand or idea so as to call attention to it or to persuade persons or organizations to buy, approve or otherwise support it.

G2   GENERAL

G2.1   Advertisements and anything advertised shall meet generally accepted moral and ethical standards.

G2.2   This appendix shall apply when *racing* and, in addition, unless otherwise stated in the notice of race, from 0700 on the first race day of a regatta until the expiry of the time limit for lodging *protests* following the last race of the regatta.

G2.3   An event shall be designated Category A, B or C in its notice of race and sailing instructions, but if not so designated it shall be Category A. However, at the world and continental championships of Olympic classes, Category B advertising shall be permitted on hulls and, for Olympic sailboard classes, on hulls and sails. After the notice of race has been published, the category shall not be changed within ninety days before the event without prior approval of the national authority of the organizing authority.

G2.4   A national authority, or a class or the Offshore Racing Council for its events, may prescribe *rules* for advertising that are more restrictive than those of a category. For a particular event, the notice of race and the sailing instructions may include *rules* for advertising that are more restrictive than those of the event's category.

US SAILING makes no prescription to this rule.

G2.5   Advertisements on sails shall be clearly separated from national letters and sail numbers.

G2.6   When, after finding the facts, a protest committee decides that a boat or her crew has broken a rule of this appendix, it shall

(a) warn the boat that another breach of the rule will result in disqualification; or

(b) disqualify the boat in accordance with rule 64.1; or

(c) disqualify the boat from more than one race or from the series when it decides that the breach warrants a stronger penalty; or

(d) act under rule 69.1 when it decides that there may have been a gross breach.

G2.7   The ISAF, a national authority, a class association or the ORC may, for its events, subject to rule G5, designate the category and may require a fee for doing so.

G2.8   The ISAF or a national authority may, for its events, prescribe *rules* and require a fee for giving consent to individual boats for advertisements, provided that such consents do not conflict with, when relevant, class rules or the rules of the ORC.

US SAILING makes no prescription to this rule.

G3   CATEGORY A

G3.1   Advertising on boats other than sailboards is permitted only as follows:

(a) The boat's class insignia may be displayed on her sails as required by Appendix H.

(b) One sailmaker's mark, which may include the name or mark of the sailcloth manufacturer and the pattern or model of the sail, may be displayed on both sides of any sail and shall fit within a 150 mm x 150 mm square. On sails other than spinnakers, no part of such mark shall be placed farther from the tack than the greater of 300 mm or 15% of the length of the foot.

(c) One builder's mark, which may include the name or mark of the designer, may be placed on the hull, and one maker's mark may be displayed on spars and on each side of small equipment. Such marks shall fit within a 150 mm x 150 mm square.

(d) The boat's type may be displayed on each side of her hull. Lettering shall not be higher than 1% or longer than 5% of the hull length of the boat, to a maximum of 100 mm or 700 mm respectively.

(e) Makers' marks may be displayed on clothing and equipment. Other advertising may be displayed on clothing and equipment ashore.

(f) The organizing authority of a sponsored event may permit or require the display of an advertisement of the event sponsor not larger than 0.27 m^2 in the form of a flag, and/or of a decal or sticker attached to each side of the hull or to a dodger on each side of the boat. In addition, when a sponsor supplies all hulls and sails at no cost to the organizing authority or competitors, one advertisement not larger than 0.27 m^2 may be displayed on each side of the mainsail. For an event of a class association or the ORC, such advertising requires approval by the class association or the ORC and, when it so prescribes, by the national authority concerned. Notice of such permission or requirement shall be included in the notice of race and the sailing instructions.

US SAILING prescribes that its approval is not required.

G3.2 Advertising on sailboards is permitted only as follows:

(a) The sailboard's class insignia may be displayed on her sail as required by Appendix H.

(b) One sailmaker's mark, which may include the name or mark of the sailcloth manufacturer and the pattern or model of the sail, may be displayed on both sides of the sail. No part of such mark shall be placed farther from the tack than 20% of the length of the foot of the sail, including the mast sleeve. The mark may also be displayed on the lower half of the part of the sail above the wishbone but no part of it shall be farther than 500 mm from the clew.

(c) The sailboard's type or manufacturer's name or logo may be placed on the hull in two places and on the upper third of the part of the sail above the wishbone. One maker's mark may be displayed on spars, on each side of small equipment and on a competitor's clothing and harness.

(d) The organizing authority of a sponsored event may permit or require the display of an advertisement of the event sponsor on both sides of the sail between the sail numbers and the wishbone and on a bib worn by the competitor. For an event of a class association, such advertising requires approval by the class association and, when it so prescribes, by the national authority concerned. Notice of such permission or requirement shall be included in the notice of race and the sailing instructions.

US SAILING prescribes that its approval is not required.

G4   CATEGORY B

G4.1   A boat competing in a Category B event may display advertising only as permitted for Category A and by rule G4.2 (for boats other than sailboards) or rule G4.3 (for sailboards) and throughout that event shall not display advertising chosen by the boat of more than two organizations or persons. A Category B advertisement shall be either one or two of

(a) the name of an organization or person,

(b) a brand or product name, or

(c) a logo.

G4.2   Advertising on Boats Other than Sailboards

(a) The forward 25% of each side of the hull may display no more than two advertisements chosen by the ISAF, the national authority, the class association or the ORC, for its event; or by the organizing authority of the event when it wishes to display advertising of an event sponsor. When both the organizing authority and one of the other organizations wish to use the space, they shall each be entitled to half the length of the space on each side. The remaining length of the hull shall be free of any advertising except for that permitted in rule G3.1(c) and except that half that length may be used for advertising chosen by the boat. If advertising is not displayed on the sides of the hull, it may be displayed on each side of the cabin, the insides of the cockpit coamings or sidetanks, subject to the same length dimensions.

(b) Advertising chosen by the boat may be displayed on sails as follows:

    (1) Advertising on spinnakers is without restriction except as provided in rules G2.5 and G4.

    (2) On one other sail, only one advertisement may be carried at a time, and it may be on both sides of the sail. It shall be placed below the national letters and sail numbers and have a width no greater than two-thirds of the length of the foot of the sail and a height no greater than one-third of that width.

(c) Advertising chosen by the boat may be displayed on the mainmast and main boom, but both displays shall be limited to the name, brand or product name, or logo of one organization. The space within one-third of the length of the mast and two-thirds of the length of the boom may be used.

(d) In addition to the advertisements carried on the boat, advertisements limited to the organization(s) advertising on the boat and one or two additional organizations may be displayed on clothing and equipment worn by competitors.

G4.3 Advertising on Sailboards

(a) The forward 25% of the hull may display no more than two advertisements chosen by the ISAF, the national authority or the class association, for its event; or by the organizing authority of the event when it wishes to display advertising of an event sponsor. When both the organizing authority and one of the other organizations wish to use the space, they shall each be entitled to half the length of the space on each side. Advertising chosen by the competitor may be displayed within the remaining length of the hull.

(b) That part of the sail below the wishbone not used for Category A advertising may display advertising chosen by the competitor.

(c) In addition to the advertisements carried on the sailboard, advertisements limited to the organization(s) advertising on the sailboard and one or two additional organizations may be displayed on clothing and equipment worn by competitors.

G5 CATEGORY C ADVERTISING

G5.1 Approval of Advertising

Advertising for a Category C event (any event that permits advertising beyond Category B advertising) shall be

(a) approved by the national authority of the venue unless the event is an international event;

(b) approved by the International Sailing Federation (ISAF) when the event is an international event (i.e., an event open to entries other than those from the national authority of the venue).

G5.2 Advertising Fees

(a) National events: The national authority of the venue may require an advertising fee for approval of Category C advertising to be paid to it.

(b) International events: The ISAF will require an advertising fee for approval of Category C advertising, and will share the fee equally with the national authority of the venue.

G5.3 Approval Fees

The organizing authority of an event with cash or cashable prizes or appearance payments totalling more than US $10,000 or the equivalent may be required to pay an approval fee. For a national event the national authority of the venue may require such a fee to be paid to it. For an international event the ISAF will require such a fee to be paid to it.

G5.4 Rules for Category C advertising shall be stated in the notice of race and the sailing instructions

APPENDIX H – IDENTIFICATION ON SAILS

See rule 77.

H1   ISAF INTERNATIONAL CLASS BOATS

H1.1   Identification

Every boat of an ISAF International Class or Recognized Class shall carry on her mainsail and, as provided in rules H1.3(d) and (e) for letters and numbers only, on her spinnaker and headsail

(a)   the insignia denoting her class;

(b)   national letters denoting her national authority from the table below. Except in an international championship, such letters need not be carried in home waters, nor are they required on boats of a class that uses a sequential international numbering system; and

(c)   a sail number of no more than four digits allotted by her national authority or, when so required by the class rules, by the international class association. Alternatively, if permitted in the class rules, an owner may be allotted a personal sail number by the relevant issuing authority, which may be used on all his boats in that class.

Sails measured before 31 March 1997 shall comply with rule H1.1 or with the rules applicable at the time of measurement.

Letters	National authority	Letters	National authority
AHO	Netherlands Antilles	BEL	Belgium
ALG	Algeria	BER	Bermuda
AND	Andorra	BLR	Belarus
ANG	Angola	BRA	Brazil
ANT	Antigua	BRN	Bahrain
ARG	Argentina	BRU	Brunei Darussalam
ARM	Armenia	BUL	Bulgaria
ARU	Aruba	CAN	Canada
ASA	American Samoa	CAY	Grand Cayman
AUS	Australia	CHI	Chile
AUT	Austria	CHN	China
BAH	Bahamas	CIV	Ivory Coast
BAR	Barbados	COK	Cook Islands

Letters	National authority	Letters	National authority
COL	Colombia	MAR	Morocco
CRC	Costa Rica	MEX	Mexico
CRO	Croatia	MLT	Malta
CUB	Cuba	MON	Monaco
CYP	Cyprus	MRI	Mauritius
CZE	Czech Republic	MYA	Myanmar
DEN	Denmark	NAM	Namibia
DJI	Djibouti	NED	Holland
DOM	Dominican Republic	NOR	Norway
ECU	Ecuador	NZL	New Zealand
EGY	Egypt	PAK	Pakistan
ESA	El Salvador	PAR	Paraguay
ESP	Spain	PER	Peru
EST	Estonia	PHI	Philippines
FIJ	Fiji	PNG	Papua New Guinea
FIN	Finland	POL	Poland
FRA	France	POR	Portugal
GAB	Gabon	PRK	Korea, DPR
GBR	United Kingdom	PUR	Puerto Rico
GEO	Georgia	QAT	Qatar
GER	Germany	ROM	Romania
GRE	Greece	RSA	South Africa,
GUA	Guatemala		Republic of
GUM	Guam	RUS	Russia
HKG	Hong Kong	SEY	Seychelles
HUN	Hungary	SIN	Singapore
INA	Indonesia	SLO	Slovenia
IND	India	SMR	San Marino
IRL	Ireland	SRI	Sri Lanka
ISL	Iceland	SUD	Sudan
ISR	Israel	SUI	Switzerland
ISV	US Virgin Islands	SVK	Slovak Republic
ITA	Italy	SWE	Sweden
IVB	British Virgin Islands	TAH	Tahiti
JAM	Jamaica	THA	Thailand
JPN	Japan	TPE	Chinese Taipei
KAZ	Kazakhstan	TRI	Trinidad & Tobago
KEN	Kenya	TUN	Tunisia
KGZ	Kyrghyzstan	TUR	Turkey
KOR	Korea	UAE	United Arab Emirates
KUW	Kuwait	UKR	Ukraine
LAT	Latvia	URU	Uruguay
LCA	St. Lucia	USA	United States of America
LIB	Lebanon	UZB	Uzbekistan
LIE	Liechtenstein	VEN	Venezuela
LTU	Lithuania	YUG	Yugoslavia
LUX	Luxembourg	ZIM	Zimbabwe
MAL	Malaysia		

H1.2 Specifications

(a) National letters and sail numbers shall be in capital letters and Arabic numerals, clearly legible and of the same colour. Commercially available typefaces giving the same or better legibility than Helvetica are acceptable.

(b) The sizes of characters and minimum space between adjoining characters on the same and opposite sides of the sail shall be related to the boat's overall length as follows:

Overall length	Minimum height	Minimum space between letters and numerals or edge of sail
Under 3.5 m	230 mm	45 mm
3.5 m – 8.5 m	300 mm	60 mm
8.5 m – 11 m	375 mm	75 mm
over 11 m	450 mm	90 mm

H1.3 Positioning

Class insignia, national letters and sail numbers shall be positioned as follows:

(a) Except as provided in (d) and (e) below, class insignia, national letters and sail numbers shall when possible be wholly above an arc whose centre is the head point and whose radius is 60% of the leech length. They shall be placed at different heights on the two sides of the sail, those on the starboard side being uppermost.

(b) The class insignia shall be placed above the national letters. If the class insignia is of such a design that two of them coincide when placed back to back on both sides of the sail, they may be so placed.

(c) National letters shall be placed above the sail number.

(d) The national letters and sail number shall be displayed on the front side of a spinnaker but may be placed on both sides. They shall be displayed wholly below an arc whose centre is the head point and whose radius is 40% of the foot median and, when possible, wholly above an arc whose radius is 60% of the foot median.

(e) The national letters and sail number shall be displayed on both sides of a headsail whose clew can extend behind the mast 30% or more of the mainsail foot length. They shall be displayed wholly below an arc whose centre is the head point and whose radius is half the luff length and, if possible, wholly above an arc whose radius is 75% of the luff length.

H2   OTHER BOATS

Other boats shall comply with the rules of their national authority or class association in regard to the allotment, carrying and size of insignia, letters and numbers. Such rules shall, when practicable, conform to the above requirements.

US SAILING prescribes that:

(a) Unless otherwise stated in her class rules, the sails of a boat not in an international class recognized by the ISAF shall, if delivered after January 1, 1990, comply with rule H1.

(b) Offshore racing boats not subject to rule H1 shall carry US SAILING numbers on mainsails, spinnakers and each overlapping headsail having a luff-perpendicular measurement exceeding 130% of the base of the foretriangle.

H3   CHARTERED OR LOANED BOATS

When so stated in the notice of race or sailing instructions, a boat chartered or loaned for an event may carry national letters or a sail number in contravention of her class rules.

H4   WARNINGS AND PENALTIES

When a protest committee finds that a boat has broken a rule of this appendix it shall either warn her and give her time to comply or penalize her.

H5   CHANGES BY CLASS RULES

ISAF classes may change the rules of this appendix provided the changes have first been approved by the ISAF.

APPENDIX J – WEIGHING CLOTHING AND EQUIPMENT

See rule 43.1(b). This appendix shall not be changed by sailing instructions or prescriptions of national authorities.

J1   The items of a competitor's clothing and equipment to be weighed shall be arranged on a rack and thoroughly soaked by total immersion in water for one minute or longer if necessary for total saturation. After being soaked, the items shall be allowed to drain freely for one minute before they are weighed. Life-jackets shall be included, but not a hiking or trapeze harness or clothing worn only below the knee unless class rules require that it be included. The rack must allow the items to hang as they would hang from clothes hangers, so as to allow the water to drain freely. Hiking or trapeze harnesses shall be weighed separately and tested for positive buoyancy.

J2   During the weighing, pockets that have drainholes that cannot be closed shall be empty, but pockets or items of equipment that hold water shall be full.

J3   When a weight recorded exceeds the amount permitted, the competitor may twice rearrange the clothing and equipment on the rack and the measurer shall again soak and weigh it. If a lower weight is recorded that record shall be final.

J4   A competitor wearing a dry-suit may choose an alternative means of weighing:

    (a) the dry-suit and items of clothing and equipment that are worn outside the dry-suit shall be weighed as described above;

    (b) clothing worn underneath the dry-suit shall be weighed as worn while *racing,* without draining; and

    (c) the two weights shall be added together.

APPENDIX K – COMPETITORS' ISAF ELIGIBILITY

See rule 75.2. This appendix shall not be changed by sailing instructions or prescriptions of national authorities.

K1   ISAF ELIGIBILITY RULES

To be eligible to compete in an event listed in rule K2.1, a competitor shall

(a) be governed by the regulations and rules of the ISAF;

(b) be a member of a member national authority or one of its affiliated organizations. Such membership shall be established by the competitor

   (1) being entered by the national authority of the country of which the competitor is a national or ordinarily a resident; or

   (2) presenting a valid membership card or certificate, or other satisfactory evidence of identity and membership;

(c) not be under suspension of ISAF eligibility.

K2   EVENTS REQUIRING ISAF ELIGIBILITY

K2.1   ISAF eligibility is required for the following events:

(a) the sailing regatta of the Olympic Games;

(b) the sailing regattas of regional games recognized by the International Olympic Committee;

(c) events including 'ISAF' in their titles;

(d) world and continental championships of ISAF international classes and of the Offshore Racing Council; and

(e) any other event approved by the ISAF as a world championship and so stated in the notice of race and the sailing instructions.

K2.2   ISAF eligibility may be required for any other event when so stated in the notice of race and the sailing instructions with specific reference to this appendix.

K3   **SUSPENSION OF ISAF ELIGIBILITY**

K3.1   After proper inquiry by either the national authority of the competitor or the ISAF Executive Committee, a competitor's ISAF eligibility shall be promptly suspended with immediate effect, permanently or for a specified period of time

(a)   for any suspension of eligibility in accordance with rule 69.2; or

(b)   for breaking rule 5; or

(c)   for competing, within the two years preceding the inquiry, in an event that the competitor knew or should have known was a prohibited event.

K3.2   A prohibited event is an event

(a)   permitting or requiring advertising beyond that permitted for Category B under Appendix G that is not approved as required by that appendix;

(b)   in which cash or cashable prizes and/or appearance payments totalling more than US $10,000 (or its equivalent) may be received by any one boat, that is not approved by the national authority of the venue or, for events conducted in more than one country, the ISAF; or

(c)   that is described as a world championship, either in the title of the event or otherwise, and that is not approved by the ISAF. (ISAF approval is not required for world championships of ISAF international classes or of the Offshore Racing Council.)

K3.3   When an event described in rule K3.2 has been approved as required, that fact shall be stated in the notice of race and the sailing instructions.

K4   **REPORTS; REVIEWS; NOTIFICATION; APPEALS**

K4.1   When a national authority suspends a competitor's ISAF eligibility under rule K3.1, it shall promptly report the suspension and reasons therefore to the ISAF. The ISAF Executive Committee may revise or annul the suspension with immediate effect. The ISAF shall promptly report any suspension of a competitor's eligibility, or of its revision or annulment by the ISAF Executive Committee, to all national authorities, international class associations, the Offshore Racing Council and other ISAF affiliated organizations, which may also suspend eligibility for events held within their jurisdiction.

K4.2   A competitor whose suspension of ISAF eligibility has been either imposed by a national authority, or imposed or revised by the ISAF Executive Committee, shall be advised of the right to appeal to the ISAF Review Board and be provided with a copy of the Review Board Rules of Procedure.

K4.3   A national authority or the ISAF Executive Committee may ask for a review of its decision by the ISAF Review Board by complying with the Review Board Rules of Procedure.

K4.4   The Review Board Rules of Procedure shall govern all appeals and requests for review.

K4.5   Upon an appeal or request for review, the ISAF Review Board may confirm, revise or annul a suspension of eligibility, or require a hearing or rehearing by the suspending authority.

K4.6   Decisions of the Review Board are not subject to appeal.

K4.7   The ISAF shall promptly notify all national authorities, international class associations and the Offshore Racing Council of all Review Board decisions.

K5   **REINSTATEMENT OF ISAF ELIGIBILITY**

The ISAF Review Board may reinstate the ISAF eligibility of a competitor who

(a)   applies for reinstatement;

(b)   establishes substantial, changed circumstances justifying reinstatement; and

(c)   has completed a minimum of three years of suspension.

APPENDIX L – BANNED SUBSTANCES AND BANNED METHODS

See rule 5. This appendix shall not be changed by sailing instructions or prescriptions of national authorities. When governmental requirements conflict with parts of it, those requirements apply.

INTRODUCTION

Doping is the taking or using by a competitor of a substance or a method banned by the ISAF. Doping is governed by rule 5, this appendix, and the ISAF *Medical Lists* (containing the official lists of doping classes and methods, medicines that may be taken, and laboratories accredited for doping control) and *Doping Control Procedures* (the medical procedures leaflet). These publications, doping control forms and the ISAF schedule of penalties are available from the ISAF to national authorities and competitors on request.

L1   GENERAL

L1.1   No testing shall be initiated by the organizing authority of an event without the written authority of the ISAF or the national authority having jurisdiction over the event, except that at an event for an Olympic class it may be initiated by the national authority of the competitor to be tested.

L1.2   A competitor selected for testing shall not refuse to be tested and shall appear at a control centre when required by a sampling officer.

L2   INITIATION OF DOPING CONTROL

The ISAF or a national authority may at any time initiate medical testing to control doping within its own jurisdiction or for competitors under its jurisdiction. A sampling officer shall be appointed to administer or supervise the testing.

L3   SELECTION

L3.1   At an authorized event, the chairman of the protest committee shall select the finishing places of competitors to be tested on the day. This may be by means of a draw or by other means decided by the protest committee. When there is more than one competitor in each boat, any or all of them may be selected. The race committee shall give to the sampling officer the names of the competitors who *finished* in the selected places. When, for any reason, no boats have *finished* in the selected places, names may be selected by means of a draw. A competitor may be tested more than once during an event.

L3.2   When the ISAF or the national authority of a competitor under its jurisdiction initiates out-of-competition testing of a competitor, it shall test only after receiving written consent from the competitor. Any such testing shall take place within the period specified in the consent.

L4   PROCEDURE

L4.1   (a) The sampling officer or his representative shall inform a competitor by written notice, in confidence, that he or she has been selected for testing and is required to provide a urine sample at the time and place specified in the notice. The notice shall also specify the name of the sampling officer appointed for the event and of the designated laboratory to which specimens will be sent.

(b) The competitor shall acknowledge receipt of the notice, and the time of its delivery shall be recorded by the sampling officer or his representative.

(c) The competitor may be accompanied by one person of his or her choice.

(d) The *Medical Lists* and *Doping Control Procedures* shall be available to the competitor on request.

(e) A competitor who fails to appear at the appointed time and place or who refuses to provide a sample shall be removed, together with the boat in which he or she was sailing, from the event and all its results. The protest committee shall call a hearing in accordance with the rules of Part 5, Section B, to investigate the circumstances and report its findings to the ISAF or to the initiating national authority, and to the national authority of the competitor.

L4.2 The sampling officer and other persons involved in doping control shall act in accordance with *Doping Control Procedures* and shall explain all procedures for doping control to the competitor.

L4.3 The competitor shall be given a copy of the doping control form and shall sign it to acknowledge that he or she has been informed of the procedures.

L4.4 The competitor shall provide a postal or fax address at which, during the 60 days following the testing, he or she may be informed of the result of the test of sample B (rule L5).

L4.5 Failure by a competitor to acknowledge receipt of the notice (rule L4.1(b)), to sign the form (rule L4.3) or to provide an address will not be grounds for cancelling any penalty imposed for breaking rule 5.

L5 SAMPLING AND RESULTS

L5.1 The competitor shall provide a urine sample which will be divided into two samples, A and B, and sent to a designated laboratory.

L5.2 When sample A is negative, the sampling officer shall so inform the competitor immediately and no further action shall be taken.

L5.3 When sample A is positive

(a) the initiating authority shall so inform the competitor and his or her national authority immediately. No race results shall be changed at this stage; and

(b) the laboratory will proceed to test sample B. The competitor or his or her representative may be present at the testing.

L5.4 (a) When sample B is negative, the initiating authority shall so inform the competitor and his or her national authority, and no further action shall be taken.

(b) When no result has been obtained from sample B after 60 days from the date of the testing, the test shall be considered void and no further action shall be taken.

L5.5 When sample B is positive, the ISAF or the initiating national authority will inform the competitor in writing at the address provided (rule L4.4) and his or her national authority. The ISAF will inform the national authority having jurisdiction over the event.

L5.6 (a) Any positive result of a medical test shall be reported promptly by the initiating national authority to the ISAF.

(b) Any penalties imposed by the national authority for breaches of rule 5 or rule L1.2 shall be reported promptly to the ISAF.

L6 APPEAL PROCEDURE

L6.1 The competitor has 20 days from the date of the communication required in rule L5.5 to appeal to the International Medical Commission (IMC) of the ISAF. When after 20 days the competitor has not appealed, his or her national authority and that of the event will be notified of this fact.

L6.2 After the last day for submitting an appeal, penalties will be applied and the scores of the competitor and the boat in which he or she was sailing shall be removed from the results of the event.

L7 EXEMPTIONS

L7.1 A competitor may ask, only in writing, for prior approval from the IMC for the use of a banned substance or a banned method for special medical reasons. The reasons shall be stated and supported with medical evidence from a doctor.

L7.2 In offshore races of more than 50 nautical miles, the use during the race of any banned substance or banned procedure for emergency medical treatment shall be reported promptly to the protest committee, which shall inform the appropriate national authority and the ISAF. The IMC may retroactively approve such use.

L8 SUSPENSION OF ISAF ELIGIBILITY

L8.1 In addition to any penalty imposed under rule K3.1, a competitor who has broken rule 5 may have his or her ISAF eligibility suspended as provided in Appendix K.

L8.2 The competitor may appeal as provided in Appendix K.

L9 COMPETITOR'S EXPENSES

Any expenses incurred in connection with this appendix by a competitor shall be his or her responsibility.

APPENDIX M – NOTICE OF RACE AND SAILING INSTRUCTIONS

See rules 87.2 and 88.2(a). The term 'race' includes a regatta or other series of races.

M1   NOTICE OF RACE CONTENTS

M1.1   The notice of race shall include the following information:

(1) the title, place and dates of the race and name of the organizing authority;

(2) that the race will be governed by *The Racing Rules of Sailing*, the prescriptions of the national authority when they apply, the rules of each class concerned, the sailing instructions and any other applicable *rules*;

(3) the classes to race, conditions of entry and any restrictions on entries;

(4) the times of registration and warning signals for the practice race or first race, and succeeding races if known.

M1.2   The notice of race shall, when appropriate, also include the following:

(1) ISAF approval and eligibility requirements (see Appendix K);

(2) the category of the event (see rule G2.3) and, when relevant, the additional information required by Appendix G;

(3) the procedure for advance registration or entry, including fees and any closing dates;

(4) an entry form, to be signed by the boat's owner or owner's representative, containing words such as: 'I agree to be bound by *The Racing Rules of Sailing* and by all other rules that govern this event';

(5) measurement procedures or requirements for measurement or rating certificates;

(6) the time and place at which the sailing instructions will be available;

(7)   any changes to the racing rules (see rule 86);

(8)   changes to class rules, referring specifically to each rule and stating the change;

(9)   the courses to be sailed;

(10) penalties for breaking a *rule*;

(11) denial of the right of appeal, subject to rule 70.4;

(12) the scoring system;

(13) prizes, including any cash, cashable prize and/or appearance payments totalling more than US $10,000 that may be received by any one boat.

M2   SAILING INSTRUCTION CONTENTS

M2.1 The sailing instructions shall include the following information:

(1)   that the race will be governed by *The Racing Rules of Sailing,* the prescriptions of the national authority when they apply (for international events, a copy in English of such prescriptions shall be included in the sailing instructions), the rules of each class concerned, the sailing instructions and any other applicable *rules*;

(2)   the schedule of races, the classes to race and times of warning signals for each class;

(3)   the course(s) to be sailed, or a list of *marks* from which the course will be selected and, if relevant, how courses will be signalled;

(4)   descriptions of *marks,* including starting and finishing *marks,* stating the order and side on which each is to be left;

(5)   descriptions of the starting and finishing lines, the starting system and any special signals to be used;

(6)   the time limit, if any, for *finishing*;

(7)   the scoring system, stated in full or included by reference to Appendix A, class rules or other *rules* governing the event.

M2.2 The sailing instructions shall, when appropriate, also include the following:

(1) ISAF approval and eligibility requirements (see Appendix K);

(2) the category of the event (see rule G2.3) and, when relevant, the additional information required by Appendix G;

(3) replacement of the relevant rules of Part 2 with the International Regulations for Preventing Collisions at Sea or other government right-of-way rules, the time(s) or place(s) they will apply, and any night signals to be used by the race committee;

(4) changes to the racing rules permitted in rule 86, referring specifically to each rule and stating the change;

(5) changes to class rules, referring specifically to each rule and stating the change;

(6) restrictions controlling changes to boats when supplied by the organizing authority;

(7) the registration procedure;

(8) measurement or inspection procedure;

(9) location(s) of official notice board(s);

(10) procedure for changing the sailing instructions;

(11) safety requirements, such as requirements and signals for personal buoyancy, check-in at the starting area, and check-out and check-in ashore;

(12) declaration requirements;

(13) signals to be made ashore and location of signal station(s);

(14) the racing area (a chart is recommended);

(15) approximate course length and approximate length of windward legs;

(16) the time limit, if any, for boats other than the first boat to *finish*;

(17) time allowances;

(18) class flags;

(19) the location of the starting area and any applicable restrictions;

(20) any special procedures or signals for individual or general recalls;

(21) *mark* boats;

(22) procedure for changes of course after the start and any special signals;

(23) any special procedure for shortening the course or for *finishing* a shortened course;

(24) restrictions on use of support boats, plastic pools, radios, etc.; on hauling out; and on outside assistance provided to a boat that is not *racing*;

(25) the penalty for breaking a rule of Part 2 other than the 720° Turns Penalty;

(26) protest procedure and times and place of hearings;

(27) denial of the right of appeal, subject to rule 70.4;

(28) the national authority's approval of the appointment of an international jury under rule 89(c);

(29) substitute competitors;

(30) the minimum number of boats appearing in the starting area required for a race to be started;

(31) when and where races *postponed* or *abandoned* for the day will be resailed;

(32) tides and currents;

(33) prizes, including any cash, cashable prize and/or appearance payments totalling more than US $10,000 that may be received by any one boat;

(34) other commitments of the race committee and obligations of boats.

APPENDIX N – SAILING INSTRUCTIONS GUIDE

This guide provides a set of tested sailing instructions designed primarily for major championship regattas for one or more classes. They therefore will be particularly useful for world, continental and national championships and other events of similar importance. The guide can also be useful for other events; however, for such events some of these instructions will be unnecessary or undesirable. Race officers should therefore be careful in making their choices.

The principles on which all sailing instructions should be based are as follows:

1 They should include only two types of statement: the intentions of the race committee and the obligations of competitors.

2 They should be concerned only with racing. Information about social events, assignment of moorings, etc., should be provided separately.

3 They should not change the racing rules except when clearly desirable.

4 They should not repeat or restate any of the racing rules.

5 They should not repeat themselves.

6 They should be in chronological order; that is, the order in which the competitor will use them.

7 They should, when possible, use words or phrases from the racing rules.

To use this guide, first review rule M2, Sailing Instruction Contents. Then delete all optional instructions that will not be needed. Instructions that are required or strongly recommended are marked with an asterisk (*). Then select the paragraphs desired where more than one version is shown. Then fill in the spaces where a solid line (___) appears, following the directions in the left margin, and select the desired wording where a choice is indicated by alternatives in brackets ([. . .]). Finally, renumber all instructions in sequential order.

NOTE: *The notes in the left-hand column contain guidance for preparing sailing instructions. Do not include them in the completed draft.*

On separate lines, insert the full name of the regatta, the inclusive dates from measurement or the practice race until the final race, the name of the organizing authority, and the city and country.

SAILING INSTRUCTIONS

*1   RULES

Insert the full names of the national authority, when applicable and of the class(es). Insert the appropriate category (see Appendix G).

The regatta will be governed by *The Racing Rules of Sailing* (RRS), the prescriptions of the ___, the rules of the ___ class(es), except as any of these are changed by these sailing instructions, and by these sailing instructions. The regatta is designated Category ___.

*2   ENTRIES

Insert the competitor eligibility conditions, if any.

Eligible boats may be entered by completing registration with the organizing authority. Eligibility requirements for boats are ___. Eligibility requirements for competitors are ___.

*3   NOTICES TO COMPETITORS

Insert the specific location(s).

Notices to competitors will be posted on the official notice board(s) located ___.

*4   CHANGES IN SAILING INSTRUCTIONS

Insert the times.

Any change to the sailing instructions will be posted before ___ on the day it will take effect, except that any change to the schedule of races will be posted by ___ on the day before it will take effect.

5 SIGNALS MADE ASHORE

Insert the specific location.

5.1 Signals made ashore will be displayed at ___.

Insert the sound signal and time.

5.2 Flag AP with two ___ (one ___ when lowered) means 'The race is postponed. The warning signal will be made not less than ___ minutes after AP is lowered.'

Insert the sound signal.

5.3 Flag B fully hoisted with one ___ means 'Protest Time has begun.' When lowered half way, it means 'There are less than 30 minutes remaining before protest time ends.' When lowered, it means 'Protest time has ended.'

*6 SCHEDULE OF RACES

Races are scheduled as follows:

Race	Day and date	Time of warning signal
_____	_____	_____
_____	_____	_____
_____	_____	_____
_____	_____	_____

Insert the days, dates and times. Include any practice races.

(etc.)

Insert the time.

No warning signal will be made after ___ on the last day of racing.

7 CLASS FLAGS

Insert the class names and names or descriptions of flags.

Class flags will be:

Class	Flag
_____	_____

8 RACING AREA

A section of a chart or other suitable map should be copied and marked for this purpose.

The racing area will be as shown in Illustration A, attached.

Insert the distances and the number of the leeward mark. Delete the last sentence when not applicable. Attach the course diagram(s). A method of illustrating various courses is shown in Addendum A.

*9   THE COURSE

*9.1   The diagram(s) in Illustration B show the course(s), including the approximate angles between legs, the order in which marks are to be passed, and the side on which each mark is to be left. Mark 1 will be approximately ___ nautical miles from Mark ___. The first and last legs will be approximately ___ longer than the distance from Mark ___ to Mark 1.

Insert the number of the leeward mark.

9.2   The approximate compass bearing from Mark ___ to Mark 1 will be displayed from the race committee signal boat.

Insert the number of the leeward mark. Include the gate in the diagram as shown below.

9.3   If the race committee sets a gate instead of Mark ___, boats shall sail between Mark ___ S and Mark ___ P from the direction of the last mark and round either Mark ___ S to starboard or Mark ___ P to port, as shown below.

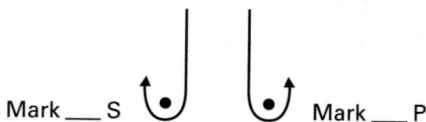

Mark ___ S   Mark ___ P

Do not use if courses may be shortened.

9.4   Courses will not be shortened. This changes rule 32.

Insert the descriptions of all marks and the instruction number. Delete any mark numbers that do not apply.

*10   MARKS

Marks 1, 2, 3 and 4 will be___. New marks, as provided in instruction ___, Change of Course After the Start, will be ___. The starting and finishing marks will be___.

Use the last part of the sentence for a multi-class regatta. Insert the number of the system, the number of minutes and the class names in order of starting.

*11   THE START

*11.1   Races will be started using rule 26, System ___, with classes starting at ___ minute intervals in the order ___.

(OR)

*11.1   Races will be started as follows. This changes rules 26.1 and 30. Times shall be taken from the visual signals; the failure of a sound signal shall be disregarded.

Title	*Signals*
Warning	Class flag, 1 sound
Preparatory	Blue flag or flag P, I, Z, or black flag; 1 sound
Starting	Flags removed, 1 sound

The preparatory signal will be displayed one minute after the warning signal and will be removed, with one sound, one minute before the starting signal. The starting signal will be made five minutes after the preparatory signal.

Succeeding classes will be started as follows:

(This is a new starting system that the ISAF hopes will be tried.)

(a) at five-minute intervals by displaying the warning and preparatory signals with the starting signal for the preceding class, or

(b) at any time after the starting signal for the preceding class by displaying the warning signal for the succeeding class.

Insert the number of the leeward mark.

*11.2   The starting line will be between a staff displaying an orange flag or shape on the race committee boat at the starboard end and Mark ___ at the port end.

(OR)

*11.2   The starting line will be between a staff displaying an orange flag or shape on the race committee boat at the starboard end and the port-end starting mark.

95

Delete the last sentence when signals will be made from the starboard-end race committee boat.

(OR)

*11.2 The starting line will be between staffs displaying orange flags or shapes on two race committee boats. Signals will be made from a race committee signal boat stationed to windward of the line.

(OR)

*11.2 The starting line will be between staffs displaying orange flags on Starting Marks A and B and between staffs displaying orange flags on Starting Marks B and C as shown below. Mark B may not be on a straight line between Mark A and Mark C. For the purpose of rule 30.1, the extensions of the starting line are the extensions beyond Marks A and C.

Mark A •   •   • Mark C

                Mark B

Use only for a multi-class regatta. Insert 'warning' when classes start at ten-minute intervals, 'preparatory' when they start at five-minute intervals.

11.3 Boats whose ___ signal has not been made shall keep clear of the starting area and of all boats whose ___ signal has been made.

Insert the number of minutes.

11.4 A boat shall not start later than ___ minutes after her starting signal.

12 **MARK BOATS**

Insert the description of the flag or shape.

Mark boats will be stationed beyond each mark. At the finish, the mark boat will be stationed beyond the finishing line. When on station only, each mark boat will display a ___. Failure of a mark boat to be on station or to display her signal will not be grounds for redress. This changes rule 62.1(a).

13   CHANGE OF COURSE AFTER THE START

A change of course after the start will be signalled before the leading boat has begun the leg, although the new mark may not then be in position. Any mark to be rounded after rounding the new mark may be relocated to maintain the original course configuration. When in a subsequent change of course a new mark is replaced, it will be replaced with an original mark.

*14   THE FINISH

The finishing line will be between a staff displaying an orange flag or shape on a race committee boat and the nearby mark at the port end.

(OR)

The finishing line will be between a staff displaying an orange flag or shape on a race committee boat and the port-end finishing mark.

(OR)

The finishing line will be between staffs displaying orange flags or shapes on two race committee boats.

Delete if the 720° Turns Penalty will be used. Insert the number of places.

15   PENALTY SYSTEM

The Scoring Penalty, rule 44.3, will apply. The penalty will be ___ places.

Insert the time(s) and class(es). Adjust for a single class regatta or for a single time limit for all classes.

*16   TIME LIMIT

The time limit will be ___ for the ___ class and ___ for the ___ class. Boats failing to finish within ___ minutes after the first boat finishes or within the time limit, whichever is later, will be scored Did Not Finish. This changes rule 35.

17   PROTESTS

Insert the time.   **17.1**   Protests shall be written on forms available at the race office and delivered there within ___ after the time of the last boat's finish.

(OR)

Insert the times.   **17.1**   Protests shall be written on forms available at the race office and delivered there within Protest Time which will begin at ___ and end at ___ .

17.2   Protests will be heard in approximately the order of receipt as soon as possible.

(OR)

Insert the time.   **17.2**   Protests will be heard in approximately the order of receipt beginning at ___ .

17.3   Protest notices will be posted within 30 minutes of the protest time limit to inform competitors where and when there is a hearing in which they are parties to a hearing or named as witnesses.

Use only when the requirements of rule 70.4 are met.   **17.4**   Decisions of the [jury] [protest committee] will be final as provided in rule 70.4.

17.5   Rule 66 is changed by adding this sentence: 'On the last day of racing, a *party* to the hearing may ask for a reopening no later than one hour after being informed of the decision.'

Insert the numbers.   ***18**   **SCORING**

The [Bonus Point] [Low Point] scoring system, rule A2, will apply. ___ races are scheduled, of which ___ races shall be completed to constitute a series.

Insert the number of races.

(OR)

The [Bonus Point] [Low Point] scoring system, rule A2, will apply, modified so that each boat's series score will be the total of her race scores, with her worst score discarded if ___ or more races have been completed. ___ races are scheduled, of which ___ races shall be completed to constitute a series.

Insert the name of the class and the rule number.

(OR)

For the ___ class, the class scoring system, rule ___ of the class rules, will be used.

19 SUPPORT BOATS

Insert 'the disqualification of' or 'points for _ _ _ additional places added to the scores of'. In the latter case insert the number of places.

Team leaders, coaches and other support personnel shall not be in the racing area from the time of the preparatory signal for the first class to start until all boats have finished or the race committee signals a postponement, general recall or abandonment. The penalty for failing to comply with this requirement will be ___ all boats associated with the support personnel who do so.

20 HAUL-OUT RESTRICTIONS

When this applies to some classes only, insert the name(s) of the class(es) between 'all' and 'boats'. Insert the time. Use (b) only when there is a scheduled reserve day.

All boats shall be afloat before ___ on the day preceding the first scheduled race and shall not be hauled out during the regatta except:

(a) with and according to the terms of prior written permission of the [jury] [protest committee]; or

(b) after the race preceding a reserve day, in which case they shall again be afloat before ___ on the day preceding the next race.

Insert the class(es) **21** **PLASTIC POOLS AND DIVING**
and time. **EQUIPMENT**

Underwater breathing apparatus, plastic pools
or their equivalent shall not be used around ___
class boats after ___ on the day preceding the
first scheduled race.

22 **RADIO COMMUNICATION**

A boat shall neither make radio transmissions
while racing nor receive radio communications
not available to all boats.

Change as required. **23** **PRIZES**
When perpetual
trophies are to be Prizes will be awarded to each member of the
awarded, refer to crews placing first, second and third in the
them by their regatta.
complete names.
State, when
appropriate, that
cash or cashable
prizes and/or
appearance payments
totalling more than
US $10,000 (or its
equivalent) may be
received by any one
boat.

Addendum A – Illustrating the Course

Shown here are examples of course illustrations. Any course can be similarly shown. When there is more than one course, prepare a separate diagram for each course and state how each will be signalled.

This course is frequently used. Options include
(1) varying the interior angles of the triangle (45°–90°–45° and 60°–60°–60° are common),
(2) deleting the last windward leg,
(3) using a gate instead of a leeward *mark* for downwind legs (not reaches),
(4) using an offset *mark* at the beginning of downwind legs (not reaches), and
(5) using the leeward and windward *marks* as starting and finishing *marks*. Be sure to specify the interior angle at each *mark*.

Start - 1 - 2 - 3 - 1 - 3 - Finish

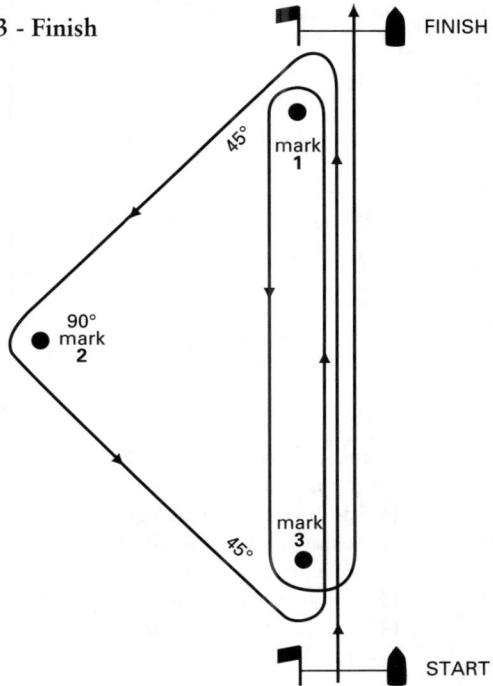

This course is frequently used. Options include
(1) increasing or decreasing the number of laps,
(2) deleting the final windward leg,
(3) using a gate instead of a leeward *mark*,
(4) using an offset *mark* at the windward *mark*, and
(5) using the leeward and windward *marks* as starting and finishing *marks*, respectively.

Start - 1 - 3 - 1 - 3 - Finish

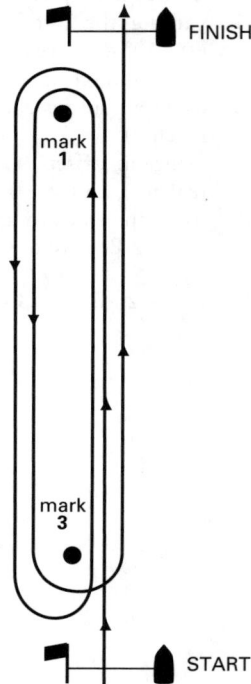

Trapezoid courses are becoming more common in multi-class regattas. Options include
(1) adding additional legs,
(2) using gates instead of leeward *marks* for downwind legs (not reaches),
(3) varying the interior angles of the reaching legs,
(4) using an offset *mark* at the beginning of downwind legs (not reaches), and

(5) finishing boats upwind rather than on a reach. Be sure to specify the interior angle of each reaching leg. It is recommended that Mark 4 be different from the starting *mark*.

Start - 1 - 2 - 3 - 2 - 3 - Finish

Start - 1 - 4 - 1 - 2 - 3 - Finish

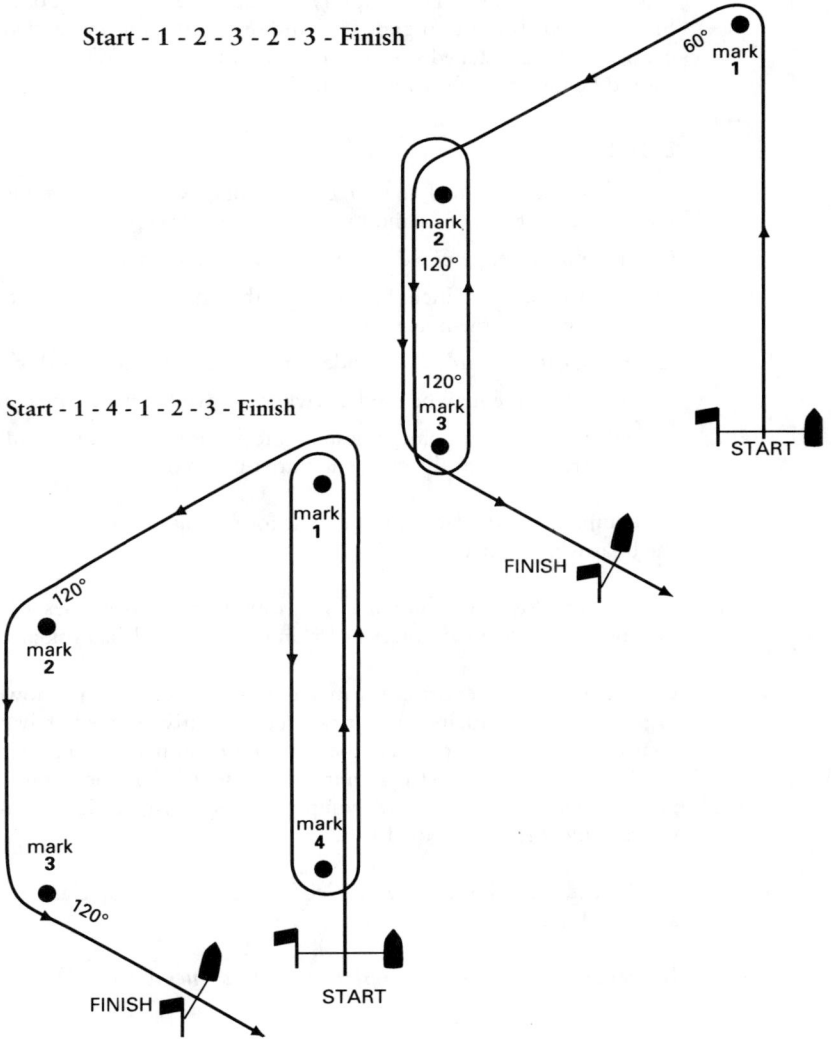

Addendum B – Boats Provided by the Organizing Authority

The following sailing instruction is recommended when all boats will be provided by the organizing authority. It can be added to, changed, or shortened to suit the circumstances. When used, it should be inserted following instruction 5.

BOATS

6.1 Boats will be provided for all competitors, who shall not modify them or cause them to be modified in any way except that

(a) a compass may be tied or taped to the hull or spars;

(b) wind indicators, including yarn or thread, may be tied or taped anywhere on the boat;

(c) hulls, centreboards and rudders may be cleaned only with water;

(d) adhesive tape may be used anywhere above the water line; and

(e) all fittings or equipment designed to be adjusted may be adjusted, provided that the class rules are observed.

6.2 All equipment provided with the boat for sailing purposes shall be in the boat while afloat.

6.3 The penalty for not complying with one of the above rules will be disqualification from all races sailed in which the rule is broken.

6.4 Competitors shall report any damage or loss of equipment, however slight, to the organizing authority's representative immediately after securing the boat ashore. The penalty for breaking this instruction, unless the [jury] [protest committee] is satisfied that the competitor made a determined effort to comply, will be disqualification from the race most recently sailed.

6.5 Class rules requiring competitors to be members of the class association will not apply.

Use when the regatta is not restricted to class members.

APPENDIX P – RECOMMENDATIONS FOR PROTEST COMMITTEES

This appendix is advisory only; in some circumstances changing these procedures may be advisable. It is addressed primarily to protest committee chairmen but may also help judges, jury secretaries, race committees and others connected with protest hearings.

In a protest hearing, the protest committee should weigh all testimony with equal care; should recognize that honest testimony can vary, and even be in conflict, as a result of different observations and recollections; should resolve such differences as best it can; should recognize that no boat or competitor is guilty until a breach of a *rule* has been established to the satisfaction of the protest committee; and should keep an open mind until all the evidence has been heard as to whether a boat or competitor has broken a *rule*.

P1   PRELIMINARIES (may be done by the race office)

- Receive the form from the protestor.
- Note on the form the time the *protest* is lodged and the time protest time ends.
- Inform each *party*, and the race committee when necessary, when and where the hearing will be held.

P2   BEFORE THE HEARING

Make sure that

- each *party* has a copy of the protest form. When copies are unavailable let the protestee read the *protest* before beginning.
- no member of the protest committee is an *interested party*. Ask the *parties* whether they object to any member.
- only one person from each boat (or *party*) is present unless an interpreter is needed.
- all boats and people involved are present. If they are not, however, the committee may proceed under rule 63.3(b).

- boat representatives were on board when required (rule 63.3(a)). When the *parties* were in different races, both organizing authorities must accept the composition of the protest committee (rule 63.7). In a measurement *protest* obtain the current class rules and identify the authority responsible for interpreting them (rule 64.3(b)).

P3 THE HEARING

P3.1 Check the validity of the *protest* or request for redress.

- Were the contents adequate (rule 61.2)?
- Was it delivered in time? If not, is there good reason to extend the time limit (rule 61.3)?
- When required, was the protestor involved in or a witness to the incident (rule 60.1(a))?
- When necessary, was 'Protest' hailed and the protest flag flown correctly (rule 61.1(a))?
- When the flag and hail were not necessary was the protestee informed?
- Decide whether the *protest* is valid (rule 63.5).
- Once the validity of the *protest* has been determined, do not let the subject be introduced again unless truly new evidence is available.

P3.2 Take the evidence (rule 63.6).

- Ask the protestor and then the protestee to tell their stories. Then allow them to question one another.
- Invite questions from protest committee members.
- Make sure you know what facts each *party* is alleging before calling any witnesses. Their stories may be different.
- Allow anyone, including a boat's crew, to give evidence. It is the *party* who must decide which witnesses to call. The question 'Would you like to hear N?' is best answered by 'It is your choice.'
- Call the protestor's and then the protestee's witnesses (and committee's if any) one by one. Limit *parties* to questioning the witnesses (the *parties* may wander into general statements).

- Invite the protestee to question the protestor's witnesses first (and vice versa). This prevents the protestor from leading his witness from the beginning.
- Allow a member of the protest committee who saw the incident to give evidence (rule 63.6) but only in the presence of the *parties*. The member may be questioned and may remain in the room (rule 63.3(a)).
- Try to prevent leading questions or hearsay evidence, but if that is impossible discount the evidence so obtained.
- Only accept written evidence when both *parties* agree.
- Ask one member of the committee to note down evidence, particularly times, distances, speeds, etc.
- Invite first the protestor and then the protestee to make a final statement of her case, particularly on any application or interpretation of the *rules*.

P3.3   Find the facts (rule 63.6).

- Write down the facts; resolve doubts one way or the other.
- Call back *parties* for more questions if necessary.
- When appropriate, draw a diagram of the incident using the facts you have found.

P3.4   Decide the protest (rule 64).

- Base the decision on the facts found (if you cannot, find some more facts).
- In redress cases, make sure that no further evidence is needed from boats that will be affected by the decision.

P3.5   Inform the *parties* (rule 65).

- Recall the *parties* and read them the facts found and decision. When time presses it is permissible to read the decision and give the details later.
- Give any *party* a copy of the decision on request. File the protest form with the committee records.

P4 REOPENING A HEARING (Rule 66)

When a timely request is made for a hearing to be reopened, hear the *party* making the request, look at any video, etc., and decide whether there is any material new evidence which might lead you to change your decision. Decide whether your interpretation of the *rules* may have been wrong; be open-minded as to whether you have made a mistake. If none of these applies refuse to reopen; otherwise schedule a hearing.

P5 GROSS MISCONDUCT (Rule 69)

P5.1 An action under this rule is not a *protest,* but the protest committee gives its allegations in writing to the competitor before the hearing. The hearing is conducted under the same rules as other hearings but must have at least three members (rule 69.1(b)). Use the greatest care to protect the competitor's rights.

P5.2 A competitor or a boat cannot protest under rule 69, but the protest form of a competitor who tries to do so may be accepted as a report to the protest committee which can then decide whether to call a hearing or not.

P5.3 When it is desirable to call a hearing under rule 69 as a result of a Part 2 incident, it is important to hear any boat-v-boat *protest* in the normal way, deciding which boat, if any, broke which *rule,* before proceeding against the competitor under this rule.

P5.4 Although action under rule 69 is taken against a competitor, not a boat, a boat may also be penalized.

P5.5 The protest committee may warn the competitor when it believes this to be sufficient penalty, in which case no report need be made to the national authority. When the penalty is more severe and a report is made to the national authority, it is helpful to recommend to the national authority whether or not further action should be taken.

P6 APPEALS (Rule 70 and Appendix F)

When decisions can be appealed,

- leave the papers so that the information can easily be used for an appeal. Is there an adequate diagram? Are the facts found sufficient? (Example: was there an *overlap*? YES/NO. 'Perhaps' is not a fact found.) Are the names of the protest committee members on the form, etc.?

- comments on any appeal should enable the appeals committee to picture the whole incident clearly; the appeals committee knows nothing about the situation.

P7   **PHOTOGRAPHIC EVIDENCE**

Photographs and videos can sometimes provide useful evidence but protest committees should recognize their limitations and note the following points:

- The *party* producing the photographic evidence is responsible for arranging the viewing.
- View the tape several times to extract all the information from it.
- The depth perception of any single-lens camera is very poor; with a telephoto lens it is non-existent. When the camera views two *overlapped* boats at right angles to their course, it is impossible to assess the distance between them. When the camera views them head on, it is impossible to see whether an *overlap* exists unless it is substantial.
- Ask the following questions:
  - Where was the camera in relation to the boats?
  - Was the camera's platform moving? If so in what direction and how fast?
  - Is the angle changing as the boats approach the critical point? Fast panning causes radical change.
  - Did the camera have an unrestricted view throughout?

APPENDIX Q – INTERNATIONAL JURIES

See rules 70.4 and 89(c). This appendix shall not be changed by sailing instructions or prescriptions of national authorities.

Q1   **COMPOSITION, APPOINTMENT AND ORGANIZATION**

Q1.1   An international jury shall be composed of experienced sailors with excellent knowledge of the racing rules and extensive protest committee experience. It shall be independent of and have no members from the race committee, and be appointed by the organizing authority subject to approval by the national authority if required (see rule 89(c)).

Q1.2   The jury shall consist of a chairman, a vice chairman if desired, and other members for a total of at least five. A majority shall be International Judges. The jury may appoint a secretary, who shall not be a member of the jury.

Q1.3   No more than two members (three, in Group M, South and West South America; Group N, Central and East South America; or Group Q, Africa – South of the Sahara) shall be from the same country.

Q1.4   The jury may divide itself into two or more panels of at least five members, of which the majority shall be International Judges. If this is done, the requirements for jury membership shall apply to each panel but not to the jury as a whole.

Q1.5   When the jury has fewer than five members, because of illness or emergency, and no qualified replacements are available, it remains properly constituted if it consists of at least three members. In this case, members shall be from different countries except in Group M (South and West South America), Group N (Central and East South America) and Group Q (Africa – South of the Sahara), where two members may be from one country.

Q1.6   When the national authority's approval is required for the appointment of an international jury (see rule 89(c)), notice of its approval shall be included in the sailing instructions or be posted on the official notice board.

Q1.7   If the jury acts while not properly constituted, the jury's decisions may be appealed.

Q2   **RESPONSIBILITIES**

Q2.1   An international jury is responsible for hearing and deciding all *protests* and other matters arising under the rules of Part 5. When asked by the organizing authority or the race committee, it shall advise and assist them on any matter directly affecting the fairness of the competition.

Q2.2   Unless the organizing authority directs otherwise, the jury shall

(a)   decide questions of eligibility, measurement or boat certificates; and

(b)   authorize the substitution of competitors, boats, sails or equipment.

Q2.3   If so directed by the organizing authority, the jury shall

(a)   make or approve changes to the sailing instructions,

(b)   supervise or direct the race committee in the conduct of the races, and

(c)   decide on other matters referred to it by the organizing authority.

Q3   **PROCEDURES**

Q3.1   Decisions of the jury shall be made by a simple majority vote of all members. When there is an equal division of votes cast, the chairman of the meeting may cast an additional vote.

Q3.2   When it is considered desirable that some members not participate in discussing and deciding a *protest,* the jury remains properly constituted if at least three members remain.

Q3.3   Members shall not be regarded as *interested parties* (see rule 63.4) by reason of their nationality.

Q3.4   If a panel fails to agree on a decision it may adjourn and refer the matter to the full jury.

APPENDIX R – DEFINITIONS FOR COMPETITOR ELIGIBILITY

Prescribed by US SAILING, *this appendix provides definitions of three groups for competitor eligibility that can be used singly or in combination by a club, class association or other organizing authority for a race or series. Several variations are possible. For example, a maximum number of competitors of a particular group permitted on each boat may be established; the group requirement for helmsmen may be different from that for crew members; or separate trophies may be awarded for different groups.*

An organizing authority that decides to use this appendix shall so state in its notice of race and sailing instructions. When particular group requirements will apply, or when requirements of different groups will apply to different competitors within the event, these requirements shall also be stated.

Although use of this appendix is not required, it shall not be changed by the notice of race or sailing instructions.

R1 DEFINITIONS OF GROUPS FOR COMPETITOR ELIGIBILITY

R1.1 *Group 1, Amateur Competitor*

A Group 1 competitor is one who engages in competitive sailing solely as a pastime, who does not benefit financially from an activity that contributes to the performance of racing boats, and who has not been engaged within the past 12 months in activity that would make him a Group 2 competitor or activity within the past 24 months that would make him a Group 3 competitor. As exceptions, the following competitors are included in Group 1:

(a) *a competitor who occasionally accepts reimbursement for reasonable out-of-pocket expenses of travel, living accommodations and meals necessary for participation in an event;*

(b) a sailing instructor who, during no more than 90 days per calendar year, teaches racing in a yacht club, sailing club, community sailing program or youth camp, or at a school or other educational institution.

(c) Paid hand employed on a cruiser-racer type yacht during no more than 90 days per calendar year, and who will not reach age 25 before the end of the calendar year.

(d) one who, for compensation, occasionally gives racing clinics not longer than one week.

R1.2 Group 2, Marine Industry Competitor

A Group 2 competitor is one who is neither a Group 1 nor a Group 3 competitor and has not been engaged in an activity that would make him a Group 3 competitor within the past 12 months.

R1.3 Group 3, Professional Competitor

A Group 3 competitor is one who directly or indirectly:

(a) is paid to race;

(b) benefits financially from competing;

(c) primarily because of sailing skill or sailing reputation, receives payment or other compensation having a value of more than US $1000 for allowing his name, likeness, sailing performance or sailing reputation to be used for the advertisement, promotion or sale of any product or service; or

(d) publicly identifies himself as a Group 3 or professional competitor.

R2 FINANCIAL BENEFITS

Financial benefits include, but are not limited to, the following:

(a) income, a gift, loan, or other direct benefit, in excess of reasonable out-of-pocket expenses as permitted in rule R1.1(a), for participating in a race;

(b) a prize of money or its equivalent, a prize readily converted to money, or a non-monetary prize having a value of more than US $1,000, other than a prize of primarily symbolic value such as a trophy or a watch;

(c) an agreement involving current or future employment based on racing activities or successes.

R3   EXAMPLES

Deleted by action of the United States Sailing Association Board of Directors on March 23, 1997.

R4   CHANGES IN GROUP STATUS

R4.1   A Group 3 competitor becomes a Group 2 competitor after 12 months during which he has not been engaged in an activity that would make him a Group 3 competitor.

R4.2   A Group 2 competitor becomes a Group 1 competitor after 12 months during which he has not been engaged in an activity that would make him a Group 2 or Group 3 competitor.

R5   PROTEST DECISIONS

R5.1   When a protest committee decides that a competitor has broken a sailing instruction that applies this appendix, it shall disqualify the boat from any races sailed with the competitor aboard and exclude him from further participation in the event.

R5.2   A protest committee acting under Appendix R shall report its decision to US SAILING and to the competitor's national authority if it is not US SAILING.

R6   US SAILING ELIGIBILITY REVIEW AND APPEAL

R6.1   A competitor may apply to US SAILING for review of his eligibility status under Appendix R, or US SAILING may initiate such a review. The competitor may be required to provide information and evidence. A competitor who applies for such a review shall pay an administrative fee ($25 for members of US SAILING; $75 for others). A panel of members of the US SAILING Eligibility Review

Committee will conduct the review and determine the competitor's eligibility status under this appendix.

R6.2　*A competitor may appeal a decision made under rule R6.1, provided he does so within 30 days of receiving the decision. Members of the Eligibility Review Committee who did not conduct the initial review will act on such an appeal and will confirm or revise the competitor's eligibility status.*

APPENDIX S – PERFORMANCE HANDICAP RACING FLEET RULES

US SAILING prescribes that Performance Handicap Racing Fleet (PHRF) races shall be governed by the Racing Rules of Sailing and the rules of this appendix.

S1 PROTESTS INVOLVING RATING CERTIFICATES

For rule 64.3(b), the authority responsible for interpreting the PHRF rules is the PHRF handicapping committee that issued the certificate, except when a Special PHRF Handicapping Committee has been appointed for that purpose.

S2 SPECIAL PHRF HANDICAPPING COMMITTEE

For an event in which boats with ratings issued by more than one PHRF are expected to compete, the organizing authority may request that the US-PHRF Rating Review Committee appoint a Special PHRF Handicapping Committee.

S3 BETWEEN-EVENT RATING CERTIFICATE REVIEWS

A request for a rating certificate review shall be submitted to the PHRF handicapping committee that issued the certificate. A request for a review of that committee's decision, unless its rules prohibit such requests, may be submitted to the US-PHRF Rating Review Committee in accordance with written procedures available from the US SAILING Offshore Office.

APPENDIX T – SOUND-SIGNAL STARTING SYSTEM

US SAILING prescribes that, when the sailing instructions so indicate, the Sound-Signal Starting System described below shall be used. This system is recommended primarily for small-boat racing and makes it unnecessary for competitors to use stop watches. Supplemental · visual course and recall signals are also recommended when practicable.

T1   *Course and postponement signals may be made orally.*

T2   *Audible signals will govern, even when supplemental visual signals are also used. (Rule 26 will not apply.)*

T3   *The starting sequence will consist of the following sound signals made at the indicated times:*

Signal	Sound	Time before start
Warning	3 long	3 minutes
Preparatory	2 long	2 minutes
	1 long, 1 short	1 minute, 30 seconds
	1 long	1 minutes
	3 short	30 seconds
	2 short	20 seconds
	1 short	10 seconds
	1 short	5 seconds
	1 short	4 seconds
	1 short	3 seconds
	1 short	2 seconds
	1 short	1 second
Starting	1 long	0

T4   *Signals will be timed from their commencement.*

T5   *A series of short signals may be made before the sequence begins in order to attract attention.*

T6   *Individual recalls will be signalled by the hail of the sail number (or some other clearly distinguishing feature) of each recalled boat. Flag X need not be displayed.*

T7   *Failure of a competitor to hear an adequate course, postponement, starting sequence or recall signal will not be grounds for redress.*

PROTEST FORM

EVENT   Organizing authority   Date   Race number

PROTESTING BOAT   Boat name   Class   Sail number

Person in charge   Member of   Signature

Address   Telephone

PROTESTED BOAT   Boat name   Class   Sail number

Person in charge (if known)   Member of (if known)

Address (if known)   Telephone (if known)

NOTIFICATION   Did the protesting boat inform the protested boat of the protest?   Circle one

yes   no

If so, how   when

Did the protesting boat display a protest flag?   yes   no
If so, when

INCIDENT   When and where   Witness(es)

Rules alleged to have been broken

THE REMAINDER OF THIS PAGE IS FOR PROTEST COMMITTEE USE ONLY

PRE-HEARING INFORMATION

	Date	Time		Parties notified of hearing	Circle one	
Protest received				Protestor	yes	no
Protest time limit				Protestee	yes	no

Protest flag observed by race committee at finish   yes   no

Objection about interested party made   yes   no

Protesting boat represented by —————————————————

Protested boat represented by —————————————————

HEARING TO VALIDATE PROTEST (Rule 63.5):

	Circle one			Remarks
Hail timely and appropriate	yes	no	NA	
Protestor informed protestee	yes	no	NA	
Proper and timely display of protest flag	yes	no	NA	
Protest flag acceptable	yes	no	NA	
Nature of incident identified in protest	yes	no		
Protest lodged within the time limit	yes	no	time limit extended	

CONCLUSION   ( ) Protest valid, hearing will continue   ( ) Protest invalid, hearing is closed

119

DESCRIPTION OF THE INCIDENT

DIAGRAM OF THE INCIDENT (One square = one boat length)

SHOW ON DIAGRAM: Wind direction and strength – Current direction and strength
Marks (or directions to marks) – Position of boats at various times

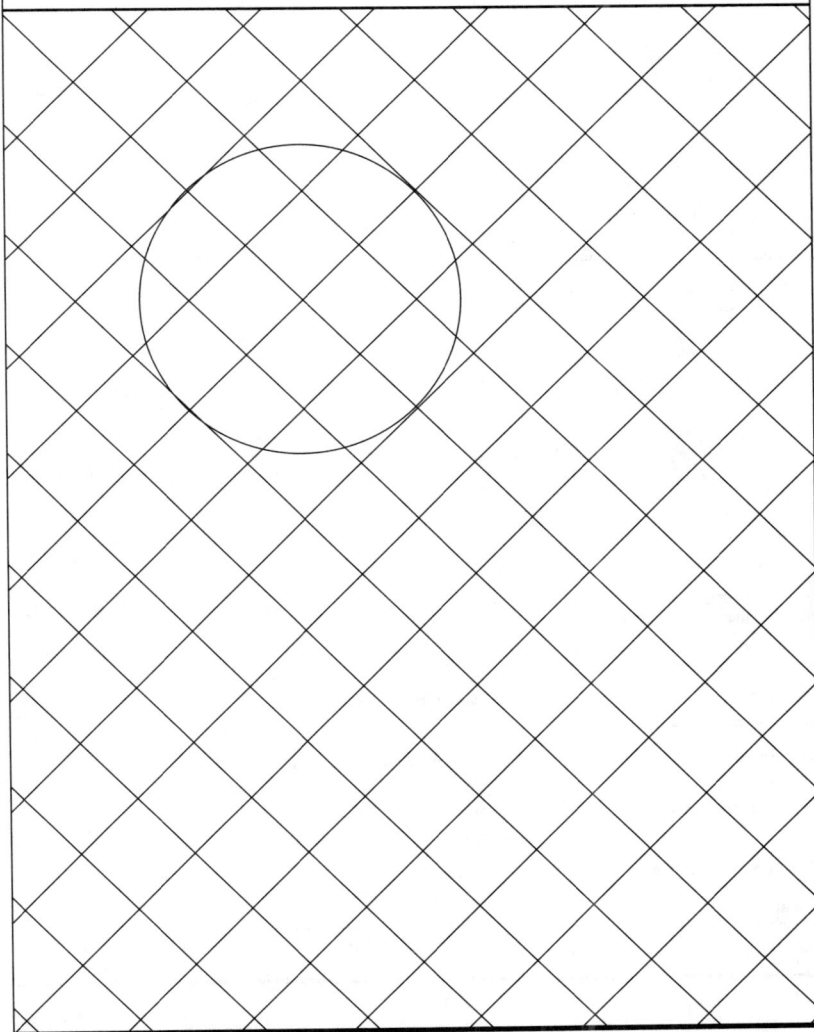

DECISION OF THE PROTEST COMMITTEE:

Facts found

Diagram   ☐   Diagram of boat _____ is endorsed by the committee

         ☐   Committee's diagram is attached.

Conclusion and rules that apply

Decision

Protest Committee members

Signature of Chairman _____

Date of hearing _____   Date of decision _____

Decision announced in presence of   ☐ protestor   ☐ protestee   ☐ other _____

Written decision requested   Date requested   Date transmitted

Protestor   yes/no

Protestee   yes/no

INDEX

References are to rules (e.g., 27.3), appendices (e.g., A1.4 or B), or sections (e.g., Introduction). Locations for sections are on the Contents page. Headings are arranged alphabetically; the references that follow them are arranged in the order in which they appear in the book. Italics are used for words that appear in Definitions. An italicized word at the end of an entry and before any subheading means that its Definitions text contains the heading word (e.g., contact: 14, C, E, *keep clear*). Appendices B, C, D, E, J, M, N and P are not indexed in detail.

Why Join US SAILING?

US SAILING Directory
(retails for $5)

10 Issues of **Sailing World Magazine**, the authority on performance sailing (a one-year subscription worth $28)

Discounts on regatta entry fees, publications, accessories and safety gear. $72 value for $40 membership

10 Issues of **American Sailor Magazine**, the official news publication of US SAILING ($24 value)

Official racing **Rule Book** or **Log Book** ($15 value)

1 800 US SAIL-1

DEFINITIONS

A term used as stated below is shown in italic type or, in preambles, in bold italic type.

Abandon A race that a race committee or protest committee *abandons* is void but may be resailed.

Clear Astern and **Clear Ahead; Overlap** One boat is *clear astern* of another when her hull and equipment in normal position are behind a line abeam from the aftermost point of the other boat's hull and equipment in normal position. The other boat is *clear ahead*. They *overlap* when neither is *clear astern* or when a boat between them *overlaps* both. These terms do not apply to boats on opposite *tacks* unless rule 18 applies.

Finish A boat *finishes* when any part of her hull, or crew or equipment in normal position, crosses the finishing line in the direction of the course from the last *mark* either for the first time or, if she takes a penalty, after complying with rule 31.2 or rule 44.2.

Interested Party A person who may gain or lose as a result of a protest committee's decision, or who has a close personal interest in the decision.

Keep Clear One boat *keeps clear* of another if the other can sail her course with no need to take avoiding action and, when the boats are *overlapped* on the same *tack*, if the *leeward* boat could change course without immediately making contact with the *windward* boat.

Leeward and **Windward** A boat's *leeward* side is the side that is or, when she is head to wind, was away from the wind. However, when sailing by the lee or directly downwind, her *leeward* side is the side on which her mainsail lies. The other side is her *windward* side. When two boats on the same *tack* overlap, the one on the *leeward* side of the other is the *leeward* boat. The other is the *windward* boat.

Mark An object the sailing instructions require a boat to pass on a specified side, excluding its anchor line and objects attached temporarily or accidentally.

Obstruction An object that a boat could not pass without changing course substantially, if she were sailing directly towards it and one of her hull lengths from it. An object that can be safely passed on only one side and an area so designated by the sailing instructions are also *obstructions*. However, a boat *racing* is not an *obstruction* to other boats unless they are required to *keep clear* of her or give her *room*.

Overlap See **Clear Astern** and **Clear Ahead; Overlap**.

Party A *party* to a hearing: a protestor; a protestee; a boat requesting redress; any other boat or a competitor liable to be penalized, including under rule 69.1; a race committee in a hearing under rule 62.1(a).

Postpone A *postponed* race is delayed before its scheduled start but may be started or *abandoned* later.

DEFINITIONS

Proper Course A course a boat would sail to *finish* as soon as possible in the absence of the other boats referred to in the rule using the term. A boat has no *proper course* before her starting signal.

Protest An allegation by a boat, a race committee or a protest committee that a boat has broken a *rule*.

Racing A boat is *racing* from her preparatory signal until she *finishes* and clears the finishing line and *marks* or retires, or until the race committee signals a general recall, *postponement,* or *abandonment*.

Room The space a boat needs in the existing conditions while manoeuvring promptly in a seamanlike way.

Rule (a) The rules in this book, including the Definitions, Race Signals, Introduction, preambles, and the rules of an appendix when it applies, but not titles;

(b) the prescriptions of a national authority, when they apply;

(c) the sailing instructions;

(d) the class rules except any that conflict with the rules in this book;

(e) any other documents governing the event.

Start A boat *starts* when after her starting signal any part of her hull, crew or equipment first crosses the starting line and she has complied with rule 29.1 and rule 30.1 if it applies.

Tack, Starboard or Port A boat is on the *tack, starboard* or *port,* corresponding to her *windward* side.

Two-Length Zone The area around a *mark* or *obstruction* within a distance of two hull lengths of the boat nearer to it.

Windward See **Leeward** and **Windward**.

ABOUT THE AUTHOR

Dave Perry grew up sailing on Long Island Sound. Learning to sail in Sunfish, Blue Jays and Lightnings from his parents and in the junior program at the Pequot Yacht Club in Southport, Connecticut, he won the Clinton M. Bell Trophy for the best junior record on L.I.S. in 1971. While at Yale (1973-77) he was captain of the National Championship Team in 1975, and was voted All-American in 1975 and 1977. Other racing accomplishments include: 1st, 1978 Tasar North Americans; 5th, 1979 Laser Worlds; 1st, 1979 Soling Olympic Pre-Trials (crew); 10th overall, 1981 SORC (crew); 3rd, 1982 Soling Worlds; 1st, 1982 Prince of Wales Match Racing Championship; 1st, 1983 Star South American Championship (crew); 1st, 1983 and 1984 Congressional Cup; 2nd, 1984 Soling Olympic Trials; 6th, 1985 Transpac Race (crew); 1st, 1988 and 1992 Knickerbocker Match Race Cup; and 1st, 1994 Ideal 18 North American Championship.

Dave has been actively working for the sport since 1977. He has led hundreds of US SAIL-ING instructional seminars in over fifty one-design classes; directed U.S. Olympic Yachting Committee Talent Development Clinics; coached the 1981 World Champion U.S. Youth Team; and given seminars in Japan, Australia, Sweden, Argentina, Brazil and Canada. He has been the Youth Representative on the US SAILING Board of Directors and the Chairman of the U.S. Youth Championship Committee, and has served on the following other US SAILING committees: Olympic, Training, Class Racing and O'Day Championship. He is currently a member of the US SAILING Appeals Committee and a US SAILING Senior Certified Judge. In 1992 he was voted into the *Sailing World* Hall of Fame; in 1994 he received an honorary Doctorate of Education from Piedmont College; and in 1995 he became the first recipient of US SAILING's Captain Joe Prosser Award for exceptional contribution to sailing education. He is currently the Director of Athletics at Greens Farms Academy, a K-12 co-ed independent school in Westport, Connecticut.

ABOUT THE ILLUSTRATOR

Brad Dellenbaugh grew up in Fairfield, Connecticut where he learned to sail at the Pequot Yacht Club. He has been coaching and teaching sailing for over twenty years. Presently an Offshore Sailing coach at the U.S. Naval Academy in Annapolis, Maryland, Brad also coached the intercollegiate team at Brown University from 1980-1990, as well as the U.S. Women's team from 1984-1987. From 1977-1980 he coached the sailing team at the Hotchkiss School in addition to teaching in the art department, and taught junior sailing from 1973 through 1982 on Long Island Sound. He continues to be actively involved in teaching junior and adult racing clinics across the U.S. both on the water and in the classroom, and lectures frequently on racing tactics and the rules.

An avid racer, Brad has been involved in three Olympic campaigns in the Soling class (including with Dave in 1984), as well as serving as tactician or helmsman in numerous national, continental and world championships in a wide variety of one-designs and offshore boats. He has won the 1988 and 1989 US SAILING Team Racing Championship, the 1989 J-24 World Championship and the 1990 and 1991 J-22 World Championship. He is a US SAILING Senior Certified Judge, and also serves as an umpire, race officer and member of several US SAILING Committees.

Brad graduated from Brown University with a major in fine arts and has pursued this interest as a freelance artist, illustrating for a number of sailing magazines and books.